Mennonite World Handbook

1990

Mennonites in Global Witness

Diether Götz Lichdi, Editor
Loretta Kreider, Assistant Editor

Published by
Mennonite World Conference
Carol Stream, Illinois USA

ISBN 1-878047-00-0
Library of Congress Catalog
Card Number: 78-69932

©1990 Mennonite World Conference
465 Gundersen Drive, Suite 200
Carol Stream, Illinois 60188 USA
Design: Glenn Fretz (Sue Meggs-Becker)
Printing: D.W. Friesen & Sons Ltd.
Printed in Canada

Cover photo credits, right to left:
EMS photo by Jim Bishop
MCC photo by Jim King, 1987
Jim Bishop photo, 1989
MCC photo by Jim King, 1986
MCC photo by Kevin Sensenig, 1987
EMS photo by Jim Bishop, 1989
MBM photo by Naswood Burbank, 1988
Goshen College photo by J. Tyler Klassen, 1989
The People's Place photo

Table of Contents

6 Vision

Directory 1990

Abbreviations

A	Old Order Amish
ADS	Algemene Doopsgezinde Sociëteit
AIMM	Africa Inter-Mennonite Mission
AMAS	Associação Menonita de Assistência Social
AMBCF	Africa Mennonite and Brethren in Christ Fellowship
AMBS	Associated Mennonite Biblical Seminaries
AMC	Asia Mennonite Conference
ASCIM	Asociación de Servicios de Cooperación Indígena-Mennonita
BA	Beachy Amish Mennonite Fellowship
BIC	Brethren in Christ Church
BICWM	Brethren in Christ World Missions
CAMCA	Consulta Anabautista Menonita de Centro América
CGC	Church of God in Christ, Mennonite
CIM	Council of International Ministries
CLARA	Centro Latinoamericano de Recursos Anabautistas
CMC	Conference of Mennonites in Canada
CMS	Council of Moderators and Secretaries
COM	Commission on Overseas Mission
CONIM	Comité National Inter-Mennonite
CPT	Christian Peacemaker Teams
EMBMC	Eastern Mennonite Board of Missions and Charities
EMC	Evangelical Mennonite Church
EMCC	Evangelical Mennonite Conference (Canada) and Evangelical Mennonite Conference Board of Missions
EMEK	Europäisches Mennonitisches Evangelisations Komitee
EMFK	Europäisches Mennonitisches Friedenskomitee
EMMC	Evangelical Mennonite Mission Conference
GC	General Conference Mennonite Church
IMK	Internationale Mennonitische Kontakte
IMO	Internationale Mennonitische Organisation
IMPC	International Mennonite Peace Committee
MB	Mennonite Brethren Church
MBM	Mennonite Board of Missions
MBM/S	Mennonite Brethren Missions/Services
MC	Mennonite Church
MCC	Mennonite Central Committee
MCCC	Mennonite Central Committee Canada
MCC U.S.	Mennonite Central Committee United States
MCSFI	Mennonite Christian Service Fellowship of India
MEDA	Mennonite Economic Development Associates
MERK	Mennonitische Europäische Regional Konferenz
MWC	Mennonite World Conference
MWH	Mennonite World Handbook
RMM	Rosedale Mennonite Missions (Conservative Mennonite Board of Missions and Charities

Acknowledgments

The first *Mennonite World Handbook* was published in 1978 at the Tenth Assembly of Mennonite World Conference in Wichita, Kansas. For the first time a comprehensive collection of historical and statistical data was available covering the worldwide Mennonite conferences and related bodies. It was widely used, and expectations were high that in time it would be followed by further editions. In 1987, traveling on a speeding bus on the Trans Chaco Highway from Filadelfia to Asunción, Paraguay, Diether Götz Lichdi and I discussed the shape and direction of the next edition. We were returning from the triennial meeting of the MWC General Council. That conversation, and many more since, led to the appointment of Diether Götz Lichdi as Editor.

Diether brings to this volume his considerable experience as editor of the *Mennonitische Jahrbuch*, widely used and highly respected as an annual informational publication among the Mennonites of Europe. He is the author of numerous historical monographs, scholar, historian, businessman, minister in the Mennonite church in Heilbronn, conference leader (Verband, Federal Republic of Germany), and member of the General Council of MWC.

In the course of shaping the outline of the book, a lengthy list of resource persons was consulted, including but not limited to the following: Wilbert Shenk, Bert Lobe, Norman Kraus, John A. Lapp, Hans Kasdorf, Walter Sawatsky, Ron Yoder, Don Jacobs, Alice Roth, Atlee Beachy, Linda Shelly, Abe Dueck, Anna Epp Enns, Cornelius J. Dyck, Dennis Martin, Dorothy Yoder Nyce, Daniel Schipani, Shirley Yoder, Adolf Ens, Gerhard Friesen, J.M. Klassen, Bernie Wiebe, Helmut Harder, Don Loewen, Jacob F. Pauls, and Mesach Krisetya.

A special tribute of honorable mention goes to Assistant Editor Loretta Kreider, a member of the MWC staff in Carol Stream, Illinois. She is eminently qualified and rightly deserves credit for the task of compiling the statistical section. Beyond that, Loretta brought to this book her careful, well-informed editorial skills, turning her computer into an extension of her knowledge. The smoothly flowing prose and consistent literary style is the result of a unique combination of tireless work and outstanding gifts as a literary stylist.

While the book is published in English, the statistical section is designed for multilingual use. Portions of the text will be printed in German in the *Mennonitische Jahrbuch 1991*. Efforts will be made to produce the material in other languages as well.

Paul N. Kraybill, publisher
Mennonite World Conference
May 15, 1990.

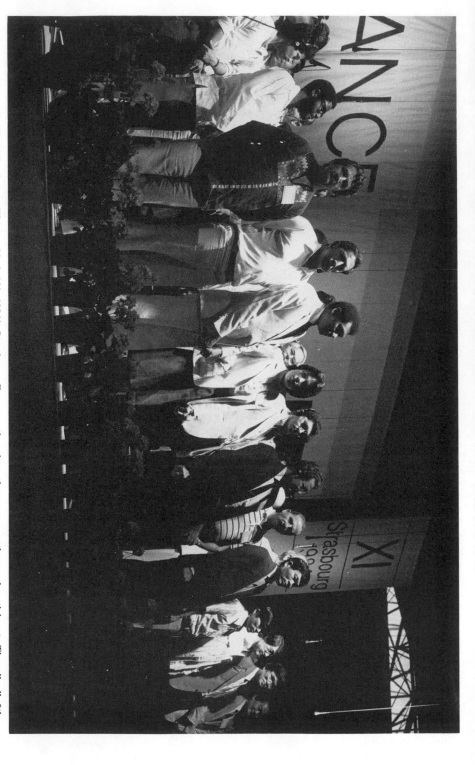

Mennonite World Conference XI Assembly, held in 1984 in Strasbourg, France, gathered together over seven thousand participants. The roll call of the participating conferences at the opening session on July 24 reflected some of the assembled seventy nations. (MWC photo by Janneke Mens, 1984)

Introduction

Mennonites in Global Witness

by Diether Götz Lichdi, Editor

The purpose

The *Mennonite World Handbook* (*MWH*) was first issued in 1978. The purpose of this second edition is to inform and update visitors to Assembly 12 in Winnipeg and, thereafter, to serve the Mennonite community throughout the world. The *MWH* seeks to acquaint readers with the diversity and the unity of the Mennonites and related groups: their stories, experiences, thoughts, and hopes. We meet sisters and brothers reporting on their experiences and describing their work in new or well-established congregations, giving insight into particular situations. We are invited to join the theological thoughts and current deliberations of Mennonite teachers. We see statistics about conferences and congregations, activities and budgets, ministries and ministers. It may strike some that most of the authors come out of the North American or European context. This disparity does not correspond with the membership figures, because the Mennonites coming out of mission during the last two or three generations will probably soon surpass their sisters and brothers of the sending churches. Therefore, it is not only desirable but necessary that Mennonites of the two-thirds world participate more and more in the theological discussion. Their differently shaped experiences, which we learn about through their stories and ministries, promise new insights and perceptions.

In a single book it is impossible to relate all the various activities that Mennonites are undertaking in the many parts of the world. The articles, sketches, and information contained in this *MWH* do not intend to be comprehensive or representative. The *MWH* does, however, try to reflect the pluralistic Mennonite world and its multicultural structures. Certainly the stories of the authors are authentic for their specific situation. They are meaningful in their context and will enlarge our Mennonite experience. They are like pieces of a mosaic, each one giving an important aspect but not the whole picture. The same applies to the discussion of theological issues. The subjects are not treated in scholarly depth or with exhaustive width. Instead, they allow us to participate in the thinking of experienced Mennonite teachers without pretending to propagate a Mennonite theology. The overall selection and treatment in the *MWH* may sometimes seem arbitrary, but the intention is to suggest a fresh look at important issues by presenting meaningful stories and reporting actual experiences. Numerous articles deal with subjects outside of the Western (North American and European) background and witness specific situations in the two-thirds world (Asia, Africa, and Latin America) through case studies describing different contexts. The *MWH* hopes to enhance future tasks and strengthen the worldwide sister/brotherhood by these stories and ideas. Opinions other than those presented here may also be relevant for discussion by Mennonites. The *MWH* asserts the necessity for dialogue and cooperation by visualizing the gospel in real life.

The statistical material is not truly comprehensive, either, since it gives limited information about Mennonites and related groups throughout the world. In connection with the figures of members and congregations, the structures and activities of conferences are on display. Although a questionnaire was carefully and precisely prepared to gather information, there may be misinterpretations and errors. Therefore, the figures may reveal tendencies more than exact statistics. Mennonite World Conference (MWC) has tried during the last decade to learn about and contact all known bodies and, with some exceptions, has been basically successful. MWC provides the only resource preparing this kind of information and, despite shortcomings, the statistics are getting more reliable from year to year.

The approach

Critical readers, pointing to the fact that there are relatively few writers representing the two-thirds world, may claim that this *MWH* still has a paternalistic attitude, which has proved so troublesome in the past. This critique may be justified and demonstrates that we are still at the beginning. There will be a long road to follow, and coming publications will have to deal with it. The change in the Mennonite world—as also reflected in the history of MWC—has been tremendous during the years since World War II. The Mennonite world has, in many respects, turned upside down. In recent years the outstanding issues have been the organizational, financial, and personal dimensions, and they were more or less handled with North American assistance. The most prominent task now is to cope with the growth that has been spiritually and theologically entrusted to us by God. It will not be enough during the coming years for Mennonite conferences in the two-thirds world to become self-sufficient, employing more and more indigenous sisters and brothers, ministering to an increasing number of congregations, and gaining independence from outside know-how and technical assistance. We should undertake joint reflections on witnessing to the biblical Christ in today's world in different contexts in a variety of situations, showing faithfulness to our Anabaptist heritage.

We obviously need not only a contextually oriented language or problem-related images but, first of all, a renewed identity reflecting our mutual solidarity, our different experiences, and our common hope in Christ Jesus. In coping with these objectives, we are still in infancy. Traditionally, Mennonites have refused theology, which they allotted to the "scribes," and meant to depend solely and directly on the Scripture itself. The relevant discussions in other denominations were denounced as hypocritical and lacking in humility and obedience. They generally believed that the gospel would immediately reveal all the wisdom necessary for a Christian life, and they considered theological deliberations a worldly arrogance. Most of them were not aware that the customary presentation of the Anabaptist past (especially in the sixteenth century) for the most part implemented a theological interpretation of the past in order to explain the presence of the Mennonites. The Anabaptist vision was to become a guideline in today's issues, and historical imagination supported some wishful thinking. Facing the growth of Mennonites in the two-thirds world today, our identity can no longer be defined by history alone. There has to be a new means for shaping the Mennonite vision. The research and description of our history was the beginning of the systematic evaluation of the gospel's meaning and challenge for us. New roads for exploration have opened since the first *MWH*.

Interconnection

As Mennonites acquainted themselves with "strange" cultural settings, the traditional vision lost its exclusive relevance for the formation of guidelines. As new sisters and brothers joined us, the old patterns and explanations failed and now need to be replaced by visions referring to the gospel and reflecting the Anabaptist heritage with enough flexibility to adjust to various cultural settings. MWC mirrors this development. Two assemblies before World War II were dedicated to historical commemoration. The themes thereafter were more general and revealed no specific Mennonite character. To compensate for this lack, common messages were sent to the Mennonite world. However, the messages ended when the unanimity and enthusiasm faded away and the presidium wanted to avoid antagonistic discussions that would create or deepen hostile feelings. Some people perceived this abstinence as indifference and insisted that MWC not only organize large assemblies but also facilitate joint reflection on the relevance of the gospel and the impact of our Anabaptist legacy. The MWC Executive Committee met this request and in 1985 appointed an international "Faith and Life Committee" to produce a study book, *Witnessing to Christ in Today's World*, prior to Assembly 12. This and similar efforts should lead to better understandings of different positions and to more cooperation in finding answers to relevant issues and defining common goals.

The *MWH* also reveals the structural changes in inter-Mennonite relations. Notwithstanding the relative decrease in the size of the traditional Mennonite community, the missionary movements are no longer going exclusively from the West to other parts of the world. Missionary operations into Europe and North America started by "new" Mennonites mark the beginning of a new era of mutuality. Even earlier there were various mission outreaches in Indonesia, Zaire, and Latin American countries opened and operated independently by Mennonites of these countries (sometimes supported by Europeans/North

Americans). Now their missionary zeal turns to the Old World, which needs the gospel. The allegedly Christian Occident is to receive the gospel anew carried by the overwhelming joy of first- and second-generation believers.

This change signals the establishment of many Mennonite centers around the world. The North American centrality of the postwar period has lost its uniqueness. The Mennonite world looks forward during the coming years to receiving influence and suggestions from unexpected directions. Mutual stimulations will increasingly form the Mennonite identity and vision. Cooperation in mission, relief, and other fields in various dimensions will be better utilized. Common issues will be handled by "old" and "new" Mennonites as well, and there will be more issues involving both groups. An exchange of ideas and visions, of gifts and goals, will enrich our spiritual life and enhance our capacity as stewards of the kingdom of God. Sharing our burdens may provoke renewal in many groups and congregations. The inter-Mennonite dialogue will give importance to many new tasks unknown today. It will facilitate the Mennonite identity despite or because of the diversity of background and pluralistic temptations; it will contribute toward a sense of unity nurtured by a common witness. Joined forces, demonstrated mutuality, and interdependence will undergird the Mennonite community.

The experience of MWC

Assembly 12 of MWC at Winnipeg may not yet justify the claim of global witness for today's world, taking into account the preponderance of North American visitors. The *MWH* tries to focus on stories and issues, on people and thoughts, to direct our attention to situations and expectations beyond the boundary of the family reunion. It wants to get its readers involved in those questions that must be answered in the immediate future and to make the reader aware of many sisters and brothers around the world.

Mennonite World Conference developed out of a modest beginning. Before World War I, when the Mennonite world was much smaller and more secluded, a proposal was first published. Mennonites then had the vision of the "Stillen im Lande" (Quiet in the Land). The majority spoke German. Almost half of them lived in Russia. There was a handful of "new" Mennonites in the mission fields in Indonesia, India, and Africa. On the occasion of the four hundredth anniversary of the first baptism upon confession of faith, Christian Neff of Germany in 1925 invited all Mennonites to the first assembly of MWC in Basel. The characterization of a world conference was somewhat overstated: besides one visitor from the United States, eighty came from Switzerland, France, Germany, and The Netherlands. Two representatives of the Russian Mennonites had to stay at the border because they could not obtain a visa.

After World War II the number of visitors increased and MWC became an all-Mennonite event. Since 1967 the Travel Fund has facilitated the visiting of more and more sisters and brothers from the growing Mennonite bodies in the two-thirds world. Nevertheless, their participation is much below their percentage of membership. This is due to lack of funds rather than lack of interest. The meetings themselves and the subsequent reports have been a valuable contribution to a global witness. The program became more diverse and included almost all facets of Christian life. Those who attended got acquainted during workshops and conversation groups. Many started to read the gospel together, to share their experiences, and to pray together. This might be a reason that MWC did not become a well-organized "super church" but developed as a network of relationships and encounters, worship and cooperation. In the next decade this tool will be shaped as the Mennonite community witnesses, like a city set on the hill, providing help, hope, and vision for everybody.

The general goals we have to take into account are

- the proclamation of Christ's kingdom in today's world.
- the construction of the local congregation as God's people.
- the strengthening and extension of mission and relief.

The special Mennonite contributions are

- the elucidation of Mennonite ecclesiology in terms of sister/brotherhood and mutual love.
- the emphasis of the Anabaptist ethic: faith is to produce action.
- the updating of the peace witness and the theology of service and sharing.

MWC will facilitate stronger ties

- to maintain an easily accessible network of information and communication.
- to enlarge meetings for various levels and occasions.
- to initiate working groups for special projects and inter-Mennonite cooperation.
- to facilitate theological studies, education, and publications.

MWC is a tool that might channel additional tasks if commissioned. The supporting bodies will have the responsibility to test the possibilities and provide for the enabling of MWC. The suggestions and initiatives of the MWC staff itself also play an important role in defining its future. Of course, MWC has to cope with the general Mennonite polity of protecting the integrity and independence of conferences and congregations. The tension of our heritage and future goals, of our autonomy and our solidarity in Christ, can be productive in mission and relief, in building churches, and in shaping new visions.

Diether Götz Lichdi, editor, Federal Republic of Germany, b. 1935, lay preacher, businessman, and editor of the *Mennonitische Jahrbuch*.

Congregation in Donskoj near Orenburg in the USSR. We see the congregation gathering after a baptismal ceremony in 1986. Today many of these people have emigrated to Germany. (Photographer unknown)

Stories

Who are we?

by Cornelius J. Dyck

There may be as many different answers to this question as there are Mennonites, not to speak of descriptions non-Mennonites would give. What follows here may appear to some as a statement of the ideal—what we often refer to as the vision or, at least, what we would like to be, not what we really are. Since 1988 at least five books have been written by Mennonites about who the Mennonites are. The following is not a summary of their analysis but a brief, personally interpretative statement based on regular reading of our papers, reports of meetings—global and national, on continuing dialogue with brothers and sisters worldwide, as possible, and on observation. Readers will need to keep their own background context in mind as they proceed.

As Mennonites we are a part of God's family, a people on the way, on a pilgrimage with Christ. We seek the fullness of the kingdom of God even as we experience it in all its earthiness in our local congregation at home and in close encounters with each other. We are a people wanting to be guided by the Spirit, a people knowing some of our own weaknesses but also knowing the overwhelming grace and love of God. In Christ we have become united; we are one in him.

We come from many lands, nations, and cultures. We have been shaped by the societies from which we have come and to which we return. We have been shaped by our heritage of faith from the sixteenth century. We have been shaped by our study of the Scriptures. We have been shaped by our own personal experiences of life, the joys and sorrows of human existence. We are a very diverse people. Yet in Christ we are, and can increasingly become, one in spirit, mind, and heart. We can celebrate our diversity because of our strong common bond in him. In him we respect each other, we learn to listen to each other, we help each other. "There is neither Jew nor Greek, slave nor free, male nor female, for you [we] are all one in Christ Jesus" (Gal. 3:28).

As a Mennonite people we affirm that we are an integral part of the Christian church. Our roots are not first in the sixteenth century but in the Scriptures and the early church. We want our congregations to be like the church in the Bible. But the faithful of the ages (and the not-so-faithful) are also a part of our history of the church. The experience of persecution has driven us into the wilderness, where we believed that we alone were the faithful remnant. We came to see ourselves as a marginal but heroic people, perhaps even more faithful than others. But God has visited us in judgment and in mercy. We need to reclaim our heritage as part of the universal body of Christ, the "una sancta," and adjust our self-images accordingly. God has no stepchildren! And there are many believers in other traditions who have not "bowed their knees to Baal."

In Anabaptism we have a unique sixteenth-century European heritage. It is a heritage that Mennonites in Latin America, Asia, and Africa also rightfully claim. It is a heritage of suffering, of struggle for freedom of religion, of the separation of church and state, and of voluntary (believers') church membership. It is a heritage in which the emphasis on discipleship is a central part of the good news of the gospel and in which a strong missionary zeal flourished. It is a heritage in which peace and justice and equality were taught and lived. It is a heritage of the spiritual, social, economic, and ultimately political struggle of our forebears, for which the most fitting monument is the *Martyrs Mirror* and, even more, the living monument of thousands of faithful, dynamic congregations around the world. We claim this heritage. It helps us to understand who we are.

On the other hand, Mennonites of European background likewise claim the history of Mennonites in Africa, Asia, Latin America, and minority groups among us as our own. As we get to know this history and identify with it, including slavery, colonialism, and paternalism, we are humbled that we too were often among the oppressors. Repentance and forgiveness open a new channel for healing and understanding. A *Martyrs Mirror* volume of the travail of twentieth-century Mennonites worldwide could fill a volume larger than the original. We are so print (book) oriented in the West. Now, as we take time to hear and tell our stories to each other across national, cultural, and dogmatic boundaries, the walls of division and suspicion come tumbling down, for Christ has broken them down (Eph. 2:14). In sharing our stories we are discovering who we are, individually and as a people.

As Mennonites we have a long-standing reputation as being a hard-working and pioneering people. From the Vistula Delta to the Ukraine, from the North American Midwest to the Chaco of Paraguay and the farms of Sumatra, we have tamed the wilderness and made the deserts bloom. We have often been tolerated because we were an economic asset. For us work is a part of godliness. And so we find it hard to understand the poor. "Why don't they work?" The many causes and shapes of poverty often elude us. A deacon's big car even had a bumper sticker that read, "I fight poverty, I work." In the past we have tended to remain aloof from those around us, and they have envied us. We tended to marry those from among our own people. Instead of winning others, we built walls around us.

But that is changing. While we originally in the sixteenth century were an urban people, we soon became almost exclusively rural. Now in 1990 we are again a predominantly urban people in most parts of the world. We have entered many professions, particularly the human service professions in health, education, social agencies, and even politics. On any given day many more than one thousand of us are working as volunteers in some area of human need at home or abroad. But the arts are also again beginning to flourish among us. Then, too, there are many successful entrepreneurs and industrialists among us who are trying courageously to apply Christian ethics in the marketplace.

In Europe, and particularly in North America, we have built many structures and institutions to sustain our life and work. We are generous, but mostly not sacrificially generous, in supporting them. In other parts of the world there is more spontaneity and day-to-day freedom. Resources there are few. Yet as people of one global family we are called to share with others as we are able (Gal. 6:10). In 1527 Ambrose Spittelmaier wrote, "How can we say, 'This house is mine, this field is mine, this money is mine' [and then pray] 'Our Father'?" Our brothers and sisters of the so-called Third World have much to teach the rest of us about love and justice.

From the first days of Anabaptism we have seen ourselves as a people of peace, "Sermon on the Mount" Christians, and have often been recognized as such. Yet throughout the centuries, and still today, many among us do not see nonresistance, or nonviolent resistance, as a part of the good news of the gospel. Jesus' death on the cross is not seen as a call to us to also overcome evil with good. Pacifism has become a luxury, available to those who live in societies that permit it; and even there a misguided patriotism often rejects it. But at the heart of our identity is the gospel of peace. Jesus' words and example still stand. And in 1990 peacemaking is becoming increasingly difficult unless it includes a concern for justice.

Mennonites have historically been a worshiping and praying people and a people of the Bible. A new study about to be released will tell us how North American Mennonites are doing in this area. Our congregations in the Third World would not be growing so rapidly if these elements were not a part of their daily life. Here and there the empowering ministry of the Holy Spirit has brought new life and witness. There are healing ministries. While the ministry of the laity continues, pastoral duties are increasingly carried out by trained leaders, including women.

And so we come together in Winnipeg as a global family, not knowing many of our sisters and brothers but wanting to meet them, to hear their stories of life and faith, to look into their eyes and hearts, to sing and to pray. It is through interaction with others, through finding our place in our large family, and through listening to God in prayer and worship that we can begin to answer the question of who we really are, alone and together.

Cornelius J. Dyck, USA, b. 1921, M.A., Ph.D., professor of Anabaptist and sixteenth-century studies at Associated Mennonite Biblical Seminaries (Elkhart, Indiana), and former executive secretary of MWC.

Mennonite Central Committee helps in many emergencies around the world. In Sudan, where this snapshot was taken, a civil war rages, unknown by much of the public. (MCC photo by Ray Downing, 1989)

Rooted in our faith heritage

by Angel M. Canon

> Always be prepared to give an answer to everyone who asks you
> to give the reason for the hope that you have. But do this with
> gentleness and respect ... (1 Pet. 3:15b)

When I received the invitation to write this article, I accepted without hesitation
because it dealt with a subject that was very clear for me. However, as I reflected
carefully about the connotations of the Mennonite faith, I saw there were roots
that were much richer and deeper than those I had considered at first. Among
them are an apostolic heritage of faith, a theology and doctrine born in the heart
of the Anabaptist Radical Reformation, and a church that, in the midst of the
twentieth century, continues to be committed to the foundations of God's reign.

The Mennonite church has a faith heritage rooted in the foundations of the
apostolic church, that is to say, in Jesus Christ, the Bible, the Holy Spirit, and the
community of believers. For the early church, Jesus, the "Word," had existed for
all eternity. He is the supreme revelation of the eternal and only God, the only
mediator between God the Father and the human race, which is alienated by sin.
By his expiatory death on the cross, he made reconciliation with God possible,
not only of humanity but of all the cosmic creation; and, by his resurrection as
Lord of life in all its fullness, he has defeated death with all its miseries (Col.
1:15–23). It was thanks to the coming of the Paraclete, the Counselor, that the
timid community was "clothed with power from on high" and launched itself to
fulfill the Great Commission. The early church was a genuine community of
discernment and discipleship, of prophetic proclamation of redemption and grace
but also of justice and punishment, of individual privileges and responsibilities
as well as commitments and fraternal solidarity. All the gifts of the Holy Spirit
were recognized and stimulated in the believers and the community for the
"edification of the body" and the extension of the kingdom (1 Cor. 12–14,
Eph. 4:11,12).

I also identify myself with the Mennonite church because its theology and
doctrine, forged in the heart of the Radical Reformation in the sixteenth century,
are in accordance with the foundations of the early church. Both the Anabaptist
Radical Reformation and the early church recognized (1) the authority of the
Scriptures as the normative principle in the discernment and interpretation of
Jesus Christ, (2) the eternity of the "Word"—Christ—from the beginning in
God, (3) the union of the Father and the Son, (4) the incarnation of Christ in a
people and race at a certain moment in history, (5) that Christ is mediator
between God the Father and God's creation, and (6) above all, that Christ is Lord
and God. Concerning the church as a community of believers, Walter Klaassen
summarizes the Anabaptist writings in his book *Anabaptism in Outline*: "The

church was now identified as the gathered congregation of believers who have voluntarily entered it by baptism upon confession of faith. Only those can be members who are obedient to Christ. Love is the chief mark of the church. ... It is a community of mutual aid in which nothing is held back from those in need."

The Anabaptist Mennonite movement was characterized, among other things, by (1) having separated itself totally from the Roman Catholic church and having dared to go beyond where the classical Protestant Reformation had gone, (2) teaching the total separation from the world, (3) living a holistic gospel, (4) baptizing only adults and refusing to baptize infants because they did not find a biblical base to do it, and (5) giving a sound no to war and arms. In that way, through the recapture and purification of biblical and Anabaptist foundations, the Mennonite church started to spread to the world of that day and has reached us through 465 years of history and pilgrimage.

Finally, I am a Mennonite because this church in the twentieth century, in spite of its limitations and imperfections, tries to continue being faithful to the foundations of God's reign and to its holistic mission. In fulfilling that vocation, the church does not curtail its missionary work. Many men and women, in gratitude and commitment to their Lord and with love for those who suffer, have sacrificed their comfort to go to become incarnated in peoples, cultures, countries, or regions in order to share God's love, exposing themselves to all sorts of poverty, disease, misunderstandings, hostilities, and even persecution and death. Others go with their own resources as volunteers to many places in the world to share themselves and their gifts with communities or churches where human beings are moaning and suffering. Many others, in accordance with their economic resources, give of their money for the construction of the kingdom. These resources are used to plant churches, build meeting places, prepare pastors and leaders, create centers for biblical formation, and found schools, health centers, homes for the elderly and for orphans, and projects of communal agricultural development. In other words, they share their bread with the needy.

This church not only announces the good news of the kingdom. It also raises its voice against all systems of injustice and violence. It is a church that says no to militarism, arms, war, and environmental contamination. No to all that goes against life, for only the Lord has dominion over life. The Mennonite church is the one that allows me to develop my gifts and grow in communion and discipleship with my brothers and sisters, knowing that "I do not consider myself yet to have taken hold of it. But one thing I do: Forgetting what is behind and straining toward what is ahead, I press on toward the goal to win the prize for which God has called me heavenward in Christ Jesus" (Phil. 3:13,14).

Angel Canon, Colombia, b. 1948, M.Div. student in Lombard, Illinois, pastor for twenty-four years, member of the conference Iglesia Evangélica Menonita de Colombia.
Translated by Margaret Schipani.

Old Order River Brethren by choice

by Stephen E. Scott

On October 5, 1969, at age twenty-one I was baptized into the Old Order River Brethren Church in a pond near Mountville, Pennsylvania. I was not raised in this church. My baptism was the culmination of a three-year search for a church home.

Perhaps it would be in order to give a bit of history of the Old Order River Brethren Church, since it is one of the smaller and less-well-known branches of the Anabaptist family. The River Brethren originated about 1780 in Lancaster County, Pennsylvania (USA). The first members were mostly Mennonites but were highly influenced by the German Baptist Brethren (Dunkers) and the predecessors of the United Brethren. The doctrines and practices of these three groups were blended to make a unique combination. They were called River Brethren because they lived close to the banks of the Susquehanna.

Like many Anabaptist groups, the River Brethren divided into liberal and conservative factions in the nineteenth century. The liberal group adopted the name Brethren in Christ. The conservative group became known as Old Order River Brethren and, unofficially, as Yorker Brethren, after York County, Pennsylvania, an early center of the group. Today Old Order River Brethren congregations are located in Lancaster County, Pennsylvania; Franklin County, Pennsylvania; and Dallas County, Iowa.

The Old Order River Brethren have traditionally met for worship in the homes of the members, although schools and other public buildings are also used. A plural, unsalaried ministry is observed. Ministers are chosen from the congregation and receive no formal training. The transition from German to English was made early in the twentieth century, but traditional, slow hymn tunes are still observed. All singing is a cappella. There is no Sunday school. Members wear distinctive plain dress. The women wear head coverings. The men wear beards.

A testimony or experience meeting is a part of every regular worship service of the Old Order River Brethren. At this time any person can tell how God is working in his or her life. A traditional practice was to relate one's Christian pilgrimage. In this spirit I will tell some of my experience—not because I want any glory, but to show how God has worked in my life.

My family has no long tradition in any denomination. To my knowledge, only one of my grandparents ever belonged to a church. My immediate family was converted at a Baptist revival meeting when I was thirteen. Large numbers of people were persuaded to accept Christ as their Savior through the efforts of this church. The fundamentals of the faith were strongly emphasized; but, as I grew in the Christian faith, I found the church to be lacking in some ways.

Early in my Christian life I became influenced by a religious group that lived close to my native Dayton, Ohio. I had seen these people occasionally when my family went on shopping trips into town. I was impressed by the black hats and long beards of the men and the women's bonnets and long dresses. I wanted to know who these people were and what they believed. I learned that local people called them Dunkards and that their official name was Old German Baptist Brethren.

I began reading about the Old German Baptists and similar groups like the Mennonites and Amish. I found that collectively they were often called "plain people" because of their distinctively simple dress. I subscribed to some of the periodicals of these groups and studied their doctrines. When I was old enough to drive I visited their churches. I was received warmly in all the churches I visited. I never got the idea, as I have heard some say, that the plain groups were closed ethnic groups that someone from another heritage could not join.

As I became better acquainted with the plain people, my connection with the Baptist church grew less. I asked my pastor and Sunday school teachers why we did not observe the doctrines and practices of nonresistance, foot washing, the head covering, and nonconformity in dress. I was given very unconvincing explanations. Ironically, when I went away to a Baptist college I severed my tie to the Baptist church.

At first I began attending a Mennonite church in my area. I appreciated their a cappella singing and kneeling for prayer. I was attracted to the minority of members who still wore plain dress. In one way I felt at home with their church program, which included Sunday school, revival meetings, and missionaries. In another way the church seemed too much like the evangelical mainstream that I had just left. The matter of nonconformity to the world was obviously diminishing rapidly. I began making a 60-mile trek to Plain City, Ohio, where I attended Conservative Mennonite and Amish Mennonite churches.

About this time I withdrew from college and decided to get my obligation to the government out of the way. With some difficulty, and certainly with God's help, I was given a conscientious objector classification. An alternative service job opened up for me at Lancaster Mennonite High School (LMH). I spent two years there as a janitor.

I was delighted to live in Lancaster County, Pennsylvania, the American homeland of the plain people. I was fascinated by the wide variety of Anabaptist groups represented in the area. I visited a number of different churches but felt most at home among the Old Order River Brethren. I became acquainted with this group through one of the teachers at LMH, Myron Dietz.

Among the River Brethren I found a warm, loving fellowship. It appeared to me that these people were truly seeking God's will in their lives and were not seeing how close they could get to the world. Their form of worship, their singing, and their style of dress were all very traditional. These traditions served to keep the church from worldly trends. Standards of appearance and behavior were not regarded as legalism but as practical applications of biblical principles.

I viewed the River Brethren as a truly spiritual people whose spirituality was a real inner presence, not merely a certain vocabulary or participation in certain activities. I was especially impressed by the lack of a generation gap. The young people seemed to be in full harmony with the older generation.

I am not trying to say that the River Brethren do not have their share of problems and shortcomings. Yes, we have our struggles. But the church as a whole is determined to work through these problems with Christian love and patience while being true to God's word and our godly heritage.

My story is not unique. There are many members in our fellowship who were not raised in the church. These people were attracted to the Old Order River Brethren for basically the same reasons I was. Compromises in our nonconformity to the ways of the world would have, no doubt, made us less appealing to seekers. Indeed, some who came among us considered that we were not "nonconformed" enough.

There are great pressures around us to take an easier way. In our minds, this is not the way of the cross. We take seriously the warning in James 4:4, "… friendship with the world is enmity with God …" and 1 John 2:15b, "If any man love the world, the love of the Father is not in him."

Perhaps our greatest challenge as a church is to effectively instill our biblically based values in our children. Yes, we do hear cries of, "Why can't I do this?" or "Why do I have to do that?" But we believe a truly surrendered heart will ask, "Lord, what can I do to serve you?"

Stephen E. Scott, USA, b. 1948, researcher-writer at Good Enterprises (Intercourse, Pennsylvania).

George R. Brunk III, dean of Eastern Mennonite Seminary, places a hood on Can Ngoc Le of Vietnam, recipient of a master of arts in church ministries degree. Dr. Brunk is the current moderator of the Mennonite Church. (EMS photo by Jim Bishop, 1989)

When I was a stranger

by Ramzi Farran

When I was a child ...

I first came to personally know the Mennonites through Mickey Mouse. I was
about seven years old and in the second grade in Jericho, then part of Jordan,
when the Mennonites came to my school to distribute Christmas Bundles. The
bundles had the usual soap, toothbrush, washcloth, towel, and school supplies.
But my most treasured possession was a fire truck with a moveable Mickey
Mouse head. It was one of the few toys I had, and play with it I did.

My sister had already worked for Mennonite Central Committee (MCC) for
several years to support our family. But through my experience with the Christmas Bundles, I began to realize who MCC was and what they were doing in the
West Bank. During the next twelve years, MCC workers often visited our home,
and I personally became acquainted with many of them. Orie Miller, William
Snyder, and Akron, PA, were common household names and places—I was sure
that Akron was a big city in the United States. MCC workers invited me to
attend their prayer services and participate in a one-week summer camp, at
which time I received my first Bible.

I was born to a Greek Orthodox family in Jerusalem in 1946. Jerusalem was
under the British mandate and was a city of turmoil, beset by both religious and
political struggles. My father, a prosperous businessman, owned a taxi company
and a large movie house in Jerusalem. One evening in the spring of 1948, the
Israeli commandos, promising that we could return home the next day, told us to
flee the city. The next day never came. My father literally lost all his properties
and businesses overnight. We became refugees. Eventually we were able to
return to my family's winter home in Jericho, where my mother still lives.

Putting away childish things

My parents wanted to protect me from the Muslim influence in the public
schools, so they made sacrifices in order that I could attend a private Catholic
school. I served as an altar boy and participated in mass daily for six years. My
family strictly observed Lent and fasted before communion. Holy Week was the
highlight of our Christian life in a land where we were a minority.

I was awarded a scholarship to attend a Quaker boarding school for the last six
years of my education—my second encounter with the peace churches. At that
time I realized that I wanted to be more than a nominal Christian, but I was beset
by both internal and external turmoil. Internally, I rebelled against the religious
practices, structure, and Greek language of the Orthodox church. On the other

hand, the peace stand of the Quakers in the midst of violence, prejudice, and hatred was like a slap across my face. And yet, when I began attending silent Quaker services, I was comforted by a faith that was expressed in the more understandable English language and where Scriptures spoke to me in a personal way. Gradually I drifted away from the Greek Orthodox masses. Externally, I was confronted by militaristic Muslim friends who could not understand how I could hold a faith based upon Israel—in a country where Israel was the enemy.

The Mennonites, however, continued to have a subtle but pervasive influence on my life. In 1965, through the help and invitation of Ernest and Mary Lehman, then MCC workers in Jordan, I accepted a scholarship to attend Goshen College, a college affiliated with the Mennonite Church. The Lehmans had known my family for over a decade and had followed my life and well-being with interest. Their return to Indiana coincided with my coming to college, where their home became my home-away-from-home. While in Goshen I became reacquainted with many MCC friends I had come to know in the Middle East. In Jordan they learned about my culture, and now they were helping me, a stranger, learn about theirs. I began to comprehend and appreciate the risks and sacrifices they had made to help others. That first Christmas, the Lehmans gave me H.S. Bender's *These Are My People*, my first serious encounter with Mennonite theology.

When I was wounded ...

During the summer of my freshman year at Goshen College, I lost my right arm in an industrial accident. I was still trying to adjust to having left my family and country, and now I was confronted with one of the most painful losses in my life. I was devastated and discouraged and was not sure how I would go on. In this pain, however, I came to understand more about Mennonite community. Many people in Goshen expressed their love and compassion for me. The surgeon and attending physician tried their best to reattach my severed arm. The head nurse led the campaign for my recovery. Factory workers, from the Amish to the prostitute, donated money for me. College friends fed me and prayed with me. Former MCC workers Wayne and Agnes Schertz picked up my soiled pajamas each evening and returned the same pair, clean and ironed, the next morning. College Church members provided transportation and comfort. I was bombarded by attorneys who suggested that I sue my employer. Viola Good, my adviser at the college, selected a Mennonite attorney who arranged for the employer to pay my medical expenses and workman's compensation. I was beginning to learn who my people were and what they believed.

Journeys with John

During the June 1967 Middle East War, fear, frustration, loneliness, and anger were my daily companions. I began realizing that I was losing connections with my home and family and would never be able to return to the West Bank. For three weeks after the war I had no contact with my family. One morning in my Christian Faith class, Ed Stoltzfus began by expressing concern for my family's well-being. He led a spontaneous prayer for my family's safety. During the class break I went to my mailbox and found God's answer waiting for me: my family was unharmed. Upon my return to class we all shared in prayers of thanksgiving.

During that summer I met John Mosemann, pastor of the Goshen College Mennonite Church. Through conversations with John, my life began to change. He listened to my experiences of physical, mental, and spiritual anguish and provided comfort in his quiet, gentle way. He understood my struggles and helped me reconcile the disparity between the Middle East events and a loving God. He emphasized that the best way to conquer my enemy was through love. He helped me to understand that Christ was the fulfillment of the Old Testament prophecies. This formed the basis for my belief that the ethnic Israel, now present in the Middle East, is different than the spiritual Israel referred to in God's plan. It also formed the basis for a new meaning of Christ's crucifixion and resurrection, the way of love and peace.

John became my friend and always greeted me, not with the usual "Shalom," but with the Arabic, "Salaam." His international reputation and involvement in the Mennonite Church did not interfere with our relationship. He took me home as a son where I also learned to know his wife, Ruth. He continued to nurture me spiritually and baptized me in 1968. His interest in my life did not end there, as he later counseled me and my prospective wife and officiated at our wedding. Both he and Ruth became adopted grandparents for our two sons. The Mose-manns' love and faith was God's love made evident to me.

Now, some twenty years later, I still struggle with loving the enemy, knowing that my family lives with oppression and suffering each day. Sometimes I grow impatient and wonder whether God is dragging his feet, or whether I am blind to see him working, or whether the Middle Eastern issues will be resolved in my lifetime. I believe in the priesthood of all believers and continue to learn from others in my congregation who model their faith in simple dignity. I believe the church must become more global and open to the strangers who surround us. We need to decrease our focus on nationalism, culture, and conferences and focus on the theology that binds us together. A strong congregational focus on Christian education is essential to provide opportunities for both strangers and those who have grown up in the Mennonite church to become who God wants us to be.

I find that I may still be a stranger in a strange land to some of the people I meet daily, but I have found that within the Mennonite church I am no longer a stranger, but part of a larger people.

Ramzi Farran, Jordan/USA, b. 1946, M.S., high school chemistry teacher and chairperson of the Lombard (Illinois) Mennonite Church education commission.

Guatemalan woman carrying her little child on her back. Guatemala has one of the highest rates of malnutrition and infant mortality in Central America. Providing health care and nutrition is a challenging task.
(MCC photo by Emily Will, 1990)

My walk through the Mennonite church

by José M. Ortiz

I would rather be called a Christian, but I have not resisted being called a Mennonite. Within ecumenical circles, I have no problem with being a generic Mennonite, but when I am with Anglo Mennonites, I have caught myself talking about "them" and keeping an ethnic distance. Therefore, it is in order to give a rationale why I am a Mennonite, and that is expressed in some simple reasons. I am a Mennonite because of history. At the time that I was entering adolescence and in a faith search, their missionaries were on hand to explain the Bible. Because the Mennonites were not allowed to send service people into China due to World War II, they opted to go to Puerto Rico—to Aibonito and to Coamo Arriba, my home community. My coming to Christ led me to obtain Bible training. The Mennonites invested in me, and I also invested in them. Once my schooling was over, a job in ministry was waiting for me. Yes, I am a Mennonite for three very pragmatic reasons, very strong reasons to remain in the church: they helped in my conversion, my training, and my professional or ministerial development. I cannot call this opportunism; I call it providential and mutual investment.

My walks through the church have led me to cherish and nurture strong bonds with Mennonites from all walks of life who have become my extended family, and that is a good feeling on this side of heaven. I cherish simplicity of life, a faith expressed in service to others, and a desire for peace and justice. That search grabs my feelings and engages my intellect. Like the psalmist, I "despise the noise of the solemn assemblies," a passive faith, but I strive for a faith that is active and reflective.

Yes, the Mennonite church has some wrinkles, and that helps us all to keep humble. We need to redirect our energies or we will lose our sense of people-hood. We have been plagued by a sense of loss when it comes to visible leader-ship. It seems that leaders are not appreciated and respected, or they are ignored, all of which creates apathy. The lack of leadership is expressed by the absence of good preachers; yes, our pulpits are suffering. Positions in our denominations are not filled on time, and disregard to appeals for committee memberships in de-nominational slots is common. The decision-making process is becoming obsolete, costly, and time consuming. At times it degenerates into indifference and inertia. The net result tends to be that the church invests more dollars but the outcome is the same or worse than previous years. There is a need for personnel, new creative ministries, and evangelistic activity that will bring an increase in church membership. If we cannot secure new converts, we are, in fact, saying that our witnessing does not make sense to the secular person. Have we become part of a religious folklore rather than an expression of the gospel, that dynamite with the power of God to transform lives! This concerns me!

North Americans are a people on the move. Over 25 percent of our population is experiencing a continuous exodus. Some of God's people move for the sake of conscience, others because of their professions, still others because of their intention to be a witness. I have lived in Philadelphia, New York City, Chicago, and Tampa in the United States, and in San Juan, Puerto Rico. All of those major cities had a Mennonite witness in progress; we have become urban. Let the intentional moving continue, but we do not have to move in exclusively with those of our own kind. More Mennonites will move, but that does not mean that they will maintain their Mennonite identity. This should not be considered a loss. Let the ones on the move help to bring a redeeming word to their spheres of government, politics, other denominations, the business sector, and the professions. Let our mobility be a way of testing the fiber of our beliefs.

As a Hispanic Mennonite, I also feel responsible for the future of the Mennonite church. I will make an effort to see that our worship together is more experiential, to look at other Christian traditions with respect, to be less colonialist when it comes to money and positions of leadership, and to enter the mainstream of American life. As we go into the world, we testify that our church has experienced Pentecost and persecution and that the church is entering the decade of the 1990s with a promise to be a faithful witness of Jesus Christ.

José M. Ortiz, Puerto Rico, b. 1939, director of Hispanic Ministries at Goshen College (Goshen, Indiana).

Yo soy Menonita

by Elizabeth Soto

"Yo soy Menonita" (I am a Mennonite) is a phrase many Latin American Mennonites like to say in a proud voice. Part of my identity is based in this sentence. As well, "Yo soy mujer" (I am a woman), "Yo soy puertorriqueña" (I am a Puerto Rican), and "Yo soy cristiana" (I am a Christian); each holds a profound meaning of who I am.

Born in Puerto Rico and partially raised in Chicago, I was a child of an immigrant family who moved to the United States in the early 1960s for employment. Twelve years later my family returned to the "promised land"—a dream of many Puerto Ricans. There I was able to rescue my identity as well as my mother tongue—Spanish. But I was a child already exposed to a second culture and another way of living. That made me a bilingual and bicultural person quite early in my life.

It was in Puerto Rico while I was a teenager that I first learned to know about the Mennonites. Why a Mennonite and not a Baptist, Methodist, or Pentecostal? As I became a committed Christian coming from the Catholic tradition, I recall making a conscious decision to move away from the faith of my forebears. I was just a teenager, but I needed a change; and this small Mennonite church, two houses away from my house, looked as good as any. In the beginning, I must confess, any other church would also have been fine. I thank God that it was not just any other church. It was a Mennonite church. In this small church I began to understand discipleship. In the midst of this evangelical church among many in Puerto Rico, I was given the opportunity to learn about Anabaptist history. I began owning the Mennonite faith. This church met my needs. It confirmed my pacifist attitudes and my yearning for a sense of community.

Bombarded by denominationalism, I was invited by members of the Alliance Church, Baptists, and Pentecostals to be one of them. The Mennonites were not well known in the northwest part of the island where I lived. "Be one of us. Mennonite is a weird name," they told me many times. Later on during my seminary training in my young adult years in the Seminario Evangélico de Puerto Rico (Evangelical Seminary of Puerto Rico), I felt the need to defend my theological stand as a Mennonite. Mennonites made up less than 2 percent of the student body, and we were challenged to prove our pacifist beliefs. Once again I found myself explaining the uniqueness of the Anabaptist belief, and as I did so my belief became much stronger. I began to believe that it was not coincidence that this small church was Mennonite. God had provided me, through his providential love, with the opportunity of my life. I then made a conscious decision to live my belief faithfully, choosing to be a Mennonite.

As I came closer to finishing my seminary training, I felt the need to study my Anabaptist Mennonite history more inductively. I transferred to Associated Mennonite Biblical Seminaries (AMBS) in Elkhart, Indiana, for my last year in 1984–85. There I was exposed more directly to the Germanic Mennonite style of worship. I was attracted to the expression of faith among the North American brothers and sisters with their sense of community, peacemaking, and simple lifestyle.

As a direct result of studying at AMBS, I slowly started my personal journey of reconciling the two faiths I was carrying, the Mennonite faith and the Catholic faith. As a child I grew up Catholic. Once I made my move to the Mennonite church in Puerto Rico, I, like almost all Latino Evangelicals who come from Catholic background, was taught to deny that I was a Christian before. This I see as one of the big misconceptions the evangelicals in Latin America have. They believe that Catholics are not Christians. This is quite ironic considering that one moves from one Christian faith to another. The intensity of self-denial and self-awareness opened my eyes to an internal need to express fully the richness of my two faiths. I became aware that I was a victim of the fundamentalist interpretations of Christianity that the evangelicals in Puerto Rico have. It was as though my past had been stolen from me and I needed to rescue it. My journey was mixed with pain and joy as I began to celebrate the Mass and to sing lively choruses in the Mennonite church in Puerto Rico. I was able to reconcile or celebrate their differences and rejoice in the similarities. I was not on a lonely journey; I had community and special friends who heard me during moments of need. Today I own a Mennonite Catholic faith. Is this possible? Yes, all is possible when we walk with our Savior.

But there are things I would like to see improved. I believe we need more exchanges of ideas between the Asian, Latin American, and African Mennonites and the North American and European Mennonites, who come from a more Germanic historical tradition. North Americans need to acknowledge the value of the faith of these Third World Mennonites and be open to the rapid church growth these churches are experiencing. They need to be challenged by this growth and allow this development to bring about a new evangelical style to their own churches. I believe North Americans, through the arrival of their ancestors to North America, have assumed a passive position against injustice. Their sense of peacemaking is narrowed down to comfortable, inactive pacifism. As Mennonites independent of our culture, language, and ancestral roots, we must search seriously to develop an active stand in denouncing injustice in our countries as well as work at bringing about peace. Our call as Christians and peace-loving Mennonites must be to embrace a theology of social justice and community based on the gospel.

I firmly believe we as Anabaptist Mennonites have much to share in this world full of pain and injustice. Several Latin American theologians have expressed their strong conviction that "Anabaptism is a theology that can speak to the people suffering reality today in the condition Latin America is found ...." I agree with that. Anabaptism contextualized to all parts of the world can well be applied to the pain and hopes of our people.

The first thing I saw in Mennonites was that they are loving people. They are a people who love people, and a people who serve with love and in the name of love. This has been reaffirmed through the opportunities I have had to work in several church agencies. As I work and worship with them, I become more certain that Mennonites are people of love, community, and peace. I feel proud to be a Mennonite. I have learned to appreciate my own faith community.

Today, because of this, I am a better Christian. I am open for new ways of expressing my faith through the gift of owning two faiths, two cultures, and two languages. This has a lot to do with why I am a Mennonite today. For this and many more reasons, I can say in a proud and humble voice: "Yo soy Menonita."

Elizabeth Soto, Puerto Rico, b. 1959, M.A. in religion, assistant secretary to Latin America and the Caribbean for Mennonite Central Committee (Akron, Pennsylvania).

Paulus Singgih is one of the founders of the Muria Synod (GKMI). He was baptized in 1934 and began to preach one year later as a lay preacher. (MWC photo by Paul Kraybill, 1989)

My personal pilgrimage as a Mennonite

by María Janeth Albarracín

Why I am a Mennonite

On August 9, 1984, a date that remains etched in my mind, I experienced a true change in my life when I welcomed the hand of the almighty God. It was the beginning of a personal and material transformation. This transformation brought me certain problems since I lived in a world, governed by human power and money, that I had to abandon. It was at that time that I had the support of the Mennonite brothers and sisters and I became a Mennonite Christian, marking the beginning of a new life full of experiences and testimony of Jesus Christ. I will continue to be a Mennonite because in that way I will be closer to the word of God, which gives my life security and confidence as I live a simple life, full of love.

Characteristics of a Mennonite Christian

Once the Mennonite brothers and sisters had taught me to live in Christ, and the peace I felt in my heart was absolutely real, I decided to leave the Mennonite community to serve as a missionary for the Lord. Because of the Mennonite foundation that Christians should help one another, I began my voluntary work in health and nutrition in Burkina Faso (Africa), allowing me to put into practice what Jesus teaches us in the New Testament and deepening my faith, peace, and hope. You shall be my witnesses, Jesus said to his disciples before he ascended into heaven, and now I feel like one of his witnesses in the community where I work.

My goals, and the direction Mennonites should move

One of my main preoccupations is the lack of personal evangelism. In other words, today more emphasis is put on sharing the message to the masses and not enough attention is given to the individual. For that reason, it would be good for the Mennonites to reflect on this situation and develop a program of personal evangelism. On the other hand, the lack of Mennonite churches in countries where there is much poverty has meant that those less favored do not have the opportunity to share the peace, hope, and love of God. I invite the Mennonite brothers and sisters to reflect on this poverty and to go to those places.

What I like and dislike about the Mennonites

It would be good for all the Mennonites in the world to communicate with each other and to know what activities they are involved in. I would like the Mennonites to support each other spiritually and to see them carefully study the Mennonite Christian beliefs in their churches. In these times in which we live, I like the work the Mennonites are doing toward peace, understanding, and comprehension of other religious philosophies, trying to become one in Christ.

One of my personal experiences while I was serving in Burkina Faso was how those of other churches totally accepted me as a Mennonite. I understood then that all the Christian churches, although they have different names, have the same focus, that is, forgiveness and salvation in Jesus Christ. I also saw that the African Christians are more united because they do not take the denomination so much into account, but instead the strongest view and concern is being one in Christ. If I can make a bit of a comparison with Christians in general, the African Christians are growing stronger in faith.

My particular conviction

I am completely convinced that it is not our religion that saves us but our faith and our intimate relationship with God. We can have this relationship wherever we are, without needing to go someplace else to find it. The Lord manifests himself through our lives for the good of humanity and, in one way or another, the Mennonite brothers and sisters provide support for beginning to live in Christ. Being a Mennonite has taught me to live faithfully. It has shown me the correct road while at the same time has provided many satisfactions and opportunities for new experiences. It is in this way that I feel whole and secure in all the facets of my life.

I give thanks to my Mennonite brothers and sisters in the Bogotá community of Teusaquillo because they were my support in every way: spiritually, morally, and in prayer from the beginning of my personal journey as a Mennonite. I give thanks to Mennonite Central Committee for their acceptance, support, and the opportunity they gave me to develop my work in Burkina Faso. And last, I thank all my Christian brothers and sisters who have kept me in their prayers. May God bless you.

María Janeth Albarracín, Colombia, b. 1959, university studies in nutrition and dietetics.
Translated by Margaret Schipani.

How I got involved

by Yorifumi Yaguchi

The first Americans I saw were the soldiers. There was a navy camp in our town and they located themselves there. And they were the first Christians I saw. Because I was a child then, I thought at that time that all American soldiers were Christians. There were two chapels in the camp. I remember that I visited one of them, which was full of soldiers, and a chaplain preached with eloquence.

But the soldiers I saw in the street or in cabarets spat, smoked like chimneys, got drunk, danced, and used abusive words. Such words as "You son of a bitch!" and "goddamned!" were common among them, and we soon learned to use them. Above all, they loved prostitutes. I later wrote some poems on those experiences.

I sometimes liked GI's …

I sometimes liked GI's,
Because they gave me chewing gum,
I learned how to chew it
And how to spit on the ground.

I sometimes liked GI's,
Because they gave me cigarettes,
I learned how to smoke them
And how to smoke out of nostrils.

I sometimes liked GI's,
Because they gave me canned beer,
And I learned how to get drunk
And how to act like a drunkard.

I sometimes liked GI's,
Because they gave me money,
When I took them to the place
Where prostitutes were living.

I sometimes liked GI's,
Because they taught me English,
And I learned how to use
"God damned, you son of a bitch," and "Jesus Christ."

Our town ...

Our town sleeps in the daytime and
wakes up at night with sudden screams.
There street-girls with dresses of
Various colors of extravagancy
Are standing
In front of all the gates of houses
All along the street.

Once soldiers come in swarms,
Girls begin to fly as mosquitoes,
Shouting "Hi, John," "Paul" or "Jacob,"
Clinging to them, and
Quickly disappearing into
The darkness within the gates,
While call-boys run in the form of bats,
Pulling Rikshas with soldiers on
To places where girls are waiting
In soft, silk-made beds.

Christianity was not an admirable religion in our town. As a matter of fact, it
was a despicable one. Many of our townspeople laughed at it. "It is a brute's
religion!" some said behind the American soldiers' backs. I felt the same. I did
not realize then that the Japanese soldiers had done far worse things in neighboring countries.

When the war was over, I lost interest in or belief in the Japanese religions. Both
Buddhism and Shintoism had been behind the Japanese government during the
war. I could not trust those religions, which had supported the war and which
had told us lies, saying that Japan was a divine country and that Japan would
never lose. And I thought that Christianity was not trustworthy either.

So, when I first met some pacifist Christians, it was a big shock for me. They
turned my world upside down. They said they had not fought but had obeyed
God. They had been critical of their own government and had been praying for
the Japanese people during the war. It was a revelation for me. Scales fell from
my eyes and I could finally see the work of Christ. And I joined the Mennonite
church.

Enlightenment

Why can't I be spiritually awakened to
understand that this world gets worse
as the inevitable result of evil
human nature? Why do I get angry with it so easily?

Why can't I retreat into a mountain
and enjoy the rest of my life, sipping wine,
looking at the moon and making haiku
like the one enlightened?

However hard and long I may raise
my insignificant voice of anger,
I know I cannot stop this stream;
but I cannot give it up.

Those who attained perfect enlightenment
yell at me from this world and the other,
"Hey! You have been a Christian for a
long time! How come you are not awakened yet!"

And I shout back to them, "Indeed, I haven't
attained enlightenment yet but I never
intend to! As long as I live, I will
continue to worry, get angry and shout!"

This is one of my recent poems. "Enlightenment" ("satori" in Japanese) is a
Buddhist term. I do not intend to attain enlightenment in a Buddhist sense. My
enlightenment is to follow Christ and go into the world. I do not want to separate
myself from the world. And in the face of mounting injustice and misery, I
would like to live with those suffering people, because Christ lives with them. I
often get lost, get angry, worry, and make cries of protest, but Christ is with me
and soothes me. And I feel solidarity with the Mennonite community.

Yorifumi Yaguchi, Japan, b. 1933, B.D., M.A., professor at Hokusei Gakuen University.

Residents of a home for disabled children in Ho Chi Minh City, Vietnam, benefit from donations made through MCC's Global Family Program. (MCC photo by Stan Reedy, 1989)

The flowering of one bloom

by Gan Sakakibara

I was baptized at the age of twenty as a Presbyterian and then became a Mennonite when I was sixty-two years old. During those intervening forty-two years I was very dissatisfied with the positions the Protestant church of Japan held on the issues of war and peace. My dissatisfaction with the Protestant church in my country increased greatly during Japan's preparations for war. During that time the weak Protestant church had no choice but to acquiesce to the government's request for support of their efforts to prepare for war in the face of commercial attacks from all over the world. My Christian conscience wanted to express its opposition to the warlike governmental policy; but as a weak, private man, that was impossible for me to do. I was very ashamed. I thought: A Christian should be a pacifist; I should be a pacifist; stand up to the government and be counted.

Facing this dilemma, I considered the actions of the Protestant people in other countries under similar circumstances. They normally cooperated with their governments and advised their young men to be patriotic and cooperate in their government's war efforts. I rationalized away my conscientious way of life. Of course, this was in direct opposition to my true beliefs, and I was always living in the midst of shame. The military defeat forced upon the Japanese people feelings of shame and humility. All the Japanese Christians became Christian pacifists, including me. But I found it difficult to be born again as a pacifist just because of a defeat in war. An additional fifteen years were necessary for me to be truly born as a Christian pacifist. This was revealed to me through my studies of the Hutterian way of life and history.

In 1960 my wife and I visited the United States for the first time. We spent one-half year visiting Hutterian communities and similar communal groups such as the Reba Place Fellowship in Evanston, Illinois, and others. At first these communities interested me as a student of political economy, but later the religious character of the members greatly attracted me. I eventually found that their strength of character was based upon the Anabaptist faith, which had been established by their forebears more than four centuries earlier. Thereafter, Anabaptism became my main interest in life, and I left the Protestant church of Japan.

My true conversion to Christian pacifism was brought along by the historical Hutterian logic used in their resistance to a military tax. This logic had been applied when the Hutterites were still living in Moravia. The emperor wanted to collect a military tax in order to establish a military force to fight the Turkish invasion. In those days, the Hutterian people were the most obedient and hard-working people and were always willing to pay their taxes. Therefore, the tax collectors expected the Hutterites to pay the tax obediently. But the reaction of the Hutterites surprised the tax collectors. The Hutterites resisted the tax using the following logic: We are blacksmiths who can make swords and kitchen knives. But we do not want to make swords because the sword's primary purpose is to kill, and to kill people is a sin. If we did make swords and those swords killed men, then we would also be responsible for the killing. So we do not want to commit a sin by making swords. But we blacksmiths also make kitchen knives for the purpose of preparing food. There might be people who would kill or wound others with a kitchen knife that we had made, but under those circumstances we would not be responsible and therefore would not have committed any sins. The same logic worked for paying the military taxes. Therefore, their Christian pacifism did not allow them to pay the military tax. This logic taught me about Christian pacifism. When I read about this, I understood the real meaning of Christian pacifism.

Christian pacifism took a great step forward in 1935 when representatives of the Mennonites, the Society of Friends (Quakers), and the Church of the Brethren met in Newton, Kansas. It was there that these churches first called themselves the "Historic Peace Churches." The most important achievement of this conference was an agreement to request that the United States government allow full recognition for conscientious objection and provision for alternative service. The government did grant this request when conscription was instituted at the time of World War II. I was very interested in the Anabaptist achievements in the fields related to peace and war, and I wrote a book titled *The Anabaptist Heritage of Conscientious Objection*.

Whenever a discussion occurs about the philosophical differences between the Protestant and the Anabaptist approaches to the problems of peace and war, I like to refer to the Puidoux Conferences. Although the Japanese Protestants are almost completely unaware of the proceedings of the Puidoux Conferences, I consider them to be among the most important meetings in history. When Japan's defeat was completed by the dropping of the atomic bombs on Hiroshima and Nagasaki, the world concluded that future nuclear wars would mean the end of mankind. This discovery of the risks of nuclear war made all the churches in the world, including the Protestants, seriously rethink their policies on supporting sovereign rights to war. All the churches of the world wanted to learn more about the position of the Anabaptist churches on this subject.

Discussions during the 1948 World Council of Churches (WCC), held in Amsterdam, showed a strong and developing concern about peace and war. Prior to this conference, the churches that would now comprise the WCC were almost all so righteous that they did not take notice of "sects" such as the Historic Peace Churches. But at the 1948 WCC conference, they dared to adopt the philosophy of those "sects"—"War is contrary to the will of God." In Amsterdam the WCC broke with tradition and started to pay attention to minority groups such as the Mennonites and the Church of the Brethren. Being familiar with the peace activities of these groups, the WCC wanted to start a dialogue on peace and war with the Historic Peace Churches and develop it to the point where they could cooperate and strengthen each other and ultimately form a "Christian position" on the rights of sovereigns to war. To this end, the 1948 WCC conference concluded that a special conference was needed.

The first Puidoux Conference was planned and opened. It ran from August 15–19, 1955, in Puidoux, Switzerland. The Puidoux Conferences were continued in 1957, 1959, 1960, 1962, 1965, and 1967. The International Fellowship of Reconciliation (IFOR) was added as a fourth peace church, joining the Mennonites, the Society of Friends, and the Church of the Brethren. This international conference was always held in Switzerland, changing towns but not changing the name "Puidoux."

The use of the atomic bomb to end World War II made people look more carefully into the risks of future wars. The opinions about the risks of war almost always pointed to the consequences of nuclear war and the wisdom of supporting the rights of sovereigns to war. The risks of nuclear war also brought about the change of attitude in the discussions at the WCC. This pacifist tendency of the WCC has been clearly expressed in the concluding declarations of every WCC since its beginning in 1948. Therefore, the history of the Puidoux Conferences should be more fully described and publicized. The Puidoux "bud" must be allowed to flower.

Gan Sakakibara, Japan, b. 1897, Doctor of Economics, professor of economics (retired) at Aoyama Gakuin University, and member of Honancho Mennonite Church in Tokyo.

Three generations of a happy family at the Woodcrest Bruderhof near Rifton, New York.
(Woodcrest Archives photo)

Becoming a Mennonite

by Marta Quiroga de Alvarez

From Roman Catholicism

I heard about the gospel from a group that I did not know was "Mennonite." I am talking about my youth, some forty years ago. Before that I had been a faithful Roman Catholic. Actually, at that time the only church that was known in each town was the Roman Catholic one, so there really were not many options. But a growing evangelical Mennonite church was starting to be known in our community. I was part of an average family. My parents were simple workers; both worked in their business making clothes for men. The four children studied and helped out at home. Little by little we noticed that our oldest brother, through friendships with other youths, was going to that church. I was frightened. What was it? What were they teaching? The priests, my teachers, had done their part to frighten me. "Do not have anything to do with those people; they are heretics," they would tell us. But after some time I was also in that group, as were my mother, my younger siblings, and, finally, my father. "Believe in the Lord Jesus, and you will be saved—you and your household" (Acts 16:31) had been fulfilled. We had been converted. We had accepted Jesus Christ as our savior and would be counted among the baptized members of the "Evangelical Church" of Bragado (a city with thirty thousand inhabitants).

As the years passed I understood that besides being "Evangelical" I was also "Mennonite." What a strange name! There were not as many denominations as there are now. The evangelical churches were grouped, as they still are, in the Federación Argentina de Iglesias Evangélicas (Argentine Federation of Evangelical Churches), and ours was among them. That was because we had something basic in common, the gospel, the good news of salvation. And that was the most important thing for us, the new generation of dissidents, that is, those separated from the church of our parents.

The first Mennonite missionaries, using good judgment, began the work where there was no other evangelical witness, preaching the Scriptures without additional traditionalisms, with only the name "Evangelical Church." At that time there was not much discussion about our differences with other evangelical groups. Actually, our yearly evangelistic meetings always had preachers from other groups. We received them as "God's servants," our brothers, and practically ignored the fact that they did not belong to our Mennonite family. Therefore, many of us were converted by the preaching of brothers from the Salvation Army or the Methodist or Baptist churches. They were of our kind, as we understood it.

I finished my high school studies and left for the city of Buenos Aires to look for work. Even though it was difficult at that time to get employment, I was able to succeed. But God had other plans for my life. "What are you doing in the capital city?" the pastor of the fledgling Mennonite church, today known as Floresta, asked me. "You should be working in your own town. In Bragado we are in need of a Spanish grammar teacher at the Bible Institute." And I left to work there.

At the Mennonite Bible Institute of Bragado

God had called me to work right on the grounds of the church where I had been baptized. Besides the hours I spent teaching language at the Institute, I took courses on Bible and church doctrine. It was then, and only then, that I could begin to understand the place God had prepared for me. I was part of a world-wide church. Its history and doctrines began to penetrate in me like something new and challenging. Then I realized that the foreign pastor who led me to the gospel was a "missionary." That word became full of meaning. Although we were a Christian community, we did not know Christ to the fullest. The missionaries had come for that reason, so that our Christianity would be by experience and not by word alone. Then the doors of a new world were opened. I became aware of fundamental details about the Christian life of the believer and realized that the Mennonite church had a positive and fundamental contribution to make to the other Christian churches.

Resistance to the mandatory military service became a subject for study and discussion among the youth. New phrases such as "conscientious objectors," "alternate service," and "voluntary service" were introduced into my vocabulary and mind. I discovered then that our group surely had a definite place among other groups. Yes, and today when "conscientious objectors" are calling at the steps of the House of Representatives of the nation, our people are in the front line. They write and sign petitions so that the government may study these options and create legal provisions for our young people who, because of their conscience, do not want to bear arms or train to bring death. In spite of sixty years of the Mennonite presence in Argentina, in spite of raising our voices against the military draft, the goal has yet to be accomplished. During the war between Argentina and England over the possession of islands in the south Atlantic, some of our youths came face to face with the problem. One 18-year-old who had been called up for military service, son of a pastor of one of our Mennonite churches, asked his father, "Dad, what will I do if I am faced with a battle and have to kill?" His father answered him, "You will have to decide for yourself. I can tell you that I would rather have a son who died in peace with his Lord than a son who has had his peace disturbed because he killed a fellow human being."

The Mennonite church in Argentina has not renounced that objective. On the contrary, in the organization of the evangelicals it is the one that leads the way because of its pacifist history that has brought so much pain and so many blessings to this world. A clear and definite law has still not been passed, but the presentation of that request continues, each time accompanied by a larger group of people in favor of peace. Now I can say that "I am a Mennonite," but I still cannot fully understand all those deaths in our history, unjust deaths of our forebears in Europe. How much blood was shed, how much pain, and how much torture, all in the name of faith and in defense of life in Christ and obedience to his teachings.

My personal temperament leads me to reject all dogmatism and, even more as I perceive the ample and generous spirit of our history, to understand the forgiveness and goodness that come from Christ himself.

The vision widens

While I was teaching at the Bible Institute, and having concluded my biblical studies there, I was given the opportunity to travel to Toronto, Ontario (Canada), as part of a delegation of Christian education personnel from the Confederación de Iglesias Evangélicas Argentinas (Confederation of Evangelical Churches in Argentina) attending a congress for Christian educators. There I was given the privilege of studying for one year in my specialty at Goshen College. My vision of the work of the Mennonite church was broadened more and more. I was a worker in the Argentine Mennonite church; I am the wife of a pastor; I was a teacher in the public school system. With all of that, my concept of belonging to an evangelical community with something to give the evangelical world was affirmed and deepened. The simple life, without luxury or boasting, and the broad concept of the brother/sisterhood of the body of believers were becoming part of my life experience. The breadth of that practice was becoming effective in my own experience of service as a Christian woman in the church.

When our three children were small, I served the Lord for fifteen years on a continent-wide radio program. My objective was to present ways to confront different alternatives that are present in the home from the point of view of a Christian wife and mother.

On several occasions I was named to be on the executive board of the Iglesia Evangélica Menonita Argentina (IEMA, Argentine Evangelical Mennonite Church). At the present time I am a member of that board. I point that out because it shows that a Christian woman can also be useful beyond her home and local church and should serve according to the divine will in whatever way God leads each individual.

New winds of spiritual renewal

In the 1970s new winds of renewal arrived, not only in our Mennonite churches but also in other evangelical churches. The IEMA was quite solidly established, and these winds of renewal produced an impact in many of our congregations. Again was seen the positive contribution of that broad vision that characterizes us. While in other groups it caused divisions, separation of the pastors, and internal struggles, our church was able to absorb that influence. It drank the fresh water of that spiritual renewal, kept all the good, and was edified. Several pastors and leaders accepted the new renewal vocabulary. More was said about the baptism of the Holy Spirit; new emphasis was given to praying for the sick and anointing with oil. The distribution of gifts by God to the members of the body of the church was talked about with more depth. More clarity was gained about the active presence of Satan and the supernatural power of God to expel and defeat evil.

As delegates from different Mennonite conferences work intensely to prepare an Anabaptist Curriculum for Biblical Studies for use in the Spanish-speaking congregations of America, the possibility of integration among different Anabaptist conferences was put into practice, thus proving that it is possible for us to come together. We are sister conferences with the same history and the same purpose for our existence!

Today in my home community of Arrecifes, besides the Roman Catholic and Mennonite church, there are five or six Pentecostal groups from various backgrounds. We are all independent of each other, but when it comes to biblical teaching, a doctrine based on the solid foundation of Christ, the small group of believers from our church presents itself with God-granted authority and influences the Christian world that surrounds it.

I am a Mennonite. At sixty-three years of age, I continue being so because this is the community where I came to know the Lord, because in my youth I learned to love him and felt his call to service in this brother/sisterhood of believers in my home town of Bragado, Argentina.

Marta Quiroga de Alvarez, Argentina, b. 1926, editorial director of the Anabaptist Curriculum for Congregational Bible Education, member of the executive board of the Iglesia Evangélica Menonita Argentina. Translated by Margaret Schipani.

I was born into the Mennonite church

by Luis Correa

I remember a few years ago that several other members and I decided to leave the church because of some arguments in the local congregation. Those of us who left were from the school in Cachipay where the General Conference Mennonite Church began its work in 1947. I was gone from the church for two years, during which time I visited several churches and congregations trying to find a place where I felt comfortable and that would meet my needs. I had spent twenty years in the Mennonite church, first in Cachipay and later in Bogotá— two years at the seminary in Montevideo, later as pastor in a small congregation in Cachipay, and eight months in the new church in Bogotá (1967). I had collaborated very actively in this last church (when the Reverend Howard Habbegger was a missionary in Bogotá), and I loved my church so much that when practices and liturgy in worship that went against our customs were introduced, we preferred to leave the church. At first glance this could seem like a negative reaction, but fortunately, with time, those of us who had left that congregation again gathered (all ex-students of the school in Cachipay). Although our original purpose was not to form a new congregation, perhaps God's plans were different. In time we invited Gerald Stucky, then co-pastor of the Mennonite church in Berne, Indiana, to return to Colombia and continue the task that he, along with other missionaries, had begun years earlier. We started meeting informally in his apartment and became known as the Mennonite Community of Chapinero, the name of the neighborhood where the apartment was located. The group grew and is now the Mennonite Community of Teusaquillo.

Why did I not join another church? Well, it could be that it was because I was born into and grew up in the Mennonite church, but actually it was more than that. For me history is very important: it is said that a people without history is a people without a future. The Mennonite church is a historical church. Having a history, having roots, having been part of the process, has a lot of value. The Mennonite church is not the result of disputes or misunderstandings among people; it represented instead a new concept of the Christian faith, a more authentic and real vision of the word of God, of a life more in touch with that word.

Its liturgy or form of worship is balanced and participatory. It is not tied to tradition, but neither does it go too far toward the Pentecostal-like forms of disorder or improvisation. The worldwide Mennonite family is quite large, but it has known how to keep its identity and brother/sisterhood over time. Identifying with the poor, and the church's projects in their favor through Mennonite Central Committee (MCC), are very valuable, particularly by denouncing the injustices that are committed against the Latin American countries. The commitment of the MCC volunteers with refugees in Central America and their stance of denunciation through the *Washington Memo* make the Mennonite church a church of solidarity and one that carries a relevant message in the situation in which we live.

In all the Latin American countries we live in a very difficult period: unjust political structures, external debts that extremely limit the minimal services to which the citizens are entitled, violence on all sides, propagation of religious sects through false messages that distract people from their reality and oppression. It is important that the Mennonite church recover the biblical message of peace and justice and preach God's plan for humanity, which is no other than life itself and, more specifically, abundant life. My worry is that the Mennonite church would quit participating in the building up of the kingdom; that it would quit being the church of the rural people, of the artisans, of the homemakers; that it would quit preaching and living the gospel within the reality of a liberating gospel.

It is very hard to leave or abandon a Mennonite congregation. I appreciate the Mennonite theology and, as I said before, the history. I appreciate the General Conference's vision of the world and their progressive ideas. I really like the friendship and fraternal ties between foreigners and nationals. I believe this last aspect has determined the success of the work. I hardly remember any serious conflicts between Colombian workers and foreign missionaries. Even when the missionaries have returned to their countries, we remember them here with much love. I like that family warmth in the Mennonite church.

Maybe what I do not like about some congregations, and I speak of our congregations, is that they have adopted liturgical or worship practices different than those of the Mennonites. I think that can lead to the loss of identity. Without falling into traditionalism, forms of worship can be found that meet the spiritual needs of the believers.

Luis Correa, Colombia, b. 1938, active member of the Iglesia Evangélica Menonita de Colombia. Translated by Margaret Schipani.

Mennonite by conviction

by Gladys Siemens

I was born in a Christian home in Paraguay. At five years of age I accepted Christ as my personal savior in the Free Methodist Church, but later my parents moved and we attended a New Testament Church (Iglesia Neotestamentaria), where I was baptized at age eleven and where I attended until I was eighteen. Then I went to Argentina to study for almost two years, and when I returned I again went to the Free Methodist Church. There I began to teach Sunday school, children, and youths; and later I was Sunday school superintendent.

After two years I felt God calling me into voluntary service work, and I went to work with the Mennonites in the Chaco under ASCIM (a mission/service organization to the indigenous communities in the Central Chaco) in Yalve Sanga as a teacher. Even though my friends thought I was crazy, I did it anyway and felt very happy in this ministry where I served for one year. Working there I received the greatest impact in my life, living in community, sharing together God's love, and teaching through daily living how to be a servant according to God's word. From then on I began to think that taking the message to others is much more than just words. A very special and much loved family for me were Katarina and Jacobo Klassen. They, living a simple and humble life, with a smile on their lips and a big heart, were my parents in the Mennonite faith. I will never forget them. Through their lives they taught me how to take the message to others, that Christ's love unites us, and that in him we are all equal.

I returned to the Chaco to work for the Paraguay Bible Society, where I had the opportunity to relate to different denominations.

In 1979 I met a student of CEMTA (Theological Mennonite Center of Asunción) whom I married in 1981. We then went to live in the city of Palmeira in Paraná, Brazil. We worked for AMAS (Mennonite Association of Social Assistance). I worked as a secretary for the vocational school, and my husband worked as teacher and as assistant pastor of the Palmeira Mennonite Church for two years. Then in 1983 we received an invitation to pastor the Sertãozinho Mennonite Church in São Paulo, where we served for six years.

Since 1989 we and our two daughters have been in the United States. We are studying in Indiana, my husband at Associated Mennonite Biblical Seminaries and I at Goshen College in the Hispanic Ministries Department.

My personal experience as a Mennonite

I am a Mennonite for two reasons. In the first place, it is because I am married to Peter Siemens, who is from a family of Mennonite tradition, but more than just a tradition of Mennonite faith. His family also lived the Mennonite faith. Second, I am a Mennonite because I have learned a great deal about the Anabaptist doctrine, community life, and pacifism (nonresistance).

I feel very happy about being a Mennonite by faith or conviction and believe I still have much to learn about its historical background. The emphasis on learning the Bible in a community of faith and believing that God's word is his maximum revelation for our lives; the focus on the lordship of Jesus Christ; the emphasis on simple lifestyle, humility, and the concern for mission outreach—all these characteristics have helped me to think daily about my relationship with God.

I do have some concerns about the Mennonite church:

- How can we better be a testifying church?
- To what extent is traditionalism good, and at what point does it cause us to become prejudiced?
- Why, in many cases, do countries that seem to have all the opportunities and resources show so little church growth?
- Why do we evangelize so little in comparison to others?
- Is our church or community the best alternative for today's world?
- What can we do to help people better understand the gospel through our Mennonite background?

I believe we must be guided more by God's Holy Spirit and let him direct all our goals. Many times we choose a capable person, humanly speaking, but the person is not chosen or led by God for a particular ministry. I also believe we must give more importance to evangelism—whether in schools, colleges, universities, or hospitals—using every possible means of communication. People are thirsty to hear the message of peace. Friendship evangelism and telephone evangelism have had good results in Brazil in the recent past. I believe we have to concentrate more on the command "… go and make disciples" (Matt. 28:19). And we must not forget that evangelizing goes along with discipling.

What I like most about Mennonites in general is that they have a deep concern for service. Where there is a need, one can be fairly sure there will be Mennonites volunteering to help. This always makes my heart glad, and I thank God for that. What I do not like is that in some countries to be Mennonite is confused with race rather than faith. A real conflict and irritation for me is when the name "Mennonite" is used to obtain certain privileges. What pains me is to see less and less value placed upon simple living while allowing materialism to gain more and more territory in our communities, permitting the world to enter in rather than testifying to the world.

There are many things that I like about my particular conference, the Associação Evangélica Menonita (AEM) in Brazil. We are concerned about all the concerns I shared above, and we are praying that God will work in us. We all have the same feeling about "unity"—unity as a conference, as leaders, as churches, and as families. We see the need for the healing of wounds of the past and to improve our interpersonal relationships. What I do not like, or, better said, what concerns me, is that in some churches I feel we are working outside of the Brazilian cultural context. We have to be aware of the importance of the Afro-Brazilian culture and the concern that exists in the areas of evangelism and spiritual growth as well as better preparation of leaders.

Juana Gladys Ojeda de Siemens, Brazil, b. 1955, university studies in psychology in Argentina, currently attending Goshen College (Goshen, Indiana) and studying Hispanic ministries.
Translated by Louise E. Showalter.

Celebrating worship in a cheerful spirit in Zaire. (MWC photo by Paul Kraybill, 1988)

Why I am a Mennonite

by Michael Banks

Prior to writing this article, I conducted a class on Anabaptism at the Ossing Correctional Facility, more popularly known as "Sing Sing." Recommendation for my participation had come from Bishop Monroe Yoder of New York, who had been contacted by the New York Theological Seminary extension campus at the Ossing facility. It happened that Sister Marian Bohen of the Maryknoll School of Theology was facilitating a course on church history, and the men in her class were intrigued with the "Radical Reformers" of the Reformation period. They requested that a Mennonite or Anabaptist minister come and speak to their questions in detail.

It was amusing to see their response when I was introduced by the instructor, and even more when they discovered that there were Mennonite churches in the Bronx. The first question fired by these initiates in church history and theology was, Why are you a Mennonite? The implication of their question was clear because of their obvious surprise. The first preconceived notion of what a Mennonite should be or look like was dissolved.

The dialogue that followed made clear the spirit of Anabaptism as our lively, sometimes intense discussions covered the areas of free will, church as community, the centrality of Christ in faith and practice, peace and justice, and discipleship. Consistently underscoring our dialogue was the interrelationship of these essential components of Mennonite faith and what that means for urban people of color—the group making up this class of fifteen. The experience reaffirmed my basic conviction that the faith and doctrine expressed through the Mennonite church at its best speaks directly to the heart and social issues of all people regardless of their ethnic origin.

In my attempt to address the purpose of this article, let me simply say that I was not born predisposed to be a Mennonite, nor was I assimilated into the Mennonite church through a long process of exposure to any of the existing denominational service projects. I became a Mennonite because of a radical conversion experience and the providence of God, who inserted at the time of my "crisis" two individuals who demonstrated a likeness to Christ that inspired me to live and learn as they did. It was in the context of a small Mennonite church in the Bronx that my spiritual formation took place. When that spiritual formation was in process, faith and practices embraced me and, in turn, motivated me to embrace Jesus Christ. Through this experience, I had to deal with all that I was and am, and I resolved to commit myself to remaining a Mennonite.

One component that continues to deepen for me is the church as community. This notion resonates with that element of my own Afro-American tradition of community and extended family. In the light of the gospel, my vision extended beyond my own Afro-centric perspective, yet I never dismissed the value or integrity of that perspective. I perceived in the church a movement toward inclusion and not exclusion.

In my times of struggling within the embrace of God and the community of faith, I have discovered a legacy of persecution not unlike the historical persecution of my people. From this foundation I continue to draw strength to respond to the hostilities of crime, racism, etc., that surround the community in which I am now called to minister. This common legacy always directs us back to the way of Christ. At times my gift to the church is to remind people of our shared roots and not to become complacent because of status or acceptance by the world.

In the embrace of God a word was formed in my heart that spoke of willingness, not willfulness. In an age of many winds of doctrines that too often tell individuals to develop their own plan of salvation, a willingness to follow Christ daily provides the empowering quality that enables one to be an agent of transformation. The message that is forged out of this experience is one qualified by hope, since I no longer need the system to name me or define me. Through willingness I am named and defined by the kingdom of God.

Finally, my experience of discipleship speaks of being accountable. That is difficult, but without it growth cannot occur. The notion of living in the light, knowing and being known, preserves us from the subtle form of self-deception that causes compromise and the disintegration of authentic kingdom living. It is from the position of inner integrity forged out of obedience to Christ that we can properly discern the principalities and powers and speak the word of the Lord against exploitation.

I remain a Mennonite to embrace those refugees fleeing the principalities of death and to direct them to an alternative way.

Michael Banks, USA, b. 1953, pastor of Burnside Mennonite Church (Bronx, New York) and leader with his wife, Addie, of Pilgrim's Way, an intentional urban community sponsored by Eastern Mennonite Board of Missions and Charities.

Chinese Mennonite who survived to tell his story

by Robert Kreider

In the 1978 *Mennonite World Handbook* for the Tenth Assembly at Wichita, Kansas, no Mennonite churches were listed in China—a blackout of information. Before World War II, Mennonite missions flourished in China, one of the missions reporting 2,500 baptized members. In 1978 a Mennonite missionary, fearing that the church had been completely crushed, declared, "If only one Christian could be found where we started churches, I would be grateful."

A Chinese Mennonite couple, presumed to have died, was found to be among the living: James and Hazel Liu of Hengyang, China. In January 1979 James, who had suffered three years of imprisonment and mistreatment during the Cultural Revolution, felt it safe to write to two missionary friends. During the past decade James has renewed his friendships with North American colleagues and the Chinese Mennonites among whom he had served as teacher and leader.

His story, along with that of his coworker, Stephen Wang, is told in a twin autobiography, *Christians True in China*. James Liu had been educated in Mennonite mission schools at Puyang (Kaizhou) in Hebei Province, studied two years at Mennonite colleges—Bluffton and Bethel, and then returned to serve his people. In 1936, the year before the Japanese invasion of China, he gave an address at the twenty-fifth anniversary of the General Conference Mennonite churches in China on an Anabaptist vision for the Chinese churches. For five years following World War II, James and Hazel Liu, who was a nurse, worked with a young Mennonite Central Committee (MCC) team in relief, refugee, and orphan work. James remembers these years as deeply satisfying. With the coming of radical changes in China in 1949, the door of communication with Mennonite friends overseas abruptly stopped. For almost thirty years no one outside China knew whether James and Hazel Liu were alive or whether a Mennonite church continued to exist in China.

Beginning in 1979, James renewed his long lapsed linkages with Mennonite friends abroad. James and Hazel began to receive a few international visitors in their home. In 1984, after a lingering illness, Hazel died. Since then James has returned to his boyhood home to visit among the people where he once helped establish and nurture congregations. In 1985 he traveled to North America to renew old friendships. Now, in 1990, James Liu at the age of eighty-six stands before us as a Christian brother whose faith glows with undiminished brightness.

James Liu, who will attend Assembly 12 at Winnipeg, will be the first citizen of the People's Republic of China ever to attend a Mennonite World Conference assembly. He comes with deep affection for his Lord Jesus Christ and for the world fellowship of Mennonites that has shepherded him in the faith. He comes with an awareness of the cost of discipleship. He can say with the apostle Paul: "What can separate us from the love of Christ? ... I am convinced that there is nothing in death or life, in the realm of spirits or superhuman powers ... that can separate us from the love of God in Christ Jesus our Lord" (Rom. 8:35–39).

Although James suffered grievously during the Cultural Revolution, one hears from him not one murmur of bitterness about the years of rejection for his faith and his friendship with foreigners. He was asked whether he ever meets on the streets of Hengyang former Red Guards who once taunted and tortured him. He answered, "Oh, yes; I tell them that they did what they had to do. They wanted to be good Chinese." James is ever the forgiving, loving teacher and friend.

In 1979 in one of the first letters he sent abroad, he wrote: "There is not a church in Hengyang, nor a house church. The only church we have here is heart-church. We have church in our hearts." A year later he reported: "The former church leaders in Hengyang have talked about starting church work, but we don't know how soon. ... We hope the sooner the better. Let's pray for it. ... How hungry the people are for spiritual food! Praise the Lord!" In Shanghai, 1980, he met J. Winfield Fretz, an old friend from Bluffton College days, who brought him Bibles and hymnals—wonderful gifts. A former MCC colleague sent him a devotional book based on a text he particularly cherished: "Whatever you ask for in prayer, believe that you have received it and it will be yours" (Mark 11:24).

In 1981, when Christians were beginning to come out of hiding, he wrote that he had heard that Christians in Puyang (formerly Kaizhou, his boyhood home and center of the General Conference Mennonite mission) were worshiping in private homes. In January 1983 he happily reported that he was one of a committee of nine to help open a church in Hengyang, which held its first service Christmas Eve. Two years later he told about two thousand believers in Hengyang and two young men sent to Wuhang for seminary study. In 1985 he received from an old pastor friend a letter that one of the counties in the General Conference Mennonite mission field, Chang Yuan County, now had thirty-four preaching places, 2,428 members with more than four hundred attending regularly, one pastor, and twenty-one people helping with the preaching. In 1985 James visited Puyang (Kaizhou), where relatives, church friends, former students, and even public officials greeted him warmly. The magistrate, who was chairman of the local People's Congress, said to James at a dinner in his honor, "Your mission and school made great contributions to the Puyang people. Many of your students are working in the government. If you have a chance to go to America again, be sure to tell the missionaries and their children. They can come any time and stay here as long as they wish. They are welcome in Puyang."

As James reflects back on his life, he recalls times of career decisions. Returning from the United States in 1932, he was urged to take a well-paid position with the government. He declined, saying "I cannot do that because I am a Christian.

God knows our need, and he will provide what we need." When he was working with MCC, he was encouraged to leave MCC to take a university position. He answered, "Right now, relief work is more important than teaching in a university because there are so many poor people along the flooded area of the Yellow River. Many of them are dying of hunger ...." He was told, "You are foolish." His answer was, "I like to be foolish." As the Nationalist government was collapsing in China, he was offered the opportunity to go to Taiwan, Indonesia, or the Philippines to serve with MCC. He felt that he was called to stay in China with his people in their need.

James Liu's days are full: helping with the housework of his son's family, Bible reading, keeping up with national and world news, writing letters, assisting in the work of the local church, conducting Bible study in his home, pastoring the families of those who were once children in the MCC orphanage, and serving as a kind of pastoral counselor by correspondence with the congregations re-emerging in the former Mennonite mission field. He has come to be a kind of conference pastor to the shepherds of the Mennonite flocks.

He receives reports from pastors of the congregations in the six counties around Puyang and Daming where the General Conference Mennonites once had a membership of 2,500. He reports as many as twenty thousand worshipers in several registered congregations and scores of house churches. In Daming four graduates of the earlier Mennonite Bible School are caring for the church. In Qing Feng the government has returned a Mennonite church building to the local congregation, which is registered. In addition, Christians meet in seven house churches. In Dong Ming a congregation of one hundred members contributes funds to rent a house for worship. The church in Chang Yuan is registered and has twenty-seven house churches in the city and countryside with about four thousand members. Some ten thousand attend services. In Puyang the church is growing rapidly with many from the local oil fields attending one of the ten house churches. They have two pastors, four less-active pastors in their eighties, and ten house church lay leaders. With a growing church, this information is already out of date.

James uses the name "Mennonite" to describe the congregations re-emerging in the six counties. And yet Chinese Protestants describe this as a postdenomina- tional era. One senses in James an abiding affection for his Anabaptist-Mennon- ite people and for the missionaries who planted the church. He is unapologeti- cally Mennonite and unapologetically a Chinese Christian. His fondest hope is that his grandsons, Paul and John, will become Christians, can study in a Men- nonite school in North America, and will return to serve their Chinese people. James Liu's eldest grandson was baptized on Easter Sunday 1990.

Robert Kreider, USA, b. 1919, Ph.D., emeritus professor of Bethel College (North Newton, Kansas), educator, historian, writer.

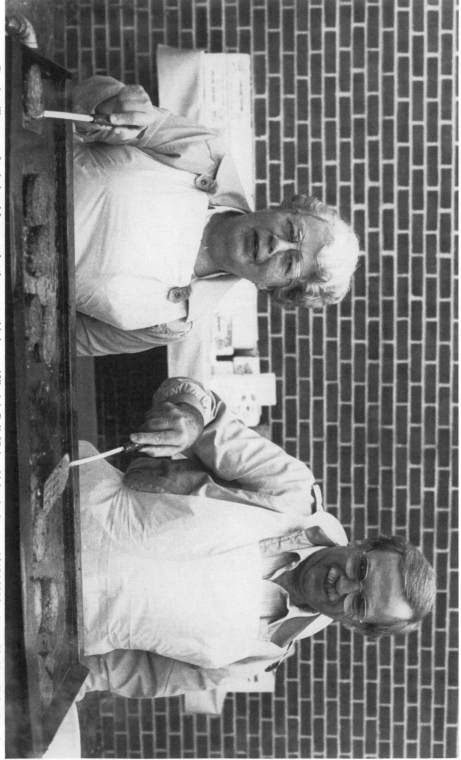

Couple grills sausage for the breakfast crowd at the twenty-third annual Virginia Relief Sale, which raised a record $184,000 for the worldwide relief and service program of MCC. (Photo by Jim Bishop, 1989)

More joy than frustration: An urban pastor today

by Peter J. Foth

For twenty years now I have been a pastor of the Mennonite church in Hamburg, a city of millions in the northern part of the Federal Republic of Germany. Approximately 540 members make up the congregation, most of them scattered widely throughout the city or even far beyond its boundaries. At the end of World War II, many Mennonite refugees from East and West Prussia came to northern Germany. That is why at present two-thirds of our members have an East or West Prussian background; only a minority are "old Hamburgians." However, adjustment problems have long since been overcome. Today we are one church body living in a secularized city and coping with its environment.

I do my pastoral service together with my wife, Elke. Ever since our three children have grown up, she has worked for the congregation both for a salary (in the church office) and in a voluntary capacity: she works at church functions in front of and behind the scenes; she joins me on visitations; she is an important encourager and critic in my work. We have been in this congregation for a long time now. Surely that has its advantages and disadvantages. One advantage is the possibility of really getting to know the members of so large a congregation and of accompanying them over a larger span of life. I try to compensate for a possible disadvantage, one pastor holding such a long term, by drawing on as many members as possible for their cooperative assistance, thereby giving room for other ideas than just my own. Seven years ago I suffered a heart attack and had to undergo heart surgery. In retrospect, I am thankful for this experience because it gave me new insights. It is quite generally my experience that, with increasing age, I am more capable of approaching people and of saying a helpful word to them in difficult situations. I believe that counseling requires at least a certain age and background of personal experience.

What is "Mennonite" about my work as pastor of this city church? At first glance, very little. Our work is largely no different than the work of pastors of other denominations. We and our church members live in the same world as the members of other churches or as those who do not attend any church. We have the same problems and hopes, the same careers, and the same life situations. Our church program, too—worship services, youth programs, discussion evenings, seminars, excursions—is hardly distinguishable from the programs of other churches. We have good neighborhood relations with the Lutheran church, which is, in our city, by far the largest Christian church, and we occasionally exchange pastors for preaching. What, then, is specifically Mennonite in the life of our congregation? We are an independent congregation with various ties and even some blood relations to other Mennonite congregations, and we have contact with the worldwide Mennonite community. However, all of this, all these primarily ethnic elements that are so typical of Mennonites, can also be

found in many other denominations. Perhaps more important, we are—despite
the employed, full-time pastor—a church of lay people and volunteer workers.
Today our Hamburg congregation fits this description better than in the decades
before World War II, when there was the tendency to expect everything from the
one hired pastor. If anything fills me with satisfaction after twenty years of
service here, it is the fact that today many more members do active lay work, not
least in preaching, than at the beginning of my term. When I was incapacitated
for one-half year because of my illness, most of the worship services were taken
over and led by our own members. Much has changed in the last twenty years,
and service by a "core congregation" is a general trend of our time. Thus,
increased voluntary work within the church is not solely to my credit, even
though I did work determinedly in that direction. It makes me happy when the
realization grows that the church is everyone's business. Only that which many
people shape and carry brings reward, above all for the workers themselves.

I like to preach. But I am also thankful that I do not have to preach every Sunday
as I did in the beginning years. Now I can take more time to thoroughly prepare
for a sermon. Often I carry an idea, a basic thought, or a method along in my
mind for weeks, and I think about it until the sermon is "ripe" (in my opinion).
Several years ago I discovered that I enjoy teaching church workers and other
members at their level of understanding. We have arranged a regular training
seminar for pastors from the entire northern area of Germany, and in our congregation we have held seminars on the doctrine of faith, historical and contemporary Mennonitism, and the Bible. Presently we are engrossed in the Epistle to the
Romans. I get a lot of pleasure out of preparing for and passing on that which I
once learned or acquired.

The cooperative work of many in our congregation leaves me with some time to
take on tasks within our conference. I am especially responsible for the contact
with our students of theology. This work is very rewarding. For several years
now Mennonites in Germany have had quite a number of capable and committed
young men and women who are studying theology and preparing for some kind
of service within the church. In fact, a certain kind of generational change has
already taken place, and though I am not even fifty years old, I find myself un-
mistakably on the side of the "older preachers." It is important that students of
theology do not lose contact with the congregations. German university education traditionally recognizes a great deal of academic freedom which, along with
its advantages, also holds dangers. One of my tasks is to arrange semiannual
seminars for students, occasionally together with the Dutch students of theology,
in an attempt to smooth the way for them into congregations.

I also have disappointing experiences. Mennonite congregations in secularized
cities in Germany live in an intellectual climate in which the church presents
only one of many options for leisure time. We live near the sea, and if a family
has just purchased an expensive boat, then the cost must be equal to its worth. In

other words, the family wants to use the boat—during the weekend, of course. Such families are practically lost for church work, at least during the summer months. Naturally in winter the boat must be overhauled ....

Being a Mennonite congregation in a city means that there is little "living in a community." Only a modest number of church members have enough contact with each other to be able to practice exchange and mutual strengthening beyond the worship service on Sunday morning. Many, far too many, do not take part in the life of the congregation other than to give their financial contribution, an indication that they do absolutely want to belong. For many in our congregation, church does not have high priority. But I have learned not to complain about those who are not there, rather to be happy with those who are there. I also regret that our congregation is too large and too scattered for me to be able to keep track of all church members and always to know for sure where crisis situations have set in. Often weeks go by before I find out that someone has been in the hospital for quite a while already. Problems within families are frequently kept hidden quite skillfully from the outside world, yes even from the church congregation. But that is each person's right, and no one should force himself on others when not desired. I am also aware that, in the past, I have not always found the right words for the right times, whatever the reasons.

In our city congregation we have practically no Mennonite Aussiedler (resettlers from the Soviet Union) as church members. Our congregation has thus been spared the difficulties, the petty, know-it-all doggedness that "mixed" congregations have had to experience and still do. Originally, German Mennonites observed the stream of Aussiedler with great sympathy and much hope. In the meantime, a disillusionment has taken their place. The right attitude now seems to be to let the Aussiedler be themselves and let them find their way around in an environment that for them is so strange and often so frightening. This can best happen in their own congregations, where there are also clashes and adjustment problems. I want to be open for everything that is mutually possible, but I do not want to force myself on anyone or in a wrong sense expect anyone to be or to do something that he cannot. I have also learned to respect and to bear the massive, but also very narrow, sometimes domineering, piety of Aussiedler churches and their leaders, but I will not be blinded by it.

I like being pastor of a Mennonite church. And as long as my congregation wants me to be their pastor, I want to do my varied, largely satisfying, sometimes frustrating work joyfully.

Peter J. Foth, Federal Republic of Germany, b. 1940, pastor of the Hamburg and Altona Mennonite Church. Translated by Anita Lichti.

Bible study in the open air in the Philippines. (EMBMC photo by Earl Zimmerman, 1988)

Confessions of a Sunday school teacher

by Leona Dueck Penner

Over the years I have taught a variety of Sunday school classes, in a variety of ways and in a variety of settings, ranging from serving as a teenage assistant in a nursery class in a small rural church in western Manitoba to being a full-fledged (though barely out of my teens myself) teacher of teenagers in a city church, to leading a mixed-age children's class in Central Africa, to team teaching both children's and adult classes in our inner city church in Winnipeg.

Looking back on that experience, I was at first overwhelmed by a feeling of inadequacy, a feeling that a thousand other teachers would have been much better qualified to write on this theme than I was, teachers who did not some-times agree to teach out of a strong sense of duty or out of a "somebody has to do it" mentality, but "real" teachers, teachers with training; teachers who planned their classes well ahead of schedule, not on Saturday night; teachers who maintained enthusiasm and inspired their students, Sunday after Sunday, not just now and then; teachers who had a sense of calling that carried them right through to the end of the year. In short, I confess, teachers quite unlike me.

But as I thought about it some more, it occurred to me (judging from the diffi-culty our church and other churches seem to have in recruiting Sunday school teachers) that a high percentage of Sunday school teachers are, in fact, like me; and, therefore, maybe it was better to hear from an "average" Sunday school teacher with whom many could identify than from one of those who would receive an "excellence in teaching award." For, to be honest, the majority of us do not have a whole lot of natural talent, nor do we have much training or the energy needed to prepare for and teach a good Sunday school class, Sunday after Sunday, after we have done a hard week's work. In spite of our best intentions, we often feel unprepared when we enter our classes on Sunday morning. Still, I believe that the average Sunday school teacher does make a significant contribu-tion to the individual students and to church life in general, because the teacher is "forced" to develop the three Christian virtues of faith, hope, and love.

First of all, teachers develop faith because they do spend extra time in Bible reading and prayer (especially the latter, because they know their need of God!). Second, they develop hope because they do have good classes—classes when the chemistry is right between subject, teacher, and students—just often enough to keep them committed to prolonging the experience and even to signing up for teaching again the following year (after a good, long summer break). And third, they develop love because they do spend a good deal of time thinking about the people in their class throughout the week as a result of the weekly, more intimate interaction with them. In addition, they create a store of personal memories that enrich the life of the teacher and, one hopes, the lives of the students and the congregation as a whole. At least, that is my experience. I would like to share some of my own most precious Sunday school memory pictures with you:

From my early teaching years, there is an image of a young, thin-faced boy named Richard who attended my class sporadically for a year or two. Richard was a boy from a poor, inner city family, dressed in shabby clothes, a boy who was hyperactive and disrupted the class, a boy who told "tall tales" (some called them lies). Clearly he was intelligent, and under that tough exterior was a good deal of sensitivity. Many years later, I wonder what became of him. Did the stories of the love of Jesus and an hour in the company of a caring, though average, Sunday school teacher make a difference in his life?

From a class in a tiny one-room school in Central Africa in the mid-1970s, I carry with me a vision of rows of black and white faces, warm from the sun, turned toward me, listening raptly to the story of Joseph. The Sunday I remember was one of those "good" teaching days when everything came together—subject, teacher, students—and all of us left feeling changed somehow by the beauty and the wisdom of the Bible.

From a class studying the Jan and Myron Chartier book, *Nurturing Faith in the Family,* a few years ago there is a picture of always vulnerable and sometimes anxious faces of moms and dads, both "new" and "old," as we talked about a subject very dear to all of our hearts. We realized very quickly that there was no sure-fire way to implant faith in our children other than modeling it the best we can and depending on the grace of God, expressed often through the love and support of friends, to lead our little ones into truth.

And, from a class in Winnipeg last fall, I have a memory of animated faces of women as they talked about stories involving the ups and downs of women's relationships in the Bible, stories of Hagar and Sarah, Mary and Martha, Ruth and Naomi, stories told from a black "womanist" perspective in a book entitled *Just a Sister Away** by Renita J. Weems, stories which, in spite of all the intervening years and changes in the cultural roles of women, still felt familiar because they reflected our own diverse lives, our own weaknesses and strengths, our own victories and failures as we participate in the building of the kingdom.

It is memory pictures such as these that keep me, an average teacher, teaching. And, I am sure, similar pictures sustain many other teachers as well.

*Weems defines "womanist perspective" as the perspective of "courageous women who are committed to whole people, both men and women."

Leona Dueck Penner, Canada, b. 1943, co-director of the Peace and Social Concerns Program of Mennonite Central Committee Canada and member of the team that plans the overall teaching ministry of the Aberdeen Evangelical Mennonite Church in Winnipeg, Manitoba.

Tools for building the kingdom

by Mario Higueros

As academic dean of SEMILLA, my challenge is to search for God's ways in the midst of human ways. Along with my coworkers I hope to become a useful tool in the midst of the community of faith in order to build up the kingdom of God. Latin American Anabaptist Seminary (SEMILLA), a formative institution of the Latin American Mennonite conferences, is a seminary by extension that serves eight Central American countries and ten Mennonite conferences in Central America. It has a total of 135 students, both regular (for credit) and auditors. For five years the seminary has been preparing members of the Mennonite congregations biblically and theologically, from an Anabaptist perspective, on three academic levels: middle and higher bachelor's degree and licentiate.

The task of dean requires a diverse number of competencies given the nature of our seminary by extension. The task begins by choosing and contacting the professors for the courses to be taught the following school year. Later we need to work together on the syllabus with every professor for each of the six courses we offer each year. Following that, the dean continues searching for texts and other adequate materials from the biblical-Anabaptist perspective of SEMILLA to gather the anthologies for each yearly course. We favor the use of anthologies, because the compilation of different articles and excerpts from books puts the student on the road to a broader and more critical development than can be achieved by a single text, let alone by programmed instruction. The board of directors, which is composed of delegates or representatives of each Central American conference, studies and designs the materials to be developed each year after determining if these meet the needs of the community of faith. The board receives recommendations from the academic council, the director, and the dean. Following these previous steps, the dean has the task of designing each anthology, supervising the printing, and sending copies to each country. Another task is to maintain contact with all the students and keep a record of their academic progress as well as student registrations and the records of the courses being completed. The dean keeps the director of SEMILLA informed and prepares two written reports for the board of directors at the time of their regular annual meetings. In addition, the dean directs the department of publications of the seminary, which is called "Ediciones SEMILLA." This requires organizing and leading the editorial council at their annual meeting and publishing the following annually: at least four books; four volumes of the seminary periodical, *Esperanza en camino*; *Raíces*; modules; and many other printed materials.

The tasks described above involve diverse activities that naturally generate anxiety and a physical toll. But when we see the reality of many other countrymen who also invest their energies in tasks that many times are poorly compensated, we feel very grateful to God that we can spend our life in service to the human beings God loves. We work with men and women whose standard of living is below the poverty level. The contrasts between the rich and the poor are extreme and offensive. The congregations are bombarded with political influences that want to make them instruments of partisan views and even orient them to an ideological interpretation of the gospel in order to legitimate selfish interests. The social projects of the congregations must hurdle many obstacles. For example, we face the traditional concept that the church's only concern is with the "spiritual" realm and also the escapist emphasis, which leads congregations to live only with the hope of the life to come and to center spiritual action only on the soul in a private fashion. Within the church as well as outside it, action that denounces violence through a concern for human life is mainly interpreted as being influenced by leftist ideology. Many doctrinal emphases presented as "purely biblical" try to push us into silence despite the evidence of social injustice. These make us accomplices of a false faith, leading us to interpret God's will as the success and comfort of only a few.

Like the majority of Central American evangelicals, I arrived at the Mennonite church from a Reformed and evangelical influence. The testimony of Mennonite Central Committee workers with whom I had contact appealed to me because they showed a way of being and different attitudes than I was accustomed to. My wife and I were attracted to their simple lifestyle, humble attitude, and not putting on airs of being "on the mission field." Later my wife and I became aware that the Mennonites with whom we were acquainted were heirs of a tradition that we did not know in our circles (nor did many Mennonites in Central America). They not only followed certain doctrines for what they meant, but followed Jesus. Furthermore, in the Anabaptist thought of the Radical Reformation we found what we had experienced in other Christian communities outside the evangelical circles. We saw that in the community life of the brother/sisterhood, charismas are not hierarchical in nature but gifts of divine graciousness. We discovered that there was a search for peace and justice without turning away from the problems of our people. We could see that a political interest existed (in its most proper form) without making any system sacrosanct. Besides, they insisted that Jesus was the only Lord and that God was the sovereign power. In other words, human life was not sacrificed at the altar of theological or political beliefs. When I was invited to work with SEMILLA, I had experienced that those beliefs were not only valid but totally biblical. All this led me to believe that a task in an institution such as SEMILLA was a way to collaborate so that it could be a useful instrument for the faith communities of the area.

The philosophy of the seminary not only coincides with my wife's and my search and our findings, but it is also consistent with the thought of the Anabaptist Radical Reformation. It is stimulating to be part of an educational institution such as SEMILLA that does not aim to be an ecclesiastical superstructure or an institution where "pastors are made" in the restricted, clerical sense. It simply aims to be a tool at the service of building the kingdom of God, in other words, to collaborate by means of this ministry so that our communities can serve all men and women rather than being centered only in our own program.

The experience of sharing with students and churches has provided me with a rich opportunity for human contacts. Because of the nature of our program and having courses in each country, I have the opportunity to perceive some of the problems, especially in this region so besieged by social, economic, and political ailments. All of that illumines the context for preparing materials that do not turn their back on the daily reality of many people at this time in our countries. I have learned, together with my brothers and sisters, that Jesus Christ is present in the world through those who accept his rule and that he is not merely a hope for the ultimate matters but for the penultimate matters as well—for the here and now.

SEMILLA, which is committed to an open-ended task, also requires constant revision. Having a program of studies that appeals to the needs of our Central American churches and communities means we always need to remain open to new methods and resources for teaching. The contents are based on the discerned needs and not a predetermined program. Besides, theological claims, in spite of their biblical grounding, are always provisional. I think that all theology is always partial and that it is a search for understanding the inscrutable knowledge of the word of God. The road of the provisional is a hard and misunderstood road, but it seems to be the heart of the character of Jesus Christ. Conformity to the status quo, which gives some security, is our constant temptation. My task as dean implies the danger of establishing immovable claims and not being sensitive to the voice of God's Spirit, who always talks through the community. Many times we are faced with the temptation of authoritarian teaching, of indiscriminately influencing the educational criteria. Performing the task in a multidisciplinary and communal way helps me avoid personalism and dogmatism. The thoughts of the Radical Reformation, which we try to restate in the midst of our Central American situation, make us confront "very dear" doctrines that need to be reformulated and questioned, but our inner being resists it. The same thing happens with some students and congregations who react vehemently when faced with an alternative biblical perspective. Some, on the contrary, although cautious of the new, are open to learning. Still others conform with a dependent education where they learn axiomatic material in a passive way.

With joy and with much effort we can say that in congregations from Mexico to Panama men and women are being raised, willing to walk together on the road of learning for life in the kingdom of God, where instead of professors we offer facilitating and encouraging agents; they are tools, fragile vessels for service, so that together we can keep finding God's way in the midst of human ways.

Mario Fernando Higueros Fuentes, Guatemala, b. 1942, licentiates in psychology and in pastoral theology, academic dean at the Seminario Anabautista Latinoamericano (SEMILLA).
Translated by Margaret Schipani.

Baptism service in Spain celebrated by San Pablo Street Christian Fellowship (MBM photo by Connie Byler, 1989)

Worship asks for participation

by Eleanor Kreider

It was like coming home. ... Everyone seems to participate actively in the service. ... It was wonderful to find local Christians praying for peace and justice. ... Worship in this church fits together the things that are often torn apart. You behave like a family, and yet you have worldwide concerns. You put piety with peacemaking. You link praise with action.

Visitors to the Wood Green Mennonite Church in North London, England, often make comments such as these. Their experiences in our worship have enabled them to give expression to important themes in our church's life: "domestic" worship in a public place, worship nurturing discipleship, and modern Christian worship as a living expression of ancient traditions.

"Domestic worship" in a public place

On Sunday mornings our congregation of about fifty adults and children meets in a large room above a community center. Pictures and equipment indicate other groups that use the space throughout the week—a daily luncheon for elderly folk, the Royal British Legion, a bingo club, and a disco. How does it feel to be a church without our own building? Sometimes we are frustrated, especially when we would like to make changes in decoration or schedule. It makes for extra work, having to carry our books and supplies in and out each week. But the advantage is that we are in close touch with the people who live locally, and we are subject to the same limitations as any other community group. How we deal with the organizing committee and the Old Guard at the community center is our first point of witness.

As people arrive for worship, they are drawn into an atmosphere that is informal and homelike. We have only half an hour to get the room arranged for worship. Visitors often find themselves drafted to help members shift tables and chairs. As starting time approaches, the instrumentalists quietly tune up, someone puts out the hymnals, others rattle teacups, setting out trays for the inevitable "cuppa" which will follow the worship service. The door to the toilet bangs each time someone goes through. At the top of the stairs, little children rush to greet their friends. Visitors take off their coats and peer past the hangers toward the semi-circles of chairs where a few are praying quietly. All of this varied activity within one room! And it is the room in which we are planning to worship. Sometimes it seems like an intent busyness, with each one doing the job at hand. But at other times it seems almost impossible to create an atmosphere of poise and peace in which we can begin our worship. That is the negative side. The positive is that this is like the atmosphere of a home. Something important is going to happen here. Everyone has to pitch in to get ready. Getting ready for church is not like producing a stage performance with everything perfect before the doors open. In the few minutes we have before each service, we need to make the rented space become home for our church. We need to settle ourselves down. We need to prepare ourselves as God's family to pray and worship God together.

But true worship needs more than a suitable space. The building does affect our worship; the structure can shape our experience. Ultimately, however, it is not the building that matters as we gather for worship. What matters is who we are as God's family. As sisters and brothers, we remember the acts and faithfulness of our Father, our reliance upon him and each other, and our responsibility to the world and our neighbors. At its best, "familial" worship can be our deepest experience of being at home, where pretence falls away and we are true—true to ourselves, true to God, true to God's world.

Worship nurtures discipleship

During our ninety-minute meeting, our worship comprises three parts. In the first part we sing, read the Scriptures, and pray in ways that people of all ages can participate. Sometimes we present Bible stories in dramatic readings. We like using flannelgraph and other visual aids. Almost every week we sing birthday blessings to someone with a song, "[Name], Jesus loves you!" Simple thank-you prayers and a song complete the first section of praise and worship. At this point the children go to a side room for their special activities.

The second part is the prayers. For many of us, this is the heart of the worship. As members of a local Christian church we are members of the body of Christ, participating in Christ's mission. That mission includes listening to the world, mourning over its pain, and interceding for its leaders. We pray about local housing issues, about European environmental questions, about unemployment or housing needs of individual members, about friends who do not yet know Jesus. Jesus taught us to pray for our enemies and our neighbors, to bless each other, to ask for healing. Jesus promised us overflowing life. In our prayers we get a foretaste of the promise. In our prayers we find Jesus in the middle of our circle. We know that answered prayers may yield surprises and perhaps give new shape to our corporate life. To pray together is our work, and it is our joy.

The concluding part of the worship varies. Once a month it is a communion service. The communion service flows on from the prayers by the peace greeting (holy kiss) and singing. We stand to hear the words from Scripture. Then two members give thanks over the bread and cup. First we break and serve to each other the unleavened bread. Then we all drink from the common cup. On other

Sundays of the month, a sermon comprises the final part of the service. We have elders, but they are not always the preachers. A number of members are gifted Bible expositors. We have relatively few outside speakers. The elders oversee the choice of topics and biblical texts, and also attempt to elicit the prophetic, the free and Spirit-given word that emerges through the life of the church.

We baptize in a small lake in Hampstead Heath, North London. Its public character makes an outdoor baptism an opportunity for witness to passers-by. We usually have members at the edges to explain what is happening to joggers and people out walking their dogs. Many will stand and watch.

Worship in our church is characterized by its familial atmosphere, with numerous common meals, and by its emphasis on corporate prayer. In worship the community discerns God's word through expository and prophetic gifts of the Spirit. In worship we express our joy and thankfulness, our weakness and need. In worship, as in no other way, we the church become the living body of Christ.

Twentieth-century Anabaptists in an early church tradition

So this is what we are: an urban European Mennonite church made up largely of people whose parents are not Mennonites. Are we, we ask ourselves, a legitimate contemporary expression of the Anabaptist tradition? We want to be Anabaptists, and believe that we are, for several reasons. Sixteenth-century Anabaptist groups, made up of adults who had chosen this way of life, expected all to participate. Bible study, prayer, exchange of counsel, mutual support, and discipline—all of these took place within a group that named each other brother and sister. A formal, "churchy" atmosphere was neither theologically nor practically possible for them. After all, they were meeting in homes, barns, outbuildings, forests, or caves. Though they had ministers, any member could speak to elucidate the word. Central to the Anabaptist groups was the communal search for an authentic life, a walk of faith in the steps of the Master. The word, the witness, the way of life—all were enlivened by the Holy Spirit.

In its small size, the full participation of its members, its fervent prayer, its communal discernment, and its "prophetic" stance, our small church in England is seeking to grow into a twentieth-century family likeness to its sixteenth-century sister groups from across the Channel. But even more striking is the similarity that both types hold to their New Testament counterparts. Those first churches, too, were small urban groups, centered around their heartfelt worship of God, their thankfulness for redemption through Christ. Their life was intertwined with their worship. The practices of the early Christians form a seamless whole, which included their belief, their radical way of life, their worship of God. It is our desire, as English Anabaptists, to continue in that great tradition.

Eleanor Graber Kreider, UK, b. 1935, M.Mus., director of Resource Centre of the London Mennonite Centre.

An African choir at Foyer Grebel near Paris where students from Africa are hosted. (MBM photo by Phil Richard, 1988)

Changing visions of worship

by Marlene Kropf

Worship in North American Mennonite churches has been changing rapidly since 1960. In the past, one expected to find similar patterns of worship in Virginia, Kansas, Oregon, Ontario, or anyplace between. Today Mennonite worship is characterized by creative ferment. Increased participation of many people, a variety of streams of spirituality, changing styles of music and language, greater attention to the Christian year, and hunger for the reality of God's presence have all contributed to renewal in worship.

Social, cultural, and religious changes have created new expectations and visions for worship. Perhaps the most significant development has been a growing awareness of the loss of the sacred in public life. In a pluralistic society, people do not share common assumptions about divine reality. Christian values no longer provide a foundation for the public or private spheres of life. Scientific and technological advances continue to alienate people from their spiritual moorings. As a result, many people, including churchgoers, experience profound emptiness. The hunger for spiritual reality is evident in many places. Fascination with Eastern religion, involvement in popular psychology movements, the pursuit of wealth and pleasure, and openness to every variety of spiritual renewal reflect a deep hunger for religious experience. As a consequence, a major agenda for North American Mennonites is the recovery of the transcendent or vertical dimensions of worship.

Just as important, however, has been an expanded awareness of the significance of the horizontal dimensions of worship. Though Mennonites would be slow to recognize the influence of worship reforms from Vatican II, the church has indeed felt the impact of the acceptance of the Constitution on Liturgy in 1963. Whereas Mennonite worship had traditionally emphasized communal discernment and lay participation, the conviction that worship is "the people's work" had eroded in many places.

Also contributing to a renewed vision of participatory worship have been the cross-cultural experiences of Mennonite Central Committee workers and Mennonite missionaries. As they learned to appreciate indigenous worship styles in many parts of the world, they brought home a desire for richer, more culturally diverse styles of worship that involve the body and heart as well as the mind.

Today Mennonites are reclaiming a vision for worship that unites the vertical and horizontal, the transcendent and immanent. People long to experience God's power and love when they gather for worship; they also want the bonds of community to be strengthened. In addition, they want worship to empower them for a life of faithful witness and service in the world.

What does the emerging vision of worship look like?

The recovery of the transcendent or vertical dimensions of worship can be seen in four major arenas:

* Attention to the essential elements of worship
* Awareness of a variety of streams of spirituality
* Appreciation for the role of symbols and art in worship
* Understanding and use of the Christian calendar

Mennonite worship has always included singing, prayer, and preaching. In recent years more attention is being given to a wider range of acts of worship that help people become aware of God's presence, hear God's word, and respond in faith and obedience. An example of this focus can be found in the work of the Hymnal Council, which is preparing a hymnal-worship book to be published in 1992 for Mennonites and Church of the Brethren in North America. Instead of organizing the new hymnal in doctrinal or topical sequence, the council has chosen to organize the music according to the acts of worship in a typical Sunday morning service. The acts of gathering, praising, confessing, reconciling, offering, hearing God's word, affirming the faith, responding in prayer, and sending can all help worshipers to focus their attention on the God whom they have come to meet.

Two elements of worship—praise and confession—reflect increased concern for the vertical dimensions of worship. In part because of the influence of the Charismatic movement, Mennonites are spending more time in acts of praise and adoration. A not uncommon pattern is for a congregation to sing songs of praise for twenty to thirty minutes at the opening of Sunday worship. Deeper than any particular stream of spirituality, however, is the growing conviction that God is the center or focus of worship. Because of being ethnic communities, Mennonites in the past may have sometimes gathered to worship for mainly social reasons. In a secular age, much more is needed. People need to experience the living presence of God if their faith is to survive and sustain them in a world that is hostile to the reign of Jesus Christ.

Along with praise, the acts of confession and reconciliation are gaining in importance. Although most Christian churches never dropped confession from the weekly order of worship, North American Mennonites have neglected these acts. Preparatory services for communion traditionally included opportunities for confession. In communities where annual revival meetings were held, people also had opportunities to publicly acknowledge their need of God and confess their sin. Perhaps a perfectionist view of discipleship among Mennonites also contributed to the neglect of corporate confession. Today these acts of worship are reappearing along with a heightened appreciation for God's grace. Prayers of confession occur in a variety of forms. In some churches, a worship leader or pastor leads the corporate prayer of confession. Sometimes the congregation prays the confession in unison (it may be a Scripture such as Psalm 51). At other times a hymn such as "Far, Far Away" is sung as a confession.

The transcendent dimensions of worship have also been enriched by various streams of spirituality influencing the church. Adoration of God is a typical emphasis of charismatic worship; the holiness and majesty of God are a focus of conservative evangelical streams; silence in the presence of mystery is a gift of contemplative spirituality. Where the various streams of spirituality are appreciated and integrated into corporate worship, they have potential to enlarge awareness of God through a rich variety of biblical images.

A third arena for expanded awareness of the transcendent in worship is the use of symbols and art. Although Mennonites fell heir to a didactic, iconoclastic wing of the Radical Reformation, many churches today are rediscovering the power of art to mediate God's presence and grace. The use of sculpture, banners, liturgical movement, drama, color, texture, music, visual art, gesture, and ritual can all contribute to more vital experiences of God's presence. Some churches plan a worship center, which visually highlights the focus of a particular service. Others have introduced simple hand or body movements to express praise or confession or supplication. Some churches train Scripture readers to proclaim the word with passion and skill. Music, of course, has always been the most important art form in Mennonite worship. Often a mode of prayer, music lifts the congregation into God's presence and expresses more than words alone can say. A wider range of songs, hymns, instruments, and musical styles has broadened the possibilities for meeting God in worship. Nor has the sermon been untouched by the desire to experience God rather than just talk about God. An emphasis on narrative theology, storytelling, greater use of images and metaphors, and more effective communication skills has made the sermon "an event in time" rather than a teaching. Preaching is not just proclamation; it is also a manifestation of God's presence and power.

The fourth arena is greater use of the Christian calendar. While Mennonites have long celebrated Easter and Christmas, many churches have paid scant attention to other events of the Christian year. An increased interest in early church worship patterns is partly responsible for more use of the Christian calendar. Another factor is renewed appreciation for the rhythms of fasting and feasting. Perhaps more significant is the recovery of the awareness of the power of the gospel to shape and transform people's lives. The Christological focus of the Christian calendar from Advent to Pentecost invites people to enter more deeply into the paschal mystery and hear the call to live as disciples. The emphasis on the church's mission in the world, which occurs in the second half of the Christian year, provides a holistic context for witness, service, peacemaking, and stewardship.

More participatory styles of worship

The emerging vision for worship among Mennonites in North America also includes an awareness that the horizontal dimensions of worship need to be strengthened. Because of ethnic ties in the past, Mennonites have experienced worship as a community event. Today the breakdown of community and the increasing cultural diversity of the church call for renewed attention to relationships. Worship is a corporate spiritual discipline. It involves the entire body of believers—all ages, races, sexes, and economic groups. True worship demands the active participation of all the people of God.

The desire to be more inclusive in worship affects structures for worship planning, styles of worship, use of language, and the involvement of all generations. In contrast to clergy-dominated patterns of worship leadership, for example, today's worship is often planned and led by lay people. Although elders or deacons may be involved in establishing worship themes and directions, the week-to-week planning is often carried out by lay people. In some churches, the pastor (or preacher) meets early in the week with the worship and music leaders. Together they plan the order of service using the Scripture focus for the week as a framework. What may be lost in expertise is gained in wider ownership of worship concerns. Worship styles are also more participatory. The congregation is involved in calls to worship, responsive Scripture readings, litanies, spontaneous prayer, and sharing of joys and concerns. Sunday evening services in the past were often more informal and participatory than Sunday morning services. Because many churches no longer hold Sunday evening services, those less formal elements have tended to become part of Sunday morning worship. For example, a children's meeting was formerly part of Sunday evening worship. Now a children's story or experience is often incorporated on Sunday morning.

Testimonies of personal spiritual experiences were also included in Sunday evening services in the past; requests for prayer were usually part of the traditional Wednesday evening prayer meeting. With the disappearance of both these settings for worship has come the desire to introduce some elements of community sharing on Sunday morning. The sharing time often follows the Sunday morning sermon and includes personal testimonies, affirmations, and concerns about health or work or relationships. Usually this time concludes with a pastoral prayer, or members gather around the individuals who have requested prayer and pray specifically for their needs.

One consequence of these additions to worship is that more time is necessary for the Sunday morning service. While an hour used to be a standard length of service, many congregations now meet for 75- or 90-minute services. A few congregations have even expanded worship to a two-hour block of time on Sunday morning.

Specific attempts are being made to include people of all generations in worship leading. A father and grade school daughter may read a Scripture together. A family may light the candles on an Advent wreath. On a certain Sunday, the youth may plan and lead worship. In one congregation an elderly grandmother who writes poetry is occasionally invited to recite one of her poems in worship. Another way worship is becoming more participatory is through increased sensitivity to language that includes all people. The words of worship must welcome the disabled, the poor, women, and racial minority groups. Even the language used to describe God is being re-examined for exclusiveness. People are also being encouraged to participate more fully in the actions of worship. They may rise to sing or hear Scripture read. In the act of reconciliation, they may turn to each other, shake hands, and offer assurances of God's forgiveness. In a few churches liturgical movement provides an avenue for fuller participation in worship. Still another kind of participation is the involvement of the whole self—body, mind, and heart—in response to Scripture. The stories of Scripture can suggest ways to concretely involve worshipers. For example, when the story of the woman at the well (John 4) was the focus, one worship planning team chose to invite the congregation to receive the water of life. After the sermon, people were invited to come forward to receive a drink of water from a punch bowl filled with icy cold water. The act symbolized their desire to receive living water from the eternal spring, Jesus Christ. Another way the horizontal dimensions of worship are being strengthened extends beyond the immediate gathering of believers. A broader social consciousness and awareness of injustice compels churches to bring the wider world into the worship hour on Sunday morning. Calls to action in peacemaking, stewardship, or community service are frequent. One congregation that has hired a full-time community worker often hears requests for prayer or immediate action on Sunday morning. Intercessory prayer may include prayers for peace in the world as well as laments for tragedy and pain. Some churches take their worship out into the street as a form of witness. On Palm Sunday they march around the church singing songs of praise to God. On Good Friday in one community teenagers carried a wooden cross through the streets from church to church for use in various services. Marchers for peace gather in public places to pray for an end to war.

In a time of much ferment and change, it is easy for worshipers to lose sight of the focus of worship: meeting God. It is also easy for conflicts to develop over various expectations and preferences. Education for worship is sorely needed in Mennonite congregations as well as training for worship leaders. To strengthen both the vertical and horizontal dimensions of worship will call for the Spirit's guidance and power as the Mennonite church in North America seeks to be faithful in the future.

Marlene Kropf, USA, b. 1943, M.A. in teaching, M.Div., staffperson for education, worship, and spirituality at Mennonite Board of Congregational Ministries (Elkhart, Indiana), part-time assistant in spiritual formation at Associated Mennonite Biblical Seminaries (Elkhart, Indiana).

Worship in Mbuji Mayi reflecting a joyous spirit. (MWC photo by Paul Kraybill, 1988)

The Sunday worship in Mbuji Mayi

by Milolo Kabalu

Very early in the morning, at about 8 o'clock, the deacons take care of arranging the sanctuary. They put out flowers, dust the benches, and hose down the sanctuary. The children then go to Sunday school, which lasts about thirty minutes. They are given special instruction based on Bible verses, and they learn songs. The Youth for Christ group has its meetings after the service.

The starting time for the service varies from one parish to another. When the bell rings, the faithful enter in order and in silence. The choir members take their places at the front. There are often four choirs in large parishes—children's, youth, women's, and men's choirs. The number of choirs varies from one parish to another.

The women have a uniform, which is not required, but the use of a head scarf during the service is recommended to all of them.

When the worship leaders have entered, the moderator reads a Bible verse, and the congregation rises to sing a hymn. At the end of the song, praise is given to the Lord by the moderator, and the faithful pray silently. The chorister then announces two collective songs, and everyone sings with joy under his direction. If the song has a four-beat measure, it will be accompanied by the clapping of hands. After a meditation on the goodness of the Lord, the moderator invites one of the members to thank the Lord for having watched over all the members during the week. The moderator reports to the members the amount of the offering and the number of Bibles and songbooks from the preceding week. He arranges for the place where the prayer groups will meet that week. He also introduces the visitors. The faithful welcome the visitors with a special song, and a member is chosen to say a prayer for them.

Now comes the participation of the choirs, who sing their melodies in the order given by the moderator. In a parish where there are four choirs, they sing alternately. The men's choirs are often accompanied by guitars and chalice-shaped drums. The women's choirs are accompanied by metal percussion instruments, the "tshipuidi" (small folk instrument made from a calabash with a small metal pipe inserted at the top for blowing into the calabash), which provides the bass voice, and other indigenous instruments. Not all choirs have the same instruments. There are others who sing only with unaccompanied voices. The songs of the women and the youth are often accompanied by dances. If not the entire body, at least the head will surely be moving. The dance always has meaning and is appropriate to the song. It always manifests praise and joy. In other choirs, only gestures are used.

Taking the offering is done in the following manner. First are the promises that the faithful have made secretly to the Lord concerning personal problems. When the problem is resolved, the person gives a testimony before the congregation. Each one gives what she or he has promised. It can be money, produce, or an animal. This part of the service has its special song. The day's balance is tallied, and everyone rises, singing and dancing. The children bring their offerings first, then the youth, the women, and the men. In this part only money is given. The tithe is given voluntarily by the people involved. This can be in the form of money, produce, or animals. A member is chosen to consecrate all the offerings to the Lord. The choirs again sing several melodies. After their songs, the moderator counts the members, the Bibles, and the songbooks.

The most important part of the service is the sermon. At this time all the children are watched carefully to see that they do not disrupt the sermon. The preacher for the day announces to his audience the author, page, chapter, and verses of the reading. He reads in a loud and clear voice. Afterward, he invokes the Holy Spirit to enlighten and hold the attention of the audience and to help the preacher during the sermon. As he preaches he directs the attention of the faithful to the subject of the day, adding verses from other biblical writers. When the chapter and verse are announced, whoever finds them first reads for the others. To ensure that the message is well understood, he sometimes uses stories, images, proverbs, or objects (didactic material) taken from biblical passages.

The length of the sermon varies from one preacher to another. If the sermon is long, it will be interspersed with verses of song that speak about the same subject in order to give the preacher a break and prevent the faithful from sleeping. The sermon does not often last longer than an hour. The singing is often improvised and can come from any member. Sometimes the preacher asks the audience short questions in order to hold their attention, and the answer is always given collectively. After ample explanation of all the points of the message, he makes a summary and gives the moral.

When the sermon is finished, a member who is chosen gives thanks to the Lord for the message; often the preacher fulfills this task. The choirs sing for the last time. Their songs correspond to the theme of the sermon. At the end, the pastor prays as a closing. The congregation sings the prayer "Our Father" and receives the blessing. Leaving the sanctuary is also done in order, and all the faithful greet each other at the door. The way we worship in Zaire is very satisfying.

Milolo Kabalu, Zaire, b. 1952, trained as a teacher, president of the women of the parish, Communauté Mennonite au Zaire.
Translated by Sylvia Shirk Charles.

Note
Mbuji Mayi is a city of approximately 100,000 people in the province of East Kasai in Zaire.

Chinese Christians meet

by Herta Funk and Ann Martin

What about Protestant Christianity in China? The China Educational Exchange (CEE), an inter-Mennonite North American agency sending people to China and hosting Chinese in North America, has been able to observe church life in China since the organization was founded in 1981. CEE teachers have attended open churches, generally as "back-benchers." One CEE couple took the initiative one Sunday to visit a group meeting in a home (because there was no open church in the city), but was quickly discouraged from continuing attendance. Consequently, CEE teachers generally cannot speak from personal experience about such informal meeting points. Most teachers have only attended open churches, but many have had contacts with members of home meetings.

Easter joy, meeting at the church

Easter 1984 came as a surprise for one CEE teacher because the outward signs leading up to it were missing in the culture. As four foreigners walked into the church courtyard in Chengdu, each got a little daisy pinned on the lapel. The church itself was already crowded, and there were probably over one hundred people sitting outside in front of the open church windows. Two university students—who came to church on a semiregular basis because they liked the "holy atmosphere" and sensed that people loved each other—immediately greeted them warmly. Then the foreign guests were ushered into the crowded sanctuary, where four British Quakers with connections in China were seated in front of them. The church was decorated with white daisies and azaleas, which, they later discovered, were contributed by an 81-year-old woman medical doctor who had spent twenty-seven years in prison—several of those years in solitary confinement. The choir came in to the strains of "O Come, All Ye Faithful." The twenty-five singers, among them quite a number of young people, wore snowy white robes with brilliant red satin sashes. Twice during the service they sang, in four-part harmony, "Up From the Grave He Arose." Dr. Li Lianke, well over 80, led the service. Then followed the baptism of thirteen people. Over half of the candidates were gray-haired women, but there were some young people as well. On the way home from church, everyone received two Easter eggs.

Church in Chengdu

This Protestant church in the city of Chengdu, Sichuan Province, was reopened in March 1980 after having been closed for over a decade. During the Cultural Revolution (1966–76) the church, like all others, was closed. The government subsequently returned the property to the church. Church structures are built around a Chinese courtyard. Worshipers enter through a gate. In this church in Chengdu, the church building is to the left. To the right, jutting into the court-

yard, is an old several-story mission house. Straight ahead is a new office
building for the Sichuan Christian Council. Mr. Hua Chengji of the church is its
general secretary. The rest of the courtyard is framed by low one-story structures. In 1980, before the church was renovated, services were held in two rooms
of the former mission house—seventy people crowded into a space for thirty. In
a few months the congregation, by then 160, had moved into the church building, filling it almost to capacity. Attendance has increased to the point that there
now are as many people sitting in the courtyard, listening through open windows, as there are inside the building. By 1988 there were three churches in
Chengdu. The senior pastor of the church is Dr. Li Lianke, a second-generation
Christian and a second-generation pastor, and a good friend of CEE folk. His
childhood memories are not without pain, because Christianity was so often
linked to Western colonial expansionism in trade and commerce. A popular
saying at the time was, "Win a convert; lose a citizen."

Dr. Li sees the nondenominational church that emerged after Liberation in 1949
as the work of God's grace. His church is part of the larger Three-Self movement in China, a movement working for a self-supporting, self-governing, and
self-propagating church. One of China's thirteen theological schools (one seminary and a dozen Bible schools with space for seven hundred students) is located
in Chengdu. Dr. Li, in addition to being the president of the Sichuan Christian
Council, is its principal. At present there is a big leadership gap in all churches
in China. In the Chengdu church there are several older ministers engaged in the
work of the church (one over ninety years old) as well as some young seminary
graduates, including a woman. Chinese church leaders talk about the way they
organized the union church in Chengdu: "In 1979 we began to contact scattered
former members. We asked the government authorities to return our church
property. Our first service was March 2, 1980. We wept for joy. The joy of being
able to worship together overcame our differences. We strongly perceived that
this could only be the wondrous work of the Holy Spirit."

Easter joy, meeting at home

Easter 1988 was celebrated by another North American teacher in China in a
home. Five young Chinese, including three singles in their early 20s and a
married couple in their 30s, and three foreign teachers met in the two-room
home of an older woman. This woman taught in the local Three-Self church and
at a key university. Like many intellectuals, she had suffered banishment to the
countryside for agricultural labor during the Anti-Rightist Campaign in the late
1950s. Her ostracism had continued through the Cultural Revolution. She
recalled names of disrespect the neighbor children used to hurl at her as she
passed by. Those years had been the crucible in which God had tested and
refined her, she told us. She was by nature proud, but the humiliations visited
upon her had been transforming. She was delighted with the opening of the
churches beginning in 1979. She was also realistic about the problems, even ob-

stacles, they encountered. She reported to the group that a pastor in another part of the province required their prayers. He was encountering resistance from some local authorities who felt the church he served was growing too rapidly.

With a small coal-burning stove and the close quarters providing warmth, the group began worship with prayer and then took turns reading aloud the Easter story and related passages. The foreigners read aloud, too, their stumblings and mispronunciations either gently corrected or ignored. At the end of the reading, the older woman asked several to share testimonies. One woman recounted two recent experiences of God's faithfulness. The first involved cooking matches. They were nowhere to be found, either in the state-run stores or at the little privately run street stalls. They were a tiny item, but without them her family could not light their gas stove to cook. She became convinced that the Bible's injunction to ask the heavenly Father for all things also applied to matches. She felt silly "bothering" God with such a trifle, but the match supply had dwindled to almost nothing, so she asked anyway. Immediately she came upon a vender with a bountiful supply. Second, she had been praying for several months that one of her factory coworkers would attend church with her. She had invited the coworker several times, but the colleague had always found excuses. The woman decided that she would not ask again; rather, she would wait for God to move her friend's heart. To her delight, the coworker came to her before long and asked which Sunday it would suit for the two of them to go to church together. Another woman, a teacher, described the encouraging role she tried to play with her students. Many felt some hopelessness about their futures and viewed her as a confidante. She said she made no secret of her Christian beliefs to her students and coworkers and that even though some viewed her as an eccentric, others were attracted by her optimism and energy. Throughout these testimonies, the older woman occasionally interjected questions or comments. She played a mentoring or discipling role for these young Christians, all young in age and some young in faith too. Her own granddaughter was not a Christian; these were grandchildren of the spirit. The tenor of the conversation revealed that these Chinese Christians considered themselves to be salt in society. They tried to model actions and attitudes that would elicit questions about "the hope that is in you," and they prayed for hearts open to hearing the response.

Christians in China and CEE teachers from abroad have appreciated the opportunity to experience the reality of all being part of one body of Christ. Chinese church leaders sometimes plead with their foreign counterparts: "Please do not divide the body of Christ in China." What they do ask for repeatedly is this: "Remember us and pray for us."

Herta Funk, Canada, b. 1935, Ph.D. in German literature, English teacher in China from 1983–87 under CEE, former coordinator of publicity and education for CEE in Winnipeg, Manitoba.
Ann Martin, Canada, b. 1961, B.A. in communications, studied and taught in China under CEE from 1985–88, assistant director of CEE in Winnipeg, Manitoba.

Taiwan Women's Choir performs at Asia Mennonite Conference. (MWC photo by David Shelly, 1986)

House churches

by Lois Barrett

House churches are composed of believers in groups that are small enough to meet face to face, groups that have covenanted with God and with each other to be the church under the authority of Christ and the guidance of the Spirit. House churches often meet in homes but may sometimes meet in public buildings or church meetinghouses. More important than the place of meeting is the closeness of relationships implied by the word "house." House churches are known by a variety of terms: small groups, koinonia groups, care groups, base communities. They differ from groups organized only for fellowship or only for Bible study in that they are free to take on all or almost all the functions of the church, including worship, pastoral care, accountability, teaching, gift discernment, decision making, and mission and service. Some congregations are made up of one house church of seven to twenty people. Other congregations are clusters of several house churches that may meet together as often as once a week or as seldom as once every seven weeks. House churches tend to be found more often in cities, where people may not have extended family or other networks of relationships with other Christians. People in house churches are looking for more caring and accountability than they might get from just attending worship on Sunday morning in a large congregation.

The congregation of which I am a part is Mennonite Church of the Servant in Wichita, Kansas (USA), a city of about 280,000. Our congregation is made up of several house churches that meet in homes during the week. The whole congregation meets together for worship on the first and third Sunday mornings of the month and on the fourth Sunday for decision making. Mennonite Church of the Servant was begun in 1976 through the initiative of the Western District Home Mission Committee (General Conference Mennonite Church). But since our beginning we have also chosen membership in the South Central Conference (Mennonite Church). Our members have come from both groups as well as from other Mennonite conferences, other denominations, and people with few previous church connections.

What is important to us

Caring and discipling—House churches have been a good place for us to combine love and accountability. We all need support from other Christians. We need people with whom we can share our difficulties and our joys. We also need people who love us enough to nurture us and to question us. Many people have lamented the lack of church discipline in many North American churches. But there has also often been a lack of a caring environment in which people can feel free to share their deepest needs and find healing for their wounds. Caring and discipline belong together. An important part of our time together as house churches is in sharing about our previous week: our relationships, life events, dreams, experiences with God. We do this sharing in a more formal way once a year when each person who wants to covenant with the church gives his or her "spiritual pilgrimage." This is a careful look at the person's past year as well as his or her current state of physical, emotional, and spiritual wellness and goals for the future.

Covenant and community—House churches are intentional churches. They do not come into being by simply adopting denominational statements of faith. They are intentional about who they are and what is the basis for their being together as a community of faith. At Mennonite Church of the Servant, we state those things in our covenant. Our covenant was drawn up at the beginning of our church. It is our confession of faith and our commitment to Christ, to each other, and to ministry in the world. Each year, after spiritual pilgrimages have been shared, we sign the covenant at a special Maundy Thursday meal. Some of those who sign are signing for the first time. Others of us are signing again. This is our recommitment to Christ and to the church for the coming year. The covenant and the "understandings," which we have written down to make the covenant more specific, are the basic guidelines for our life together as a Christian community. We encourage community in a variety of practical ways: through about half our group living in the same neighborhood, through potluck meals, through sharing various personal possessions, through a mutual aid sharing fund.

The ministry of all members—With our baptism and our covenanting, we also commit ourselves to ministry within the body of Christ. Each person has a ministry in and through the church. Part of our annual cycle is gift discernment. In his or her house church, each member reviews abilities, resources, and preferences. Then the house church in consultation with the whole church helps each person discern one or more roles in which he or she can serve the church. The roles for some people are leadership roles. But even then, leadership is shared rather than hierarchical. Each house church has one or more shepherds who take responsibility for the overall life of the house church and for the pastoral care of its members. They also serve as a kind of board of deacons or elders for the whole church. My role in the church is that of teacher/preacher and shepherd to the shepherds.

Worship and decision making in the power of the Spirit—Our worship times as house churches and as a whole church are an important part of our life together. In worship we declare our allegiance to God as our ruler and our commitment to each other as God's people. Our worship times are informal. They include a lot of singing, accompanied by whatever instruments people bring. There is teaching, the Bible applied to our life. There is prayer for each other, for those we know, for the world. About once a month we have communion as our recommitment to the body of Christ and as a celebration of our life together in the Spirit of Christ. Decision making is also an important part of our life together. In the

Bible the word for "church" is used primarily for the church as a worshiping body and the church as a decision-making body. We have monthly "church life" meetings to make decisions as a whole church. We use the consensus method, meaning not necessarily total agreement but willingness for the church to proceed. We have found it important to look not just for human agreement but for all of us to be listening for what the Spirit of God wants to say to us.

Prayer and mission—We are committed to integrating spirituality and action. Some of us may lean farther to one side or the other. But true prayer grows out of the events of our lives. And true mission grows out of our prayer and a strong awareness of the presence of God through us in the world. A weeknight prayer group sees its mission as inner healing for whoever comes to the meeting. One house church has worked intensively with a Central American refugee. As a whole church, we are involved in Churches United for Peacemaking, Mennonite Housing Rehabilitation Services, a Mennonite Voluntary Service unit, and Window to the World, a shop that sells SELFHELP Crafts obtained through Mennonite Central Committee.

Churches have met in houses since New Testament times. (See Acts 2:41–47; 12:12; 16:15,40; 17:5, Rom. 16:5, 1 Cor. 16:15,19, Col. 4:15, Philem. 2.) Wherever renewal movements have sprung up, people have met in homes to share the gospel. In sixteenth-century Europe the Anabaptists also met in homes, not only because of the persecution but because of the opportunity to read the Scriptures together and teach each other. There is no current, accurate estimate of the number of house churches among Mennonites in North America. The 1986 *Mennonite Yearbook* listed forty-six "church communities" in the United States and Canada, but some congregations were included that were not communities or house churches and other house churches were not listed. In addition to the congregations that are made up strictly of one or more house churches, many larger Mennonite congregations have several "house churches" or "small groups" performing many of the functions of house churches.

Wherever they are, house churches provide a sense of being part of God's family. In societies that have become more impersonal and fragmented, where extended families no longer live close by, where people sometimes attend services in large churches without actually speaking to anyone else, house churches help create a new Christian family with both love and accountability. We tell people, "We will teach you not just to go to church, but to be the church."

Lois Barrett, USA, b. 1947, M.Div., teaching minister at the Mennonite Church of the Servant (Wichita, Kansas).

Leónidas Saucedo (left), moderator of the Iglesia Evangélica Menonita Boliviana, prays for Julia Masai, a new believer.
(MBM photo by Gerald Mumaw, 1988)

The charismatic experience in Amor Viviente

by Marco Antonio Ulloa

In the 1970s many Christian churches and denominations found themselves exposed to what is known today as the Charismatic movement. This was a movement rooted in the belief in a spiritual experience known as the baptism in the Holy Spirit, which was an anointing of power from above to become witnesses of Christ and which opened a way to experience the supernatural gifts of the Holy Spirit, specifically those named in 1 Corinthians 12:8–10. Amor Viviente was not an exception. From its very beginning in Honduras, it found itself under the influence of this movement, which happened to be a positive influence in this case. In the following paragraphs I will present a short historical review of the charismatic beginnings of this church named Amor Viviente together with a description of some particular characteristics that such influence has had through the years.

The beginnings of the charismatic influence in Amor Viviente

The charismatic experience has been in Amor Viviente from the very start, as specifically manifested in the life of its founder, the Reverend Edward King. A missionary from the Eastern Mennonite Board of Missions and Charities, Brother King started to feel a tremendous burden for the life of Honduran youth who were without hope and without Christ in their daily lives. Feeling incapable of helping them (in charismatic terms, we could call this the lack of anointing and power), Brother King found himself asking God to perform a radical change in his own life due to the fact that the burden was very heavy and he could do nothing to make it lighter, even when he tried—without much fruit—to bring the message of Christ to these Honduran youth. God's answer, as Brother King used to tell, came very soon. Through another Mennonite missionary, he came to know and had a talk with a person who had experienced what he called the baptism in the Holy Spirit. Trying to understand all the details related to the experience, Brother King argued a lot with this person, only to finally come to the conviction that he needed that experience. That very night he received the baptism in the Holy Spirit, and his ministerial life was radically changed. He had such anointing of the Spirit that the message of Christ flowed with power through him, touching the lives of many young people. As a result of his own experience, Brother King brought the charismatic influence to Amor Viviente— which means "living love" in Spanish. It is important to notice that he actually founded the church after he received the baptism in the Spirit. From the very first years there were retreats and camp meetings where dozens of people came to know Jesus, receiving at the same time the charismatic experience. In other words, they were receiving not only salvation but also the anointing of power through the baptism in the Holy Spirit.

This was not an experience that the people received and then forgot. It expressed itself in a radical change of life. All of a sudden they found themselves freed from the power of drugs and alcohol and capable of restoring family relationships that had been destroyed. Healings, deliverance, prophetic words, speaking in tongues, and the radical change of life to serve Jesus with power were common experiences at the beginning of Amor Viviente. All these produced (and still produce) a tremendous expression of gratitude, which was shown in a powerful praise and worship experience based on a full conviction of the greatness of God. The spirit of power and praise was apparent in all meetings, not only retreats. Church meetings used to begin at 6 p.m. and often lasted until midnight due to the praise and worship experience—which was alive and rich—and the power of Jesus moving among the people. The gifts of the Spirit were revealed in many ways, usually bringing the people to a higher commitment and searching of God's will for their own lives.

Characteristics of the charismatic influence in Amor Viviente

Apart from the characteristics already mentioned, there are some particular charismatic characteristics in Amor Viviente that deserve to be described in this article, for we cannot deny that the effects of the Pentecostal experience are different in every church. The characteristics discussed in the following paragraphs have stayed and developed through the years:

1.   In Amor Viviente the Pentecostal experience brought a tremendous awareness of what it means to be the body of Christ, that is, the need to work as a team. What do we mean by that? If we read very carefully the Scripture passage that mentions the gifts of the Holy Spirit (1 Cor. 12), we will notice that these are not presented in a context of an individual and egocentric experience but in the context of the body of Christ. The gifts are given for the good of all members and for the building of the church; they are given to each one for mutual benefit. The one who prophesies does it for the rest of the body and not for himself, and this can be applied to every gift that God provides to any of the members. This awareness came to Amor Viviente as a result of the charismatic influence and has produced tremendous effects through the years. Individual members have always sought out "their own" place in the body, the specific functions that God has shown them they can and must perform. The result of that awareness, today, is this: a church of a few thousand people, where the majority of its members perform clearly defined and productive functions according to their own natural and spiritual gifts. It is impressive to see hundreds of people going to church not to receive a message passively while they sit on a bench but, on the contrary, to present their gifts in an active way for the building of the body of Christ. One important element of this awareness is that it has completely eliminated the mistaken idea that the pastor is the person who does all the work, being some kind of an octopus or a superman, gifted in all areas of church work. Instead, each member finds his or her own place, takes responsibility, and performs

actively and efficiently as part of a big team of servants (ministers) called the body of Christ.

Amor Viviente grows and goes forward as this big team of ministers of Christ, not only the leaders but each and every member. The growth numerically, spiritually, and as an institution is the result of the work of the whole body of believers. There are ministries for counseling, children, music, and teaching as well as a Christian education center, a radio station, and many other projects and church programs. The duties for each of these activities are performed by church members, most of whom put forth all that effort only because they love Jesus and his work.

In order to provide a good environment for the use and development of gifts, Amor Viviente functions through growth groups, groups of five to ten believers. These groups stimulate growth and mutual edification while providing practical ways for each member to develop his or her own particular gifts. These groups are the center of Amor Viviente. Simply attending the general church meeting (worship) does not make someone a member of the church; rather, going to a growth group makes him or her an active member of the body of Christ.

2. The charismatic influence brought to Amor Viviente a free and spontaneous worship experience that involves the whole person. Due to the manifestations of the Spirit, praise and worship have always been important in the life of Amor Viviente. Christ has always been exalted as the center of worship. This worship experience has evolved through the years. Especially during the last few years, Amor Viviente has been experiencing a tremendous change in relation to worship. Many charismatic songs that were actually to gratify our own souls and not to exalt Jesus Christ have been put aside. Today most of the songs are centered on God and his works and are solely for his exaltation and glory. This change has produced tremendous effects in the spirit of the praise and worship.

3. The charismatic influence also brought the burning desire to consecrate one's life to Christian service. This desire was the foundation on which a whole program for leadership training was built. Members who were filled with the Spirit had a burning desire to serve. This brought Brother King to the point of finding a way to give people the stable foundation necessary to serve as leaders on different levels. The training system was called discipleship meetings. After many years of development, these discipleship meetings have grown into a complete three-year program in which those who show qualities for leadership receive practical training on spiritual as well as administrative and ministerial issues, together with a definition of lines of authority in the body of Christ. In one of our churches (Amor Viviente in Tegucigalpa, the capital city of Honduras), the program currently trains more than six hundred people in three different levels. This is a result of the charismatic influence.

4.   The charismatic influence also brought a tremendous emphasis on personal evangelism performed by Spirit-filled members of the body. From the beginning Amor Viviente was characterized as an evangelistic church because members actually believed that one of the purposes of the baptism in the Spirit was to give the believer power for witnessing (Acts 1:8). Evangelism is done not by well-known preachers but by members of the congregation. This is derived from the conviction that all believers are called to save lives, not only through the spoken message but also through their own lives once they are filled with the Spirit. This implies a tremendous responsibility, for it calls for a change of life (personal, familial, and professional) in an underdeveloped environment not accustomed to responsibility, discipline, and some other things. Evangelism means not only words; it means living in accordance with those words. That is what makes evangelism "in the Spirit," and this idea has created an important sense of stewardship in the members of Amor Viviente. Today all the evangelism is done through the growth groups, which eliminates the need for special activities such as evangelistic campaigns and, at the same time, provides a balanced and continuous numerical growth. The spirit of evangelism manifests itself not only locally but also in mission work. Today Amor Viviente has more than fifteen national churches and two international churches, one in New Orleans (USA) and the other in Alajuela (Costa Rica).

5.   In Amor Viviente, the charismatic influence has always provided a clear, up-to-date, and fresh vision, not only as a body but also at the personal level. From the very beginning there has been a place for the prophetic word. In such a way the vision has grown and kept current. The missionary work is a result of that; it is based on prophetic utterances received from the Lord. Every year Amor Viviente has a week in which most of the members fast for six days to update personal and corporate vision for the year and find guidance from the Lord on every level of life. In this week there are prophetic messages to give guidance and allow the congregation to move forward as a unified body.

We have seen some characteristics of Amor Viviente that are a result of the charismatic influence. Without doubt, in this particular case, the influence has been very positive and full of purpose. We thank the Lord for the life and ministry of the Reverend Edward King and for his vision, openness, and desire to serve the Lord, which brought him to the Pentecostal experience. Without those elements, Amor Viviente would not have existed or experienced the tremendous blessings it has today from the power and anointing of the Holy Spirit.

Marco Antonio Ulloa, Honduras, b. 1953, M.Div., minister of music in the Amor Viviente congregation in Tegucigalpa, and academic dean of the Amor Viviente Christian education center.

Empowered Ministries, Mennonite renewal

by Calvin Kaufman

Empowered Ministries—the result of merging Mennonite Renewal Services (MRS) with the Church of the Brethren Renewal Services (BRS) and other related congregations—encourages renewal in groups with an Anabaptist orientation and maintains regular contact with church leaders. We thereby try to improve communication and understanding between us and to foster and facilitate renewal events at churchwide, district, and local congregational levels.

Beginning of the Charismatic movement

The roots of the Charismatic movement can be traced to the Pentecostal (holiness) churches that began in 1901 in Topeka, Kansas, and in Los Angeles, California, in 1906—reaching Chicago, New York, London, and Scandinavia by 1915. The Charismatic movement started in the early 1950s with the formation of the Full Gospel Businessmen's Fellowship in Los Angeles. In 1955 Mennonite minister Gerald Derstine in Minnesota and, in 1957, Dennis Bennett, an Episcopalian minister in California, received what most charismatics call the baptism with the Holy Spirit. Not until 1972 was there official recognition given to the work of the Holy Spirit in the Mennonite Church in North America. Early in 1972 there was a convocation of the Holy Spirit at Eastern Mennonite College, Harrisonburg, Virginia, and in June a festival of the Holy Spirit at Goshen [Indiana] College. In the 1975–77 biennium, the Mennonite Church studied the life and work of the Holy Spirit, and a summary statement was adopted in June 1977 by the Mennonite Church General Assembly.

Today Pentecostals are referred to as the first wave of the Holy Spirit and the charismatics as the second wave. Beginning about 1980, there is now a third wave, mostly among the evangelicals. Together these groups number approximately 350 million Christians worldwide, in spite of the fact that approximately 80 million have dropped out or have become post-charismatics since 1960. This movement is the largest and the fastest-growing (19 million a year) renewal movement in the history of the Christian church, according to the *International Bulletin of Missionary Research* (July 1988). While the Pentecostal movement flourished among the small town and urban poor—a reason why the Pentecostal movement has not been taken seriously by many Christians—the Charismatic movement tends to be more middle class in orientation, although it is found among all socioeconomic levels.

Holy Spirit renewal within the Anabaptist groups

In the mid-1960s only a few Mennonites and Brethren gave witness to an empowering of the Holy Spirit, but by the late 1960s and early 1970s many

Brethren and Mennonites entered into this experience. Mennonite Renewal Services began as an organization in 1975 as we saw the need for an annual North American gathering on the Holy Spirit and for involvement in the 1977 Kansas City transdenominational meeting on the Holy Spirit. The North American annual conference soon gave way to regional conferences in some fourteen areas. Today there are six regional annual conferences and four that meet periodically, including a Mennonite Brethren group in British Columbia. Empowered Ministries desires to have contact with Mennonite Brethren, Brethren in Christ, Evangelical Mennonites, and other Anabaptist groups. We also have contact with and mail our *Empowered* magazine to Central and South America, Asia, Europe, and Africa. Harold Bauman, formerly with the Mennonite Church (North America) Congregational Ministries, estimates that 10 to 50 percent of the Mennonite Church members are involved in the Holy Spirit renewal, including 25 to 35 percent of pastors. In one conference within the Mennonite Church, about two-thirds of the congregations are involved in this renewal movement.

Many Mennonites and Brethren have left the church over the past twenty-five years and have become involved in independent charismatic churches; in the United States, these now number about thirty thousand congregations. In northern Indiana the church has lost about eight hundred members, and eastern Pennsylvania about one thousand. Lancaster Conference (Pennsylvania) reports that some are now coming back into the conference as their churches are becoming more and more open to renewal (such as charismatic worship styles, etc.).

In recent years we have witnessed the rise of apostolic and prophetic ministries, which are helping to give leadership to this renewal movement within our Anabaptist groups. Apostolic ministry helps to provide visionary leadership to thrust the church in new directions spiritually and geographically. It also strengthens and stabilizes the local congregation and the church at large. Apostolic ministry functions in conjunction with prophetic ministry (Eph. 2:19,20). Apostolic ministry must be functional in that it is doing the ministry and not merely a title or office. Paul did not refer to himself as the Apostle Paul but as Paul, an apostle of Jesus Christ. Renewal is also moving from individual to more congregational and corporate renewal. Renewal networks are springing up in various parts of North America. We believe these networks should move alongside existing conference relationships.

What attracts people to Holy Spirit renewal

Among the expressions and contributions that attract people to this movement are the following:

- Hunger for an intimate relationship with the Father, Son, and Holy Spirit.
- A desire to encounter Jesus as Lord in transformation of the old self and as the baptizer with the Holy Spirit.

- A desire for movement beyond the rational intellectual to the intuitive, with the awakening of one's personal spirit in communion with the Lord Jesus.
- Worship that releases one's personal spirit as well as the gifts and fruit of the Spirit such as the prophetic word, emotional and physical healing, and the ability to deal with demons.
- Prayer that engages one in warring against the spiritual forces of the enemy.
- A desire for a greater empowerment for witness and ministry.
- Training for ministry, including members ministering to one another.
- A greater unity in the body of Christ with a genuine love and acceptance of those from different denominational streams.

Unfortunately, excesses and imbalances have also marked this renewal movement; not least have been pride, rejection, and divisiveness. We understand these problems not as the work of the Spirit but the work of human immaturity and, therefore, acknowledge our need for grace to maintain mutual respect and a deep awareness of our spiritual poverty before God as we seek the kingdom.

The recovery of the Anabaptist spirit

In the history of the church there have been many waves of the Holy Spirit, and Anabaptism is one. They made a major contribution to the sixteenth-century Reformation through their emphasis on the life and ministry of the Holy Spirit. In September 1988, the Lancaster Mennonite Assembly adopted a conference statement, from which the following excerpt was taken:

> Menno Simons was called the "reformer of the Holy Spirit" because he emphasized the work of the Spirit more than many other reformers. In the study of the Anabaptist movement, some have noted that many of the marks of the present charismatic renewal, with its emphasis on freedom of worship and the exercise of spiritual gifts, were evident among early Anabaptists. To the extent that we have neglected these aspects of spiritual life, we have failed to meet the spiritual needs of our people. We would do well to rediscover the power and freedom of the early Anabaptists. We need the anointing and power of the Holy Spirit as taught in Scriptures.

Mennonite theologian John Howard Yoder has said, "Pentecostalism is in our century the closest parallel to what Anabaptism was in the sixteenth" (*Concern* magazine, July 1967).

The Anabaptists were a recovery of the New Testament church in both word and spirit. To be as effective as the early Anabaptists were, we must serve and minister under the anointing and power of the Holy Spirit as they did. The Lord greatly blessed their life and ministry because they placed Jesus in control.

Some primary issues

One of the areas of disagreement concerns conversion and baptism with the Holy Spirit. Some renewal leaders draw from Pentecostal theology, while others affirm our historical-theological understandings of the baptism with the Holy Spirit, emphasizing that we need to encourage the infilling and release of the Holy Spirit for ministry within our churches. The rise of the apostolic and prophetic ministries also is questioned by some church leaders, but we believe these ministries can interact with pastors and congregations relationally and not governmentally. These ministries must come to congregations and pastors with hearts of submission to the local elders and pastors. These ministries should complement local resources and the ministry of the overseer-bishop, perhaps functioning within or alongside denominational and conference structures. There is also some disagreement regarding women in ministry. All would affirm that God gives women for ministry and wants to release their gifts, but some would put limitations when it comes to leadership with authority over men. We believe the Lord wants the integration of this renewal movement with the other four or five renewal movements within the Anabaptist family of churches such as the spiritual formation, peace, justice, church growth, and stewardship movements.

Vision for the future

The Lord is indeed renewing his church and preparing us for the consummation of all things in Christ. We need to rekindle the flame of the Spirit-filled life. We need the empowering release of the Spirit for witness and ministry, including the supernatural gifts experienced by the Anabaptists of the sixteenth century. The three primary goals for Empowered Ministries are mission, unity, and renewal.

Mission—"Lift up your eyes, and see how the fields are already white for harvest" (John 4:35b). Renewal is for mission and outreach, and the renewal churches are attracting many diverse people.

Unity—Jesus prayed for the unity of his followers, "that they may all be one … so that the world may believe" (John 17). The unity of the disciples and the effectiveness of the mission are closely related. Our community that we have in Jesus Christ as a Mennonite people needs to be expressed by our love for each other and by our working together under the rule of Jesus Christ.

Renewal—It is our conviction that districts, conferences, and indeed whole Anabaptist denominations will experience renewal and transformation as Jesus Christ is manifested more and more among us. We all need to continue to rediscover the Anabaptist spirit that placed Jesus at the center of life.

Calvin Kaufman, USA, b. 1936, B.A. in religion and postgraduate seminary studies, interim pastor at Trinity Mennonite Church (Morton, Illinois).

The shape and function of pastoral ministry

by Ralph A. Lebold

Major forces have influenced the shape of pastoral education and pastoral ministry in the last three decades. Mennonites in North America have shifted from reliance on leaders with minimal formal education to an assumption that seminary education is the norm. The leadership structure has changed from a multiple ministry pattern to one where the single pastor with deacons/elders has become common. This shift has been accompanied by rotation of leaders often resulting in shorter terms of service for pastors. The perception of who leaders are has changed so that an employee mentality has become all too common. Consequently, problems related to leadership evaluations, involuntary terminations, and related personnel issues have become common agenda items for denominational committees.

The office of pastoral ministry has lost the respect it once held in the community. This shift is similar to that experienced by other professional groups and is not unrelated to the undermining of authority systems in the larger society. The office is often viewed in functional or service terms without the concept of the call of God as a transcendent reality. These are a few of the major influences and changes in our Mennonite denominations. How have the denominations responded?

Called to the pastoral ministry

Central to the Anabaptist-Mennonite faith was the view of the church as a community of believers bound together in a common commitment to Jesus Christ. Even though Anabaptists did not follow Luther's terminology of the "priesthood of all believers," they emphasized a similar point: all people share the responsibility to witness and to serve Christ. Consequently, they became a dynamic missionary movement. In the midst of this witnessing and serving, church pastoral leaders maintained a central and vital role in all areas of the Anabaptist movement. The three-fold ministry—bishops, ministers, and deacons—emerged as a pattern for the congregations.

Even though with the resurgence of Anabaptist studies this reality of designated leadership was often down-played, the fact is that the office and role of pastoral ministry was and is central to the life of the churches. Even as we acknowledge the importance of the general ministry of all Christians, we at the same time affirm the importance of the spiritual ministry (pastoral leadership) roles of the church. Consequently, calling individuals to the vocation of "the ministry" remains as an important task. Increasing attention is being given to the task of calling and discerning individuals for this important task, particularly at the district conference and congregational levels. The ministry inquiry program initiated by the General Conference Mennonite Church is a denominational effort to encourage young college students to consider pastoral ministry as a vocation. This emphasis represents a recent shift and has been occasioned by the dearth of leaders for congregations.

Qualifications and training

Our denominational groups have varying emphases in the discernment, selection, and training of leaders. Central to all groups is the concern that individuals have a deep and personal commitment to Jesus Christ and to the church. The ministry vocation is a demanding role that calls people to provide spiritual leadership in the church with vision and courage. There is an assumption that a knowledge of and love for the Scriptures is present. Preaching and teaching ministries are important; therefore, churches look for good verbal skills and an ability to communicate well. Relational skills are central. In a church that stresses community and mutual care, leaders are expected to listen well, to relate meaningfully with others, and to model ways of communicating the love of God to those in need. Leadership skills and organizational abilities are an asset in a time when congregations and district conferences have more complex organizations and programs. Given the demands of the pastoral office, the qualities of compassion and caring are a must. These resources are rooted in a meaningful walk with God. Therefore, time for meditation, study, and prayer are increasingly emphasized in a day when burnout is becoming a familiar occurrence.

A current issue in calling and placing leaders is whether women are acceptable to serve in these pastoral leadership roles. The General Conference Mennonite Church and the Mennonite Church are ordaining, commissioning, and licensing women to the pastoral ministry. Other groups have not followed this trend to the same extent. In the groups mentioned, women are also serving in major district conference and denominational roles. Currently the moderator of the General Conference Mennonite Church (USA) is a woman.

The training for ministry in the church is taking various forms. As noted in the introduction, seminary education is the norm, although in some Mennonite groups fewer than one-half of the ordained ministers have had seminary education. For nearly two decades the statement published in the book *The People of God* by Ross T. Bender has provided guidance for the General Conference Mennonite Church and the Mennonite Church in pastoral and theological education. There is continuing ferment as to what constitutes adequate preparation for ministry in the church.

Pastoral education can be viewed as a combination of educational modalities and emphases. In the tradition of theological education, a thorough grounding in Scripture is assumed as well as an understanding of theology, church history, and ethics. In the stream of professional education there is a focus on the development of a pastoral theology, the development of pastoral, interpersonal, and leadership skills. In recent years there has been a renewed emphasis on the development of spiritual disciplines—prayer and meditation—as well as giving attention to personal and pastoral identity concerns.

In view of the fact that some people are ordained to the ministry without seminary education, there has been a range of programs designed to provide the training pastors need. For approximately ten years a number of district conferences have participated in a conference-based theological education (CBTE) program in cooperation with Associated Mennonite Biblical Seminaries (AMBS) and Eastern Mennonite Seminary (EMS), both in the United States. The focus of each conference program varies, although there are some common elements. A number provide seminary or college credit courses leading to an academic degree. Continuing education and enrichment courses are shorter in length. They are designed to assist pastors in working at congregational ministry issues or on areas of personal and professional growth. Several CBTE centers have developed various types of supervised pastoral education programs, normally based in congregations. Other program emphases include a mentor-trainee teaching model (Paul-Timothy programs), which combines reading and reflection in the context of ministry experiences.

The clinical pastoral education movement (CPE) has influenced seminary training models, and these training resources have been utilized by many pastors and seminary students. In one district conference more than one-half of all the active pastors have had some CPE training. Urban ministries training programs have also been promoted among Mennonite leaders. An action-reflection learning style is common both to urban training programs and to CPE. Theological education by extension (TEE) is another form of pastoral training more common in Central and South America. Possibilities are being explored by North American groups on ways to adapt this approach to the North American setting.

Denominational pastoral ministry issues

Our various Mennonite groups are not all at the same place regarding leadership issues. There are, however, some common concerns.

1. As noted in the introduction, the office and role of pastoral leadership has been viewed as having less credibility in recent years, as has ordination. With the emphasis on servant leadership, there has been a tendency to interpret the role primarily in functional terms. The sense of the divine call to serve and the significance of the office have often been down-played. Fortunately, in recent years these issues have been re-examined with the result that there is a renewed emphasis on the significance of the office and the role of the pastor as a spiritual leader called of God in the context of the church. There is a recognition that the emphasis on the general ministry of the whole people of God stands alongside

the special ministries of those who are called to the vocation of pastoral ministry in the church.

2.   Leadership styles have become an important issue when addressing the theological vision of servant leadership, when exploring the concept of team ministry, or when contemplating the leadership needs in larger or smaller congregations. It is assumed that central to a vision of servant leadership is the attitude that the role provides a context for service and that it is not a context to control or rule over others. To be a servant means that pastors give leadership, but do so for the good of the body and not to maintain positions of power. It is also generally recognized that personalities differ; training and contexts will shape the way leadership is exercised.

3.   Personnel policies have evolved over the last number of decades. There is an increasing call for common practices in screening and placing candidates for ministry. Given our varied denominational polities, further definition is needed as to the relationships of authority among congregations, district conferences, and denominations. Who screens and ordains the pastor? When there are problems between the pastor and the congregation, it is not always clear what role and authority belongs to the district conference. Denominations have developed codes of ethics for pastors, but a code of ethics is needed for congregations.

4.   Some groups are developing guidelines for the support, nurture, continuing education, and accountability of pastoral leaders. Where these are in place, pastors generally have adequate resources to undergird their ministries.

5.   Pastor-congregational relations are not always healthy. Involuntary terminations are unfortunately all too common. Currently the pastorate project (General Conference-Mennonite Church) is a research study to work with approximately sixteen congregations to explore the systemic factors that contribute to healthy or unhealthy pastor-congregation relations.

Church groups are investing substantial time, money, and personnel in the calling, preparation, and support of leaders. In the last three decades, we have witnessed major changes and stresses at many levels of church life. As we enter the last decade of this century, it is the writer's belief that we will witness a time of consolidation and clarity in relation to the issues addressed in this article.

The apostle Peter's words to the elders in the churches in Asia Minor are a fitting word to all those called to serve in pastoral ministries: "Be shepherds of God's flock that is under your care, serving as overseers—not because you must, but because you are willing, as God wants you to be ..." (1 Pet. 5:2).

Ralph A. Lebold, Canada, b. 1934, M.Th., D.Min., director of external programs at Associated Mennonite Biblical Seminaries (Elkhart, Indiana), and past moderator of the Mennonite Church General Assembly.

Las comunidades cristianas de Burgos

by José Gallardo

Origins

In 1975 a very dynamic evangelistic movement arose with an interdenominational group of Christian young people in Burgos, Spain. The importance they gave to art (music, theater, mime, dance) as evangelistic means was noteworthy. They were known as comunidades cristianas (Christian communities or fellowships). John Driver was invited to teach on pacifism, church history, the Sermon on the Mount, and so on. In 1977, through Driver, I came into contact with the movement. After a time of thinking it over, I joined them in June of 1978 with the purpose of opening a rehabilitation center for drug addicts in the village of Quintanadueñas, which is 6 kilometers north of Burgos. We created a community to which people with great need began coming: couples whose marriage was disintegrating; the sick, both physically and psychologically; outcasts and misfits; drug addicts, delinquents, and prostitutes; and some who came because they had nowhere else to go.

Meanwhile, in the city of Burgos, certain problems arose among the young leaders of the comunidades cristianas. The movement began to disintegrate. Later, with the arrival of Dennis and Connie Byler and their children in 1981, this weak and fragmented body was able to reorganize. Dennis and Connie came from the Fellowship of Hope in Elkhart, Indiana (USA). Through their leadership, service, attitude, and love they were instrumental in helping these youths toward stability and maturity. Currently they continue to serve in Burgos under Mennonite Board of Missions (MBM).

Evolution

The comunidades cristianas movement in Burgos had been able to unite elements that are often separated in Christian churches: social action and spiritual renewal, evangelism and creation of employment opportunities, the charismatic dimension and a community approach to Christian life. At the beginning the comunidades had an ecumenical character, and some of them met in Roman Catholic parishes. The remnant of the original comunidades today has an evangelical character. It is mostly made up of young married couples and some singles. Most of the recent converts come from traditional Roman Catholicism with little or no personal commitment to it. (In Spain, everyone is considered to be Roman Catholic unless the contrary is demonstrated.) From the beginning there was a vision for the unity of the Christians in the city. An evangelical church, with Baptist origins, also embraced this vision for unity. Now we have jointly constituted the Comunidades Cristianas Unidas de Burgos (United Christian Fellowships of Burgos). This church has a nondenominational, evan-

gelical character, though some of us maintain a special relationship with the
international Mennonite brother/sisterhood. We have a good relationship with
the Christian Gypsies in Burgos, though they have their own style and organization. However, we have not managed a solid fraternal relationship with the local
group of Plymouth Brethren, who strongly oppose our charismatic dimension, or
with the Roman Catholic church.

This does not stand in the way of a group from our comunidades participating in
a prayer group with Roman Catholics. Likewise, a group of brothers and sisters
from the comunidades, particularly from the rehabilitation center, frequently
attends the daily meetings of the Gypsy brothers and sisters.

Characteristics

Over the years we find a series of characteristics that define important aspects of
the life of the comunidades cristianas of Burgos. The most important have been
rehabilitation of outcasts and misfits, prison ministry, community lifestyle,
creation of employment opportunities, evangelism, peace, and unity.

Rehabilitation of outcasts and misfits—This arose out of pressing need at a time
when the problem of drugs and delinquency was growing at an alarming rate in
Spain. At the time, 1978, there were few Christian rehabilitation centers and
even fewer state centers. Some of today's members of the comunidades met the
Lord Jesus through their liberation from drugs during these years. Through these
rehabilitated youths, other members of their families have also experienced
conversion. In other cases, the youths have returned to their cities of origin,
joining evangelical churches. Some have become leaders there. Such is the case
of José Peláez. We met José in prison, and when he was released he came to
spend some time in rehabilitation at Quintanadueñas. At the end of this time he
was already an important help for us, and he is currently in Castellón, working
actively in the evangelical church with which he had previously had some
contact. Other youths have stayed as part of the team of the rehabilitation center.
One of these is Oscar López, who after five years was given oversight of the
center. His life in contact with drugs, prison, and delinquency has given him an
appropriate background for dealing with outcasts and misfits. After a time of
instruction, he has begun to carry some pastoral responsibilities in one of the
comunidades and is considered a fine preacher. Currently we continue to receive
outcasts and misfits. Most of them come out of drugs or prison. When deciding
whom to admit, the drug addicts continue to have first priority.

Prison ministry—Our first contact with the prison came when some of the
youths in the rehabilitation program had to go to jail because of previous of-
fenses. Such was the case of Oscar López, the present director of the center. He
was AWOL (absent without leave) from the Legion, a branch of the military he
had joined in order to flee from trouble in his hometown. The police were

searching for him, and we advised him to turn himself in so as to put his life in order. He did this, and once he was in prison we were able to visit him as if we had been his family. He impressed the authorities with the change in his life, and it was he who developed a vision for witnessing among prisoners. That was in 1981. Since then we have been advancing steadily. Though we began with a small group and many reservations, there was fruit that remains to this day. A group that witnessed in the women's prison had no success. But the team for the men's prison has grown and is currently made up of twelve men who visit the prison four times a week, two or three people at a time. There they meet with a group of prisoners who are willing to receive the word of God and change their lives. We currently have much freedom to witness in the Burgos jail. We frequently organize activities for all the prisoners such as concerts, films, and talks. We have had very good experiences and also some difficulty. Some of those who had changed backslid when they regained their freedom. Still, others have persevered. Such is the case of José Antonio, a youth who experienced a profound conversion from the start. In spite of his long sentence (thirty-eight years), he was allowed to leave the prison one day in order to be baptized together with his mother. Today, five years later, he is regularly given days of prison leave. We believe he will soon be granted the possibility of living and working in our rehabilitation center, needing only to spend the nights in jail.

Community lifestyle—This was always an important element. At first it was easy. Most of the members were single. At one point there were fifty people sharing their possessions. One of these communities, at Quintanadueñas, gave rise to the rehabilitation center. In spite of mistakes and changes, the dream of community remains in place. New steps are currently being considered. We have a project for setting up several apartments in the city for singles. One is already functioning. Here it will be possible to go through a period of adaptation after leaving the rehabilitation center. These apartments will also serve as points for receiving others who are contacted through evangelism and who may need a place to stay. Some families live close to each other, which makes for enhanced communion and hospitality. Furthermore, some Christian homes have been open to receiving people who are in need of a family context.

Creation of employment opportunities—An important element within a society that at one point came close to a 20-percent unemployment rate has been the search for employment opportunities. To this end, several brothers have begun businesses in cleaning, plumbing, painting, wooden toy manufacturing, and so on. These businesses employ, for the most part, members of our comunidades who were unemployed and would have had a hard time finding employment otherwise. Some have come out of drug abuse or prison. There is also a desire to create new businesses, which could generate money for supporting those who might sense a missionary calling or who might dedicate their full time to ministry, be it pastoral, rehabilitation, or whatever.

Evangelism—Right from the beginning, evangelism has been an important element. Lately we have gained even more ground. For the first time in Burgos, we are able to hold evangelistic campaigns without having to request permission to hold them under the guise of "cultural events." We are regularly out with evangelistic activities in the "plazas" doing theater, singing, witnessing, and so on. People are generally respectful, asking occasionally whether we are Jehovah's Witnesses or some other cult. (In Burgos, anything other than Roman Catholicism is considered sectarian.) One of these evangelistic activities resulted in the creation of the comunidad in Gamonal. The film *Jesus, the Man You Thought You Knew* was shown in one of the neighborhood theaters and was seen by a large crowd. We handed out questionnaires at the end and organized groups, which met in homes to review short sections of the film on video and discuss the life of Jesus. The result has been the formation of a congregation of fifty members, some of which previously belonged to the other two comunidades and some of which are recent converts. The Gamonal comunidad is now strong and active. Some of its members have come from a problematic past and prison.

Peace—The witness for peace through a commitment in favor of conscientious objection existed in our midst even before the latter was established by law. The group of COs was granted amnesty, since at the time it had not been possible to carry out civilian service. Today it is even possible to do civilian service in our rehabilitation center. Some people are in contact with pacifist groups, both national and international, such as the Movement of Conscientious Objection, Church and Peace, and International Fellowship of Reconciliation.

Unity—It has not been easy. Still, today we have three Christian fellowships, which function together under a group of pastors and leaders recognized by all. Besides the activities held by each comunidad, there are joint meetings: evangelism groups, Bible classes, youth meetings (including a coffee house ministry), activities organized for older children and young teens, and a common fund. We also meet together every week as a united local church. In spite of the difficulties, we have been blessed by the Lord through these steps toward unity. Each comunidad is experiencing a growing vitality, and together we are witnessing a growing work of the Holy Spirit.

The vision that God is placing in our heart for the future is to make way for an increase in the number of comunidades in other neighborhoods and in nearby cities. We even dream of sending missionaries to other parts of Spain and to other countries. Important aspects of our prayer commitment include growth in consecration, the call for people to work full time, and the emergence of more communal groups. We consider ourselves a young church with much to learn. We want to take seriously the task of becoming the kind of church that the life of Jesus and the New Testament teach.

José Gallardo, Spain, minister in the Comunidades Cristianas Unidas de Burgos.

Proclaiming Christ's way of peace

by Richard Blackburn

The Lombard Mennonite Peace Center (LMPC) is a ministry that shares Christian peace education programs and resources with churches of all denominations, schools, and other organizations. Since its inception in 1983, LMPC has grounded its peacemaking in a biblical understanding of salvation and Christian discipleship. The original vision of awakening non-Mennonite Christians, as well as others, to the gospel imperative of peacemaking continues to guide LMPC's sense of mission and outreach.

The peace center grew out of a long-standing commitment of the Lombard Mennonite Church (Illinois, USA) to follow Christ faithfully in the way of peace. It continues as one of the most vital and far-reaching programs of this congregation of about 150 members in the western suburbs of Chicago. The church's peace commission serves as the peace center's board of directors, and many church members work as volunteers in various aspects of the peace center ministry. Three full-time staff people guide LMPC's day-to-day operations.

LMPC addresses a variety of issues, from biblical foundations for peacemaking and interpersonal conflict resolution skills to global peace and justice concerns. Since 1983, over 850 educational programs have been given in various settings. In 1989 alone, the peace center presented 173 such programs. In addition to its program activity, LMPC also shares audio-visual and literature resources. Having found broad interest in its various resources, the extent of LMPC's outreach efforts has spread from the Chicago area to include much of the midwestern United States and beyond.

In tandem with its educational work, LMPC also coordinates Friends for Peace, an ecumenical network of churches working and praying together for peace. The network consists of over forty cosponsoring churches and other peace and justice organizations. Using LMPC staff resources, Friends for Peace sponsors four ecumenical peace and justice events during the year: worship services in conjunction with Central America Week, Peace Pentecost, and Hiroshima-Nagasaki Day as well as an autumn peace/arts event. The latter has usually consisted of a concert with a guest artist or a musical production with a cast of local volunteers, such as *Alice in Blunderland: Reflections of a Nuclear Age* or *Lazarus*, a musical drama created by Bread for the World about hunger and poverty. LMPC created Friends for Peace largely out of a desire to support those individuals in other churches who have heard Christ's call to peacemaking. Although several denominations have drafted important position statements on peace and justice issues in recent years, the commitment to such issues rarely finds expression at the congregational level. Individuals or even committees who seek to address the peacemaking agenda often feel lonely and isolated in their own congregations.

Friends for Peace thus provides such people with a meaningful way to live out their call to peacemaking and invite their congregations to do the same.

Since 1985 LMPC has also functioned as the Midwest affiliate of the Mennonite Conciliation Service, headquartered in Akron, Pennsylvania. In addition to providing training in conflict resolution and mediation skills, the peace center has a growing mediation service. Churches of various denominations are increasingly calling upon LMPC to intervene in divisive congregational disputes. Currently LMPC staff members are working with a Lutheran, Nazarene, Congregational Unitarian, and Mennonite church as well as a Benedictine community of Roman Catholic nuns. Every case is different, but a typical situation in which we would be called to mediate might focus on the role of the pastor:

> In this imaginary congregation, one group is criticizing the pastor's performance and is determined to force the pastor to resign. As LMPC intervenes, we look beyond the immediate issues that are being articulated and help people to communicate their basic, underlying interests. As we identify those concerns, we are able to explore alternatives and invite problem solving. Concerns might be such issues as preaching performance or why young people are leaving the church, or dissatisfaction with the way decisions are made. As people engage in problem solving, bringing resolution to their concerns, most of the hostility is dispelled. But if hostility remains or if there is reluctance to participate in the problem solving process, that is a sign of deeper, more systemic issues at work. We then try to deal with those dysfunctional patterns. …

Indeed, such consulting and intervention work in the area of congregational conflict is currently the most rapidly expanding aspect of the LMPC ministry.

Also growing out of its conciliation work, LMPC has recently begun a school initiative project, working with both public and private schools to train teachers in conflict resolution skills. Such faculty in-service training is designed to equip educators to teach conflict resolution skills in the classroom and, ultimately, to set up conflict manager programs. Conflict manager programs train students from third grade through high school to serve as mediators in addressing student-to-student conflicts on the playground and throughout the school environment.

We have found that training in conflict resolution skills has widespread interest because all people have conflict in their lives. Everyone is anxious to learn skills to handle conflict in the home, place of work, and church. In that way LMPC can first meet people at their level of need. Then we help them to see that the skills we teach for use in interpersonal relationships are analogous to the skills and strategies that we advocate for addressing community and international conflict. As people catch the vision for peacemaking on the interpersonal level, they create a basis upon which we can help them to see the broader possibilities for peacemaking.

The peace center has also set up a victim-offender reconciliation program (VORP), working with local police departments as well as DuPage County probation and court officials. Modeled after the various VORP programs previously set up by Mennonites and others throughout North America, DuPage VORP receives referrals from the criminal justice system and facilitates a process whereby victims and offenders are brought together in the presence of a trained mediator to talk through the facts and feelings of the case and to come to a restitution agreement. Presently DuPage VORP is handling only juvenile cases, although it will soon expand into working with adult offenders. Established as a separate organization with a community-based board of directors, DuPage VORP presently employs a half-time coordinator who is also a member of Lombard Mennonite Church.

Although not directly related to the peace center ministry, Lombard Mennonite Church has also established a Mennonite Central Committee SELFHELP store in Glen Ellyn, another western suburb of Chicago. Staffed by two members of the church and many volunteers, Cross Cultural Crafts complements the global education efforts of the peace center by marketing craft items made by Third World producers.

In all of its various peace and justice ministries, the Lombard Mennonite Church has sought to lift up God's kingdom vision of shalom and be a witness in the community. In addition to the above activities, the congregation also supports various justice initiatives coordinated by other churches in the community: the local food pantry, a community clothes closet, an overnight shelter for the homeless, and a free-dinner program. Over the years Vietnamese, Hmong (from Laos), and Ukrainian refugees have also been sponsored by the congregation. Given its active commitment to Christian discipleship, it is not surprising that a number of current members have indicated that they were first attracted to become a part of Lombard Mennonite Church as a result of being exposed to the peace center or one of the other programs mentioned above.

Central to the success of the Lombard Mennonite Peace Center has been the specifically Christ-centered nature of its vision. Our central message is that Christ's way of nonviolence is relevant for resolving conflict in all areas of our lives: in the home, the church, the community, and the world. Through all that we do, we seek to glorify the one who has brought us into a reconciled relationship with God through his atoning death and resurrection victory. We seek to honor the one who has already triumphed over all powers and principalities and who simply bids us to follow his example in accepting the way of the cross. The LMPC ministry seeks to proclaim that Christ is the path to peace.

Richard Blackburn, USA, b. 1951, M.A. in art history, director of the Lombard Mennonite Peace Center (Lombard, Illinois).

Louise Yoder teaches Quechua children Bible stories in Cusco, Peru. (EMBMC photo by Howard Yoder, 1988)

Life and faith in Casa Horeb

by Alba and Rafael Escobar

Our story is filled with surprises, both beautiful events and tragic moments; but it is our story, our experience, in a wonderful country called Guatemala in Central America. Ours is a country with many wonders and many lively, happy people accustomed to surprises because, among us, anything can happen. We are a people with a desire to speak, a people who suffer, a people with hope.

Our church community was born at a time when our country was going through an acute sociopolitical crisis. Just two years before, a strong earthquake had devastated our country, destroying more than a million houses and causing more than 125,000 deaths. Help arrived, but the people have continued living with an acute crisis. Military regimes have followed one after another, bringing agony in a country where terror, violence, death, and kidnappings are everyday occurrences. By the work of a very active Mennonite pastor, Gilberto Flores, a reflection group was formed by families from the Catholic tradition who wanted to study and learn from the Bible. With patience and perseverance, a growing community that was enthusiastic, dynamic, and expressive was brought to life. It grew very fast and after two years existed as a well-integrated congregation, the Iglesia Menonita Casa Horeb (Mennonite Church Casa Horeb). About 1980 this fledgling community composed of several families from the middle class and some from a lower economic class made a formal decision to join the Conference of the Mennonite Churches of Guatemala, which was accomplished at the 1983 convention.

In Guatemala, areas of conflict have forced inhabitants of villages and towns to abandon their homes and lands, causing great numbers of the rural population to flee to the capital of Guatemala City. This causes the well-known problem of slums on the outskirts of the city, which are separated from the basic services and guarantees of everyday life. Added to this are the armed conflicts in other Central American countries, leading to many more Central Americans arriving in our country daily to stay or pass through on their way to North America. Given these realities, we have emphasized two purposes: (1) encourage the knowledge of our faith, and (2) serve our society.

After analyzing our journey and our faith, and in order to reach these objectives, we decided to carry out our community and church work from a more Anabaptist perspective. We are giving life to our faith through the community and by means of five ministries that correspond to our vocation of service and redemption. Always searching for a more biblical Anabaptist way, we have brought together the resources, the experiences, and the thoughts of these ten years of existence. The men, women, youths, and children who are a part of the faith community all participate in the practice of our faith.

We appropriate the vision of Acts 2:42, which tells about the active life of an early community, guided by the Holy Spirit. We have taken their action as an example and are engaged in the following ministries:

1.   Proclamation—A team of men and women mobilizes our community in the essential task of proclaiming the message of the gospel of the kingdom through any valid means that do not involve manipulation or the mere aim of proselytizing. Our thrust is to bring about new ways of proclamation that respect individuals as human beings.

2.   Christian service (Diakonia)—A team of men and women gives testimony of our faith and hope, serving in practical ways to assist people with their needs until changes bring about social transformation (widows, the sick, the displaced, strangers, orphans, care in emergency situations, creation of socially productive projects, and community development).

3.   Teaching—A group of men and women maintains the principle of faith-community education so that the community can be educated and transformed, liberated by the knowledge of the gospel of the kingdom. We must do our theology from our own context while taking advantage of courses, workshops, seminars, and whatever else facilitates the discovery of our faith and Anabaptist tradition. Every facilitator or person responsible for this communal action should participate sometime in our Latin American seminary for leadership training— SEMILLA.

4.   Communion (Koinonia)—A team of men and women fosters a spirit of care in human relations as well as encouraging a concept of holistic spirituality that leads to a healthy relationship with the Lord and with God's word but also with all people. This team is responsible for carrying out ways to help in conflict resolution; they plan activities, workshops, dialogues, retreats, and all sorts of things that will help keep alive our unity.

5.   Administration—A group of men and women responds to the views of the kingdom community with a mentality of service and vocation for the development of the community. They responsibly manage our resources and encourage the blessing of sharing for the benefit of all.

These practices also reflect our ideas about structures, which we view as necessary but not determinative of our actions. We desire to follow the model of the Lord Jesus, who challenges us to be suffering servants, avoiding the temptations of the authoritarian or punitive models by using a participatory model of unlimited responsibility, self-discipline, and interdependence. We give thanks to God for all of this, but it is only the beginning. We have faith that we will soon see greater things that are more in tune with our reality. And yet, already we are experiencing signs of the kingdom.

We give support and aid to those people displaced by the war. We give them material help and also accompany them in this time of pain and anguish. Brothers and sisters, with financial help from several others, are developing this project. We have opened a small store for the service of the community, with basic products at fair prices, so that members and nonmembers can be helped in the midst of the economic crisis we are experiencing.

A group of brothers and sisters makes up a team to help communities that suffer in emergencies such as earthquakes, mud slides, etc. With the help of our standing committee of social service, we have opened a medical clinic in one of our base communities, Boca del Monte. There is spiritual work there, but it is also a response to the health needs of that community. Many of our leaders have participated or are now participating in various organizations that promote development and transformation.

As a local church, we support each other through what we have called the faith communities: small groups or clusters of brothers and sisters who meet during the week to nourish and support each other and to grow through teaching, praying, and witnessing to the neighborhoods. Currently our pastoral team comprises seven members (four men, two women, and one youth). This team is in charge of ministering to the spiritual and moral needs of the congregation. The major decisions are made in another community setting called the local council where the majority of the members take part when they are called on to make group decisions. Our goal is to develop several faith communities in Guatemala City and outside of it. This year we will develop ten new faith communities. Through our delegates in a wider organization, we are participating in a national dialogue that is striving to reconcile the parties in conflict in the midst of grave national problems.

Each person contributes to give life to a community that believes in the kingdom, that believes we are the ones who need to give evidence and signs that this kingdom is among us now, although not yet in its fullness. In the meantime, we work with the hope that one day our life will be better and death will no longer bring grief to our homes.

With this simple article we want to encourage the global Mennonite community to participate in life, breaking old frameworks that teach us that the only thing of consequence is the human soul while disregarding the whole person's practical needs in the here and now. For that reason we announce a gospel that also denounces injustice and oppression. Let us not forget that the Lord is faithful and has entrusted us with the great task of reconciliation and shalom. Today, more than ever, that means peace with God, with our neighbors, and with nature, which also cries for its liberation. To God be the glory for ever and ever. Amen.

Alba and Rafael Escobar, Guatemala, b. 1954, 1947, pastors.
Translated by Margaret and Daniel Schipani.

Kenneth J. Nafziger, professor of music at Eastern Mennonite College, and EMC student John Mbatta of Tanzania play recorders during a humanities class. (EMC photo by Jim Bishop)

Opting for poor children

by Milka Rindzinski

The child-feeding program "Benjamin" is in its fifth year of operation. It was born on June 24, 1985, thanks to the initiative of the Mennonite Church of La Paz, Canelones, Uruguay. On the average, between fifty and sixty children receive a daily meal there. For many it is their only real meal for the day.

Gestation and birth

For the church in La Paz, a small congregation whose membership is primarily composed of people with modest means, the first half of 1985 was spent largely in an attempt to understand its social responsibility as a Christian community.

In reality, the social problems of the larger community were knocking on its door—unemployment, child beggars, malnutrition, sickness, homelessness, etc. And the gospel began to confront them. One member of the congregation put it this way: "In our study of Mark's Gospel, we were able to see the Lord Jesus with a new clarity; and as he faced situations characterized by suffering and injustice, he was moved to action as well as compassion." This was the beginning of a time of fraternal discussion and seeking of the Spirit's leading in order to discern those areas of need to which they were being called to serve and to share their time and their resources. During this process of following Jesus in opting for the poor, and the children in particular, the congregation decided to open its feeding program. Both the search and the decision were made by the community as a whole. The same has been true of the implementation of the program.

The brothers and sisters of the congregation set to work immediately. While some tried to find the material resources they needed, others did a census of the surrounding community to determine the family conditions of the children in order to offer the services of the church. Parents and others they contacted were quite specific in stating that they wanted nothing to do with "religion." Preference was given to those children who were being raised by their grandparents, those whose parents were unemployed, and children of single mothers. Mothers who were breast-feeding an infant or who were expecting another child were also invited to the feeding program.

Individual records containing basic personal and health information were kept for each child. The sisters in the congregation formed teams of volunteers, which took turns preparing and serving the meals. As the program began, they depended entirely on donated food. The need was so urgent that even half a kilogram of food was a significant donation. "From one day to the next we did not know whether there would be sufficient food to meet the needs, so we learned to trust God all the more," one of the brothers remembers. "To pray for the daily bread of these children was a serious thing."

Although the program began with thirty children, the severity of that winter soon brought the number of children being fed daily to sixty. Since there was not enough food for everyone who needed help, the waiting list grew. But as word got around, help began to arrive from other congregations. Moreover, some of the store owners in the vicinity, moved by the spirit of the program even though they were not members of the congregation, became interested in contributing. By the end of the first year a refrigerator had been donated to the feeding program.

Growth

During the winter of 1986 the number of children grew, sadly enough, to a record of 112 daily. The workload increased, but so did the maturity to face it and to confront the many problems inherent in all types of social service. The project had outgrown the economic resources of the congregation, so at that point they began to seek the help of other social service organizations. Looking back, one can see that the feeding program has survived thanks to three significant factors: (1) the faithfulness of the volunteers, (2) the contributions of the National Institute for Nutrition, and (3) a donation from the National Council of Churches, USA.

Stability and additional services

During 1987 and 1988 the number of preschool and school children fed each day averaged sixty. The feeding program became affiliated with another organization with a similar purpose (Coordinadora de Ollas Populares). This provided them with a forum for sharing experiences and resources as well as receiving donations of food, which made it possible to increase the rations of each child in the program. The sewing circle in the local congregation began to receive and mend used clothing and shoes for the children. They began to make plans for adding the services of a social worker in order to contribute in a more integral way to the well-being of the children. Early in 1989 a donation from the Mennonite churches in Germany made possible the remodeling and equipping of the kitchen. Later, two more services were added: a barbershop and medical assistance. Throughout the years all of these services have been rendered by volunteers and are free.

Initially the main objective of this project was to alleviate the nutritional deficiencies rampant among the children of the community. This, in itself, would have been sufficient reason to justify the existence of the program. But in this process a number of other things began to happen. The congregation discovered that it was possible to make a significant, though small, contribution to society.

It learned the cost of commitment and the discipline of being faithful. At the same time, it experienced again the faithfulness of God in providing resources, in answering prayer, and in restoring energies spent in his service. As they completed the first step of obedience, they perceived new needs and challenges and have met them as they have been able.

Although a rejection of "religion" was clearly expressed by the people of the neighborhood at the beginning, many of the children began freely attending the meetings of the congregation and Sunday school. Some of the parents also came to the church, were converted, and were baptized. Rather than being discouraged by the initial rejection, the congregation understood the response as a natural reaction of people to the preaching of the gospel out of context, which separates the kingdom of God from human history, the soul from the body, the historical Jesus from the risen Christ, and which emphasizes the need for the salvation of the individual without a corresponding emphasis on a salvation that is collective or social.

In contrast, the church in La Paz, in responding to a self-evident local need, tries with its feeding program to express its solidarity and commitment through service to "the least of these, my brethren." They seek to constitute a Christian presence in society as a sign of hope, a sign of the gospel, and a testimony to the justice of God, which at the same time is a judgment that leads to repentance. This Christian presence begins to transform individuals and society. And that transformation attracts some people while provoking others to wrath who, feeling themselves judged, do not want to repent.

The challenge facing the church in La Paz is to resist the temptation to give up its commitment to service when all sorts of difficulties arise. At the same time it must continue trying to reach the parents of the children with at least a rudimentary education in the fundamental aspects of life: the rights and duties of individuals, health and preventive hygiene, and also Christian faith and commitment.

Milka Rindzinski, Uruguay, b. 1932, librarian and director of the Study Center of the Mennonite Church in Uruguay, and a member of the pastoral team of the Floresta Mennonite Church.
Translated by John Driver.

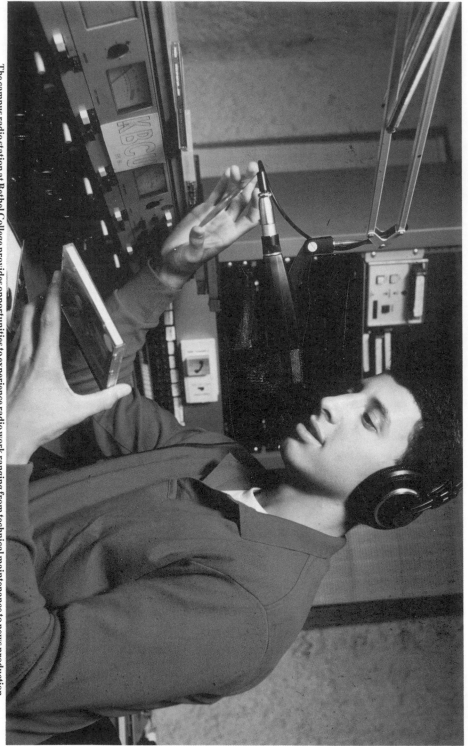

The campus radio station at Bethel College provides opportunities to experience radio work ranging from technical maintenance to news production. (Bethel College photo)

Our congregation in Dar es Salaam

by John O. Nyagwegwe

How the congregation was established

From 1934 to the 1960s, Mennonite missionaries worked in the rural areas of
Musoma and Tarime Districts, Tanzania. The first-generation Mennonites were
rural peasants who worked on their lands with their families. During those years
the church cared for spiritual needs through the congregations. They also served
bodily needs by opening mission schools and hospitals. The sons and daughters
of those who accepted Christ were brought up in mission schools and molded to
become today's church in Tanzania. At the same time the young people had the
opportunity to work on their parents' lands. Those who could not make it to
higher education were able to go back and work on the land, remaining good
Christians. In the latter 1950s many young people from the Tanganyika Mennonite Church (TMC) were moving to the towns for higher education and employment. Many of them went to the capital city of Dar es Salaam. Their parents
became concerned for their spiritual welfare. Orie O. Miller, then secretary of
Eastern Mennonite Board of Missions and Charities (EMBMC), was also alert to
this. He nudged the TMC General Church Council, and they promptly assigned
Pastor Mahlon Hess and family to Dar es Salaam. Hess sought the Mennonites
by going through a list of one hundred names. In May 1963 in a room in Arna-
toglu Hall, eight people gathered for the first Mennonite service.

Goals and issues

1. Ministry to newcomers—This small congregation has an important ministry
to Mennonites who are coming to the city for the first time. The newcomers
present themselves at the pastor's apartment or turn up at a worship service. The
church gives them a warm welcome and every possible assistance. In this way
they make their first contact with their friends, whose dwelling places they do
not know. They learn how to go about looking for employment and/or schooling,
how to find housing, how much rent to pay, where to get food, how to make new
friends, whom and what to avoid. Quickly they get an overview of the rudimentary problems of city life. Church members become friends, fathers, mothers,
sisters, and brothers. The congregation becomes a place of worship, a source of
Christian nurture, and a fountain of spiritual energy.

While Mennonite congregations back home in the Mara region are comprised of
a majority from the given local tribe, urban churches have members from all
those tribes. We are a national church in the capital city, Dar es Salaam, using
only the national language, Swahili. Most of the church members are youths and
young adults. Many of us knew each other before we came here. Some of us
grew up together and were schoolmates in primary, middle, and secondary

schools. This contributes to good understanding among ourselves; our congregation experiences unity and cooperation.

2.   Youths seek advancement—We also have problems. Like others, Christians flock to cities and towns for a variety of reasons. Young people seek self-identity and self-actualization. Dissatisfied with life in the rural areas, they explore new possibilities. They hope for good jobs and salaries that will free them to become masters of their own lives. They seek advancement in education and technical skills. However, they discover that city life is expensive. They have to depend on the money-based economy for everything. Often salaries are insufficient. Housing becomes a problem. Transportation to and from work and to church becomes a headache. Neither the congregation nor the pastor is in a position to help. Some of the young people become frustrated and disheartened. They become weak and spiritually cold. But others give themselves in church ministries: some form a youth choir and others establish groups for church development.

3.   Providing a church building—For twenty-five years the congregation has worshiped in a classroom in the pastor's residence. While 150 people can be packed into that room, on important occasions attendance reaches four to six hundred, and many people listen from the outside. Sometimes prominent individuals and government dignitaries attend a service. We need a proper place of worship to make them feel at ease and comfortable. After a long period of fund raising at the church level, a series of grants from Eastern Mennonite Board and some special contributions have brought the new building near to completion at a cost of TSH. 3,500,000 (US $25,547.45).

4.   Strengthening the leadership team—The Dar es Salaam congregation sensed the need for an additional pastor and a deacon. From its inception the Mennonite Church in Tanzania (or "KMT," reflecting its Swahili name) grew and expanded through lay ministry. But this is not adequate in our towns, particularly in a city like Dar. People in the city want to know with what authority one speaks. They are not used to listening to untrained preachers. God answered the prayers of his people. In 1984 John Nyagwegwe, leader of the congregational outpost in the suburb of Ukonga, was ordained deacon, and in 1985 Josiah Muganda as an associate pastor, besides Daniel Sigira, pastor since 1982. We would like to do all we can to strengthen the congregation and expand evangelistic outreach.

5.   Planting more congregations—Church members in urban Africa face special problems. Transportation is costly, and many members have to travel long distances to the church. In 1982 a committee of elders was formed to look for ways to plant more churches within the city. God answered our prayers: within the year a church was started at Ukonga. In 1985 another was opened in Morogoro, 200 miles from Dar es Salaam, under local leadership. In 1987 Zakayo Mawera opened Sinza near the University of Dar es Salaam, and in 1989 Mwana-Nyamala was opened.

6.   Outreach to Muslims—The population of Dar es Salaam is half Muslim and half Christian. In the latter part of 1988, Kent and Teresa Shirley joined our team. They are looking for ways to serve some of the needs of our Muslim neighbors. We want to learn from them and share with them.

Leadership committees

The congregation is being led by a team of pastors, deacons, church leaders, young people, and women. Our team works through committees that look after the daily affairs of the church and assist the pastor.

*   Evangelism Committee—They make regular visits to fellow members, assess spiritual needs in the district, and plant more churches.
*   Planning and Finance Committee—This group monitors receipts and expenditures, plans for fund raising, and makes regular reports to the congregation.
*   Education and Youth—This committee is responsible to provide training opportunities and youth activities within the district.
*   Economic Development Committee—Seeking to help the church grow financially, this group also oversees the building of new churches and houses for leaders.
*   Women's Committee—This committee promotes development of the gifts of our women and arranges appropriate activities in the district.
*   Social Committee—This group looks after poor people, contacts visitors, and arranges social functions within the district.

We accept our obligation to mold an urban church that will meet the needs of tomorrow's generation. This involves providing for the life of the congregation plus operating schools and other projects that will serve our members and the surrounding community. In our sister churches, the Catholics, Lutherans, and Anglicans, we see what is possible. They started one hundred years earlier and are now dispersed across the nation. They have had strong missionary involvement and financial and material support. Even the Muslims have launched social ministries. In fact, we could lose our children to churches who have resources for both spiritual and bodily needs. To strengthen the economic base of our church, we have decided to establish a poultry project and small gardens at Ukonga. At our central church we want to provide tutoring for primary and secondary pupils and also provide Bible classes and social activities.

While our congregation and its three outposts cater basically to people with a KMT heritage, we want to reach out and win people from other backgrounds into our fellowship. To remain faithful to the author of our salvation, we dare not neglect this.

John O. Nyagwegwe, Tanzania, b. 1948, ordained pastor and treasurer of the Kanisa la Mennonite Tanzania, Dayosisi ya Mara Kaskazini.

Community development in Burkina Faso. (MCC photo by Mark Beach, 1985)

Regional Christian radio work

by Gotthilf Horsch and Michael Schid

Jesus Christ clearly said, "Make disciples of all nations ...." The validity of that commission continues for his church today. After thousands of years it has lost none of its significance for the contemporary situation; ever anew it must be reflected in the culturally up-to-date forms of the day. Today in Germany, at a time characterized by a previously unknown diversity of media, we, as disciples of Jesus, are faced with the challenge of using the new media, in our case that of private radio broadcasting. In this way the good news of the love of God can be presented to individuals and to the public in a most effective manner.

As a result of new regulations, private, local, and regional radio stations have continued to come into existence since the middle of the 1980s. Whereas all radio stations were controlled by the different federal states until recently, it is now the goal of these private initiatives to produce programs for listeners who are especially interested in that which happens in their own city or village. Since it is rather expensive to produce good programs, so-called "supplier groups" continue to spring into existence. These groups consist of many individual program suppliers who jointly occupy a common station and frequency and who divide the twenty-four hours of the program among themselves.

In spite of considerable opposition on the part of commercial programmers, the free churches have the legal right to participate in the initiatives of private radio and thus bring the gospel in modern packaging to listeners within a radius of 20 to 80 kilometers. When the availability of the communication stations in our federal state was announced in 1986, several free church congregations considered taking advantage of this opportunity. A single congregation would not have been in the position to undertake such radio work on its own. But with eight congregations united in prayer and with God's help, pooling our joint resources and personnel, we had the courage to take the risk. Thus "Media Vision Rhein-Neckar e.V." was formed, consisting of the two Mennonite Home Missions congregations of Heidelberg and Mannheim and six other free church congregations of the region. We were then able to apply to the Landesanstalt für Kommunikation (Institute of the Federal State for Communications) for broadcasting for six hours a week.

After much difficult negotiating with the main suppliers of the Mannheim station, we received permission to transmit a fifteen-minute program once a week. Our transmission time was reduced to that, but we were thankful to God for this beginning. Also, we had to adapt our programs to the style of the station. The radio programs have to consist of two-thirds music and one-third spoken word. Everything has to be submitted, ready for broadcasting, three days prior to transmission.

Our first program was broadcast in March 1986 at 5:45 a.m. on the regional station of Heidelberg, Radio Regenbogen (FM 102.8), which can be heard within a radius of up to 80 kilometers. Since then we have had a weekly fifteen-minute program. From the beginning we have experimented with many possibilities to try to produce the optimum programs. We wish not only to inform our listeners or to encourage them to reflect but, if at all possible, to enter into a continuing dialogue with them. We want to offer help to those considering life issues. And the listeners are supposed to receive at least a brief introduction to congregational life so that perhaps they will join a congregation. We have divided transmission time proportionally among the cooperating congregations. The congregation taking its turn also determines the topic for the program, assumes the responsibility for the main part of the program, and takes care of the follow up.

The programs are inserted between segments of the regular early morning broadcast between 5:30 and 6:00. Possibly the listeners are still in bed, or else they are either just getting up or in their car on the way to work. We have to adapt ourselves to this situation. Most important of all, the program has to be so interesting that no one will think of turning off the radio. So we offer lively Christian music, short segments in interview style, etc. The program is quickly introduced by our signal and identification. After that comes music, a word of welcome, and perhaps an announcement of the topic of the program. The moderator directs the program and provides the transitions from one part to the next. We deal with such topics as the following: Love—Is It Simply a Word? How Do You Cope With Grief? Are There Answers to Prayer? Experiences With Asylum Seekers, Healing, Our Congregation, Our House Groups, Life After Death, Abortion, Peace, Joy, Euthanasia, Christmas, Pentecost, etc. We also announce special events where individuals can receive help in matters of faith and life. The programs are put together by voluntary assistants from the congregations. Frequently the pastor of the respective congregation speaks to some specific contemporary issues in an interview. Lively testimonies of members of the congregation are inserted into the programs, for example, how someone was freed after years of alcoholism. Jesus is victor and Lord over sin, sickness, need, and death. We desire that those who listen will experience with us that Jesus can help. Thus many in our congregations are challenged to live consciously with Jesus and to learn to pass their experiences on to others in a brief and lively format. At the conclusion of the broadcast, we give a telephone number to call. It is always the number of the congregation responsible for that particular program. Frequently we also offer a small pamphlet on the topic, free but in limited quantities.

Inasmuch as the broadcast time is presently so early in the morning, listener response to the programs is not yet optimal. Depending on the program and the given circumstances, on the average approximately four people call in. A woman contemplating suicide because the authorities threaten to take away her child may call. These are cries to come and help. Others seek contact so that someone will support them with spiritual or pastoral care. Frequently there are those who stop their car and run to the nearest telephone to request some literature that was offered. We have also had programs after which fifteen people called. We believe, therefore, that this is a valid service and that much of what is happening will not be heard this side of eternity.

The monthly operating expense has amounted to about DM 1.500,- until now. This has been divided among the eight congregations, with Mennonite Home Missions bearing 20 percent of the total expense, i.e., DM 300,- per month. So far we have been able to record and assemble the programs in a rented studio. By the end of 1989, however, we will need to find a different solution, since we have been notified that the studio will be sold. We would like to acquire this used studio for DM 15.000,-; but if we do not get it we will require about DM 25.000,- to furnish a new studio. We hope to receive the needed funds for this on time. We need coworkers, as well as individuals and congregations, who will support this with their prayers and their donations. We cannot operate without donations.

There is much interest in local and regional programming. In restaurants these stations are frequently playing all day. In spite of TV there is a trend toward listening to the radio. We would like to pray for more radio time at a better time of the day. We would like to train and prepare more coworkers so that we can produce even better programs. Gospel Broadcasting offers various seminars for this. Additionally, we would like to develop a spiritual counseling network so that we can help even better. Because other local stations could also broadcast our programs, we would like to contact these and negotiate with them for some cooperation or exchange of programming.

All of the cooperating congregations agree on the common goal of reaching more people with the good news about Jesus, to help where it is possible, and to offer individuals the possibility of becoming part of the large family of God.

Michael Schid and Gotthilf Horsch, Federal Republic of Germany, church planter/evangelist.
Translated by Gerhard Reimer.

Lively discussion at Associated Mennonite Biblical Seminaries. (AMBS photo by John Bender, 1989)

Highlights of Mennonite history 1945–1990

by Wilbert R. Shenk

The year 1945 marks the end of World War II and the beginning of an era of drastic change that affected all the peoples of the world. The war seemingly had the effect of intensifying the pace and scope of change that had already become the hallmark of the modern world. No one was exempted from its impact. The Mennonite and Brethren in Christ churches have been reshaped in important ways by the forces of change of these past forty-five years. This essay will consider seven sources of change that have been particularly important.

Missions

The Mennonite and Brethren in Christ story must be seen within the wider context. The present size, geographical dispersion, and multicultural complexion of the groups that comprise Mennonite World Conference are a direct result of the modern missionary movement. This story is but one chapter in a much larger saga. In 1800 world population stood at about 902 million. Christians made up approximately 24 percent of that total, but 86 percent of all Christians were of Caucasian ethnic origin. Just at this time a new impulse began to be released into the churches in Great Britain, Europe, and North America. This quickly gave rise to the modern missionary movement with mission sending societies being founded, missionaries being recruited, and missionary parties being sent to distant parts of the world where there was then no Christian church. By 1914 and the start of World War I, world population had surpassed the 1.6 billion mark, and Christians now claimed almost 35 percent of this total. The proportion of Christians of Caucasian origin was now 76 percent, while Christians of other ethnic backgrounds had risen to nearly 24 percent.

The impact of this trend becomes even clearer if we observe the situation in 1980. World population had grown to 4.3 billion in 1980, with the Christian portion of the total being nearly 33 percent. But the Christian population was now almost equally divided between Caucasian and other ethnic backgrounds— 50.5 percent and 49.5 percent respectively. Furthermore, given the trends of the past two centuries, it was evident that by the year 2000, 60 percent of all Christians would be found outside the West. This means that we are witnessing a momentous change, with the center of gravity having now moved from the historical heartland of the Christian faith in the West to various parts of the world. Africa will soon claim the single largest number of Christians of all the continents. The largest national Roman Catholic church is found in Brazil.

The Mennonite and Brethren in Christ story parallels the main Christian movement. The first Mennonite missionary initiative was taken with the founding of the Dutch Mennonite Sending Society in 1847. By the turn of the twentieth century, all the larger Mennonite and Brethren in Christ groups in Europe and North America had formed mission organizations and were engaged in sending missions to Asia, Africa, and North America. In 1945 Mennonite and Brethren in Christ churches were to be found in Europe, North America, Central and East Africa, Argentina, India, China, and Indonesia. Mennonite settlers from Russia had come to Paraguay, Uruguay, and Mexico. The Great Depression, which held the major economies of the world in its grip in the early 1930s, had damped mission activity. Some mission boards were forced to retrench, while others tried to at least maintain their present programs. World War II disrupted everything. No new missionaries could be sent out, and programs had to be carried on under considerable hardship. But the war had an important further effect, for it concentrated concern on the world as a whole. Once the war ended, scores of people offered themselves for ministry in other lands. As a result, 1945–60 was a period of unparalleled mission expansion. Brethren in Christ and Mennonite workers were sent to many countries where they had not been before. This extension has continued in the 1970s and 1980s but at a somewhat slackened pace.

Refugees and migration

Migration "for conscience sake" has been a part of Mennonite experience since the sixteenth century. That continues to be an important theme in the story right up to the present. It is estimated there are ten million refugees in the world today. Many of these refugees are the victims of the ravages of war, ideological conflict, interethnic strife, natural disasters, and economic deprivation. Mennonites have been caught up in these tragic tides on several continents since 1945.

In the aftermath of World War II, thousands of refugees needed to be resettled. North American Mennonites and Brethren in Christ worked together through Mennonite Central Committee (MCC) to assist these people. At least twelve thousand have been settled in Canada and South America since 1943. Most of these people came out of Russia. An additional twenty-five thousand left the USSR between 1987 and 1990. Another wave of refugees from the USSR started in the 1970s and has continued through the 1980s. Approximately fifteen thousand Aussiedler have come to the Federal Republic of Germany. The recent policy of glasnost has made it relatively easy for Mennonites still in the Soviet Union to leave. It is possible that virtually all Mennonites who wish to leave the Soviet Union will have done so shortly. This could mark the end of any organized Mennonite church life in the USSR—after more than two hundred years of Mennonite presence in that land.

Although we have only fragmentary information about events in China in the years following the Communist victory in 1949, it is known that many people were affected by the purges there. Christians were singled out for harassment, and many were imprisoned or relocated. Brethren in Christ and Mennonites in Zimbabwe and Zaire have endured deprivation and suffering as a result of civil war and the struggle against colonialism in the 1960s and 1970s. Refugees from Angola settled in Zaire and while there affiliated with the Mennonite churches. In the 1980s many of these people have returned to Angola as Mennonites. Some of the members of the Vietnamese Mennonite Church left Vietnam and settled in the United States as the war was coming to an end in 1974–75. In the 1980s the Central American isthmus was the scene of armed conflict and harassment of civilians. Ideology played an important role. The churches found they had to take a position against the injustice and violence being perpetrated on their people. Considerable numbers of people have migrated from Central America to Canada and the United States during the past ten years.

There continue to be smaller groups of Mennonites who migrate from one country to another to escape the demands of the sociopolitical order. Some have gone from the United States or Canada to South American countries. Others have migrated from South or Central America to the United States or Canada in order to find an environment more congenial to their convictions.

The "new" churches

We have already noted above how the modern missionary movement has led the way in spreading the Christian faith worldwide, with the result that Christians are now to be found in every country of the world and the number of Christians outside the historical heartland now outstrips those within. Mennonite and Brethren in Christ churches reflect the impact of this movement. In several cases the "daughter" church now has a larger membership than the "mother" church. The following summary gives a rough idea of these developments.

Mennonite and Brethren in Christ membership by continent:

	1974	1978	1984	1990
Europe	94,313	96,100	92,700	68,600
North America	297,538	313,000	340,000	380,500
Total	391,851	409,100	432,700	449,100
Asia and Australia	63,444	74,300	113,600	147,600
Africa	68,510	85,900	107,300	176,500
Caribbean, Central and South America	34,450	44,300	75,300	83,400
Total	166,404	204,500	296,200	407,500
Grand total	558,255	613,600	728,900	856,600

This table highlights growth in numbers, but it tells us nothing of the processes of development over the past forty-five years. To get at this part of the story, we must take into account both the world political changes of the past one hundred years as well as the stages through which the churches have come.

The founding of the Indian National Congress Party in 1885 is frequently taken as the start of the nationalist movement that spread throughout the countries that had come under domination by European colonial powers. In one country after another nationalists began to assert their claims to political autonomy. In some cases these movements had to operate underground, but their presence was always felt. By 1945 the handwriting on the wall was clear. The colonial era had effectively ended. Indonesia declared its independence from the Dutch in 1945, and India became an independent state in 1947. The next twenty years saw the steady dismantling of most of the colonial governments and the transfer of sovereignty. The list of member states of the United Nations grew dramatically.

These political developments are important to our understanding of the emergence of the newer churches. In a number of instances, the struggle for national independence had a direct impact on the mission-church relationship.

The Javanese Mennonite Conference (Gereja Injili di Tanah Jawa) was formed just before the outbreak of World War II and the military occupation by the Japanese in 1942. But this formal change had been made none too soon. Throughout World War II and the war of revolution from 1945–49, the Mennonite church had to struggle to prove both its loyalty as citizens of Indonesia and its fidelity to the kingdom of God. It endured great hardship during those years as it came under suspicion from both colonial and nationalist forces, which repeatedly overran the area.

For Christians in China the dilemma was even deeper and longer lasting. The Chinese nationalist movement broke apart in the 1920s with the Kuo Min Tang ousting the Communist faction. When the Communists finally got the upper hand in 1949, they sought to purge the land of all "foreign" elements they deemed to be a threat to the Communist ideology and its program for China. Christians came under attack for their alleged dependence on foreigners or being tools of foreign interests. Virtually all contacts with churches abroad were cut off, and the churches in China came under strict controls. The churches founded by Mennonite mission efforts do not exist as Mennonite churches in China today. The remains of these earlier efforts have either been incorporated into the united Christian church made up of many Protestant groups or they have joined the independent house church movement. Some limited contacts have been made in recent years with individual Chinese who were members of pre-1949 Mennonite congregations.

The transition from mission to church in India followed a quite different path. Although it was not widely known at the time, soon after India became an independent state in 1947 the prime minister decided to eliminate missionaries from India but to do so gradually. This had the same effect as the abrupt intervention by the Communists in China, but it allowed for a more orderly evolution. By the early 1970s the number of missionaries in India had declined dramatically.

In Zaire the transfer was made in the early 1960s when the country went through several years of war. Much of the work missionaries had been doing was disrupted, and many of them left the country even though there were too few Zaireans trained to staff all the hospitals, clinics, and schools the missions had sponsored. It was a difficult time for all concerned.

The transition from mission to church has taken a different course in countries with no history of colonialism. That is not to say there have been no tensions, but the process has been less burdened by the national political agenda that inevitably comes into play where there has been prolonged political struggle.

Thus far we have been observing the processes of development from mission to church where there has been a parallel process of gaining political independence from a foreign power or as the result of ideological struggle as in China. But independence means more than ecclesiastical autonomy. Indeed, it has been suggested that it is never proper to speak of the church being autonomous—i.e., self-governing. For the head of the church is always Jesus Christ, and we ought to speak only of "Christonomy" or of the church living in relationship to the true head. The coming to independence must be understood, therefore, as the process of a local body of believers coming to full understanding of their privileges as members of Christ's body and exercising their spiritual gifts in witness, service, worship, and fellowship. Although it is important to highlight the emergence in these past forty-five years of a growing number of sister churches within the Mennonite and Brethren in Christ family, it is even more urgent that we take account of the ways these churches are responding to Jesus Christ as their head.

In the mid-1960s the Muria Christian Church in Indonesia became more intentional about witness. They formed a board for the purpose of enabling members to engage in mission and service. Thus PIPKA was born. It has been the means by which international workers could team up with Indonesian colleagues to engage in outreach. When PIPKA was first formed, the Muria Christian Church was almost exclusively made up of ethnic Chinese. Twenty years later the church had grown so that 40 percent of its membership was drawn from a variety of other ethnic groups.

Another measure of growth in relationship to the head of the church is the way a local church makes an evangelical response to its socioeconomic and political environment. The Mennonite and Brethren in Christ churches in Costa Rica, Nicaragua, Honduras, Guatemala, and El Salvador have faced over the past decade immense physical and spiritual risks. Rather than seeking to escape either by isolating themselves from the situation or leaving the region, they have increasingly insisted on bearing witness to the reality of the reign of God precisely where there is violence by demonstrating the relevance of the way of the cross of Jesus Christ in their daily lives.

Theological developments

In December 1943 Harold S. Bender delivered as his presidential address to the American Society of Church History a statement of "The Anabaptist Vision." In this address Bender was countering the prevailing scholarly interpretation of Anabaptism, but he also succeeded in challenging those who thought of themselves as descendants of the sixteenth-century Anabaptists to recover for contemporary church life the essential elements of the Anabaptist vision of the gospel. Harold Bender was not alone in his quest for a clearer understanding of the roots of the Anabaptist movement. The Dutch Mennonites had a long tradition of historical scholarship, and several German Mennonites had laid a foundation for future scholarship. Bender was in touch with these European colleagues. If Bender's statement of "The Anabaptist Vision" provided the broad framework for the next generation of Mennonite theological development, Guy F. Hershberger's contribution was to steer that development toward a deeper and broader understanding of the evangel as "the gospel of peace." In short, the cutting edge for Mennonite theology in the period since 1945 has been the theological foundation and ethical implications of the call of Jesus to be peacemakers in the world. Hershberger began his pioneering research and writing around 1930. He produced two books in which he systematically developed his understanding—*War, Peace, and Nonresistance* (1944) and *The Way of the Cross in Human Relations* (1958). But he produced numerous articles for various church periodicals regularly and thus kept bringing before the church his insights and challenge.

The relevance of what Hershberger was doing was underscored by the emergence on the horizon of new war clouds. Memories were still fresh in the minds of many who as conscientious objectors had faced hostility and, in some cases, physical abuse when they refused to bear arms in World War I. They were concerned that steps be taken in advance to prepare the church for this further test.

In retrospect, one can only give thanks that in the providence of God a generation of young scholars placed themselves at the service of the church at a time of critical need. They succeeded in bringing together a renewed awareness of the historical and theological roots of the Anabaptist tradition that undergirds Mennonite and Brethren in Christ church life along with a passion to see the church renewed in its commitment to Jesus Christ and in obedient discipleship. As editors Willard M. Swartley and Cornelius J. Dyck point out in the preface to the *Annotated Bibliography of Mennonite Writings on War and Peace: 1930–1980*, "... the sixteenth-century Anabaptist convictions about peace had fallen prey to traditionalism, acculturation, social withdrawal, and other corroding influences to such an extent that few writings could be found across the span of several centuries. ... And when writings did appear they were primarily concerned with Mennonite self-preservation." Thus Mennonites and Brethren in Christ had become content with a greatly reduced vision of the gospel. Their experiences of persecution over the generations had encouraged them to seek for a mode of living, but this resulted in a failure to explore the full scope of the gospel in any given time and place.

Guy Hershberger began to ask a series of questions in light of his understanding of the evangelical task of peacemaking: What does the gospel of Jesus Christ mean for race relations, serving refugees and administering relief programs, the resort to law by the Christian, social action on behalf of the disadvantaged and dispossessed, tax resistance, civil disobedience, abortion, amnesty, development, labor unions, and lifestyle? When one begins to struggle with these issues, which confront whole societies as well as the disciple who is seeking to be faithful, the old framework of a theology geared to self-preservation is totally inadequate.

In the generation following Guy F. Hershberger, John Howard Yoder has provided decisive leadership through his numerous writings, lecturing, and ecumenical debate. His seminal work, *The Politics of Jesus*, is undoubtedly the most influential work by a Mennonite to be produced in the past generation. It has exerted influence far beyond Mennonite circles. Yoder succeeded in holding together responsible biblical scholarship, historical acuteness, and contemporary witness. He led the way in seeking to lay on the conscience of the wider Christian church the call to follow Jesus Christ in rejecting a resort to violence.

It might be thought that the course of Mennonite theology since 1945 has been unduly narrowed by this attempt to recover a theological heritage. In fact, this fresh focus has inspired a wide range of historical and theological work, but the lodestar has been the vision of a faithful church committed to following its crucified and resurrected Messiah in missionary witness to the world.

Institutionalization

One of the marks of modern industrial and urban society is the way it creates a range of institutions to perform a wide variety of services. Although the building of institutions as such was not an issue among Mennonites and Brethren in Christ, there has been an explosion of institutional development in the years since 1945 that has touched life at all levels and in all areas. We can do no more here than note some examples to illustrate this phenomenon.

As a result of the experience young conscientious objectors had serving in government mental health hospitals in the United States during the Second World War, a conviction developed that the church ought to engage in providing psychiatric services and to do so out of Christian compassion and spiritual sensitivity. As a result, Mennonite Mental Health Services was founded in 1947, and eventually seven mental health centers were established in the United States. Canadian Mennonites have similarly become involved in the mental health field. In certain cases a program has been created to meet a specific objective for a limited period of time. An example of this is the Teachers Abroad Program (TAP), which Mennonite Central Committee started in the early 1960s when many new African nations could not adequately staff their secondary schools and teacher training colleges. They needed short-term help, and TAP helped fill this need. The program was discontinued when this phase had passed. After thirty years of limited contact with the rest of the world, in 1979 China began opening her doors to various kinds of contact. It was made clear from the outset that China would not allow foreign program agencies to sponsor projects in China for purposes of Christian mission. But China did welcome opportunities for exchange. Five North American program agencies plus Mennonite colleges formed the China Educational Exchange in 1981 to sponsor the sending of teachers, doctors, and other scholars to China and the receiving of Chinese teachers and students who wished to come to Mennonite campuses to teach and study. At present this seems to be the most effective way of relating to China. The Mennonite Economic Development Association has been a pioneering attempt by Mennonite businesses and professional people to use their financial resources and expertise to stimulate economic development on several continents. The Mennonite Disaster Service came into existence when Mennonites in Kansas in the late 1940s felt compelled to offer themselves to help people in times of disaster. This network now covers the North American continent and has enabled Mennonites to respond to emergencies in many places.

The creation of institutions is taking place wherever Mennonite and Brethren in Christ churches seek to respond in new ways to needs around them. Over the past twenty years many churches in Latin America and Asia have begun producing their own local radio programs as an extension of their congregational witness. Some of the mission-founded hospitals have, under national leadership, continued to expand their services and upgrade their facilities, such as Mennonite Hospital in Taiwan and Dhamtari Christian Hospital in India.

Another form of institutional development has been the proliferation of inter-Mennonite programs. Prior to 1945 there were a limited number of such agencies, including Mennonite Central Committee. In a survey made in 1987, more than 120 such inter-Mennonite agencies were identified in Canada and the United States alone. This number would be considerably augmented if similar inter-Mennonite agencies on other continents were to be added.

One of the important features of many of these newer agencies is that they have been organized by lay people in response to practical needs or as a means of increasing lay participation. The MCC SELFHELP shops that have sprung up in the past twenty-five years are a typical example.

Institutionalization among Mennonites and Brethren in Christ has ranged across the spectrum from the most highly professional of services, such as that rendered through psychiatric centers, to projects organized at a community level as an outlet for dedicated lay people to put their faith into action in practical deeds.

Renewal movements

Concern for the renewal of the church has been present continually over the past forty-five years. In times of rapid cultural change, it is easy for the church to lose her sense of balance and direction. Some congregations have suffered decline and died out. The church must always struggle with its relationship to the world, or she will be co-opted by the world.

Several kinds of renewal movements have influenced Mennonite and Brethren in Christ churches since 1945. For many congregations in North America the traditional evangelistic meetings, usually conducted annually, continued to be held until about 1960. Several Mennonite evangelists during the 1940s and 1950s conducted large-scale evangelistic campaigns, but these often were geared as much to the needs of the people already connected to a church as those who had no church relationship. In the early 1950s a small group of North Americans who were either studying or working in Europe formed what became known as the Concern Group. They were dedicated to fostering the recovery of the Anabaptist vision, especially in relation to congregational life and discipline. One of the fruits of their concern was the formation later of what became Reba Place Fellowship in Evanston, Illinois (USA), with its commitment to radical discipleship as a community of life and goods. This movement continued to exert influence into the 1980s, but the several communities have modified their form of community life. What has become known as the Charismatic movement has touched Mennonites and Brethren in Christ on most continents over the past thirty years. Sometimes the results have been negative when it has led to schism, but on the whole the impact of this movement has been constructive. Indonesian Mennonite churches experienced renewal in the early 1960s followed by a period of rapid church growth. The impact of this movement has been reported in Europe, the Middle East, Latin America, Asia, and North America. One of the fears that has frequently followed this kind of renewal movement has been that it emphasizes experience at the expense of theological grounding. Some Mennonite renewal leaders have tried to exert a constructive influence at two points: to keep renewal positively related to the church, and to integrate experience with our best theological insights.

Ecumenical involvements

Several tendencies can be observed among Mennonite and Brethren in Christ churches regarding how they relate to Christians of other traditions. There are those who treat with considerable suspicion any effort to fraternize with people of other traditions out of fear they might identify themselves with those who are apostate. Another group takes precisely the opposite viewpoint. They believe that we should relate to other Christians even if there are serious doctrinal or ecclesiastical differences out of the conviction that that is precisely why we should be in conversation with other Christians. The Conference of Mennonites in Canada (CMC) has been an observer in both the Canadian Council of Churches and the Evangelical Fellowship of Canada for several years. In 1990 the CMC is proposing to its delegates that the CMC become an associate member of both groups. A third position is taken by those who identify with a more general theological or ecclesiastical tradition and thus affiliate with ecumenical organizations. Examples of this position would be the Mennonite Brethren, who have long participated in the National Association of Evangelicals, and the Brethren in Christ, who have been active in the National Holiness Association. The Dutch Mennonites have been active in both the Dutch and World Council of Churches. Among the newer Mennonite and Brethren in Christ churches, the attitude they take with regard to how they should relate to other Christian bodies generally reflects what they have been taught by Western colleagues.

But it would be misleading to gauge the extent of ecumenical involvements solely on the basis of whether Mennonites accept membership in certain ecumenical bodies. No one has done a thorough survey of the range of cooperative relationships Mennonites have with other groups. Here we will note several current examples. Mennonites and Baptists cooperated in a project to translate and publish Bible commentaries for the use of Baptists and Mennonites in the Soviet Union. A total of 10,600 sets of Barclay New Testament commentaries have now been sent to the USSR. A by-product of this project has been closer relations between Baptists and Mennonites in the West. Over the past several years a series of dialogues has been conducted between representatives of the World Alliance of Reformed Churches and Mennonite World Conference with a view to studying issues on which we remain divided. Professor Thomas Finger had represented North American Mennonites for some years in the Faith and Order discussions of the World Council of Churches to present a believers' church viewpoint. Over the past decade, especially in Latin America, some of the most vigorous "Anabaptist" thinking has been done by Roman Catholics and evangelicals who are struggling to articulate a vision of the faithful church in their time and place and have found in Anabaptist writings moral support for the position they have come to espouse.

Wilbert R. Shenk, USA, b. 1935, Ph.D., director of Mission Training Center at the Associated Mennonite Biblical Seminaries (Elkhart, Indiana).

Three Goshen College students team up, working together on a problem of common interest. (Goshen College photo by J. Tyler Klassen, 1989)

Historical time line
by David Shelly, MWC

Asia	Africa	Europe

1940

1940 Indonesian Mennonite synod (GITJ) 1945 World War II ends 1947 Independence of India 1948 Independence of Indonesia; Indian Bihar Mennonite conference; Mahatma Gandhi assassinated 1949 Communists win Mainland China; Missionaries leave China; Nationalists flee to Taiwan	1945 Zairian Mennonite Brethren conference (CEFMZ) 1948 Ethiopia agrees to Eastern Mennonite Board (EMBMC) mission work	1945 World War II ends; Many Mennonites repatriated to Soviet Union; MCC begins postwar relief services 1946 Death of MWC leader Christian Neff 1947 European Mennonite Conference at Elspeet, The Netherlands; Marshall Plan; International Refugee Organization 1948 World Council of Churches 1949 Federal Republic of Germany constituted; Internationales Mennonitisches Friedenskomitee (IMFK)

1950

1953 Union Biblical Seminary opens at Yeotmal, India 1954 Mennonite Central Committee (MCC) first North American agency in Vietnam 1959 Taiwanese conference	1950 French mission in Chad 1952 Dresser Bible School founded at Nazareth, Ethiopia 1953 EMBMC enters Somalia; Bible Institute opens at Tshikapa, Congo 1955 Widespread famine in Congo 1956 Mennonite Board of Missions (MBM) West Africa work in Ghana 1957 Decolonization era begins in Ghana 1959 First church council of Meserete Kristos (Ethiopia) meets in Nazareth; MBM Independent Church work in Nigeria	1950 European Mennonite Bible School, Basel 1951 European Mennonite Mission Board (EMEK) 1952 MWC Assembly at Basel, Switzerland 1953 Luxembourg Mennonite conference 1956 German Mennonite Peace Committee (DMFK); First North American Mennonite delegation visits USSR; French Mennonites take charge of children's home 1957 Soviets launch Sputnik; MWC Assembly at Karlsruhe, Germany

1960

1963 Mennonite Christian Service Fellowship of India (MCSFI) 1964 Tokyo-area conference; Japanese Mennonite Brethren conference; Japanese General Conference 1965 Abortive coup in Indonesia; Theological school opened at Pati, Indonesia; Famine crisis strikes India; PIPKA mission agency in Indonesia 1968 Indian Brethren in Christ conference; India's all-Mennonite gathering at Shamshabad 1969 Vietnamese conference	1960 Independence of Congo; war erupts 1962 Africa Mennonite and Brethren in Christ Fellowship (AMBCF); Baluba in Congo migrate to South Kasai; Mennonite Evangelical Community (CEM), Congo; Ghana conference 1964 Luo migrate from Tanzania to Kenya 1965 Congo Mennonite Brethren centers destroyed in violence; Inter-Mennonite and Brethren in Christ conference in Rhodesia 1969 MWC Presidium in Kinshasa, Congo; AMBCF in Kinshasa	1960 Austrian Mennonite Brethren conference 1961 German Democratic Republic Mennonite conference; Berlin Wall erected 1962 Second Vatican Council 1963 First congress of All-Union Council of Evangelical Christians-Baptists (AUCECB) in USSR; Intermenno Trainee Program 1966 Some Mennonite Brethren join AUCECB in USSR; French dedicate Mont des Oiseaux children's home 1967 International Mennonite Organization (IMO); MWC Assembly at Amsterdam, The Netherlands

Caribbean/ Central America	South America	North America
1948 Canadian migration to Mexico; Puerto Rican conference	1945 Missions in Colombia 1947 Neuland, Volendam Colonies established in Paraguay 1948 West Prussian refugees arrive in Uruguay; Period of religious persecution begins in Colombia	1945 Mennonite Biblical Seminary started in Chicago 1946 Mennonite Mental Health Services 1947 Canadian Mennonite Bible College in Winnipeg 1948 MWC Assembly at Goshen (Indiana) and Newton (Kansas)
1951 Aibonito hospital opens in Puerto Rico 1958 Mennonites from Mexico migrate to Belize 1959 Castro takes power in Cuba; Jamaican conference; MCC opens hospital in northern Haiti	1952 Colombian General Conference; Km 81 Hospital opens in Paraguay 1955 German General Conference, Brazil 1956 Seminary opens in Montevideo, Uruguay 1957 Evangelical Mennonite Association in Brazil 1958 Kornelius Isaak stabbed to death in Paraguay 1959 Mental hospital opens at Filadelfia, Paraguay	1950 MCC International Visitor Exchange Program 1951 Mennonite Disaster Service; MCC PAX Program 1955 Mennonite Brethren Biblical Seminary in Fresno, California 1956 Evangelical Mennonite Conference (Canada) 1957 First Mennonite relief sale at Morgantown, Pennsylvania 1958 Mennonite Biblical Seminary moves to Elkhart, Indiana; Associated Mennonite Biblical Seminaries; Council of Mission Board Secretaries 1959 Evangelical Mennonite Mission Conference in Canada; *Mennonite Encyclopedia* completed
1961 Hurricane Hattie devastates Belize 1962 Cuban missile crisis brings world to brink of nuclear war 1965 Honduran conference 1968 Goshen College launches Study Service Trimester in Jamaica	1960 German Mennonite Brethren conference, Brazil 1961 Alliance for Progress; German Mennonite Brethren conference, Paraguay; Trans-Chaco road completed 1963 Uruguayan Mennonite Brethren conference 1966 MWC Presidium visits four nations; Brazilian Mennonite Brethren conference 1967 Paraguayan General Conference 1968 Migrations from Mexico and Belize to Bolivia 1969 Colombian Mennonite Brethren conference	1960 Mennonite Brethren/Krimmer Mennonite Brethren merger 1961 Conrad Grebel College founded 1962 MWC Assembly at Kitchener, Ontario; MWC president H.S. Bender dies 1963 MCC Canada; Civil Rights Movement in USA 1968 Vietnam War protests 1969 Moon landing

Asia	Africa	Europe
1970		
1970 Indonesia Mennonite Seminary enters new facilities at Pati 1971 First Asia Mennonite Conference in Dhamtari, India; Japanese Mennonite Fellowship; Japanese Brethren in Christ conference; Independence of Bangladesh 1974 Asia Mennonite Services; Philippine conference 1975 Communists control South Vietnam 1976 MWC Presidium in Semarang, Indonesia 1977 Tokyo Anabaptist Center 1978 Charles Christano (Indonesia) becomes first Asian president of MWC 1979 First Australian congregation	1970 Nigerian Civil War ends 1971 Congo becomes Zaire 1972 Congo Inland Mission becomes Africa Inter-Mennonite Mission (AIMM) 1973 Million Belete (Kenya) becomes first African president of MWC 1974 AIMM work with African Independent Churches in Botswana 1977 Kenyan conference 1979 Tanzanian conferences /80 established	1972 Belgian Mennonite council 1974 Russian Mennonites migrate to Germany; Mennonite European Regional Conference (MERK) in Bienenberg, Switzerland, marks 450 years of Anabaptism 1977 MERK meets at Elspeet, The Netherlands
1980		
1980 Goshen College Study Service Trimester in China; Second Asia Mennonite Conference and MWC Executive Committee in Osaka, Japan; Australian conference 1983 Union Biblical Seminary opens at Pune, India 1986 Asia Mennonite Conference in Taiwan	1980 Burkina Faso conference in Orodara 1981 MWC General Council in Nairobi, Kenya 1982 Persecution in Ethiopia 1984 Famine in the Sahel zone makes global headlines 1987 National Inter-Mennonite Committee (CONIM), Zaire 1988 Leadership change in the Mennonite Community of Zaire (CMZ)	1981 MERK meets at Enkenbach, Germany; Italian Mennonite conference; MWC office moves to Strasbourg, France, for three years 1982 Mennonite Brethren conference, Spain 1983 Large-scale missile protests 1984 MWC Assembly at Strasbourg, France; Mission consultation, Strasbourg, France; Bilateral Mennonite/Reformed Dialogue in Strasbourg, France 1985 Bible commentaries to USSR; First Gemeindetag in Germany 1987 Two Federal Republic of Germany conferences agree to joint efforts 1988 Dramatic increase of Russian Mennonites migrating to Germany; German Bibles to USSR; MERK meets at Tramelan, Switzerland 1989 International Mennonite Peace Committee (IMPC) meets in Switzerland; 200th anniversary of arrival of Mennonites in Russia; Berlin Wall torn down; Communist regimes in Eastern bloc countries dissolved

Caribbean/ Central America

1971 Panamanian conference
1972 Earthquake devastates Nicaragua
1974 Costa Rican conference; First meeting of Central American Anabaptist-Mennonite Consultation (CAMCA); Fraternity of Evangelical Mennonite Churches of Nicaragua
1975 Mission consultation and MWC Presidium in San Juan, Puerto Rico; Belizian conference
1976 Guatemalan conference; Earthquake devastates Guatemala; Faro Divino in Dominican Republic
1977 Nicaraguan Brethren in Christ conference

South America

1971 Paraguayan Evangelical Mennonite Brethren conference; MWC considers canceling 9th Assembly at Curitiba, Brazil
1972 MWC Assembly at Curitiba, Brazil; Uruguayan Spanish conference
1974 Montevideo, Uruguay, seminary closes
1975 Nivaclé conference in Paraguay
1977 Seminary opens in San Lorenzo, Paraguay (CEMTA)
1978 Lengua conference in Paraguay
1979 Venezuelan conference

North America

1971 Mennonite Church restructured
1972 Yoder v. Wisconsin, US Supreme Court decision on education
1974 Meeting of charismatics at Landisville, Pennsylvania
1976 Council of International Ministries
1977 Old Colonists from Mexico settle in Texas; Foundation Series released by Mennonite publishers; New Call to Peacemaking
1978 MWC Assembly at Wichita, Kansas; Mission consultation, Hesston, Kansas
1979 General Conference tax assembly in Minneapolis, Minnesota

---

1980 Guatemalan Kekchi conference; IMPC holds first meetings in Nicaragua and Colombia
1983 JELAM (Latin American Mennonite Broadcast Executive Board) media ministry terminates
1984 Trinidad and Tobago conference
1986 Mission consultation in Guatemala
1987 CAMCA issues statement on war

1987 MWC General Council in Filadelfia, Paraguay; Latin American Conference of the Southern Cone meets in Paraguay
1988 World Mennonite Brethren conference at Curitiba, Brazil
1989 Latin American Conference of the Southern Cone meets in Bolivia

1980 MCC U.S. holds first meeting; Draft registration reimposed in USA
1983 Tricentennial of Mennonites in USA; First Mennonite Church/ General Conference joint meeting at Bethlehem, Pennsylvania
1985 Mennonite Church adopts "Vision 95" strategy
1986 Canadian 200th anniversary; Christian Peacemaker Teams approved; Freeman (South Dakota) Junior College closed; General Conference campaign for Kingdom Commitments
1987 United Nations declares conscientious objection a human right
1988 Triple district conference merger in Ontario
1989 General Conference/ Mennonite Church joint conference at Normal, Illinois; Bilateral Mennonite/Baptist conversations in Philadelphia, Pennsylvania
1990 *Mennonite Encyclopedia* supplement, Vol. V, published; MWC Assembly 12 at Winnipeg, Manitoba

Paul T. Yoder, overseer of the Harrisonburg District of Virginia Mennonite Conference, gives the ordination charge to Ruth Brunk Stoltzfus (age 74), who is the first woman in this conference to be ordained. (Photo by Jim Bishop, 1989)

The search for a Mennonite theology

by J. Denny Weaver

For much of this century, Mennonites have been searching for a systematic theology. That quest has proceeded under several headings. In earlier decades it went forward under the guise of listing Bible doctrines or describing a historical identity. Only recently has the theological task become identified explicitly as the development of a systematic theology for Mennonites.

The search for a theology has paralleled and reflected the interaction of Mennonites with the modern world and, in particular, with various elements of modern theology. Befitting the recent entry of Mennonites into the discipline of theology as theology, we are still in the process of sorting out the history of the interaction of Mennonite theology with the several options in the wider theological world. In fact, that sorting out of the history of Mennonite theologizing is one of the major tasks related to developing a theology for contemporary Mennonites. This essay contributes to the process of discerning some of the trends in Mennonite theologizing in this century. The analysis will suggest a direction for the future development of Mennonite theology, both as it relates to other Christian theologies and as the focus of Mennonite theology shifts from a predominantly North American to a global context. Mennonite theologizing consists not of uniform development but of a number of intersecting and overlapping trajectories reflecting influences from several domains and resulting in a variety of responses from within. The following uses a schematic approach rather than a detailed description of that complexity.

The Fundamentalist-Modernist controversy

In the 1920s and 1930s, American Protestant theology became rather polarized around the issues of the Fundamentalist-Modernist controversy. In its most elemental form, a "fundamental" constituted a doctrine necessary for salvation. The Fundamentalist movement defended a cluster of issues including the inerrancy of the Bible, the virgin birth of Christ, the substitutionary atonement, and Christ's bodily resurrection and return. Theological liberalism and Modernism as a movement sought to redefine much of the theological tradition on the basis of post-Enlightenment reason and empiricism and was open to new ideas such as evolution. For Fundamentalists the new formulations and the openness to new ideas seemed to relativize and undercut the fundamental truths of Christianity.

By one theory, the Fundamentalist movement developed as a combination of two elements: (1) premillennialism, as defined first by J.N. Darby and later popularized by C.I. Scofield, and (2) the idea of biblical inerrancy as taught at Princeton Seminary in New Jersey. A more broadly based definition of Fundamentalism formulates it as a loosely knit coalition of militant Protestant evangelicals whose unity lay not in their doctrine but in their militant reaction to Modernism. This anti-Modernist outlook expressed a world view tied to a version of Common Sense Philosophy, which assumed that truth existed in one form, accessible to any person of common sense in any age and culture of the world. Accordingly, Fundamentalists saw Modernists not as suggesting alternative interpretations of the Bible but as rejecting truth known to all reasonable people.

Mennonite theology during this epoch reflects the debate in American society. While the first definition of Fundamentalism did not always fit Mennonites, a good deal of Mennonite theology was characterized by the second definition, anti-Modernism. Although not nearly as much Modernism existed among Mennonites as some leaders feared, there were those with generally orthodox positions on individual issues who exhibited more liberal attitudes toward culture and the more experiential underpinnings of Modernism. Historically Mennonites had used confessions of faith as a way to discover things on which they agreed. They had stressed the practical dimensions of faith rather than focusing on creeds and requiring precise doctrinal formulations. Adopting the doctrinal outlook of Fundamentalism thus caused some theological tensions, which were not always recognized or articulated.

One point of tension concerned the location in the theological matrix of the historic Mennonite commitment to nonresistance and the rejection of violence. Prior to the advent of the doctrinal era, nonresistance belonged inherently to the heart of the gospel of Christ. Conversion or acceptance of salvation meant taking up the life of God's people, modeled on Christ, living the nonresistant life in community. In the doctrinal era, gospel became defined in terms of the personalized plan of salvation, which focused primarily on removal of the guilt and penalty of sin and tended to separate ethics from faith. In Daniel Kauffman's books on Bible doctrines, nonresistance was separated from the gospel and moved to a category called "restrictions." Restrictions referred to practices adopted after being saved and whose function was to prevent Christians from straying. They included such things as nonconformity to the world, avoidance of worldly amusements, rejection of the oath, and nonresistance. Such a formulation provided a definition of salvation that did not inherently include nonresistance or other aspects of lived faith.

Premillennialism

Premillennialism illustrates another set of tensions. Contacts with teachers and literature from Moody Bible Institute in Chicago led some Mennonites to adopt various versions of premillennialism. Premillennialists believed that at his return Jesus would establish and rule a kingdom on earth for one thousand years—a millennium—prior to the Last Judgment. Meanwhile, until the return of Jesus, evil held sway in the world. The dispensational version of premillennialism divided history into a series of epochs or dispensations, in each of which God established a different way of relating to his people. In the most extreme form of dispensationalism, the teaching of Jesus belonged to the final dispensation, the future millennium.

These premillennial teachings posed challenges to the idea of a lived faith in general, and to the historic Mennonite commitment to nonresistance and nonviolence in particular. A premillennialist world view concedes the control of institutions and structures to the kingdom of the world and tends to understand Christian ethics and following Christ—discipleship—in primarily individual terms. That is, it is assumed that the life and teaching of Jesus have individual, but not social, implications. The gospel message deals with individual salvation, and Christian ethics become primarily avoidance of the evil in the world while awaiting the return of Christ. That outlook can result in accepting the status quo of society and blunts the impulse to see the church as an institution that poses a genuine social alternative to the world. More particularly, the Mennonite commitment to nonresistance can appear without much foundation. In the extreme form of dispensational premillennialism, Jesus' words simply do not apply to Christians now. Even in less extreme forms, when premillennialism concedes history to the rule of Satan, nonresistance may apply to individual Christians but has no real meaning as a social policy. Personally nonresistant Christians may defend military might as necessary for the preservation of the society around them. In this case, they actually expect other people to do the killing that they will not do for themselves. When premillennialism became a controversial subject for Mennonites, the primary debate concerned whether or not it was biblical. The problematic theological dimensions noted here have become much clearer now than when Mennonites were first introduced to the doctrine.

The Anabaptist Vision

Fundamentalists and Modernists had different assumptions of authority. Fundamentalism lodged authority in a book whose truth was guaranteed by a doctrine of inerrancy and inspiration. Modernists located authority in human reason. The idea of the inerrancy of the Bible was meant to defend theological truths against the challenges of Modernist redefinition and relativism. Inerrancy was thus an assumption underlying and attached to other doctrines important to Fundamentalists, and it became the ultimate line of defense for a doctrine such as premillennialism. For Fundamentalists, those who had questions about a doctrine such as premillennialism could be accused not only of doubting the Bible but even of calling into question the entire Christian faith. This Fundamentalist approach appears to make the truth of Christ depend not on the authority of Christ himself but on a definition of inerrancy and a claim about the Bible. Further, it requires Christians to accept only one set of language and thus fails to recognize the extent to which language reflects a particular historical context.

For a time, particularly for Mennonites of Swiss tradition in the United States, the Fundamentalist-influenced doctrinal formulations could serve purposes of Mennonite identity. Bench marks such as the devotional covering and the ordinances of the church joined a Mennonite list of Bible doctrines (or fundamentals). As long as it remained strong, ethnicity could function as a reminder to Mennonites of their commitment to nonresistance, even when relegated to the category of "restrictions." The decline of ethnic identity, however, posed the potential to focus on the plan of salvation while abandoning nonresistance, which had been switched to another point in the theological outline.

In the wake of the doctrinal era, Harold S. Bender offered a way to define Mennonite theology while avoiding the Fundamentalist-Modernist polarization. Bender defined Mennonite faith in terms of the "Anabaptist Vision." Appealing to Mennonite origins in the Anabaptist movement of the sixteenth century, Bender said that the essence of Mennonite faith consisted of three things: (1) discipleship, a "transformation of the entire way of life of the individual believer and of society so that it should be fashioned after the teachings and example of Christ," (2) a concept of the church that included voluntary membership, nonconformity to the world, suffering, and love and brotherhood, (3) "love and nonresistance," which he called "a complete abandonment of all warfare, strife, and violence, and of the taking of human life." This Anabaptist Vision was a kind of return to the idea of a lived-out faith of the predoctrinal era. Bender assumed orthodox positions on the issues of concern to Fundamentalists, but did not make those doctrines the essence of Mennonite faith. He avoided discussion of the doctrine of inerrancy.

Other options

In the 1950s and 1960s the theological writings of J.C. Wenger and Gordon Kaufman represented two other kinds of Mennonite options. While Wenger and Kaufman do not represent the Fundamentalist and Modernist camps in the earlier sense, their writings may represent Mennonite developments in those lines of thought. Wenger's *Introduction to Theology* (1954) was strongly Bible based, and he continued the affirmation of orthodox definitions for the issues of concern to Fundamentalism. However, his theology had much softer edges than Fundamentalism and much greater willingness to allow for a variety of expressions of doctrine. For example, rather than insisting on the substitutionary atonement alone as did Fundamentalism, Wenger listed several atonement motifs; and he made a gentle affirmation of amillennialism without stridently opposing premillennialism. Following the earlier pattern, nonresistance is mentioned in sections on church discipline and "A Successful Christian Life."

In contrast to Wenger, Kaufman's theology appealed much more to reason and to human experience as that which validates truth. His concern in *Systematic Theology: A Historicist Perspective* (1968), a work from which he apparently distanced himself later, was to establish the extent to which theology corresponded to a rational, history-based foundation. In this work Kaufman was willing to redefine issues such as the fall or the resurrection of Jesus. At the same time, he integrated nonresistance into the discussion of incarnation as well as the life of believers and the church.

John H. Yoder inaugurated a new era in Mennonite theology. Yoder's *Politics of Jesus* (1972), his *Preface to Theology*, an informal publication of class lectures at Associated Mennonite Biblical Seminaries (Elkhart, Indiana), and other writings posed a different kind of foundation for Mennonite theology, based on neither a theory about the Bible nor an appeal to human reason or empiricism. Yoder argued that ethics and theology are located in the story of Jesus, which includes the establishment and formulation of a new, alternative society. An inherent characteristic of this new society based on Jesus Christ is the rejection of violence. In one sense, this stress on the church as alternative society continues the emphasis of Bender's Anabaptist Vision. Yoder took it a step farther, however. While he underscored the importance of the church as a visible, alternative community in the world, Yoder also suggested that this emphasis on the church might have an impact on the formulation of the list of orthodox doctrines. It was not a call to reject these doctrines but to ask how Mennonite ecclesiology and ethics might influence the shape of these doctrines. For example, in light of the fact that the classic creeds were formulated by the church in the fourth and fifth centuries, after the church had become established and abandoned the idea of being an alternative to the social order, one can ask whether the believers' church, which is shaped by its foundation on Jesus Christ, has a unique perspective on those creeds.

Elements shaping modern theology

One question in the modern debate about the foundation of a Mennonite systematic theology concerns whether or not Mennonites have a theological tradition. Since Mennonites have only recently begun to pursue formal education in theology, some have argued that Mennonites do not have a tradition of systematic theology. It follows from this view that when Mennonites begin to do systematic theology they need to supplement their inadequate theological tradition by borrowing—learning from—the theological traditions of other denominations. Others have argued that Mennonites do have a kind of theological tradition. It is said that Mennonite writers of all epochs have expressed themselves on the classic questions such as Christology and atonement. Even if these earlier formulations were not particularly original or even very good theology, the argument goes, one can still observe that their formulations were shaped by their assumptions about such things as discipleship, the visible church, and nonresistance. The conclusion then follows that those assumptions should continue to shape Mennonite theology in an explicit way as we begin formally to do systematic theology. This approach argues that Mennonites should have a unique theology, reflecting their particular understandings, rather than validating Mennonite theology by describing its conformity to that of another tradition.

Modern Mennonite theology is characterized by a great deal of diversity, reflecting the pluralism of the modern world. One recent analysis listed fourteen different suggestions for the proper orientation for a Mennonite theology. I would suggest that this variety of contemporary Mennonite theologies can be placed in three clusters of positions. Each cluster contains several varieties, and the following descriptions are precursory rather than definitive.

Cluster One emphasizes that Mennonite theology is Christian theology. This cluster assumes that Mennonites have little theological tradition of their own and should therefore quite appropriately borrow from and stress agreement with other traditions on core doctrines. The Mennonite theologians in this cluster emphasize the ways that Mennonite theology can agree with theology in other Christian denominations and traditions. Those comfortable with earlier Fundamentalism constitute one subgroup of this cluster. Another subgroup consists of those who emphasize Mennonite agreement with evangelicals and evangelical theology. A third subgroup consists of those theologians who stress classic Nicene and Chalcedonian creeds and formulas as defined by Roman Catholicism and Protestant orthodoxy. Each of the subgroups in Cluster One seeks to define Mennonite theology in terms of the theology of another group or Christian tradition. None of these subgroups acknowledges in a fundamental way John H. Yoder's point that the established church context in which the borrowed doctrines originated can have an impact on the shape of those doctrines.

On the issue of nonresistance and pacifism, this first cluster reflects the earlier discussion about Fundamentalism and the plan of salvation. For Neo-Fundamentalists and evangelicals, nonresistance belongs on the list of doctrines undergirded by biblical authority. For those who stress Catholic or Protestant orthodoxy, nonresistance and pacifism constitute a doctrine that one affirms in addition to the common core shared with Christendom. In each instance, nonresistance is not an integral part of the core shared with all Christians.

The treatment of nonresistance and the rejection of violence create some tension within the way Cluster One approaches Mennonite theology. By posing nonresistance as a Mennonite addendum to the theology of another tradition, it implies either that the other theology is incomplete—which that tradition will not accept as a self-definition—or that rejection of violence does not really belong to the essence of Christian theology—a claim the Mennonite tradition has refused to accept. I would suggest that Mennonites develop a theology that makes rejection of violence an integral and constitutive element while also allowing the non-Mennonite theology to exist as a complete tradition with which Mennonites can dialogue.

Cluster Two consists of various kinds of liberation and feminist theologies. Feminist theology is a kind of liberation theology, which has developed its own identity. From one perspective, these theologies provide expression for the justice and social concerns of Mennonites. They also pose the temptation to confuse the concerns and activity of political processes with Mennonite ethical and social concerns.

In terms of the foundation for a Mennonite theology, these liberation theologies also constitute a kind of borrowing. They use criteria from human experience and the world as the norm for validating the truth of theology. The truth of an idea or an act depends on the extent to which it advances the cause of liberation—liberation of the poor, of the oppressed, of women, and so on. Liberation theologies have varying degrees of radicalism. Some would appeal to Jesus Christ as the source or inspiration of liberation. Moderate feminist theology attempts to appeal to Jesus Christ as a source for the liberation of women. Radical feminist theology rejects the authority of Jesus, claiming that the liberation of women cannot be linked to a male savior.

On the question of the rejection of violence, liberation theology often affirms nonviolence as a method of liberation, but holds open the possibility that violence could advance the cause of liberation. Appeals can be made to Jesus as the foundation for such violence—Jesus the liberator supports any liberating action, even a violent one.

On the question of whether Mennonites have a theological tradition to draw upon, Mennonite advocates of liberation theology and feminist theology may find a mixed score. On the one hand, they can appeal to a radical tradition in the sixteenth century. There is some justification for arguing that if sixteenth-century Anabaptists were not yet at the stage of granting full equality of men and women, Anabaptists were nonetheless ahead of other sixteenth-century movements in acknowledging the contributions of women. The cluster of liberation and feminist theologians has a more pessimistic appraisal of recent Mennonite history and theology, and they are more likely to affirm that Mennonite theology needs to learn radical social and feminist equality from outside of the Mennonite theological tradition.

This cluster of liberation and feminist theology shares one characteristic with Cluster One. Like the first, Cluster Two also uses borrowed models to evaluate the truth of Mennonite theology. If Cluster One holds Mennonite theology up to the bar of a theory of Scripture or to creedal statements from the fourth and fifth centuries, Cluster Two evaluates Mennonite theology at the bar of the human experience of liberation.

A third cluster of theological opinion, following the lead of John H. Yoder, offers the most promising option for the development of a systematic theology for modern Mennonites. This cluster has much in common with what is currently called narrative theology. Perhaps it could be called a normative theology in recognition of its affirmation of the story of Jesus as the foundation and the norm for Christian theology. This approach recognizes the entire story of Jesus—life, teaching, death, and resurrection—as the proper stuff of theology. It recognizes that the uniqueness of Jesus is given not by abstract statements but by the description of his life. When God is present in history in the person of Jesus Christ, it is not in later creedal statements but through the description of his life and teaching that Christians see what the will of God is. The life of Jesus and the manner of his death show incontrovertibly that the rejection of violence belongs to the essence of the kingdom of God. Violence played no role in the community established by and built on Jesus Christ. This focus on the life, death, and resurrection of Jesus constitutes the most appropriate foundation for a Mennonite theology on the verge of the twenty-first century.

Such a narrative-based theology will keep an eye on the issues of concern to Evangelicalism and to Catholic and Protestant orthodoxy. Suggesting a narrative foundation is not a call to reject those theological concerns. It is a recognition that the creedal formulations have presuppositions and contexts that neglect the foundational character of the entire story of Jesus. Thus, we do not need to be bound to or limited by those creedal formulations in expressing the story of Jesus and in applying that story to our lives today.

A narrative-based theology will need to keep in mind the social and justice issues raised by liberation and feminist theology. The concerns of those theologies are issues addressed by the gospel, by the story of Jesus Christ. In fact, it is precisely in examining the life of Jesus that one discovers that the community founded on Christ is concerned for the poor and the oppressed and for equality of women. Calling for a narrative theology based on the entire life, teaching, death, and resurrection of Christ is not to avoid the issues raised by liberation and feminist theology but rather to underscore that Jesus Christ, and not human experience, constitutes the norm of theology. Focus on the life, teaching, death, and resurrection of Christ shows clearly that violence is unacceptable as a means of seeking liberation. It also avoids a class definition of what it means to be Christian. If the poor or the oppressed as a group constitute the children of God, that is to use a standard based on social class as the validation point of Christian truth. Focus on the life, teaching, death, and resurrection of Jesus Christ shows clearly that Jesus Christ is the norm of all truth.

The narrative-based approach to Mennonite theology offers an answer to those feminist theologians who claim that liberation cannot be linked to a male savior. If the foundation of theology is the story of Jesus, the uniqueness of Jesus and the salvific work of Jesus appear in the way he related to individuals and the way he submitted to death. The story shows that he had concerns for the poor and oppressed, that he accepted women as full participants in the kingdom of God, that he rejected violence as a means of liberation or defense. None of those is an inherently male activity or characteristic. The uniqueness of Jesus was not a product of his maleness but a matter of how he made visible the kingdom of God. While this way of depicting the unique and the salvific dimensions of Jesus' work will not satisfy the most radical feminists, it is an approach to theology that accepts the equal status of women and men as followers of Christ and as participants in the church, which makes visible the kingdom of God on earth.

Avoid labels

Some observers will no doubt want to identify the three clusters as modern versions of conservative, modernist/liberal, and moderate theologies, or as theologies representing right, left, and center. For several reasons, however, I suggest that we avoid such labels. For one thing, these three do not really exist on a continuum. Each cluster contains whole, integrated theologies, each with its own kind of integrity. Sharp arguments among proponents of the several clusters ought not blind us to the wholeness and integrity of each system. Further, it is unclear in every case what is being conserved or changed (made more liberal). The theologians in each cluster appeal to the Bible and to Jesus Christ. They differ on the nature of that appeal: Cluster One preserves certain creedal or doctrinal statements about Jesus; Cluster Two claims the liberating impulse of Jesus; while Cluster Three conserves the story of Jesus. On the other hand, proponents of each of the three clusters use concepts and theological language not found in the Bible. Thus, each of these clusters is part of an evolution of doctrine and doctrinal formulation; all in some way participate in adapting theological language to address postbiblical contexts. Therefore, I suggest that we discard as imprecise and nonfunctional the terms "conservative" and "liberal" when discussing the location of ideas in the theological matrix.

As this essay reflects, much of Mennonite theology has developed within a context dominated by the North American theological scene, and in particular that of the United States. We are only at the very beginning of understanding how that North American and United States ethos has shaped Mennonite theology. I offer here one suggestion.

The United States prides itself on being a melting pot, a cultural setting in which various immigrant and ethnic groups blend together into one national identity. That monocultural identity has a powerful civil religion that attributes a great deal of divine providence—although stated in secular terms—to the United States as a nation. When Mennonites have thought about theology in such a context, the impulse has been to formulate a theology that posed a comprehensive theological identity for the church over against a monolithic national religion. Continuing to exist as a faithful church meant defining the church in terms that prevented it from being subsumed under the unofficial but very real civil religion of the nation.

Other contexts have provided a quite different setting in which Mennonite theology has developed. Canada, for example, has an officially multicultural society. In mission contexts, Mennonites have found themselves in societies not shaped by Western Christendom and working shoulder-to-shoulder with Christians of other traditions. In these contexts, a natural impulse is to search for a theology that can transcend the divisions among Christians.

I suspect that Mennonite theologians representing these two differing cultural contexts—a monolithic civil religion and a multicultural environment with several Christian alternatives—have sometimes talked past each other and to some extent have misunderstood theological statements shaped within the other cultural settings. For example, when a theologian within the American context has articulated a theology for Mennonites that should be "over against the world," to someone in the multicultural context that theology can sound like one of the small groups asserting itself over other Christian groups. In contrast, when someone from a multicultural context has expressed the need for an ecumenical theology that transcends group differences, to someone in the monocultural context that call can sound like a surrender to the common civil religion or an abandonment of the uniqueness of the Mennonite theological tradition.

As we continue to think about the future of Mennonite theology, we need to keep such cultural contexts and national character in mind. The same theological statement can be understood quite differently depending on one's social location. Developing a Mennonite theology for the twenty-first century is not a matter of deciding for one or the other of these kinds of cultural contexts. We do need to take the particular ethos into account, however, and be willing to seek for multiple ways to express the same point. We are still at the beginning of learning to incorporate and account for cultural diversity while preserving a normative theological tradition. That learning constitutes one of the most important future theological tasks as Mennonites become increasingly a worldwide fellowship.

J. Denny Weaver, USA, b. 1941, Ph.D., professor of religion at Bluffton College (Bluffton, Ohio).

The church and women

by Christina van Straten-Bargeman

The title for this article was suggested to me by the editor, and I was free to choose another. I did not, for this title nicely shows what it is all about: we, women, are a problem. You will never find a man who thinks it should be "The Church and Men." Apparently women and men are not equal—not in the church or in society. We women are deeply hurt by this inequality as it is expressed in many ways in the life of our congregations. This has to do with the way men have been thinking and speaking about women through the ages. In a book by a Mr. Weininger—which first appeared in Germany in 1913, had twenty-five reprints in ten years, and was translated into many languages—we read: "Woman is neither profound nor high-spirited, neither sharp-witted nor honest; rather, she is the exact opposite of all this. She is, as far as we can see now, without any sense at all; she is totally non-sense, nonsense."[1] This very day women are still being given to understand that they do not make sense and, therefore, should shut up. This hurts even more deeply when it happens in the church—as it often does. The hurt generates anger, and anger drives us to question the traditional thinking that can so horribly distort God's purpose of creating man in his own image, male and female. Does it not belong to that image that God is like a mother who comforts us (Isaiah 66:13) and like a mother who gave us birth (James 1:18)? Often the Bible is cited against us. But women, too, read the Bible.

Two thousand years ago Jesus Christ equally invited men and women to a new covenant with God and to do the will of God. God became human in Jesus Christ in order to show and teach us how to live together and to liberate us from the power of evil, which is the distortion of the reality God wants for us. Martha, the sister of Mary and Lazarus, confesses it: "I now believe that you are the Messiah, the Son of God, who was to come into the world" (John 11:27). This confession, coming from a woman, seldom gets the same attention as that of Simon Peter: "You are the Messiah, the Son of the living God" (Matt. 16:16). Yet Martha is explicitly invited by Jesus to express her faith, just as in another story he invites her to leave the role traditionally allotted to women—that of serving men—and instead come and sit at his feet like her sister Mary and be a disciple (Luke 10:38–42). Some of Jesus' other female disciples are mentioned by name in Luke 8:1–3. Not only did they and many other women share the journeys of Jesus and the Twelve, they also financed them (Luke 8:3).

Women also preach the gospel (the Samaritan woman in John 4:29,30) and not without results (John 4:39). The disciples were surprised to find Jesus speaking with a woman—a sign that by treating women as equal to men Jesus acted against predominant tradition. After the resurrection Jesus first met with women, who again became the first to preach the gospel of the risen Lord. But, coming from women, this was thought a nonsensical story by the apostles; they were able to believe it only after Peter confirmed it. Jesus took the women seriously. The apostles did not. But Luke recorded it in his Gospel (24:11), the same Luke who recorded that burst of joy coming from Mary (1:46–55) about the liberating and renewing power of the word of God, which lifts the humble.

In the history of the church, equality of men and women has been nearly nonexistent. Inequality has often been defended with words from the Bible, as slavery and racial inequality also have been. Paul's words in 1 Cor. 14:33–36 are often cited without attention to the context. But citing these words out of context is not only devastating for women and our dignity as people created in God's image, but it also badly damages the image we have of Paul by making him contradict Jesus. For many of us women, that damage has been done. Paul has been made our enemy. We do not feel secure with him as we do with Jesus. Jesus told a woman, "Go to my brothers and tell them that I am ascending to my Father" (John 20:17), telling her to do what Paul would forbid her. Paul may have been using the traditional language and ideas of his time to convey the message he had to bring, but I do not believe he pretended to know better than Jesus, his and our Lord. So I want to say a few things about 1 Cor. 14.

In the community of Corinth things are very wrong. The congregation is deeply divided (1 Cor. 1:12). Their worship meetings are disastrous (11:17–34). There is no unity, no love, and Paul has to instruct them on these things (12–13). They cannot agree on the relative importance of the language of ecstasy and prophecy (talking in tongues and bringing God's message). Trying not to be too blunt, Paul opts for the clear, understandable language of prophecy (14:1–25). Then Paul proceeds to tell them in the rest of Chapter 14 that their worship meeting should be conducted "decently and in order." That people (men and women) have, at times, to be silent during the meeting is stressed three times (verses 28, 30, and 34). In the Greek original, the same word for being silent is used in all three verses.[2] Apparently, the meetings have the character of a shouting match in which the divisions show. There is disorder and quarreling where order and peace should reign (verse 33). All members of the congregation can prophesy, but one at a time (verse 31). Now how can this statement (and how can Jesus' attitude to women) be reconciled to verses 33–35? Only if, here again, a particular (and not general) problem had to be addressed. Therefore, I think that in the Corinthian congregation there were some women who disturbed the meetings by interrupting the speakers with disruptive questions. Paul, probably like a lot of men and women in that congregation, lost his patience with them and told them, in strong words, to shut up. But this chapter is not about the position or rights of women; rather, it is about speaking out of turn. It is about orderly worship meetings in which all members can prophesy, both men and women, and in which all members have to know when to be silent, both men and women. It might well be that the overemphasis on verses 33–35 has prevented some churches (both Mennonite and non-Mennonite) from learning the real lessons of this chapter. Those verses have been lifted from their context and used to silence women in the church and reduce them to second-rate members of the congregation. In fact, it has become so normal for us women to be unequal that we have come to accept our suffering and loss of dignity. How can we escape from the explanation handed down by tradition? It is normal for men and women to accept women's second-rate position—isn't it?

Not quite. Time and again there have been courageous women and men who questioned every explanation handed down by tradition. Roman Catholic tradition was questioned in such a way, in the early sixteenth century, that people broke away from that church and formed new communities where quite different concepts, like the priesthood of all believers and the spiritual partnership of husband and wife in marriage, opened up new paths for women and men. Anabaptist women clearly showed their independence when they had to give witness to their persecutors. As we read in *Het Offer des Heeren* (*Sacrifice unto the Lord*) and the *Martyrs Mirror*, they were quite able to hold their own in the discussions with their interrogators. A good example is Elisabeth Dirks, killed in Leeuwarden in 1549. She had been apprehended because she was a teacher (preacher) in the Anabaptist congregation of Leeuwarden. The interrogators asked her to tell by oath whether she had a husband. Elisabeth answered, "We ought not to swear, but our words shall be yes, yes and no, no; I have no husband." The lords asked, "We want to know what people you have been teaching." Elisabeth replied, "Oh no, my lords, leave me in peace about this and ask me about my belief; it would please me to tell you about that."[3]

It was a dangerous and exciting time, but soon different times came. Influenced by what went on in society and in other churches, Mennonites forgot about the equality of men and women in their congregations. They became "the Quiet in the Land." Women receded into the dark background again, but the ferment was there. In the second half of the eighteenth century, women in the Mennonite congregations of southern Germany had voting rights.[4] In The Netherlands women became visible again in the congregations during the nineteenth century, and in 1911 Anna Zernike was ordained as teacher (preacher, minister) after having studied theology at the Mennonite Seminary in Amsterdam. Though in the beginning people found it strange, soon having female preachers became as normal as having male preachers among Mennonites. (Other Dutch churches followed much later or not at all.) Now all functions in the congregations and at the conference level are open to both the brothers and the sisters; not their sex but their abilities and their willingness to serve are important. And when, in 1980, the Dutch brotherhood celebrated its four hundred fiftieth birthday, the conference was chaired by a woman. This is a situation of equality that women in other churches and many parts of society still long for. The United Nations, recognizing the existing inequality, proclaimed 1975 "International Women's Year," which was followed by the "U.N. Women's Decade." Already in 1974 the World Council of Churches had convened a world consultation on discrimination against women: "Sexism in the Seventies." Sexism was named and recognized as oppression, as the refusal to give women their place in church and society. This led to studies within the member churches. In 1981 the Central Committee of the World Council of Churches agreed that "women make up over half the constituents of the member churches and half of the human family; the principle of men and women in partnership means equal participation." In 1988 the World Council of Churches started its own decade, the "Ecumenical Decade of Churches in Solidarity with Women." This could be the beginning of an era of hope for many women around the world for whom oppression and denial of dignity, both in church and in society, are still a daily experience.

The present-day situation of Mennonite women around the world is summed up by Nancy Heisey and Paul Longacre in their final report for the Mennonite International Study Project (July 25, 1989). After two years of studying and traveling all over the world, they wrote the following:

> Despite the writers' good intentions, we found it difficult in many places to have interviews with women. At times women were not present in meetings. At times they were present in the background, busy with the arrangements for hosting us—cooking, serving food, or preparing beds. At other times, they were included in interview sessions, but men answered questions for them even when the questions were directed to the women. Occasionally when we met with women alone we were hindered by their shyness or our lack of ability in their languages. Yet many of the women we talked to spoke clearly, with wisdom and refreshing perspectives. In every place, we heard that women are the heart of the church at the congregational level. They are the people who attend worship services regularly and bring children to church. Women do most of the work of primary evangelism with their neighbors. In African settings we also heard of women going in groups to visit and witness in areas farther away from their villages. Women function prac- tically as deacons, arranging for material assistance and moral support for Christians and other neighbors going through times of crisis. Often women contribute a large percentage of the congregation's budget. In some places women have their own organizations within the overall church structure. Only in rare cases do they take leadership roles in the church as a whole. There are at least two reasons for this; one is the fact that most church people are closed to the involvement of women in such roles. The other is that the demands on women to provide for the needs of their families are so great that they have no extra time for formal church work. (Quoted by permission.)

From my own experience in serving on international Mennonite committees, I know that female committee members sometimes are not really seen. Their opin- ion is not asked, and when they do make a contribution it is met with surprise.

Often they are only expected to serve the coffee or write the minutes. But I also know that things are changing. Slowly. Too slowly for all of us who are still being denied our full share of human dignity. But change there is, and to under-line that I gratefully cite from the Message of the Ninth Mennonite World Conference, held at Curitiba in 1972:

> We confess that the church is truly whole only when every brother and sister can share fully and equally regardless of race or class or nation. ... any witness for peace and for the service to the needs of humanity and taking of a responsible and critical position should be the concern of the whole church and of all its members, so we cannot but promote this need for a personal involvement and decision by all our brothers and sisters wherever they live or work. The message of reconciliation puts before the church the reality that a ministry of reconciliation can only be effective if the church itself is a reconciling community .... If we be ser-vants to one another we can stand the test of our ability to serve the world. Our mind has to be reshaped to the mind of Christ (Phil. 2) ....
> As followers of Jesus Christ we do raise a prophetic voice against all exercise of violent repression, persecution and unjust imprisonment, torture and death, particularly for political reasons. We object to racism and other forms of discrimination whether in our churches or in society at large. As Mennonites who in their history have experienced what persecution represents, we feel that the thankfulness for a quiet and undisturbed life cannot close our eyes to the many inequities that are in-herent to the social and economic structures of today's world. These structures have a violence in themselves and tend to lead men into dependency and exploitation. They cause the loss of self-respect and identity and they prevent the development of a community life. In a world in which the rich tend to become ever richer and the poor ever poorer, the gospel of Jesus Christ cannot but point a way to a human dignity in which all men could share. This human dignity finds its basis in the love of God for all men alike.[5]

If "men" in these last sentences can be read as "people" (and not as "males"), then I will say amen to this. For women are people. We really are.

Christina van Straten-Bargeman, The Netherlands, b. 1931, former teacher and current representative of the Dutch conference on several committees.
Translated by Ed van Straten.

Notes
1. Weininger, *Geschlecht und Character*, 25. Aufl. 1923, as cited by F.J.J. Buytendijk in *De Vrouw*, Spectrum, 1958: "Das Weib ist weder tiefsinnig noch hochsinnig, weder scharfsinnig noch geradsinnig, es ist vielmehr von alledem gerade das Gegenteil: es ist, soweit wir bisher sehen, überhaupt nicht sinnig: es ist als Ganzes Un-sinn, unsinnig."
2. In verse 34, the New English Bible translates "should be silent" as "should not address." It is the translator who says this, not Paul!
3. *Het Offer des Heeren*, Documenta Reformatoria I, Kok 1960.
4. *300 Jahre Mennonitengemeinde Weierhof*, 1982.
5. Paul N. Kraybill, editor, *Mennonite World Handbook*, Mennonite World Conference, Lombard, Illinois, 1978, pp. 6–8.

**This Thai woman is weaving baskets to be sold in SELFHELP Crafts stores in North America.
(MCC photo by Doris Daley, 1988)**

Why do Mennonites need theology?

by A. James Reimer

Theology has to do first and foremost with God. Theology is a human activity, subject to error and change, but it is about God. The prior question to "Should Mennonites have a theology?" is, "Do Mennonites believe in God?" The answer is not as self-evident as it might at first appear, particularly in the modern scientific age, and yet it is critical. Behind the question of God is the following: Is there something larger going on in the cosmos than human agency? Or are we on our own in our strategies to expand the church? to save the planet? to fight for social justice? to serve and give aid? to develop love and understanding among family, tribal, national, and ethno-religious groups? To say that we believe in Jesus, or in the church as a community of love, or in peace and nonresistance, or in social justice and human solidarity, is not the same as saying we believe in God. If we do not believe that a transcendent God creates, grounds, bears, and preserves the world and that this God is revealed in the historical person of Jesus Christ, and if we do not believe that God is present to us in the church and in the world as Holy Spirit (the very Spirit of Christ and of God), then there is no need for theology. For Christian theology is precisely the human attempt to reflect upon and understand what these three affirmations about God mean in our time.

Mennonites do not need a theology in the sense of striving after a separate, sectarian theology: a believers' church theology or an Anabaptist-Mennonite theology. Mennonites need to do Christian theology from the perspective of a group of ethno-religious traditions that call themselves Anabaptist-Mennonite. This collection of traditions can no longer be limited to those of Swiss, German, and Dutch ancestry but include, among others, a variety of African, Indian, Indonesian, Caribbean, and Japanese groups. What makes a theology Christian and what gives such a Christian theology an Anabaptist-Mennonite perspective are two of the basic questions facing us as a world conference of Mennonites meeting in Winnipeg in July 1990. The first is more important than the second.

What is Christian theology?

Theology is "faith seeking understanding" (Anselm). It is not faith itself. Nor can it replace faith. Faith and Christian experience (the direct encounter of individuals and groups with God) are primary. Theology as rational reflection on the various aspects of faith is secondary. Theology is faith trying to understand itself in the context of the modern world, in the light of its own ground: God as the trinitarian mystery of the world, revealed in Jesus Christ, and present to us in the Holy Spirit. It is nevertheless imperative that the Christian church, including the Mennonite church, engage in such second-level theological reflection. It is not sufficient to exegete the Bible and to understand the Bible in its various social and historical contexts. Nor is it sufficient to know the history of the church, with all its wrinkles, and our heterogeneous Anabaptist-Mennonite origins, with their variety of pacifist and nonpacifist wings. It is essential, to be sure, to give serious attention to the contraries of the biblical texts and the diversities of history, to what the text really says or does not say, or to what freight the historical data can or cannot bear. Biblical scholars and social historians need to keep theology honest, keep it from distorting the facts for its own purposes. The whole point of Christian theology, however, is to seek to understand the unifying work of God behind, underneath, or in the midst of all this past and present diversity without destroying that diversity. Theology seeks to understand and address the question, What is God doing in the world? It seeks an answer to this question assuming that the one God loves the diversity of ethnicities, cultures, and religious expressions while at the same time moving as the Holy Spirit to unite all in Christ.

In an interesting 1948 article, "Philosophy in the Mennonite Tradition," Mennonite educator and churchman J.E. Hartzler argued that philosophy is a good thing and that Mennonites have and ought to have a definite philosophy.[1] The task of philosophy, he said, is to seek "meanings, interpretations, of things and events; meanings in history; meaning of God in human experience; meaning of truth and reality. Philosophy means interpretative insight." Hartzler had too sanguine a view of reason and science. The atrocities of the modern period, domination, exploitation, oppression, economic disparity, the continuing nuclear threat, the havoc wreaked on the environment by modern science, technology, and rapacious human consumption have all contributed to a disillusionment with the unqualified confidence in human rationality implicit in Hartzler's call for Mennonite philosophizing. Nor is there sufficient place given in his article to the role of the social sciences for philosophy and theology. Hartzler's basic point, however, needs to be heard by the Mennonite church today: we need to "become more vocal in the Christian interpretation of history and the world movements of today." Hartzler calls this the task of philosophy. I consider this the task also of theology. But what distinguishes Christian theology from philosophy is that it is much more specific in the categories it uses to interpret "things and events; meanings in history; meaning of God in human experience; meaning of truth and reality." It is not free-floating interpretation of events; it is interpretation through Christian categories that emerge from the biblical texts themselves and have been developed and refined in the history of the church through the centuries, particularly in its early classical period. Those who disregard the wisdom of the ages in the interpretation of the biblical texts bear the burden of proof.

What are these Christian theological categories? They are what I would call the classical Christian doctrines that find expression in the confessions of the early

New Testament and patristic church and are elaborated upon by the various Protestant confessions of the modern period (from the Reformation to the present), including the myriad of confessions and catechisms produced by Mennonites from the sixteenth century to the present. These are the traditional foci of systematic or dogmatic theology, organized around the three central affirmations in the Christian doctrine of God: God as transcendent creator of the world, God as historically revealed in Christ, and God as immanently present in the world as Holy Spirit. The one God in three modes of being. This threefold affirmation about God is the essential element of all Christian theology. All the other doctrinal categories of classical theological reflection (Creation, Fall-Redemption, and Consummation, including a variety of subdoctrines) grow out of these three core affirmations. That these categories emerge from the kerygma of the early New Testament community itself and are not forcibly imposed on the early tradition by the later church is attested to by passages such as John 1, Acts 2:22–38, 1 Cor. 8:5–6, Phil. 2:5–11, Col. 1. In short, Christian theology begins and ends with God. History and human action are important for Christian theology only as they reflect what God is doing in the world.

The two tasks of Christian theology

The task of theology is twofold: criticism and mediation. The first, criticism, is the prophetic-eschatological function of theology in which theology examines critically the tradition—classical texts, doctrines, institutions—and contemporary, idolatrous distortions of the tradition in the light of the anticipated kingdom of God. All forms of religion, including the Christian religion, need constantly to be subjected to such theological criticism, because religion (including the Mennonite religion) is particularly prone to idolatry—the absolutizing of human language; human doctrines; human interpretations; human cultures, customs and ethnicities; and human projects. In fulfilling its critical role, theology expresses God's "No" or judgment on all human pretensions and acts as a radical trans-forming and reforming force in church and society in the light of what once was and what ought to be. Here the preacher and theologian call for repentance, conversion, and nonconformity. It is this prophetic quality that characterizes in a special way the Anabaptist-Mennonite perspective. The second task of theology, mediation, might be called the priestly-sacramental function. It seeks not so much to pronounce judgment and stand over-against as to be comprehensive, to integrate, and to conciliate between conflicting positions. In this role theology stresses the positive aspects of what God is doing in individual lives, the church, and the world—God's "Yes" to creation. A preacher, counselor, or theologian who emphasizes God's love, grace, mercy, forgiveness, and acceptance is operating within the mediating sphere of theology. While both the critical and the mediatorial are important tasks for theology, I would like in the remainder of this article to reflect on the mediating function of theology with reference to three areas: the Bible, history, and the contemporary situation.

Theology and the Bible

The Bible is the primary classic for all Christian theologizing. It is "the authoritative word of God, and through the Holy Spirit ... the infallible Guide to lead men to faith in Christ and to guide them in the life of Christian discipleship" (Dordrecht Confession, Article 2). To make this affirmation is to say that the positions we take on issues such as abortion, homosexuality, divorce and remarriage, ordination, capital punishment, the use of violence in policing, biomedical ethics, politics, and business ought ultimately to be grounded in the Scriptures. This is where difficulties begin, however, because on many contemporary issues the Bible does not speak directly or with one single voice. It is this fact, and not simply apostasy, that has been responsible for many of the divisions within the universal Christian community and within the Mennonite communion.

The fact is that the Bible is a collection of sixty-six books: thirty-nine Old Testament and twenty-seven New Testament, with a series of disputed books entitled the Apocrypha (incidentally, accepted by most Anabaptists as canonical). The Old Testament books, more accurately known as the Hebrew Scriptures, are composed of materials written over approximately one thousand years and divided into legal, historical, wisdom, and prophetic literature. The New Testament writings, written over about a seventy-year period (A.D. 50 to 120), are made up of a variety of types of books—gospels, letters, epistles, apocalypse—not to mention the multiplicity of literary genre incorporated into the books (confessions, hymns, liturgies, narratives, parables, etc.). The church's decision as to which of these books should be included in what we call the canon itself took two to three hundred years. The point is that this library of books we call the Bible was written over a period of over a millennium and consists of a great diversity of material written in widely divergent historical, social, and political circ: :nces from many different historical and religious perspectives.

How is one to hear the word of God through all this diversity? I suggest that we read the whole Bible, beginning at the beginning and ending at the end, and then turn it upside down and read it again. I suggest that we enjoy the diversity and let our imagination play with the material, making connections here and there—backward and forward, upward and downward. Struggle with it. Fight with it. Disagree with it. But take it seriously as the authoritative texts that must be engaged on every level: the literal, historical, analogical, and imaginative. Particularly those parts that we do not understand or that go against our personal inclinations or against the assumptions of our age need to be engaged. It is precisely the diversity—the seeming contraries, the many dimensions—that make the Bible so comprehensive and universal in its scope. But why is theology so important for reading the Bible? Because theology seeks to understand God as transcendent mystery of the world, God as addressing us historically in Christ, and God as empowering us as Holy Spirit. It is this fundamental trinitarian affirmation that for Christians finally makes of this library of books a canon (an authoritative standard) for the church. The Bible is not God; it is the vehicle by which God addresses us individually and corporately. It is theological from cover to cover. It is faith seeking understanding. To understand what the Bible is all about, we too need to think theologically. The biblical writers did not neutrally record historical facts; inspired by God, they selected which historical events they were going to record and interpreted those events from the perspective of faith—that is, on the basis of what they believed God was doing in the world. Theology is important in bridging the diversity within the Bible itself and finding the themes that unify the multiplicity of literary units and seemingly contradicting stories, moral injunctions, and religious experiences into a whole.

What are the common themes that bind all together? From its earliest reflection on this question, the Christian church has asserted that the Bible needs to be read as a great drama: the drama of Creation, the Fall, Redemption, and Consummation. This is a theological reading of the Bible, for it assumes something the pure historian cannot: it believes that behind all the social, historical, political, and economic diversity contained within the Bible there is a God who created the world and continues to act upon and in the world, and that this God addresses us through the Bible. When we read the Bible, we believe we are not only learning about ancient cultures, or how God acted upon and was experienced by those cultures, but we believe that God is speaking to us right now through the words of the Scriptures. We believe that through prayer, openness to the leading of the Holy Spirit, and individual and communal reading and reflection on the Bible we can learn what God can and is doing in the world, the church, and our own lives.

Like their sixteenth-century Protestant counterparts (the Lutherans and the Calvinists), the Anabaptists emphasized the authoritative centrality of the Scriptures for the church rather than popes, councils, dogmas, and traditions. But diversity among the Anabaptists on how exactly to view and interpret the Scriptures quickly became evident. There were those who interpreted the Bible quite literally as a guide for Christian doctrine and church life and organization. Others distinguished between the "outer word" and the "inner word," emphasizing the priority of the inner voice of God, or the eternal word over the written Scriptures. The external words of the Bible were, they believed, important signs pointing to the living word of God.[2] The point is that while for early Anabaptists the Scriptures were normative, there was considerable diversity of opinion on how the Scriptures were authoritative. The role of theology is to provide us with thematic categories by which to mediate between the diversity within the Scriptures themselves, between different interpretations of the Scriptures, and between the Scriptural texts and every new generation.

Theology and history

Much of what we have said about the Bible can be said about history and the historical method. History is messy; it consists of an abundance of seemingly disconnected historical facts, capricious events, and conflicting movements (religious and secular). The historian's task is to describe these phenomena as fairly and objectively as possible without distorting them ideologically or seeking coherence where there is none. To be sure, the historian is interested in causes, influences, and connections; but he cannot as historian methodologically bring into his analysis metaphysical or supernatural factors. Yet the urgent moral issues facing us in the modern world demand that we move beyond such purely descriptive and empirical analysis of historical events. If we are to act as responsible human beings in the world, we will need to address the normative questions that history raises for us: What is right and what is wrong? What ought we to do? To see ourselves as moral beings with the freedom to make moral decisions is to presuppose suprahistorical or spiritual dimensions to existence that transcend historical necessity or caprice. At the point where the historian ventures into this prescriptive and normative area, he is moving out of his discipline into the field of philosophy or theology. We need systematic theology to address such normative questions: What ought we to believe and do? Where do we go from here?

Mennonites have an ambivalence toward tradition and history. Our leading Mennonite theologian and ethicist, John Howard Yoder, has written a provocative essay, "Anabaptism and History," which illustrates this ambivalence.[3] On the one hand, Yoder's emphasis on historical discontinuity and suspicion of ongoing tradition appears to reflect a historical approach. He urges the Christian historian in the Radical Reformation tradition to adopt the term "Restitutionism" as the proper word to describe the Anabaptist-Mennonite attitude toward history. Restitutionism represents a "thought pattern" with three historical stages: (1) the "normative" state of the Christian church (representing New Testament Christianity); (2) the "Fall" of the church (Constantinian and post-Constantinian Christianity—the alliance of church and state, conformity to the world most clearly manifested in the rejection of early Christian pacifism in favor of the just war; and (3) "Radical Renewal"—not simply a return to the past but "a continuing series of new beginnings [elsewhere described as a 'looping back' in the analogy of a vine]."[4] Furthermore, "The visible church defined by succession," he says, "has apostasized. There can be no cure in continuity with what is, because the organ of continuity is itself in enemy hands and must not be granted control of the peace or shape of reformation."[5] On the other hand, Yoder argues that Radical Reformation Christianity was not ahistorical or apolitical, as is frequently charged, but truly historicist: (1) history is seriously studied to see what went wrong in the fourth century; (2) the freedom and responsibility of human beings to make choices within history and determinative of history is affirmed; and (3) a historical criterion ("the very particular story of the New Testament") is used as the standard by which to criticize later historical development ("state/church linkage, episcopacy, and pedobaptism"). According to Yoder, "the claims of Christ, by virtue precisely of their historical objectivity and distance, enable a genuine catholicity [accessible equally to all]. Pointedly said: only the mental structure of restitutionism can be at once Christian and serious about history."[6]

Yoder's historical theology does justice to one legitimate task of Christian theology: the critical (prophetic-eschatological) role of theology; but it does not, in my opinion, adequately express the equally important mediating (priestly-sacramental) function of theology: theology that detects the historical continuities within each of a variety of historical ethno-religious traditions as reflected in the ongoing gracious presence of God in the ordinary institutional, family, and economic life of peoples with all the frailties and foibles of human existence.

In the modern world we tend not to think of time as enfolded in eternity but as linear, historical movement from past to present to future. We define things, people, and movements horizontally in terms of their historical beginnings and future potentiality rather than vertically in their relation to natural or supernatural reality. We have absolutized history as the arena of human freedom. Much contemporary theology also has taken history, historical action, and forward directionality as definitive for Christian thinking about God. History is important, and human freedom is to be theologically affirmed. Nevertheless, Christian theology must continue to insist that time and history are temporal realities that take on meaning only within a theocentric framework: God as both the transcending and grounding mystery of the history of the world, God as personally incarnated within history, and God present to history as Spirit. Theology reflects on what makes history meaningful in the light of this threefold affirmation.

Theology and the contemporary situation

A primary responsibility of theology is to proclaim the Christian message to the contemporary world in language that the world can understand, with answers to the genuine questions that the world is asking. In order to do this, however, theology needs to understand the modern world, to analyze and diagnose the age with the help of all the various disciplines and skills available to the church. One of the difficulties of knowing how to address the present situation is that people disagree on what the most pressing problems and questions of the world are.

Three of the primary issues facing us, I believe, are (1) the global triumph of modern technology and its negative consequences for our planet; (2) growing economic disparity, political oppression, and social injustice; and (3) religious pluralism and the question of truth in a relativistic age. The first might be called the neoconservative agenda. Here the assumptions of modern science, historical progress, and unlimited human freedom are seriously questioned. There is a yearning for transcendence and the re-enchantment of nature. The second is the radical agenda. Here the primary problem is not technology but poverty, exploitation, and marginalization, particularly of the Third World by the First World. This agenda calls precisely for that which the first agenda tends to reject: historical freedom to change things and shape the future, frequently through technological means. The third, or liberal agenda, is more concerned with intra-Christian and interreligious dialogue, understanding, and tolerance. Each of these has its theological advocates in the Christian community, including the Mennonite church. Each reflects legitimate concerns of our age even though they represent competing interests and frequently conflict with each other.

To cite chapter and verse or to draw on any particular variety of sixteenth-century Anabaptism alone will not give us adequate answers to these pressing scientific, ethical, and religious issues. What is needed is serious theological reflection that stands in continuity with the Scriptures and historical wisdom. I suggest that the three articles of the *Credo* are a fruitful starting point for just such theological reflection on the above three contemporary agendas. The issues raised by modern technology might be addressed by reflecting on God as transcendent mystery of the world and the Judeo-Christian doctrine of creation, a doctrine that has not received nearly enough attention by Mennonites. The second—social and economic justice—could be considered under a doctrine of Christ in which "the dangerous memory of Jesus" is kept alive. The doctrine of the Holy Spirit—God's working in the world in ways not easily definable by religious and denominational boundaries—offers interesting possibilities for the third set of issues: religious pluralism and ecumenical concerns.

Mennonites can no longer claim that they are not part of contemporary culture. As recent sociological studies show, Mennonites participate in virtually every level of modern societies: big business, political office, civil service, academia, the full spectrum of professional careers, blue collar jobs, union work, and so on. How is the Mennonite Christian to live with the ambiguities of modern culture on the one hand and the moral and ethical demands of Jesus in the face of poverty and injustice on the other. This is where the Mennonite church now needs the mediating and critical power of dogmatic and systematic theology. For theology is not primarily individuals privately reflecting on the great truths but the church seeking understanding in the light of the Bible and its own history. I agree with Ivor Shapiro when he says in a recent critical analysis of The United Church of Canada, "Without dogma, the church has only one dynamic—social activism."[7] Dogma is the church reflecting on and expressing theologically what it believes and stands for. We need this kind of theology as Mennonites.

A. James Reimer, Canada, b. 1942, M.A. in history, Ph.D. in theology, associate professor of religious studies and theology and director of graduate studies at Conrad Grebel College (Waterloo, Ontario), and adjunct professor of theology at Toronto School of Theology.

Notes
1. J.E. Hartzler, "Philosophy in the Mennonite Tradition," *Mennonite Life*, Vol. III, No. 2, April 1948, pp. 43–45.
2. Walter Klaassen, editor, *Anabaptism in Outline*, Herald Press, Kitchener, Ontario, 1981, pp. 140–142.
3. John Howard Yoder, "Anabaptism and History," *The Priestly Kingdom: Social Ethics as Gospel*, University of Notre Dame Press, Notre Dame, Indiana, 1984, pp. 123–134.
4. Yoder, "The Authority of Tradition," *The Priestly Kingdom*, p. 69.
5. Yoder, "Anabaptism and History," p. 125.
6. Ibid., p. 130.
7. Ivor Shapiro, "The Benefit of the Doubt," *Saturday Night*, Vol. 102, No. 3, April 1990, p. 40.

Mennonite identity

by Rod J. Sawatsky

Who are the Mennonites? What does it mean to be a Mennonite? These are questions of Mennonite identity that are repeatedly asked both inside and outside the Mennonite community. Perhaps as Mennonites we have greater difficulty in defining who we are than do other Christian communities. Even if identity is not a peculiarly Mennonite problem, identifying some of the reasons why Mennonite identity is at least frequently ambiguous will prepare us for an unapologetic formulation of Mennonite identity.

Mennonites are first and foremost Christians, even "radical" Christians. The Mennonite movement began with the sixteenth-century Anabaptists. These Anabaptists agreed that the main-line reformers such as the Lutherans, Calvinists, and Anglicans were not radical enough; that is, they had not gone to the root of the problems in the church and society and to the root of the answers as found in the Scriptures. Those Anabaptists with whom contemporary Mennonites identify insisted that such a radical reform required a recovery of Jesus—his life and teachings, his death and resurrection—as normative for each individual Christian and every gathered community of believers. Because their radicalism challenged both church and state, especially the union of church and state, they experienced extreme persecution.

Although these earliest of Mennonites shared common commitments and emphases, they were not united around a common leader as were the Lutherans. Menno Simons gained considerable authority in northern Europe for some time, but his leadership was not accepted by nearly all. Neither did the Anabaptists accept any other authority besides the Bible, although attempts were made to gain unity around other writings such as the Schleitheim Confession, the *Martyrs Mirror*, and the Dordrecht Confession. As in their scattered communities of worship and discipline they sought to be faithful to Jesus as revealed in Scriptures, the Anabaptists exhibited considerable independence of thought and resistance to compromise even at the expense of unity. The tendency to divide into subgroupings, or at least not to unite—a characteristic of much of Mennonite history—is, accordingly, rooted in its Anabaptist origins. Differences on detail as to what it means to be faithful disciples of Jesus and to be the true church of Jesus Christ have divided the Mennonite community and added complexity to defining Mennonite identity.

"Mennonite" is ambiguous in definition for several other basic reasons. Again dating back to its beginnings, the Mennonite tradition embraces an inherent tension between sectarian separation from the world and missionary responsibility to the world. Some of the many Mennonite subdivisions emphasize one or the other of these two, while other Mennonite groups seek a synthesis of them.

Accordingly, the term Mennonite identifies those strictly separatist groups known for their rejection of modern culture including, for some, modern technology. These are the most visible Mennonites, and hence they influence the understanding of "Mennonite" by the general public out of all proportion to their numbers. In fact, sociologists frequently look to them as archetypical sectarians. By contrast, "Mennonite" also identifies adjectivally a number of denominations identified less by their separatism than by their active involvement worldwide alongside many other Christian denominations in education, publishing, mission, and service. Almost innumerable institutions and organizations labeled Mennonite pursue this denominational agenda. The vast majority of Mennonites are of this less separatist and more activist persuasion, yet the former create the more identifiable public image.

"Mennonite" is also ambiguous because it has both ethnic and religious connotations. The quest to nurture their vision of the true church in peace and quiet and to separate themselves from a hostile and evil world has encouraged Mennonites over the centuries to pursue a strategy of relative ideological and geographical withdrawal. Assisted by the practice of marrying within the group and other mechanisms of boundary maintenance, the Mennonites over time developed a sense of being a unique people—even an ethnic group. Indeed, the sociologist E.K. Francis developed his seminal definition of ethnicity on the basis of a study of the Mennonites in Russia and southern Manitoba. The fact that frequent migrations, undertaken either voluntarily or under pressure, had robbed them of a national identity further assisted this process of creating a Mennonite ethnicity. Although the ethnicity was based on religious rather than racial or national distinctives, that idea of Mennonite has had, at least until quite recently, both religious and ethnic meanings, particularly in Russia and in North and South America. This cannot be denied.

Mennonite ethnicity is, however, not uniform. In the past Mennonites divided essentially into two ethnic groupings—the Swiss/South German/Pennsylvanian and the Dutch/North German/Russian—each with various subgroupings. Prior to the twentieth century at least two ethnic traditions of Mennonite language, customs, dress, art, food, etc., are identifiable. For various historical reasons, however, in North America the Dutch tradition became the more ethnic while the Swiss remained the more sectarian. But the processes of acculturation, especially in the twentieth century, are rapidly transforming both traditional Mennonite ethnicity and sectarianism. Additionally, and most importantly, as a product of Mennonite missions since the late 1900s, numerous other ethnicities now share the name Mennonite, with the result that "Mennonite" is increasingly becoming ethnically heterogeneous. A Mennonite identity that is characterized as a Germanic ethnic subculture still remains in certain areas, but is increasingly anachronistic in the face of contemporary reality. If present growth patterns persist, the original two European ethnicities will before long be minorities in the larger Mennonite family.

But if Mennonite, at least in some areas, still refers to an ethnic group entered by birth as well as a religious community entered by adult decision, who is then a Mennonite? The confusion is related to the rite of becoming a member in a Mennonite church. While it is clear that one becomes a Mennonite upon baptism into a Mennonite church as an adult, the children born into Mennonite homes tend also to be considered Mennonite until they are baptized. Frequently, even if they do not choose to be baptized, they continue to be considered or to consider themselves to be Mennonite. Emphasis upon the Christian family and on Christian nurture encourages a more inclusive definition of Mennonite than the strong emphasis on adult voluntarism might imply. This same issue arises in those countries where Mennonites have gone in mission and added numerous other ethnicities to the Mennonite household. Is a child or grandchild of a Mennonite community in India, who is herself only nominally Christian, considered to be a Mennonite, particularly if this person has been acculturated into the uniqueness of the Indian Mennonite subculture and become distanced from the regional Hindu culture in the process? This so-called "second generation" reality is the fourth factor complicating the meaning of "Mennonite," even though it is hardly unique to Mennonites.

Further reasons could be cited for the ambiguity of the term "Mennonite," e.g., the variety of theological, political, and cultural perspectives found under the Mennonite banner. The Mennonite community worldwide embraces the entire spectrum from theological liberal to evangelical, social activist to separationist, "high" culture to folk culture. Furthermore, as already noted, the word Mennonite is used in so many different ways: as an adjective, as a noun, as an adverb, and even as a verb—it is seemingly possible to "Mennonite your way," i.e., stay with other Mennonites while traveling.

Because the term Mennonite embraces such variety and ambiguity, some Mennonites periodically argue that the name may be more a hindrance than a help. In North America at least two formerly Mennonite denominations have dropped the label and no longer identify with the larger family of Mennonites represented in Mennonite World Conference. Recently some leaders of the Mennonite Brethren Church in Canada have asked if the Mennonite label compromises their evangelical message. A number of congregations in this denomination no longer identify themselves as Mennonite, apparently to avoid the ethnic and perhaps separatist connotations of the term. A current proposal is to identify themselves as Evangelical Anabaptists, thereby emphasizing the theological orientation rather than all the additional associations tied to the word Mennonite.

Most Mennonites worldwide seem, however, not to be particularly troubled by the Mennonite label. Indeed many, and perhaps most, carry it with considerable pride. (Even though Mennonites are to be humble!) For these people the ethnic dimension of "Mennonite" has little relevance or is not problematical; and, more importantly, the variety embraced by the term Mennonite is not a cause for alarm but of celebration. This celebration of Mennonite variety and this pride of being Mennonite does not deny the limitations and even contradictions of the Mennonite "earthen vessel," but strongly affirms the "treasure" of this particular Christian tradition.

Having acknowledged some of the variety and ambiguity of this earthen vessel labeled Mennonite, what for most Mennonites today is the treasure that is the essence of Mennonite identity? Mennonite identity is:

1.   Located in community, particularly in local communities of faith and worship, love and mutual aid, entered voluntarily through adult baptism; communities that support and are supported by the family, the primary building block of God's work in the world; and communities that invite all people near and far to share the embrace of God's love and peace.
2.   Shaped by history, God's activity in history throughout time, especially as recorded in the Bible; a particular story of shame and glory spanning nearly five centuries, beginning with the Anabaptists; a story that embraces an ever-widening circle of races, cultures, and ethnicities; and a story that will conclude only when God makes all things new.
3.   Defined by the incarnation, Jesus Christ who lived among us and taught us the way of life, who died and rose from the grave, thereby shattering the principalities and powers including death; God with us in full and complete revelation inviting us to faith and faithfulness as disciples of Jesus.
4.   Inspired by the kingdom, the kingdom of God, which is God's rule of righteousness and peace and justice on earth as it is in heaven; the primary loyalty above any worldly (ideological, political, economic, cultural) allegiance; calling for nonconformity and nonviolence and for the active pursuit of God's rule in all the world.
5.   Expressed in service, utilizing all our gifts in vocations, avocations, and specialized ministries for building the church, seeking the kingdom, and enriching culture and society; generously contributing time, talents, and financial resources to establishing and supporting the numerous agencies of service to respond to the needs of all human beings both near and far.
6.   Empowered by the Spirit, who by God's grace works in, among, and through us to transform us; who chides and encourages us to lives of faithful discipleship without regard to race, sex, or ethnicity; and who makes possible personal and communal growth toward the high calling of becoming God's sons and daughters and of being the body of Christ—the church.
7.   Rooted in God, who was, and is, and ever shall be; who created all things and calls us to ecologically responsible stewardship of all creation; and to whom be praise and glory in all our worship and work now and evermore.

This is Mennonite identity.

Rod J. Sawatsky, Canada, b. 1943, Ph.D. in history, president of Conrad Grebel College (Waterloo, Ontario).

Mennonites: A confessional Christian people?

by Marlin E. Miller

Mennonites have likely written and adopted more confessions of faith than any other group that came out of the reformation movements in sixteenth-century Europe. Some European and many North American Mennonite confessions of faith fill a large book (Howard John Loewen's *One Lord, One Church, One Hope, and One God*, 1985). Mennonites on other continents have also written statements of faith. In some instances, Mennonites have adopted already existing confessions of faith. For example, Indonesian Mennonites have adopted the Apostles' Creed, one of the earliest and most widely recognized Christian confessions of faith. In still other cases, Mennonites have become members of interchurch organizations and have subscribed to their confessional statements.

The occasions and purposes of Mennonite confessions of faith have varied rather markedly over the centuries. Some of the early "confessions" were written by individuals such as Hans Denk, Balthasar Hubmaier, Pilgram Marpeck, Dirk Philips, Peter Riedemann, and Menno Simons. Sometimes these confessional statements responded to specific accusations of heresy from other church groups or theologians. Sometimes they served to defend Anabaptist and Mennonite convictions during court trials. Sometimes they summarized central beliefs and practices for instructional purposes in the congregations.

Other confessions of faith were originally consensus statements about Christian beliefs and practices. They were written to resolve internal controversies, to build unity between church leaders and the groups they represented, and to summarize teachings and practices that may distinguish Anabaptists and Mennonites in relation to other church groups.

Frequently the same consensus statement served several of these purposes. For example, the [Swiss] Schleitheim Articles of 1527 express agreement on specific points of controversy among several Anabaptist groups and on matters where they differ from the Reformed churches: baptism, the ban, the breaking of bread, separation from evil in the world, pastors, the sword, and the oath. The [Dutch] Dordrecht Articles written at a "peace convention" in 1632 also sought to resolve controversy and to move several groups toward consensus and unity. The eighteen articles summarize agreement on central beliefs and practices, beginning with God and creation, and terminating with the resurrection of the dead and the last judgment. They also include all the points treated in the Schleitheim Articles. Partly because Dordrecht is more comprehensive than Schleitheim, it has frequently been used for instructing new believers in some Mennonite congregations in several countries since the seventeenth century.

Two North American Mennonite groups are presently working on a common confession of faith as a means of developing consensus on central Christian beliefs and practices. The General Conference Mennonite Church and the Mennonite Church began to discuss a common confessional statement in 1984. They are planning to complete the process in 1995, God willing, when the two delegate bodies will consider whether to adopt the proposed statement. In the meantime, preliminary drafts of specific articles are being discussed and tested within the two church bodies. The preliminary drafts will also be tested with several sisters and brothers outside North America for advice and counsel. The present format of the statement and the process of developing specific articles for the confession of faith are designed with a view to developing consensus on central Christian beliefs and practices from a Mennonite perspective.

The current draft of the article on baptism can illustrate the content as well as the format and process for developing a confessional statement as a means of building consensus in the church:

Baptism

The baptism of believers with water is a sign of their cleansing from sin and a pledge before the church of their covenant with God to walk in the way of Jesus Christ through the power of the Holy Spirit. Believers are baptized into Christ by the Spirit, water, and blood.

Baptism is a testimony to God's gift of the Holy Spirit and the continuing work of the Holy Spirit in the lives of believers. Through the Holy Spirit we repent and turn toward God in faith. The baptism of the Holy Spirit enables believers to walk in newness of life, to live in community with Christ and the church, to offer Christ's healing and forgiveness to those in need, to witness boldly to the good news of Christ, and to hope in the sharing of Christ's future glory.

Baptism by water is a sign that a person has received forgiveness from sin, died to sin (Rom. 6:1–4), repented, and renounced evil through the grace of God in Christ Jesus. Thus cleansed, believers are incorporated into Christ's body on earth, the church. Baptism by water is also a pledge for service to Christ and for ministry as members of his body according to the gifts given to each one. Jesus himself requested water baptism at the beginning of his ministry and sent his followers to "make disciples of all nations, baptizing them in the name of the Father and of the Son and of the Holy Spirit" (Matt. 28:19). Baptism is necessary for believers as obedience to Jesus' command and as a public commitment to identification with Jesus Christ, not only in his baptism by water, but in his life in the Spirit and in his death in suffering love.

The baptism of blood, or baptism of suffering, is the offering of one's life, even to death. Jesus understood the giving of his life through the shedding of his blood for others as a baptism (Luke 12:50). He also spoke about his disciples' suffering and death as a baptism (Mark 10:38). Those who accept water baptism commit themselves to follow Jesus in giving their lives for others, in loving their enemies, and in renouncing violence, even when it means their own suffering or death.

Christian baptism is for those who confess their sins, repent, accept Jesus Christ as Savior and Lord, and commit themselves to follow Christ in obedience as members of his body. Baptism is for those who are of the age of accountability and who freely request baptism on the basis of their response to Jesus Christ in faith.

Commentary

First John 5:6–8 summarizes three central aspects of baptism: "There are three witnesses, the Spirit, the water, and the blood; and these three agree." This passage refers, first of all, to Jesus' baptism and also throws light on the baptism of all believers. The witness of the New Testament as a whole is that believers are to identify with Jesus: those who share his ministry will also share his suffering and know the power of the same Spirit.

The baptism of the Holy Spirit: According to the New Testament, water baptism and baptism with the Spirit are closely connected, though not always in the same way. The Holy Spirit rested on Jesus at the time of his baptism (John 1:33), and John the Baptist called Jesus the one who would baptize with the Holy Spirit (Mark 1:8). In the Acts of the Apostles, new believers received the Holy Spirit before, with, or after water baptism. The gift of the Holy Spirit is an "advance installment" of believers' participation not only in the death of Christ, but also in his resurrection (Eph. 1:13–14).

The baptism of water: Baptism has its roots in the Old Testament practice of ceremonially washing what was unclean, whether that uncleanness came through disease, moral sin, or other cause. Through ceremonial cleansing, those who had been unclean came into fellowship with God and with the community (see the book of Leviticus: for example, Lev. 14:1–9; 17:15–16; 18:24–30). Gentiles who accepted God's commandments and the Jewish faith were initiated into the covenant people with proselyte baptism. John the Baptist, the Apostle Peter, and the early church stood in this tradition when they proclaimed that baptism meant repentance. Christian water baptism signifies the cleansing of the person from sin and incorporation into the new community of faith.

Scripture also refers to baptism as a pledge to God (1 Pet. 3:21) and as a commitment to faithfulness and ministry. Jesus' own baptism can be seen in the light of this pledge. In the New Testament, baptism follows a person's faith, in the sense of faith in, and faithfulness to, a covenant-relationship. Baptism therefore is for those who are ready to enter a faithful relationship with Christ and the church.

Thus, baptism is always to be done by the church and its representatives, publicly if possible. Baptism means a commitment to membership and service in a particular congregation. Since baptism involves commitment, water baptism is to be reserved for those old enough to make such a pledge. Children have no need for baptism, since they are safe in the care of God. When they reach the age of accountability, they are able to make the church's faith their own.

The baptism of blood: Baptism by water is also a pledge of the believer's acceptance of the baptism of suffering and death. The Apostle Paul refers to water baptism to speak of our identification with Christ in being buried with him "by baptism into death, so that as Christ was raised from the dead by the glory of the Father, we too might walk in newness of life" (Rom. 6:3–4). Those who are baptized with water make a covenant to follow Jesus' way of the cross.

Recommendations in areas of differing practice:
(1) The mode of baptism may be by pouring, immersion, or sprinkling of water. Each of these signifies the cleansing of baptism. Immersion emphasizes the believer's participation in the death and resurrection of Christ (Rom. 6:3–4; Col. 2:12), while pouring and sprinkling emphasize the pouring out of the Holy Spirit upon the believer (Acts 2:17; Titus 3:5–7). (2) Persons who have been baptized as infants and wish to become members of a Mennonite congregation will normally be encouraged to request water baptism as a sign of accepting the meaning of Christian baptism. Churches may consider the transfer of membership unaccompanied by baptism if applicants for membership who were baptized as infants have since publicly confessed or confirmed faith in Jesus Christ, have long been living a life of faith and Christian witness, have been actively participating in a Christian congregation, and commit themselves henceforth to teach and practice baptism for those of an age of accountability who freely request it.

Note first of all that the article is divided into two parts: a statement on baptism itself and a commentary on the statement. The first part summarizes the meaning of baptism. The second part, namely the commentary, gives the basis and further background for the content of the first part. The commentary thus serves the consensus-building process by elaborating what the confession of faith committee had in mind in preparing the proposed statement. The commentary implicitly invites broader conversation and evaluation of both the statement itself and of the basis for the statement. (This draft of the article has already made several revisions based on the discussions at a joint churchwide conference in the summer of 1989 and on counsel received from several people from the two church groups. The committee has also taken some of the advice as confirming the initial draft and has therefore not made some changes that some people have suggested.)

Note secondly that the commentary contains two parts, namely the commentary as such and recommendations on points where practices currently differ among congregations. These recommendations are included in the commentary rather than in the statement on baptism because they carry less weight than what is said about baptism in the statement itself. At the same time, because these differences in practice are both significant and controversial, the proposals for developing greater consensus are put in the commentary to test them as valid implications of what is said about baptism in the first part of the article. In the case of baptism, the differing practices occur within each of the participating church groups rather than between them. Developing a confession of faith in this way is therefore intended to build greater consensus within as well as between the participating church groups.

Third, the proposed article on baptism illustrates the attempt to move toward consensus on theological issues. For example, the "baptism of the Holy Spirit" and its relation to water baptism has become a disputed issue among some of the congregations through the influence of Neo-Pentecostal and Charismatic movements in the last two decades. The article refers to baptism by the Spirit before speaking about the bap' m by water and by suffering. This order makes the theological point that God's initiative precedes and enables human response without replacing it. The commentary also observes that, in the New Testament, baptism by the Spirit and baptism with water are closely connected and that both may occur together or the one may follow the other. According to Scripture, therefore, experiences of spiritual renewal that occur after water baptism should not be elevated to the normative understanding of baptism by the Holy Spirit (as would be the case in some Neo-Pentecostal and Charismatic views). Simultaneously, the article states that "baptism" includes both baptism by the Spirit and baptism by water rather than assuming that baptism by the Spirit is automatically given and guaranteed by water baptism (as would be the case with some sacramental views).

Fourth, the article on baptism illustrates an effort to incorporate Anabaptist and Mennonite emphases into the proposed statement on Christian baptism. For example, several Anabaptist writers understood the meaning of baptism to include the readiness to suffer for Christ's sake. Mennonites and other Christians have frequently forgotten this emphasis, even though it is based on the New Testament and on an understanding of the Christian life as following Christ in life. Another example is the view of baptism as a "pledge." Anabaptist and Mennonite traditions have underlined this dimension to supplement and correct sacramentalist understandings, which tend to exclude the believer's commitment from the churchly act of baptism. These distinctively Anabaptist and Mennonite emphases are included to preserve the best in this particular tradition. They are also included as a means of encouraging conversation with other Christian groups about baptism. That is to say, the emphasis on baptism as including the readiness to suffer and a pledge to follow Christ should be seen as Christian and not only as peculiarly Mennonite views. Taking this claim seriously means that Mennonites would commend this understanding to other Christians. Taking this claim seriously also means that Mennonites would be open to testing this understanding with and learning from other Christians.

Fifth, the final form of this proposed confession of faith may or may not include the commentary. One reason for having commentaries on each article is to encourage movement to broader consensus. If that purpose is met by the time the confessional statement is adopted, the commentaries may no longer be needed. Another reason for having the commentaries is, however, to provide broader background for the statement itself. This purpose may remain even after the proposed confession of faith is adopted. The commentaries may then make the confessional statement more useful for instructing new believers. And the commentaries may also make the confessional statement more helpful as a means of conversation and possible consensus building with other Christian groups.

In both Dutch and North American Mennonite history, confessions of faith have sometimes also become statements of church doctrine that have taken on obligatory, dogmatic authority. This was particularly the case in Holland during the latter part of the seventeenth century and among some groups in North America during the first half of the twentieth century. When this has happened, unquestioning assent to the confessional formulations has been the primary means of determining right belief and practice for congregations and ministers. In these instances, specific statements of faith have taken on an authority that Mennonites have generally considered excessive. Usually they have then reacted against this excessive authority of confessional statements by claiming that Mennonites are a "noncreedal" people who simply accept the Bible as the only standard for faith and life.

When Mennonites argue more carefully against the authority of "creeds" and claim to be a "noncreedal" people, they usually mean that specific formulations of belief and practice should always be subject to Scripture and to the Holy

Spirit's leading, particularly in church renewal and ethical discernment. No creedal formulations should therefore be considered to be above further testing by Scripture and by the leading of the Spirit in the church. Nor should all reformulations or new ways of speaking about central Christian beliefs and practices be ruled out simply because some creeds have already been adopted by the churches (Mennonite or other churches). Mennonites, for example, have traditionally accepted the "Apostles' Creed." Some have formally adopted it; some have incorporated it into their confessional statements or used it in other ways. But very frequently they have omitted the phrase "He descended into hell" from the Apostles' Creed, because its biblical basis remains problematic.

Perhaps the best way to understand confessions of faith from a Mennonite perspective is to see and use them as consensus statements that help to regulate the faithful church's teaching and practice until they are corrected or replaced by other such statements. New consensus statements or reformulations of traditional language may be needed to meet new challenges to the church's faith and life from the contemporary world. They may be needed because of the church's missionary witness, which gives birth to faith communities in new cultural contexts. They may be advisable because earlier formulations should be corrected or modified in the light of the Spirit's leading and of better understandings of Scripture. They may be needed in order to help counter heretical beliefs and practices that were not dealt with in earlier statements. They may be required in order to strengthen genuine unity of faith and life between divided churches. In such instances, confessional statements have a very important role in helping to build consensus and providing communal norms of belief and practice. As statements to help regulate the faithful church's teaching and practice until corrected or replaced by other such statements, confessions of faith have a needed, even if interim, role in the life and teaching of the Christian church.

In this sense, confessions of faith can help Mennonites and Christians more generally become a genuinely confessional people rather than a conglomerate of ethnic peoples. Confessions of faith as consensus statements should symbolize the truth that the Christian church is a faith community whose existence depends on a shared faith rather than primarily on a shared cultural or ethnic heritage. Confessions of faith as interim communal norms of faith and life should symbolize the reality of the church as a faith community whose existence depends on a common faith that breaks down ethnic and cultural barriers rather than reinforcing them. Confessions of faith as expressions of Christian unity should symbolize the fact that the church is a people that has been constituted and that continues by a common faith in Jesus Christ in the midst of a world where there are many different ideological and religious movements and groups.

Marlin E. Miller, USA, b. 1938, Th.D., president and professor of theology at Associated Mennonite Biblical Seminaries (Elkhart, Indiana).

Child in a church-sponsored day camp in Miami, Florida. (MCC photo by Jim King, 1987)

Jesus Christ, the servant-king

by C. Norman Kraus

Today in the broader Christian world, the subject of Christology is very dynamic and fluid. In some Christian circles the centrality and relevance of Jesus Christ for life in the world is being sharply questioned. In a world of pluralistic cultures and religions where many "saviors" are acknowledged, some theologians are saying that we can no longer hold to the exclusive saviorhood of Jesus. In a world of ethical pluralism, the relevance of the teachings and example of Jesus are challenged. Some radical feminists even question whether a male Jesus can save women. And Mennonites, who are now from many cultures and countries, are affected by these questions much more than they would have been fifty years ago.

At the beginning of the Anabaptist-Mennonite movement, all the leaders were concerned to make Christ central again in the life of the church. Conrad Grebel wrote to Myconius about his "mighty hope for a renaissance of Christ and the gospel" (Harder, 1985:113). Menno Simons adopted 1 Cor. 3:11 as his golden text: "For other foundation can no man lay than that is laid, which is Jesus Christ." There were variations in emphasis as they sought for new understanding and perspectives, but most of them attempted to stay within the boundaries of creedal orthodoxy, i.e., the full deity and humanity of Christ. But despite variations, virtually all the Anabaptist writers held to the centrality of Christ's authority for the church in contrast to that of the Pope or magistracy.

Because so much has been said about the biblicism of the Anabaptists, we need to underscore this prior point of Christ's centrality in their theological approach. Papal Christianity had, in effect, transferred the authority of Christ to the Pope as his churchly "vicar." The primary concern of all the reformers, and in a special way the Anabaptist reformers, was to reclaim the authority of Christ in the church. And in order to make Christ the final authority in the church, the Scripture's authority over papal tradition had to be asserted.

Today the Anabaptist-Mennonite church family around the world shares this same concern for the centrality of Christ in the midst of theological diversity. It is no secret that among those who fervently espouse their Anabaptist heritage there are many points of view on the specific theological and ethical issues raised in Christology. In his report of the Christology Seminar held in conjunction with the joint General Conference-Mennonite Church General Assembly at "Normal 89," Daniel Hertzler observed that even after the conference, "Mennonite Christology [is] still elusive" (*Gospel Herald*, Aug. 22, 1989, p. 608). However, the Brethren in Christ and Mennonite denominations participating in the conference pledged their continuing loyalty to "Jesus Christ our Lord in mission and discipleship."

Contemporary options

Contemporary Mennonites have not projected a self-consciously Anabaptist image of Jesus, although such an image may be implicit in their ethical emphasis. Rather, they have borrowed from the many theological options available in religious cultures surrounding them. Nearest at hand is the conservative Protestant tradition, which understands Jesus to be God's Son, who came from heaven to earth to be our high priest and the sacrifice for our sins. Also available are the liberal images of him as the prophet and social reformer, the master teacher, and the martyr example who challenges us to follow in his steps. Or the neoliberal image of him as the "new being" and the beginning of a new humanity. Liberation theology has pictured him as the savior who came to free people from social and psychological slavery as well as spiritual depression. Some feminists have suggested that we need a feminine image of Jesus, or at least one that is neither male nor female. To these more serious theological images we can add a profusion of popular images spread by radio and television preachers. There is Jesus the great psychologist, who helps us restore a positive self-image. Or Jesus the miracle-working healer, who constantly intervenes to solve our problems. Or the indulgent Jesus, who wants all his children to be rich in worldly goods as well as in spirit. Or the politically conservative Jesus, who blesses a multitude of rightist causes from public school prayers to anticommunist, terrorist activities. Each of these theological descriptions has its accompanying view of salvation. The conservative traditions have interpreted Jesus' salvation as an individualistic spiritual experience of justification with little emphasis on the social dimensions of salvation. The liberal traditions have stressed a "social gospel" and social salvation. Liberation theology has tried to combine these two in a viable biblical model. Postliberal pictures give him the status of an existential, mythical, or eschatological savior who inspires courage and hope for the daily struggle.

All of these positions have had their impact upon the Mennonite churches around the world. Some churches praise the blessed miracle-working Jesus. Some preach Jesus the savior, who justifies us and saves us from hell. Some feel comfortable with the liberation Jesus as he is understood in the Base Church movement. Some preach Jesus the exorcist and healer. Some emphasize following the example of Jesus as his disciples. Some experience Jesus in the fellowship of his body, the church, and worship him as the "head of the church." But in all this variation, one senses that from South and Central America to Africa, from the Asian churches to Europe and North America, there is an undercurrent of agreement: the authentic New Testament Christ can only be recognized as God's Servant Messiah who came not only to save individual souls but also to reconcile and heal the tragic alienation and injustice that afflict humanity. And implicit in this conviction there emerges an image of this "Wounded Lamb" (Rev. 5:6) as the very Son of God suffering in solidarity with us and for us.

The current situation

For many years our Mennonite discussion has been upon the identity and role of the church as the community of Christ in the world. The church is the body of Christ and the continuing mission of Christ. The assumption has been that Jesus Christ of the New Testament is the head of the church calling her to a martyr-witness in the cause of the kingdom of God. (This position has been freshly restated in John E. Toews' keynote address at the 1989 Christology Conference.) But there was little discussion of the explicit Christological issues. With very few exceptions, Mennonites simply accepted the Christ pictured in the fourth- and fifth-century creeds as these were interpreted in the conservative Protestant tradition. Until recently they did not develop the Christological implications of their more distinctive insight that Jesus came as the messianic servant-king. In this connection one must also note that even though our emphasis has been upon ethics and discipleship, little attention has been given to the practical question of who Jesus is for building contractors, insurance salespeople, doctors, chemistry teachers, and the like. The rote confession that Jesus is the Son of God, the second person of the Trinity, has had little relevance for actual discipleship. It does not inescapably involve the call to "leave their nets and follow" this one like the fishermen of old who confessed him to be "the Messiah of God."

More recently at the scholarly level several seminars have been held, and a number of papers have been written on the theme of Christology in an Anabaptist tradition. In 1986 and 1987 two full books appeared on the subjects of atonement (John Driver) and Christology proper (Norman Kraus). In 1989 Thomas Finger concluded his Christological discussion from an eschatological perspective in his second volume of theology. A range of positions is being advocated by Mennonite scholars. At the conservative end of the continuum is the strictly fundamentalist, literal biblicist position. Perhaps the greater part of our Bible and theology teachers would take a more centrist "kerygmatic" stance. They use biblical terminology as they understand it to have been used in its historical context. A few others are making a renewed appeal to the great creedal tradition as the starting point for defining Christology. Still others would argue that one or another of the contemporary theological positions, e.g., process theology, should be used as the systematic framework for a definition. And a few in America and Europe would take a more humanistic approach. At the moment it would be difficult to state a definitive Anabaptist-Mennonite position.

Current issues in Christology

As we have begun to discuss the Christology question explicitly in the Anabaptist-Mennonite tradition, a number of basic questions have come to the fore. Some of these concern the method of approach to the doctrine. Some touch on philosophical presuppositions. Others are related to our concepts of salvation and the church. Let me enumerate some of the important ones.

First, the authority and relevance of the early church creeds of Nicea and Chalcedon as the universal norm for Christological statements have been questioned. No one questions their historical significance in the church; but how do their ancient, metaphysical categories, which speak of Christ as "one substance with the Father" and "the eternally begotten Son," apply in our modern context? Some would generalize their meaning into a summary statement that Jesus was "fully God and fully human." Others would insist on keeping more of the metaphysical language.

Another methodological question concerns the interpretation of Scripture itself. Those who hold to the doctrine of scriptural inerrancy insist on a literal meaning of the text as understood in our twentieth-century Western culture. Others call for a historical and literary reading of the texts. When read this way, the biblical interpreter first inquires into the original context and intention of the author. Building on this the theological interpreter, like a translator, asks what its "dynamic equivalent" might be in present-day cultures. These two approaches give us different but complementary pictures of the Christ.

A third question concerns the relation of Christ's "person" and "work." The traditional approach first defined Christ's metaphysical status, i.e., essential deity and humanity. Then, coincidentally, it asked what the work of this God-man was. This is sometimes called approaching Christology "from above." Today many theologians and Bible scholars are beginning "from below." They begin with the historical Jesus Christ and then ask who he is in light of such a work. This approach has appealed to some of those in the Anabaptist-Mennonite tradition who feel that the biblical Jesus cannot be known apart from the character of his work and teachings. They relate his divine status (person) to the ethical and spiritual character of his life and work and not merely to a unique metaphysical event like the virgin birth.

A fourth issue concerns the definition of Jesus as "savior." All agree that Jesus is the savior. But what kind of savior is he? How did he effect our salvation? And what kind of salvation does he offer? This issue stems from the Reformation itself! In the sixteenth century, the issue was stated as justification by faith versus works. Does salvation include regeneration and sanctification as well as justification? Today in evangelical circles the same issues are being debated under the question of whether Jesus can be our savior without being our lord. Mennonites have held that lordship and saviorhood cannot be separated. They have stressed the lordship of Christ and discipleship as the authentic expression of faith.

A fifth issue that has re-emerged with some urgency is the exclusiveness of Jesus' saviorhood. Those raising the challenge do not question that Jesus is the unique savior of Christians but whether he is the only savior for all the world's people. Do other religious figures like Moses, Mohammed, and Buddha have a place in God's economy as saviors? If so, what is the relation of Jesus' salvation to theirs? This question has a crucial bearing on the mission of the church to those of other religious cultures, and our theologians are just beginning to wrestle with the issue.

In the area of discipleship, the nature of Jesus' example becomes an issue. Just what in his life and ministry are we to follow? To what extent should we try to follow Jesus' commands to radical servanthood—to actually love others as we do ourselves? And are we to take his mission of exorcism and healing as part of the pattern? Jesus himself promised that the disciples would do greater things than he had done. Is the way of the cross and martyrdom the exclusive requirement (Mark 8:34–35)?

Finally, the issue of "contextualization" has become a crucial one as we attempt to proclaim Christ in a pluralistic world. Mennonitism is now a worldwide phenomenon spanning many different cultures. Is there only one way for Mennonites to define Christology? Must we use the same theological terminology in the shame-oriented cultures of Asia as in the guilt-oriented cultures of the West? Must we speak of incarnation in the same way in the Hindu cultures of India as in Africa, South America, or North America and Europe? In the multiple contexts of our world, how shall we talk about the mystery of God in Christ as it is disclosed in the Bible? Is there a "universal" theological formula?

Affirming the centrality of Christ

Is it possible within the cultural pluralism of worldwide Mennonitism to affirm the centrality and normativeness of Jesus Christ for the world? I think that it is, although we may not be using the identical terms and phrases in every context. And what are the central convictions that we share and wish to affirm as Anabaptist-Mennonites? Let me suggest a few for the ongoing dialogue.

First, we believe that Jesus truly is God manifesting himself in our historical existence. The New Testament bears witness to this in many different ways. It calls him "Immanuel, God with us." It speaks of him as the definitive "word of God ... full of grace and truth." He acts with the full authority and power of God over evil to heal and exorcise demons, to forgive, to command, and to teach. He has authority even over the sabbath and the Mosaic Law. In theological language we say that Jesus is the Self-expression, or Word of God. He is more than a prophet who speaks words about God. He reflects the very character of God in his own life, death, and resurrection. This was true to the degree that he could say, "Anyone who has seen me has seen the Father" (John 14:9). From a human point of view, two very surprising things are revealed in this divine self-revelation. First, God discloses himself as a servant of humankind (Mark 10:45), not a dominating ruler. The Son of God did not come as a dictator, warrior, or judge but as a suffering servant who washed his disciples' feet. And second, as the servant-king he demonstrated that the power of God is the power of love, not violence. He showed us that God's ultimate way of dealing with evil in the universe is the way of crucifixion and resurrection, not violent revolution. In our ongoing discussions of Christology, we must be careful to keep the definition of Christ's divine "person" and "character" together in our witness to him as "the Son of God." He is the self-disclosure of God to us because, as the writer to the Hebrews puts it, "he bears the very stamp of his character" (1:3). And it is this essential self-identity with God that makes him central and normative for Christian faith. It is a strength of liberation theology that it keeps Jesus' character as savior of the poor and disenfranchised in the forefront of its definition of his person.

Second, we believe that Jesus was fully one with us in our humanity. His humanity reveals what it means to be created "in God's image." Paul called Jesus the "last Adam" and clearly thought of him as the prototype of "the image of God." He said, also, that Jesus was made "in the likeness of sinful flesh," and Hebrews adds that he suffered temptation and "learned obedience through suffering." Nevertheless, he fully submitted to the will of the Father. He was "sinless." Thus we confess that he completely identified with us in our humanity and that he is definitive for our understanding of what it means to be human. Through his solidarity with us in our sinful humanity, he accomplished for us what we could not do ourselves. That is why we speak of salvation by faith in Christ. His solidarity with us has enabled us to attain a new self-understanding through identity with him. Through our identification with him in his "suffering," we are assured of being raised to new life with him in his resurrection (Phil. 3:10–11). And our hope is that "when we see him we will be like him" (1 John 3:2). Thus Christ's humanity is closely linked with our own possibilities for authentic self-fulfillment as God's covenant creatures. As we continue our search for proper terms to express the Christological mystery, we must not lose sight of this essential connection, which was first enunciated by our Anabaptist predecessor, Pilgram Marpeck. Jesus Christ is the normative example of God's intention for humankind.

Third, however we may try to express it, we must not allow the normative uniqueness of Christ's saviorhood to be muted. The name Jesus means "God our Savior." Indeed, just as Yahweh was the covenant name of God for the ancient Hebrews, so Jesus is the new covenant name of God. And the new covenant sealed with his blood is a universal covenant of salvation. As savior he calls all peoples to be reconciled to God and each other. We are convinced that his life, death, and resurrection have established a precedent and a pattern of salvation that has universal relevance and effectiveness.

This does not mean that we must be judgmental of other "saviors" as we bear witness to the unique saviorhood of Christ. The New Testament itself offers us at least two suggestions of how to deal with this issue. John identifies Jesus Christ as the embodiment of that Word, Light, and Life of God that has always been present among humankind saving it from destruction (John 1:4–5,9–10). Thus, wherever we meet the light and love, the grace and truth manifested in Jesus, we are certainly entitled to recognize the presence of "Christ" as savior. Paul has a somewhat different approach in Romans 2–3. He suggests that there is a kind of inherent law of the Creator within the universe that the human heart recognizes (conscience). This law is not contrary to the word that has been spoken in the Mosaic Law and in Jesus Christ. And Paul suggests that God will judge people who sincerely obey this law by their "works" when they are ignorant of the historical covenants made through Moses and Jesus Christ. Paul in no sense displaces the centrality and necessity of Jesus as savior, but he also does not attempt to make judgments that belong only to God our savior. This is an area of great sensitivity in our world of clashing ideologies and religions. Christ came as the powerless one, yet he exercised the power of God for our salvation. He washed the disciples' feet, yet he was acknowledged as "Master." He came without academic and political credentials, yet he dared to challenge the Law of Moses. He allowed himself to be executed, yet he "arose on the third day." How shall we bear witness to this one who makes no claims and demands for himself but demonstrates the authentic authority and power of God?

Fourth, we confess Jesus to be the "firstborn from the dead" and the head of his body, the church. A confession of Jesus Christ as the self-disclosure of God and savior in human likeness must involve a clear self-understanding of the church as the locus of his continuing presence. The church as the body of Christ continues to embody the meaning and reality of Christ's presence. Paul can even speak of the church as "the fullness of Christ" as Christ is "the fullness of God" (Eph. 1:22–23). This means that a correct and effective confession of Christ as Lord and Savior must include a continuing demonstration of his saviorhood and lordship in the life of the church itself. Here the theological task is to give primacy of place to Christ as the head of the church. The church is not the full expression of Christ's continuing presence. Christ is not equated with or limited to the sacramental presence of the church in the world. But the church does claim to be a primary locus and demonstration of his effective presence in the world. Thus its own self-understanding and mission in the world are bound up with our understanding of Jesus as the Christ of God.

Finally, the proclamation of the centrality of Christ must include the proclamation of hope in his final victory. It was his resurrection that "declared him to be the Son of God" (Rom. 1:4). Just so it will be his eschatological victory over sin and death that will be the manifestation of his lordship and the vindication of our claims. We need to reclaim a strong witness to Jesus Christ as the hope of the world.

Clyde Norman Kraus, USA, b. 1924, Th.M., Ph.D., writer, retired college teacher and missionary.

Chapel of the Sermon on the Mount in Elkhart, Indiana, which belongs to the Associated Mennonite Biblical Seminaries. (AMBS photo by John Bender)

The church—a pilgrimaging people

by C. Hugo Zorrilla

If we would ask—What is the church? What is the function of the church?—
without a doubt we would find many divergent and contradictory answers. The
fact that today many Christians do not have a clear concept of what the church is
should not surprise us. Some Christians think the church is the building in the
neighborhood where believers meet week after week, each Sunday and each
Wednesday. Others advance a little and accept that the church is the believing
individuals who have an active and almost elitist function in the course of the believing community. Although they do not accept the idea of ecclesiastical
hierarchy, they believe there is a nucleus of people with authority and the power
to make decisions. Other Christians accept that the church is the assembly of
baptized members, or those who have "a name" in the history of their community. For these people, the concept of the church does go beyond the boundaries
of the denomination. For other Christians the idea of church is defined in the
function of the task for which the Lord has placed them in the world. The reality
of being sent by the Lord to be his servants in the world as signs of the kingdom
of God identifies them as church. The most appropriate and correct approach
would be to see what image of the church the New Testament gives us. It is
enough to mention here that the New Testament does not define the church.
Neither does it present a systematic overview of all the doctrines of ecclesiology.
The fragmentary and occasional writings of the New Testament present ecclesiastical topics intimately united to all the topics related to Christ, his ministry,
and the obedient commitment of all disciples.

The identity of the church from the biblical text

In the Gospel of Matthew—The church is the assembly founded by Jesus. God
identifies himself with her by means of the Messiah promised to be in her midst
and to remain with his own forever (1:23; 18:20; 28:20). By his words and
deeds, Jesus shows his kingdom in the world. The kingdom now is "near." The
followers or disciples have to be proclaimers of the truth. Of course, an obedient
and faithful discipleship is required to follow the Lord (4:20,22; 8:23).

In the Gospel of Mark—It is evident that in Mark the church was also begun
with the nucleus of disciples who had been with Jesus. He sends them to preach
and to heal with authority because the kingdom now has come (3:13ff.). The
Twelve were chosen as the nucleus of a new community. They are called
apostles, which means "sent" to the world as servants. Neither privileges nor
power are offered to them. They have their Teacher as an example of service,
who "did not come to be served, but to serve, and to give his life as a ransom for
many" (10:45). The disciples are exposed to the violence of the world. Therefore
they will drink the same cup as their Master and will be baptized with the

baptism with which he was baptized. In other words, for Mark, to be a sign of the kingdom of God means that the church should travel the same path of Jesus' sacrificial surrender in obedience.

In the Gospel of Luke—The reality of the church fills the historic space between the resurrection of Jesus and his imminent return. The church is the exclusive work of God and the obvious demonstration of messianic times. God in Christ is the creator of this believing community. This truth is evidenced by the presence and the manifestation of the Holy Spirit. For Luke the time of the Spirit is the fulfillment of the messianic promises. The time of the Spirit coincides with the time of the church. Both realities are evident with the coming of Jesus. He begins his ministry with the power of the Spirit (Luke 4:18). In it the origin of the church at Pentecost is assimilated. The Spirit of God is upon Jesus and upon the church to fulfill its ministries. Thus the church began with the resurrection of Jesus. It is continued through the ministry of the Spirit in the lives of its members. These extend the gospel, not as a whim or by human strategy, but according to the will and the power of the Spirit (Acts 4:31; 5:32; 11:15,16; 19:6).

In the Gospel of John—The fourth Gospel alludes neither directly nor explicitly to the concept of the church. Nevertheless, the life of a congregation of Christians is vibrant in this Gospel. They have to be faithful and remain in his word and in his love. At the same time they will suffer and will be hated by the world. It is basic for John that among the members of the community of Jesus a relationship of love exists among them and with their Master. He promises them and gives them his Spirit so that they will be continuators of the mission for which his Father sent him. With specific characteristics the Gospel describes the community of those who have come to Jesus. All the figures of the church in John are always in relation to Jesus. That is to say that ecclesiology has its roots in Christology. Thus, those who have come to Jesus are believers and also are called "sons of God." They are also branches because Jesus is the true vine. The community should be the grain of wheat, the flock of the Good Shepherd, the bride of the Husband, his own, his possession, the friends of him who gave his life for them.

In the writings of Saint Paul—An analysis of the Pauline idea of church must begin with a background vision that all ecclesiastical reality, whether local or universal, is based on the redemptive work that the believers find in Christ. The foundation of the believing community is Jesus Christ. The images that Paul uses to refer to the church enrich this concept, and they help us understand the power and seriousness of Christian service before the world.

1.   The people of God—Since their beginnings, Christians have judged themselves heirs and continuators of the true people of God. Although they were continuators of the people of the Old Testament, this continuity overcame all ethnic, cultural, and nationalistic ideals. The new Israel emerged from a faith

according to the Spirit and in accordance with the promises for messianic times (Rom. 9:6ff.; 11:5ff.). If the church is the people of God, as Paul expresses, the messianic times have already begun. The people of God can be found in each congregation of believers. In like manner, the whole church as a universal reality has in itself the representation of the people of God in each local church. In the Gentile or Greek world, for "church" Paul uses the expression "ekklesia" as a synonym for "laos," or "people of God." Ekklesia is the translation into Greek of the Hebrew expression "gahal." With this the community of Israel and its assembly was designated. All the historical meaning is found in ekklesia when Paul expresses, "to the church ... in God the Father and the Lord Jesus Christ ..." (1 Thes. 1:1). The Gentile members of each church, in its quality as "the people of God," are grafted by faith into the chosen trunk of Israel (Rom. 11:24ff., Eph. 2:11ff.). This surpasses all classes of ethnicism and nationalism. Also, Paul strengthens his idea in affirming that the believers are of the lineage of Abraham (Rom. 4:11,18, 2 Cor. 6:16ff., Gal. 3:16).

2. The pilgrimaging community—The events in the desert in Exodus are constituted as types or models for all those who, in the messianic era, share the promises of God (1 Cor. 10:6). As an assembly in the desert, the community began their wanderings by faith in the Lord. To be disobedient to Christ is the way to idolatry, which breaks communion with the cup and the bread (the blood and body of Christ) (1 Cor. 10:7,14). On the other hand, this community is composed of elected members. These are called to be chosen as saints or separated for the service of God (Rom. 1:6, 1 Cor. 1:24, Col. 3:12). This truth breaks the duality between laymen and hierarchies. That is to say, here there is no room for clerics. All believers are the community of Christ. There is no place for pressure groups or certain families with decision-making power.

3. The body of Christ—Paul uses this expression as a metaphor for unity. With it he describes the organic relationship that exists between Christ and the believers. In Colossians and Ephesians it is seen that this body is of Christ, where he is head (Eph. 1:22; 4:12–16; 5:23,30, Col. 1:18,24; 2:19). In this body which is the church, Christ exists. The church belongs to Christ. Furthermore, he is presented in the world through her and in her. Because Christ is the head of this body, the church must be subordinate to him. With Christ being the head, each member must keep watch to maintain a healthy relationship in the body. Thus a relationship of mutual dependency among members is created (1 Cor. 12:12, Rom. 12:4ff.). The harmony of the members of the body of Christ is manifested by the gifts of the Spirit. These are given to the members to function within the body, united and joined together in love.

4. The spiritual building—The church is not a building in itself. It is built when its members are built up or edified in love by way of manifestations of the Spirit. At the same time the members are edified when they dedicate themselves to the service of others. They grow as a spiritual building, and by grace they are made

the dwelling place of God (Eph. 2:19, 1 Cor. 3:9–15). Thus the assembly of believers comes to be the place where the spiritual sacrifice of praise is offered and where all its members are edified and built on the foundation of Christ.

5.   The temple of God—The metaphor of the temple is also given in the figure of the building. The glory of God is no longer in a building of stone. The believers are the temple, not an external temple but a most holy place where the glory of God is manifested (1 Cor. 3:16, 2 Cor. 6:16). All believers as a body should give themselves to worship, to praise, and to surrendering themselves as living offerings within the temple that is the church (Rom. 12:1). As a consequence, each believer is holy, that is, separated for the service of Christ, since also his personal body is a holy place of the Spirit (1 Cor. 6:19).

6.   Other metaphors for the church—Paul establishes a relationship of love between Christ and his church. That is why he uses the figure of a wife to whom Christ presents himself as the faithful, loving husband who is interested in her destiny. Thus it is evident that Christ is with her and will not leave her alone (2 Cor. 11:2, Eph. 5:28). The idea that Christ broke all nationalism and cast down all ethnic arrogance causes the apostle to accept that the church is formed from all races and cultures. All by faith in Christ are members of the same family, the family of God (Eph. 2:19). Before the Father, all are sons and all have gifts and receive the same demands. Another figure that Paul uses to define the church is that of planting or of cultivation (1 Cor. 3:6–9).

In the Epistle to the Hebrews—The author of this Epistle identifies the congregation of believers as the "house of God." The Son has prepared this house and he presents himself as the High Priest, superior to the old order represented by Moses (3:3–6). The believers journey to a city yet to come because they have no permanent dwelling place in this world (13:14). In this way the church is revealed as a pilgrimaging people who advance in liberty and confidence in a new exodus, by a new and true way, which Christ has opened once and for all. The church is a pilgrimaging community that should continue in the Way (4:1ff.; 10:20; 12:12,25; 13:15,16).

In the first Epistle of Peter—The church has its origin and identity in the answer to the call to believe in Christ and to participate in his sufferings through doing good. The believers are a pilgrimaging people, in exile, dispersed and chosen by the grace of God. Here the heart itself of their identity as the true Israel is found, a holy nation, a royal priesthood, the lineage of Abraham (2:9). The church as the people of God is also a spiritual building as has been seen in Paul. In this way the church is built as a spiritual house (2:4ff.). The believers are living stones that are cemented in Christ as a precious stone. As opposed to the old temple of Jerusalem, the believers are united to form a spiritual house where spiritual sacrifices for the glory of God are celebrated. Although they live in the midst of a hostile world, they are called upon to practice good works. For this they suffer as if they were malefactors, just as Christ suffered once and for all, the just for the unjust (3:17ff.).

Task of the church from a total testimony

The church has a specific command from the Lord: to go to the world and make disciples. But how are the churches witnesses in a world full of injustices? Today the concept of Christian testimony has been reduced to a minimum, so much so that everything has been left to proclamation and to the repetition of a conceptual, abstract theology without any direct and historic relationship with the people who listen to these decontextualized theological formulations.

Toward a total testimony—The testimony of the churches has entered into a crisis for external and internal reasons. We have reduced the testimony in the world to evangelization in the style of the electronic religion of the televangelists. We have used the Christian testimony as an easy formula for proselytism, and we have denied it its creative power of life in the Lord. What does it mean to witness, to evangelize in the world today, where 40,000 children die daily of hunger, where there are some 500 food wars throughout the countries the missionaries are sent to evangelize? How can we be a witness in the United States, where 4 of every 7 people live at that nation's poverty level, where 900 children under age 5 die of malnutrition each month, and where 6 million children live in the streets of its large cities? Presently in the world there are 500 million hungry people; 1,700 million people with a life expectancy of fewer than 60 years; 1,500 million who will never have medical assistance; 500 million with an annual per capita income of under $150. And data continue showing us a world where we Christians have to be a presence and an announcement. Cruel reality brings us to think that we have to witness to the world in a more Christlike manner; we have to change the ecclesiastical and missionary structures so that the evangelization task will be, in word and deed, creator of life. The truth is that the evangelizing practices of the Mennonite churches show none of the distinctive Mennonite beliefs. The Anabaptist churches have good theology; but their missionary practices, the majority of the time, do nothing more than copy the American way of doing missions, which in itself is a copy of the American method of promoting multinational companies. It is as though the church is selling soap or hamburgers or soft drinks rather than proclaiming the gospel of the kingdom of God.

To be signs of the kingdom demands that Christians exercise a critical evaluation of all political dominion in such a way that terms like peace, justice, liberty, life, and reconciliation take on a more concrete meaning for those who suffer the negation of those qualities at the hands of the powerful. Of course, some will say, "Let's give the gospel to the world and not mix ourselves in the things of this world." Perhaps they forget that to testify of Christ is to find Christ where he said he would be—with the poor of this world.

Many of the rulers of our countries know the usefulness for their own interests of a testimony that collaborates with their way of thinking and diverts the mind. To a reduced group of preachers in opposition, the [former] prime minister of South Africa once said, "People should not abuse the pulpit to reach South Africa for political reasons. Thus I appeal to you again, to return to the heart of your preaching and announce to your community the word of God, the gospel of Christ." With words like these many Christians feel very comfortable today, since they see the gospel as something socially aseptic and morally private, so that it serves as a coating of piety for their governments while these governments continue their politics of injustice.

In the churches' Christian practice, three groups of Christians can be identified:

- Many Christians continue perpetuating a dualistic world view, inherited from a Gnostic concept of reality. This position separates faith from works, the gospel from service, a pastoral ethic from a political ethic.
- Other Christians opt to remain "neutral" or on the margin so as to "not compromise the gospel." They do not realize that this supposed neutrality in itself is a naive but political position that permits the dominating class to continue their politics of aggression against the most elemental rights of human beings. In the presence of hunger, torture, oppression, growing arsenals, illiteracy, war, consumerism, exploitation, the accumulation of riches—can we be neutral?
- Other Christians do not separate faith-works, words-deeds, Christian practice-Christian testimony, because they perceive that their evangelical commitment emanates from the historical purpose of the kingdom of God for all people.

Toward faithfulness in spite of persecution—What degree of commitment do we show to the communities that we want to reach with the gospel when we are secure and assured of the privileges and the power of the strongest? What does the fact tell us that because of our passivity many of the important and often op-pressive decisions that affect the world are made in the societies from which we come, decisions that dehumanize those societies we go to evangelize? I believe that the death of many Christians in our day, the torture, and the missing persons show us that to testify in the world is a risk that the Lord warned us about: "If the world hates you, keep in mind that it hated me first" (John 15:18). Later he says: "If they persecuted me, they will persecute you also" (John 15:20b).

It is not strange to anyone that the position of peacemakers and reconcilers is seen as a threat to the powerful. This can create persecution, and perhaps be-cause of this we think that it is better not to continue on in a holistic evangelism, but rather to be neutral. We should realize that the persecutors and people in power try to make their own definition of what a Christian testimony is all about. What comes out is a definition that is not biblically Christian. They try to manipulate the Christian faith in such a way that many Christian groups fall into the trap of accepting the "official" version of the Christian testimony. The Christian testimony is the first, the fundamental, and the founding action of the church. It defines the task and the mission of all Christians as the people of God. It is first because it was before the church. The gospel is not a mere means to found a church or to make it grow. The people of God are the means to make the kingdom of God present. This is the final goal. The church is the means or the sign of the kingdom. In this project, all Christians are obligated to participate if they want to be faithful followers of Jesus. The Christian task in the world is not the role of a few specialists, not the task of privileged groups in the church. It is the combined work of all the people of God. The presence of the kingdom of God is shown to the world presenting the total gospel of Jesus, that is, Jesus himself as the gospel of God. He is the content itself of the gospel. This is the point of beginning to define how to witness to the world, synthesized as follows:

- Witness is at the service of the kingdom of God.
- Witness shows the kind of church we Christians are.
- Witness is the good news from Jesus for those who are in sin and suffer from the sins of others in society.
- Witness demands words and deeds that are integrated in the witness' life.
- Witness should show a sacrificial following of Jesus.
- Witness should give a believable sign of hope to those who suffer, because we are witnesses of their anguish and cry to heaven.
- Witness is a calling of faith also to those who are already Christians, so that with humility we give the Spirit of God opportunity to re-evangelize us. This obligates us to support the project of God in his kingdom. Multitudes continue waiting for us Christians to live what we believe. Let us get out of our church groups or cliques, and let us meet Christ where he said he was going to be: with the least of his brethren, with the hungry, the thirsty, the refugees, the naked, the ill, the prisoners (Matt. 25:31ff.).

The local church and the universal church clearly underscore the idea of community, of corporation. This suppresses all sentiments of selfish individualism. Each believer is incorporated by faith into the body of Christ. The Spirit empowers them to live united and to grow with the whole body. In being formed of people, the church is in the world where it has to be a sign of the kingdom of God. For this, it has to know the context of this world so that the message of the gospel will continue being pertinent. As Christians, we must confess our limitations, arrogance, and mediocrity in the church. Finally, the churches not only have to be in the world, but must know how to be in the world as servants of a gospel expressed in words and deeds.

C. Hugo Zorrilla, Colombia, b. 1940, Doctorate in New Testament, professor at Fresno Pacific College (Fresno, California), former missionary to Spain.

Judy Edmister and Seleha sift impurities from split soybeans as part of a job creation project in which soybeans are used to make a nutritious snack called soy nuts. (MCC photo by Charmayne Brubaker, 1989)

Good news of the kingdom coming

by John Driver

Biblical eschatology is concerned with the ways in which God will act decisively within history, as well as at the end of history, to consummate his purposes for all of creation.

The kingdom of God is, without doubt, the principal image for setting forth the biblical vision of eschatological hope. The kingdom of God provides the context for all that Jesus said and did. Jesus initiated his ministry with the announcement, "The kingdom of God is at hand" (Mark 1:15, Luke 4:43). But nowhere in the New Testament do we find an exact explanation of the meaning of the "kingdom of God." We may suppose, however, that the term was not new to Jesus' first-century Jewish hearers. There was a long-standing tradition among the Jewish people that God would someday establish his rule on earth. On this Old Testament understanding, Jesus built his vision of the kingdom of God.

Although the use of the term "kingdom" in relation to God is rare in the Old Testament writings, the concept of God's kingly rule is everywhere present. Ancient Israel confessed God's reign over the universe and over the nations as well as over his own people. God's kingly rule is all encompassing (Psalm 103:19). The fact that Yahweh is king over his people Israel is especially prominent throughout the Old Testament. The first specific mention of God's kingship occurs in the context of Israel's exodus experience of salvation. "The Lord ... is my salvation. ... The Lord will reign for ever and ever" (Ex. 15:2,18). This reality was engraved in the words of the covenant given at Sinai: "You shall be my own possession among all peoples; for all the earth is mine, and you shall be to me a kingdom of priests and a holy nation" (Ex. 19:5–6). There is a close relationship between God's saving activity toward Israel, reflected in the exodus and the covenant, and his kingly rule over all. The exercise of God's kingly rule was not a vague abstraction. God's reign has to do with the concrete forms that life takes among his people. God's kingdom is manifested in the social relationships practiced in response to his intention for his people (Psalms 145 and 146). The elements of God's reign include an unflagging covenant faithfulness, bringing justice to the oppressed, providing food for the hungry, setting prisoners free, opening the eyes of the blind, lifting up the bowed down, watching over the sojourners, sustaining the widows and orphans (Psalm 146:6–10).

The Old Testament story contains many indications of the social structure of God's rule. The Decalogue is undoubtedly the most concise and clearest description of God's intention for human relationships. The preamble makes it clear that life under God's kingship is determined by the very character of God himself, who liberated Israel "out of the land of Egypt" (Ex. 20:1, Deut. 5:6). The sabbatical and jubilee provisions offer another example of relationships under God's rule (Lev. 25, Deut. 15). The land is to be left fallow as a reminder that the earth and its resources are the Lord's. These are given to his people so that all, and the poor in particular, may be nourished (Ex. 23:10–11). Indebtedness is to be forgiven and indentured slaves released, because God has redeemed Israel from slavery (Deut. 15:2,12–18). Inheritances lost over the years are to be restored, because the earth is the Lord's and everyone in Israel, from the king to the most lowly, is a child and subject of Israel's loving and faithful Lord. Here again, the salvific actions of the King are to determine the shape of all relationships, social and spiritual, in the kingdom. God's kingdom embraced concrete political and social events. This is clear from the descriptions of life under God's rule. It is also clear from the prophetic vision of the future of God's kingdom. They expected God's rule to become universal, including the nations (Micah 4:1–3). They foresaw a submission to God's rule that would bring about the cessation of warfare. This would mean the conversion of weapons into instruments for the production of food (Micah 4:3). The fear and deprivation so common under evil rulers would be superseded under God's righteous rule (Micah 4:4).

This kingdom vision shared by the prophets was primarily historical. In all probability they were not thinking of a fulfillment beyond history as we know it. But this does not mean that they envisioned the kingdom coming as a result of mere cause and effect in human history. It would be the result of the sovereign activity of God, who had saved his people in the past and whose coming anew was continually awaited. The prophetic vision of God's kingdom of the future is characterized by a radical newness (Isaiah 65:17ff., 66:22). This kingdom, which has no end, is present in God's just and compassionate ordering of human relationships. God's rule is characterized by wholeness of life as he has always intended it to be, in marked contrast to the social injustices and the suffering of which Egypt was a paradigm in Israel's experience.

God's people returned from Babylonian captivity with high expectations. However, their hopes that God's rule would manifest itself in Israel's midst were not realized. Apocalyptic writers during the period between the two testaments shared their visions of when and how the kingdom would come. They almost despaired of God acting redemptively in history to restore his righteous rule and concluded that history is dominated by evil. Hope lies only in the future, they said. God would again visit his people to deliver them from evil, but only at the end of history. The earlier prophetic vision of God's rule, which held history and eschatology together in a dynamic tension, had been all but lost in Judaism. Rather than waiting for a future kingdom that could come only following the cataclysmic end of history, many Jews were tempted to set the stage for God's rule by forcibly driving out the enemies of God's people who occupied their land. There were frequent attempts to cast off the yoke of the Roman oppressors in order that God's rule might be restored. Even among Jesus' disciples this dream seems to have been nurtured right up to the eve of Pentecost (Acts 1:6).

Jesus began his messianic mission proclaiming the presence of the kingdom in the context of this wide gamut of prophetic and apocalyptic expectations and the popular tendency to understand God's rule in nationalistic rather than universal dimensions (Mark 1:14). The Jewish people in general expected that the Messiah would establish God's kingdom, vindicating the righteous and destroying Israel's enemies. However, Jesus' perception of the kingdom differed from the popular views. He began his ministry making clear that God's kingdom is for all peoples. In the synagogue in Nazareth, Jesus read the prophetic vision of messianic fulfillment from Isaiah 61:1–2a. But he stopped short of the next part: "and the day of vengeance of our Lord." Instead of announcing divine judgment on Israel's enemies, Jesus went on to recall God's gracious dealings in the past with foreigners, including the widow from Sidon and Naaman the Syrian. Jewish opposition was so violent that Jesus barely escaped with his life. Scholars have suggested that Luke 4:18–30 may well have been intended as a brief preview of Jesus' messianic mission. His announcement of the kingdom as God's new universal community of salvation and his daring willingness to commit himself to its realization did, in fact, eventually lead to his death.

Two more ways in which Jesus' perception of the kingdom differed from popular understandings are reflected in his response to Pilate, "My kingdom is not of this world" (John 18:36). This text has often been interpreted to mean that the kingdom has nothing to do with social structures. This interpretation is probably more attractive to modern readers than it would have been to Jesus' contemporaries, who generally viewed God's rule as a concrete social reality, if not present, then at least future. First, Jesus' response to Pilate is perceived as a reference to the world to come, in contrast to this world. This view understands the kingdom of God as a reality to be experienced beyond the scope of history. However, it seems to contradict the plain sense of the words of Jesus recorded by both Matthew and Luke, "But if it is by the Spirit of God that I cast out demons, then the kingdom of God has come upon you" (Matt. 12:28, Luke 11:20). The sense of the verb here leaves no doubt that Jesus viewed the kingdom as a present reality. Second, the kingdom is often perceived as an inner, spiritual reality, the right relationship of an individual with God. Jesus' words in Luke 17:21 are interpreted, as indeed some translations have done, "The kingdom of God is within you," as referring primarily to an inner, personal experience. It would seem to be more in line with the intent of Jesus here to interpret Luke's text, "The kingdom of God is among you" or "in your midst."

From the context of John 18:36, the meaning of Jesus' words becomes clear. His kingship is not of this world in that he does not resort to coercive violence, either for self-protection or for the establishment of the kingdom. So God's rule does affect the political, social, and economic decisions of his people, not by withdrawal into one's inner spiritual nature or by projection into a future beyond history, but by values that offer a radical alternative to those of the world.

According to the New Testament, the power of the new age is already operative in Jesus. Everything he says and does is related to the coming of God's kingdom. Jesus' exorcisms are prime examples of the way the rule of God is being inaugurated. In his messianic mission Jesus has assailed and overcome the Evil One (Luke 11:21–22). In effect, the mission of Jesus has been to reverse the consequences of evil in the world: disease; demon possession; the hostility of nature; social, religious, and ethnic rivalries; hunger; economic exploitation; empty religiosity; alienation; death. The conflict that characterizes his ministry is, in reality, the struggle of the new age to displace the age of sin and death. Wherever the kingdom of God is dynamically present, the values and structures of the present age will be radically reversed (Luke 1:51–53). Therefore, Jesus' followers rejoice at the signs of Satan's fall. Wherever the values and structures of evil are being effectively challenged and are being radically turned around, there we see a sign of the dynamic presence of God's kingdom.

The consummation of God's kingdom at the end of the age has been anticipated by the dynamic presence of his rule among humankind in Jesus' person and mission. Jesus surprised his contemporaries with an eschatological vision that broke with traditional stereotypes. However, Jesus' followers eventually caught this vision with admirable clarity. Inspired by the Spirit of Jesus himself, they set about making disciples of all nations and changing their social structures in the direction of God's intention for his people. They were drawn on by the hope of their Lord's appearance at the end of history to bring to its ultimate consummation God's rule, which had already been inaugurated among them.

During the first centuries of our era, Christians continued to believe that the prophetic vision of the "latter days" had, indeed, been fulfilled in their midst by the coming of Jesus and the ongoing presence of his powerful Spirit among them. In their debates with the early Christians, the Jews charged that if nothing had really changed in the world, the Messiah could not have come according to Isaiah 2:4. Therefore, since the world was still filled with warfare, Jesus could not have been the Messiah. In their response, Christians rejected the idea that God's kingdom would come only at the end of the world. They also refused to believe that the kingdom comes invisibly and without concrete changes. They insisted that the Messiah had come and that the world had, in fact, been changed. The prophetic view of God's peaceable kingdom had become a reality in the church. This vision was shared by the principal leaders of the early church. As Origen commented, "We no longer take up sword against nation, nor do we learn war any more having become children of peace for the sake of Jesus."

However, the church did not retain this vision of the kingdom for long. In the fourth century the "Constantinian shift" occurred. Augustine became a spokesman for Christians of his time and, for that matter, for most Christians since his time. Because the visible community no longer reflected with any credibility God's rule, Augustine held that the true church is the invisible, heavenly city of

God. Meanwhile, Christians are essentially aliens awaiting the future appearance of the kingdom. The church is a gathering of those rescued from this world for life in the next. In Augustine's thought, the realization of God's rule was postponed into the future, and the mission of the church was largely reduced to preparing individuals for participation in that future. Another aspect of this Augustinian heritage is the individualization that has plagued the church throughout its history. Rather than yearning for the coming of God's kingdom, Augustine's deepest desire became "to know God and the soul." Postponing into the future the dynamic presence of the kingdom has almost inevitably led to an individualistic vision of kingdom salvation. This futuristic, individualistic eschatological legacy has so influenced the mission of the church that Jesus' gospel of the kingdom is all but silenced in our witness. The social structures and practices of kingdom citizenship here and now give way to the preparation of individuals for a future and purely heavenly kingdom.

A more recent movement, which has been particularly influential among conservative Protestants and has been widely accepted among Mennonites, is Dispensationalism. The Dispensationalist interpretation of Scripture has been formulated and popularized in North America largely through the Scofield Reference Bible. It is essentially a system of biblical interpretation based on a particular understanding of salvation history. The kingdom that Jesus announced to the Jews was rejected. Therefore, the offer of the kingdom was postponed until the millennium, when it will again be offered to the Jews. Meanwhile, the church emerged quite apart from the gospel of the kingdom proclaimed by Jesus. For eschatology this means that the kingdom of God is not a present reality but a future one. Meanwhile, true believers will assemble together for communion and await divine intervention at the parousia. The absence of a vision of the dynamic presence of the kingdom of God, held in tension with a lively hope of its consummation at Jesus' appearing, has contributed to a futuristic, otherworldly, and individualistic eschatology among many Christians.

Although this is very difficult for most modern Christians in the West to understand, the suffering of the faithful is an eschatological sign—a sign of the kingdom coming. Paul told the early Christians that "through many tribulations we must enter the kingdom of God" (Acts 14:22). The suffering of God's people is directly related to the coming of the kingdom of God, and Jesus himself is the model for our suffering (1 Thes. 2:14, 2 Thes. 1:4–5, 1 Pet. 2:21; 3:14–18).

Jesus suffered for his prophetic witness, and he reminded his followers that they would be persecuted just like the prophets who went before them (Matt. 5:12). Jesus suffered as a prophet because he challenged the way the Jerusalem establishment was exercising power. Religion was used to put down the common people and to exploit the poor. The formation of a messianic kingdom community as an alternative to official Judaism was such a threat to those in power that they did away with Jesus. Jerusalem was the killer of the prophets (Luke

13:33–34). Rather than simply being the consequence of a divine decree, Jesus' death and suffering, as well as that of his followers, was the result of the violence of those who rejected the promise of the kingdom come.

There is also the sense in which Jesus' suffering was in solidarity with humanity in its need. Jesus' defense of, and solidarity with, the poor, the strangers, the lepers, and other social outcasts was a direct threat to those in power. Jesus' courageous defense of the foreigners and the poor in the temple cleansing episode was crucial in a literal sense. It led directly to the cross. In its understanding of the meaning of Jesus' suffering and death, the New Testament depicts him as a Representative Man. In his authentic solidarity with sinful and suffering humanity, Jesus was called the Second Adam, the Pioneer of salvation, the High Priest in touch with human weakness, the Forerunner on humanity's behalf, and the First Born among many brothers and sisters in God's kingdom. But this solidarity with the despised and oppressed was not without its price.

Jesus' suffering on behalf of the enemies of God's righteous kingdom resulted in their rescue. Peter Chelcicky, the radical reformer among the Czech Brethren of the fifteenth century, perceived that the salvation of the oppressors would come about only through the suffering of the oppressed. He caught a glimpse of the salvific nature of vicarious suffering to which the apostles had witnessed, "For Christ also died ... the righteous for the unrighteous, that he might bring us to God" (1 Pet. 3:18). Leonardo Boff, the Brazilian Franciscan, insists that suffering and death freely assumed in behalf of the oppressors can be truly salvific. Even though suffering cannot be avoided, violence will not have the last word. To act in a conciliatory way toward those bent on destroying fellowship introduces a saving element into human relationships. To forgive and to assume freely the cross of suffering and death that is forced upon us is to redirect history itself toward that ultimate reconciliation, which will finally include even God's enemies. The innocent and vicarious suffering and death of Christians in our time is not an unmitigated tragedy, even though it results from crimes perpetrated against humanity and should be energetically denounced. When suffering is freely assumed in the cause of Christ's kingdom, it takes on salvific dimensions. Radical Christians have traditionally understood their suffering for the cause of the kingdom as "birth pangs" of the new era being born. The suffering of the messianic community as well as the "groaning" of creation is a sure sign that the consummation of God's rule is near (Luke 21:31, Rom. 8:18–25).

The eschatological hope of the early church is summed up remarkably in the text with which John climaxes his Apocalypse (Rev. 21:1–22:5). Here we catch a vision of the consummation of God's intention for the entire universe. It takes the form of a new creation (21:1,5). The New Jerusalem appears in juxtaposition with Babylon. Rather than understanding these as literal cities, John seems to intend them to be pictures of two distinct realities. Babylon symbolizes fallen humanity with structures characterized by deceit, injustice, greed, terror, and death. The New Jerusalem is a picture of the kingdom of God where peoples live in harmony, justice, and peace in the light of God's glory. While it is true that the New Jerusalem will be consummated in all of its fullness after the fall of Babylon, the relationship of the two realities is not merely chronological: the New Jerusalem can appear only after the disappearance of Babylon. These two cities coexist in history. Therefore, God's people are to "come out" of Babylon and neither to "take part in her sins" nor "share in her plagues" (Rev. 18:4). The future will be a new creation, probably not all new things, but all things made new (Rev. 21:5). It will bear the characteristics of an earthly paradise restored. The "water of life" provides fruit for sustenance and healing. The curse that fell over the first paradise will be lifted in the new paradise, where there will be neither "mourning, nor crying, nor pain any more" (Rev. 21:4). Tears will be dried and death itself will be vanquished. The future that God is bringing will take the form of a new covenant. In the words of the biblical covenant formula, "They shall be his people, and God himself will be with them and be their God" (Rev. 21:3). God sets his tabernacle in the midst of humanity and extends the blessings of sonship, not only to the Messiah but also to the entire messianic community (Rev. 21:3,7). God's future offers renewed and perfect community. The fraternal and egalitarian social structures that characterized Israel under the Sinai covenant and the messianic community under the new covenant point to the perfect future of God's consummated kingdom.

God's kingdom comes "prepared as a bride for her husband" (Rev. 21:2). Babylon, characterized by deceit, exploitation, and violence and symbol of the empire of evil, had, in her unfaithfulness, prostituted herself to the power-hungry rulers of the world. This is the same image the prophets of Israel had employed in order to call God's people to faithfulness. By contrast, the people of God, characterized by their faithfulness in following the Messiah, have been invited to the marriage supper of the Lamb "as a bride adorned for her husband" and "clothed with ... the righteous deeds of the saints" (Rev. 21:2, 19:8). The consummation of the kingdom will bring the definitive union of God with his people.

Together with the faithful of old, we are invited to rejoice over the signs of Babylon's destruction. We are called to follow the Lamb in a new exodus of liberation from Egypt's seductive charms. In contrast, God's pilgrim people find their salvation under God's gracious rule within history. And to "follow the Lamb wherever he goes" is the only sure path to participation in the consummation of God's kingdom at the end of history. A truly biblical eschatology will save the church from temptations to take short cuts and to settle for lesser goals in its mission. Only those kingdom values that anticipate the future in which all creation shall be made new will be of ultimate consequence.

John Driver, USA, b. 1924, missionary, teacher, and writer in Latin America and Spain for thirty-eight years under Mennonite Board of Missions, recently retired.

Seed is distributed as part of an MCC-sponsored program for farmers in Ethiopia. (MCC photo by Ken Litwiller, 1986)

Thoughts on family ethics

by Ruth Krall

Personal prologue

In preparing for this article, I realized that I have multiple windows into Mennonite family life. Although I am a single adult woman without children, my personal experience of family life has two dimensions. First, I am a member of the family into which I was born. In that family I experienced parental relationships, sibling relationships, and a deep embeddedness within a stable network of extended family relationships. In that family I developed both a personal and a familial identity. It was within my extended birth-family that I developed awareness of my religious and ethnic identity as Mennonite.

As a North American woman, singleness was a feasible option for my life as I left college. Decisions about singleness yielded the realization that I would never recreate the secure stability of life patterns represented by my parental home. Instead, over the past twenty-five years, I have carefully constructed an alternative family of close friends. This friend-family is multigenerational, multiethnic, and includes both men and women. It includes single mothers, married couples, divorced or widowed individuals, people who have made personal commitments to live together as a family, and other single people without children. Within this alternative friend-family I most closely replicate the family life of married couples. Within the friend-family I celebrate birthdays, holidays, informal gatherings, and transitions of life. Within this friend-family I mourn the deaths and losses of adult life. Within this group of friends I make ongoing decisions about my life and also help others to make their own decisions.

These initial windows into Mennonite family life remain important to my life. In my birth-family I am old enough to find pleasure in new generations being born. In my friend-family I am included as friends make personal decisions in all arenas of their adult life. I am included in discussions about the daily parenting of children as well as in discussions about the care of aging parents. Careers, health, money, recreation: all of these become topics of mutual concern.

As a single person I am aware that the daily textures of my life differ from most of my friends and acquaintances. Yet I also know I am not an "only." At any given time in the United States, one-third of all adults over age 18 are single. My mother, for example, who was married for nearly thirty-five years and raised three children, has had more years of single life than I. After my father's death she needed to create a new family for herself, a network of relatives and friends.

Other windows than personal experience exist to create awareness of Mennonite family life. As a psychiatric-mental health nurse specialist, I worked in two

distinctly different Mennonite mental health hospitals—the first in an area
settled predominantly by the Mennonite Church, the second in an area where
Mennonite Brethren and General Conference Mennonites were more typical.

In more recent years, classroom and counseling contacts with college students at
Goshen College have provided the opportunity to listen to young Mennonites.
Many of these students are attempting to sort out identity issues for themselves.
Many are actively engaged in questions of "faith and people." They want to
know who they are. They also want to know what a community of faith means
for their own lives and their decisions.

It is from this multishaped vantage point that I write of family ethics in the
Mennonite church. I am not summarizing a research study, nor am I a certified
expert in family relations. Rather, I am an observer of my own life and the life of
families within the North American Mennonite church.

Concerns

> A young woman sits opposite me. She says, "The lecture yesterday
> about divorce statistics in the United States made me furious. My
> parents were such good Mennonites. Yet last month they told me they
> have separated and plan to get a divorce. What about all that religious
> teaching about marriage as a lifelong commitment in good and bad
> times?

This student is no longer alone in her pain, anger, and questioning. The impact
of divorce in the Mennonite church continues to grow. There are fewer and
fewer congregations that have never had a divorce decision made by a member
couple. The Church Member Profile II (1989) of five denominations in the
United States and Canada (Mennonite Church, General Conference Mennonite
Church, Mennonite Brethren Church, Brethren in Christ Church, and Evangelical Mennonite Church) reveals that divorce has quadrupled since the 1972
survey. In 1972, 1 percent of the original survey's respondents reported divorce.
By 1989, 4.2 percent did so. Twice as many divorces are found among Mennonites in urban areas as among those in rural areas. Increased education, increasing
assimilation to the values of the dominant culture, and rising expectations for
marital happiness may all be factors in these statistics. (Personal conversation,
J. Howard Kauffman, February 1990)

> A young man sits in my office and cries. He says, "My dad is gay. Ever
> since I've been six or seven years old, I have felt something was differ-
> ent in my family. Now my mom tells me that Dad has a male lover. She
> doesn't want a divorce and says he doesn't want one either. I really love
> both my parents. How could he do this to her? How could he do this to
> me? Mom told me that the church was going to intervene. But what

good will that do? They will just make a bad situation worse. They can't make my dad love my mom again. They can't make him "not gay."

In the 1989 Church Member Profile, more than 96 percent of respondents reported a heterosexual orientation while less than 4 percent reported a bisexual or homosexual orientation. Mennonites are not in agreement about the acceptability of a homosexual lifestyle or upon the acceptability of a homosexual orientation. Neither official church structures nor individual church members all agree on the meaning of homosexuality in the lives of Mennonite individuals. The presence of a gay caucus in the Mennonite church signals most clearly this difference of opinion. When gay men and lesbian women met daily at a church conference (Normal, Illinois, 1989) in a public prayer and praise meeting, they challenged the opinion of official structures and the majority of church members as well. The church press in both countries reports strongly held but widely divergent views on this matter. Yet individuals and families within the church struggle to understand themselves and those they love. Many attempt to maintain strong ties with the church. In a climate of dialogue where opinion is strongly polarized, they often struggle in secret and in isolation.

A young woman sits in my living room and comments, "I had an abortion a year ago. I was raped by my date after our graduation party. I never have told anyone about the rape. And I never told anyone about the abortion until it was over. I always thought abortion was sinful until I was pregnant after that rape. All I could do then was to think about suicide or abortion. I decided I wanted to live. That meant I had to have an abortion. I don't know any other Mennonite woman who has had an abortion. I need to talk with someone who understands what I've been through. Do you know any Mennonite woman who would be willing to talk with me about her experience with abortion?

Abortion is another one of the family life issues about which church members and church structures disagree. Church publications editorialize that abortion is not acceptable to Mennonites. The anti-choice movement among Mennonites gets strong support in the Mennonite press. (See *Gospel Herald*, Editorial, February 21, 1989.) Many Mennonite lay people feel that abortion is always wrong. Yet some Mennonite women seek abortions, and other Mennonite women and men support the pro-choice movement. Women who are pregnant and who need to make decisions about pregnancy continuation or termination often feel they must make these decisions alone. They also feel as if they must live in silence with their decision.

A married friend calls on the phone and says, "I need to talk. You know we have been trying to get pregnant for the past five years. Nothing has worked. I really want a baby of our own and so does he. Now the doctor tells me we could try a new fertility drug. But it is going to be very expensive, and we might end up having several babies. I can't handle the idea of giving birth to several babies, some of whom may not be able to live outside the womb. And I'm not sure I think it is right to spend this much money to try to get a baby and perhaps still not get pregnant.

The presence of reproductive technologies in North America means that individuals and couples can make decisions about pregnancy that were not possible a decade ago. In addition to the technologies that are used to facilitate conception, others have been developed to diagnose problems. According to a special issue of *Newsweek* (Winter/Spring 1990), physicians are already able to identify some 250 genetic defects, "not only in the blood of a potential parent but in the tissue of a developing fetus. The result is that, for the first time in history, people are deciding, rather than wondering, what kind of children they will bear" (p. 94). Looking to the future, it is anticipated that science will eventually be able to "[discern defects] five days after fertilization, before the embryo even implants in the uterine wall" (p. 95).

The technological capacity to identify fetal gender is now in place, permitting individuals or couples to select the sex of a baby. *Newsweek* reports that sex selectivity has begun to be practiced in the United States. In 1973, only 1 percent of American geneticists considered it morally acceptable to abort fetuses of an undesired gender. By 1989, nearly 20 percent approved in any situation and, in a 1985 survey, 62 percent said "they would screen fetuses for a couple who had four healthy daughters and wanted a son" (p. 100).

> Over coffee a good friend breaks down in sobs. She says, "My granddaughter has just accused her father of sexually molesting her when she was an adolescent. I am so upset I don't know what to do or think. One moment I want to tell her she is lying. The next, I want to comfort her. I can't believe my son did something like that. But I can't believe she is lying either. What are we to do? What am I to do? I just can't make any sense out of it all."

Incest, sexual molestation, and rape are present in Mennonite families in North America and Canada. In addition, spouse abuse is also present. In the 1989 Church Member Profile, 10 percent of respondents report physical abuse as children; 6 percent report sexual abuse as children; nearly 4 percent report forced intercourse before marriage; and almost 4 percent report spouse abuse. The pain and turmoil caused by these violations of the human body and spirit are gradually being made known among us. Articles in the church press, for example, the September 4, 1989, edition of the *Mennonite Reporter*—"My Crucified Childhood: The Horrors of a Christian Upbringing"—remind us that the pain and psychological damage of child abuse, spouse abuse, and sexual violence are not readily healed for victims of such violence and abuse. In addition, family members and friends are also wounded by the presence of victimization in any given set of human family relationships.

> A letter arrives from a college classmate. She writes, "This has been a very hard year for us. Our marriage has not been very satisfying to either of us for the past five years. But we have both been working at it ... or so I thought. Now I find out he has been having a fairly open affair with his secretary. Many of his friends knew but never told me. I found a note to him from her in the laundry and asked him about it. That's how I found out. He promises me the affair is finished. But I am having great difficulty believing him. He betrayed our marriage vows. Why should I trust him at all? I am depressed and hurt by all of this. Maybe I would feel better if I also had an affair and paid him back in kind. However, I probably would only feel worse. I don't know what I am going to do about all of this. So far, I haven't told the children and hope we never will need to do so.

Ethical concerns

In each of the vignettes above, individuals are struggling with family life issues. Real life relationships have created moments of pain, anger, hurt, or struggle. Each individual within these vignettes represents a relationship that has an ethical dilemma present within its core.

What happens to children when parents divorce? Divorce does not only reflect a couple's wishes for happiness. It also reflects their pessimism about being able to be happy together. Divorce affects both individuals in a couple. It also affects their children. In addition, it affects grandparents and the extended family. Divorce is not a private decision. It is profoundly familial.

What happens to families and individuals within families when one member recognizes that he or she is a homosexual? When any issue is politicized in the way that homosexuality has been politicized among Mennonites, polarization occurs. The impact of that polarization may have more effects on the individual than does the initial awareness of her or his difference from the majority.

Abortion, likewise, is a decision that has been politicized and polarized in our thinking as a people. For many church members, abortion is always wrong. For others it is a difficult but necessary choice. As with other debated issues in church life, the impact of strong pro-choice and anti-choice positions has created a situation wherein a woman's pain and suffering remain hidden.

Decisions about reproductive technology involve decisions about the creation of life and the destruction of life. In addition, the presence of these technologies also raises stewardship issues among us. How will a family, committed to a communal faith in the people of God, make decisions about spending money for reproductive assistance?

Having begun to recognize the sexual violence among Mennonites, we are now faced with the need to make decisions about it. In what ways do we need to work with victims of such violence, and in what ways do we need to work with the victimizers? What is the essential message of repentance that is needed? Is there a message of forgiveness and reconciliation that will not further betray the victim?

Finally, when sexual betrayal is discovered within a marital relationship, what is needed by all individuals affected by the betrayal? How is healing brought about for the couple, for the third person, or for any children involved? What is the message of repentance and reconciliation? In what way can the church, as the communal people of God, represent the mercy of God as people attempt to reestablish their lives?

As we enter this new decade on the edge of a new millennium, challenges to family ethics will continue to multiply. The presence of technology will continue to expand possibilities for choice. Specific texts of Scripture or tradition may no longer appear able to guide us. Genetic engineering, for example, was not a possibility in the biblical era. Today we are making genetic decisions about childbirth and abortion. Many of these decisions are made privately and without consultation within the church. However, if we claim to be a communal people of God, we are bound together by fibers of accountability. What is the nature of that accountability as we face issues of reproduction?

One of the unresolved issues of North American Mennonite life is how we will define accountability to God and people. When specific issues divide us—for example, homosexuality or abortion—how will we begin to discern God's will? Once discernment has occurred, how will we enforce the belief of the majority group? How will we respect the consciences of those who represent minority opinions? As we North American Mennonites are once more engaged in active evangelism within our own North American cultures, life-realities similar to those of the vignettes above will continue to emerge with their implicit demands for understanding and action. On what basis will we begin to assist individuals and families to cope with these life-realities? What spiritual growth is called for in a time of pluralism of choice?

Ruth E. Krall, USA, b. 1940, M.S. in nursing, Ph.D. in theology and personality; associate professor of religion, psychology, and nursing and director of peace studies at Goshen College (Goshen, Indiana).

Note
The case vignettes in this article have been created by the author and do not represent any actual individuals or situations.

A theology of mission in outline

by Mennonite Board of Missions

Shown below are excerpts from a document initiated and endorsed by Mennonite Board of Missions in 1978. As Wilbert R. Shenk points out, any outline of the theology of mission is incomplete. It must be filled out. It is restricted by the limited ability of whoever attempts to understand and interpret what God is saying to his people in their time and place. Yet such attempts are necessary to sharpen the issues and to focus the task more clearly.

The present outline is one such effort. It is the product of a process of search, discussion, and testing. It draws both on present practice and the vision of what missionary faithfulness ought to be. It is intended to be read alongside the Bible in a spirit of prayer. It is offered as an interim statement—in anticipation of further growth in vision and commitment.

1.   God's ultimate purpose is to "unite all things in Christ"—the redemption of mankind—"to the praise of his glorious grace" (Rom. 8:20–23, Eph. 1, Col. 1:15–20, Rev. 4:11; 5; 7:9–12, Ezek. 36:16–32, Isaiah 43:7).

4.   The people of God are witnesses. They respond to God's mission through specific efforts in time and space. These missions represent God's mission faithfully to the extent they extend the rule of God. To the degree missions promote ethnocentrism, secular power patterns, a spirit of conquest or result in cultural enslavement, they impede God's mission (cf John 17:18; 10:21b).

5.   As the reconciled community, the people of God become a sign and firstfruits of God's rule and kingdom. As they manifest the fruits and gifts of the Spirit, they are the new humanity living amid the old. When this happens God's people portray the message of the gospel and thus become a part of the good news (Rom. 8:23, Eph. 1:11–14).

6.   Church and kingdom are not synonyms. Kingdom refers to God's rule or reign. God's rule creates the church and the church witnesses to the kingdom. The church is God's people to whom the keys of the kingdom have been given in order to open it to all peoples. Thus the church is the instrument of the kingdom. The missionary message, as Jesus himself showed, is that the kingdom of God in Jesus Christ has now come among humanity and is moving toward final victory over the powers of this world (Matt. 4:17, Mark 1:14ff., cf Acts 8:12; 19:8; 20:25; 28:23,31).

7.   The people of God are ambassadors of the kingdom of God and witnesses to God's mighty acts in history. They proclaim and demonstrate kingdom concern for freedom and reconciliation, for righteousness and human welfare. They call

men and women to receive God's salvation through Jesus Christ by accepting his rule and lordship (Acts 2:14–36, Rom. 14:17, 2 Cor. 5:20, cf Luke 4:18–21).

9.   Mission emerges out of worship. In worship the people of God discover the grace, righteousness, judgment, and holiness of God. The people of God become authentic when they live in repentance. When the people encounter God, acknowledge their need and turn, they are changed into God's likeness. This experience of God's grace and glory will lead the people of God to identify with the divine missionary purposes. This is the source of missionary dynamic (Psalm 67, Isaiah 6, John 3:16, 2 Cor. 3:18).

10.   Throughout biblical history God continually breaks into human experience in order to redeem fallen humanity. God is the God who in the Exodus led the people out of Egypt, gave them the law at Sinai, and formed a covenant with them. God made them a people by rescuing them from obscurity, saving them from their sins, and delivering them from their enemies. God restored them to fellowship with himself so that they might live in shalom. Adam-in-alienation is superseded by Abraham-in-fellowship (Gen. 12:2, Deut. 10:12–22; 26:5–11, Luke 1:46–55, cf 1 Pet. 2:9–10).

11.   God is disclosed to humanity most fully in the incarnation of Jesus Christ. The incarnation revealed divine love personally and directly. God reaffirmed creation in the incarnation; as the final redemptive initiative, God took on human form. The incarnation is fundamental to God's mission as the mode of missio Deo (John 1; 14:8–11, Phil. 2:5–8, Heb. 1–2, 1 John 4:7–11).

12.   Jesus Christ entered human history as the Messiah, the Anointed One, the Suffering Servant, announcing the advent of the kingdom of God. He began his ministry by proclaiming that the kingdom had become reality in himself and was now to be accepted. It was the message of hope and salvation to a hopeless, dying world. This is the essential missionary message (Matt. 4:17,23, Mark 1:14ff., cf Matt. 11:4–6, Luke 4:18–21; 11:14–23; 17:20ff.).

15.   Central to God's redemptive mission is the calling out of a people who, in turn, are sent as envoys of God's kingdom. In the covenant with Abraham, God promised that through Abraham the peoples of the world would be blessed. The purpose of the people of God is fulfilled in their life in him and in their being sent out. Whenever the people of Israel renewed their covenant with God, they recognized that they were renewing their obligation to the orphan, the widow, the weak, and the stranger. Worship was a time for covenant renewal—when God's people deepened their commitment to the divine purposes. Because God sends, they came to understand themselves as a sent out people and consecrated themselves to be witnesses among the peoples to what God was doing (Gen. 12:1–3; 17:4–8, Isaiah 42:6ff., John 20:21b, Acts 2:38–40; 3:25, 1 Pet. 2:9ff.).

16. Jesus set forth his manifesto for the new community in the Sermon on the Mount. He addressed his message to his own people but met unbelief. The few who responded he gathered into this new community to be that people who live in the new reality of the kingdom where God is leader, and who participate in extending the kingdom through Messianic activity and witness (Matt. 5–7).

21. The ascension of Jesus and Pentecost ushered in the time when the work of Christ took on new dimensions. The Holy Spirit is God dynamically present and at work in the world, carrying out the ministry of Jesus Christ until his purposes are fulfilled (Acts 1:8).

22. The Holy Spirit is extending Christ's rule by overcoming all forms of sin and the "dividing wall of hostility" (Eph. 2:14b)—racism, sexism, tribalism, nationalism—and binding together as one new people individuals from many peoples. The urgency of mission is the urgency of the Holy Spirit responding to the whole creation which is in travail awaiting "adoption as sons." The missionary witness is marked by both the urgency and joy of the Spirit as God's people are led out in mission (Rom. 8:19–23; 10:12ff., Gal. 3:28, Eph. 1–2, Col. 3:10ff., Rev. 5:1–14; 7:9–12; 21:22–22:5).

28. The people of God are called to mission. The mission is God's and the people are God's. When they daily pray "thy kingdom come," they reaffirm God's lordship and commit themselves to missionary obedience.

29. This is the missionary age. In it the disciple community continues the mission Jesus himself began on earth. Following the resurrection Jesus commissioned his disciples to take the gospel of the kingdom to the ends of the earth until the end of the age, calling men and women to become his disciples. He linked this mandate to mission, however, directly to the coming of the Holy Spirit. The Spirit, then, provides the power and direction to the Messianic community in its witness to Jesus Christ in the world. The kingdom which was prefigured in Jesus' ministry is now being extended in this age among all peoples (Matt. 28:18–20, Mark 16:15ff., Luke 24:46–49, John 20:20–23, Acts 1:8).

30. This age must be understood eschatologically. The Holy Spirit is extending the Messianic reign, but that reign is establishing within history a part of the reality which is to be disclosed fully in Christ's second coming. The Messianic community is that group which is already living in the context of the reign of Christ, even though it does so in a world hostile to Christ's claims. This is the focal point of missionary action: faith in the Messiah challenging unfaith or rejection of the Messiah. The evangelistic task is to announce the good news that Jesus Christ has come in love and saving power. Now is the time for all to repent and be saved and become a part of God's people (Acts 2:14–36).

31. In order to share the good news of God's rule, the people of God must cross linguistic, social, and political boundaries to reach people who have not heard the gospel. Although the Holy Spirit sovereignly endows each member of the body of Christ with spiritual gifts, some gifts contribute most immediately to the nurturing and maintenance of the body, while others are for purposes of witness and service across various boundaries. The church is challenged to respect each Spirit-given gift. Apostolic gifts are to be released in order that the whole church will be led in sharing the gospel of the kingdom in the world. Those gifted to be apostles and preachers feel the "fire burning in their bones." For them not to proclaim the good news is to act against their very nature for "the love of Christ controls" them to share what they know (Jer. 20:9, 1 Cor. 9:15–18; 12; 14, 2 Cor. 5:14, Eph. 4:1–16, cf Acts 13:1–4).

32. Jesus himself announced the missionary message at the start of his ministry. He defined it in terms of the prophetic message of the Old Testament—the rule of God and his justice. Jesus Christ, as Messiah, began to fulfill what had been promised long before. He set before men and women an alternative, calling them to repent and "turn from" the bondage of the world. He enables them to live in the new order of salvation where the weak, oppressed, disinherited, enslaved, and morally bankrupt are empowered by God's Spirit (Matt. 4:23; 9:35, Luke 1:46–55; 4:18ff., cf Jer. 31:31–33).

33. Consistent with the Jubilee paradigm, Jesus emphasized lifting up the weak and poor, healing the sick and releasing the prisoner. He pronounced judgment on the rich and powerful who had no compassion and insisted that for them to live under God's rule required repentance and turning to a new way of life (Matt. 11:2–5).

34. The foundation of this new order is love and self-sacrifice rather than coercion and self-fulfillment. The message of the kingdom is the gospel of peace: a gracious, loving God reconciling unworthy individuals to himself and thereby to one another. Love, the means of humanity's reconciliation to God, is both the basis for reconciliation among people and the path of obedient discipleship, even to the extent of loving the enemy. Only on this basis is it possible to create out of all nations one new people (Eph. 1–3).

35. The fundamental mode of mission is incarnation, the embodiment of the gospel in a particular cultural context. The gospel addresses every culture from within rather than from without.

36. Mission is carried out within history. Mission interprets history Christologically and, therefore, seeks to create a new history by introducing a new order. True meaning in history is found in the work of Jesus Christ. Mission is the basic means by which God in Jesus Christ has chosen to achieve the divine purposes (Col. 1:15–20, Heb. 1:2–4).

37. Missionary action is always addressed to people in specific cultural contexts. The gospel does not despise culture but judges every culture. The incarnation maintained the tension between the divine and the human. Jesus, the Christ, was perceived as an authentic human being, identified with a particular people in a given locale. Yet he focused God's love and judgment on human nature and culture (Matt. 13:53–56).

38. The biblical view of mission includes both the personal and the social, both humanity and the cosmos. Human sin has led to the defacement of nature. Mission leads to the restoration of what has been lost through sin. The eschatological summing up of all things in Christ signifies the new creation in which the power of sin is overcome and a new order is established. Within this new reality individuals experience salvation already because they have begun to live as members of the new creation, a new order (Col. 1:15–23, cf Rev. 21:1–4).

39. The strategy for mission derives directly from the structure of the life of the people of God. This strategy is based on the new peoplehood. The Messianic community lives the gospel. It demonstrates how both the individual and the community take repentance seriously by submitting their structures and lifestyle to the lordship of the Messiah. The gospel is thereby embodied in the human situation. Mission thrusts the Messianic community outward, dispersing it among the peoples of the world. It is a movement of sojourners and pilgrims moving through history and throughout the world witnessing to the kingdom of God and incorporating into the movement all who accept Jesus Christ as Lord (Matt. 28:18–20, Mark 16:15ff., Luke 24:46–49, John 20:19–23, Acts 1:8, 1 Pet. 2:11).

40. This strategy calls for the apostolic witness to be expressed through multiple forms: word, deed, and presence. The church's vocation in the world includes preaching, healing, witnessing before authorities, teaching, living in fellowship, recounting God's mighty acts and applying that message to life, and suffering for the sake of the gospel. The church is not called to assure a certain outcome in history or work for its own success. The church is not called simply to serve the world. Beyond good works and humanitarian efforts, it points to the claims of the kingdom from whose existence and dynamic it springs. It knows that God is doing a new thing in history and testifies to that action. The church, therefore, takes the reality of sin seriously. In its daily walk the church knows the continuing struggle against the power of sin in the church and in the world. It is only by grace that God's people exist, but their existence as a miracle of grace brings God's kingdom near. The presence of the kingdom poses before men and women the possibility of life rather than death. It is always an invitation to accept the new and liberated life in Christ. The witness to the kingdom has power and authority because it is given in the mighty name of Jesus Christ and the power of the Spirit (Acts 4:10–12, 2 Cor. 5:11–12).

Exceprts from March 1978 statement by the Mennonite Board of Missions.

Honduran Mennonite pastor Adalid Romero of the San Pedro Sula Central Church and Francisco Calix of the San Pedro Sula Aurora congregation baptize a new member. On this day, thirty-nine believers were baptized. (MCC photo by Mark Beach, 1986)

Ministries   5

PIPKA mission

by Yahya Chrismanto

History

The Indonesian Muria Christian Church (GKMI), the church from which PIPKA originated and takes shelter, was born in 1920 on the initiative of Tee Siem Tat, a Chinese businessman in Kudus, Central Java. For almost forty years the GKMI grew only in the cities around the Muria Mountain, in the northern part of Central Java, among the Chinese communities.

In the late 1950s there were new, young synod leaders who had received theological education. Two of them were Herman Tann (Tee's grandson) and Sie Tjoen An. They believed that evangelism limited by racial and geographical boundaries was not biblical. By their encouragement, in 1958 the GKMI Jepara Church planted a church in Semarang. It became the first church outside of the Muria area. In 1964 the Evangelism Commission of the synod, under the leadership of Sie Tjoen An, also planted a church in Surakarta, in the southern part of Central Java. In order for this "new movement" to move faster and more effectively, both of the above synod leaders, together with Thio Tjien Swie, founded a mission body on May 15, 1965, in Semarang called "Pengutusan Injil & Pelayanan Kasih" or PIPKA, which means "Sending the Gospel and Charities." From the viewpoint of GKMI evangelism history, PIPKA is an "eye spear" of GKMI for reaching out of the Muria area. But from the viewpoint of mission history in Indonesia, PIPKA is the first mission body belonging to a church conference and also a unique mission body, doing the church's task/duty wholly.

Motivation

As a Mennonite mission body in Indonesia, PIPKA is called to take part in the church's main task: to carry out the Great Commission of Jesus Christ (Matt. 28:19–20). Moreover, almost 90 percent of the Indonesian people have not received the good news yet, the grace of salvation in Jesus Christ. Many of them are still living in darkness, poverty, backwardness, and injustice. The motto of Tee, the GKMI founder—"Freely you have received the gospel, so share the gospel freely also"—has motivated PIPKA too. To fulfill the Lord's mission, PIPKA carries out its mission for building up the people both physically and spiritually through the following programs:

1. Church planting—This includes sending missionaries to preach the gospel, pioneering new churches, and ministering to the churches until they become established churches of GKMI. The programs encompass the Five M's: Mengutus (Send), Memberitakan (Preach), Membuka (Plant), Membina (Minister), and Mendewasakan (Lead to Maturity).

2. Charities—We provide community development through social services such as agricultural system instructions, health and nutrition improvements, economic and environmental development, and children's education.

Leadership

As a mission body under the Muria Synod, the PIPKA Board is elected in the Synod General Conference every three years. The Board consists of a Main Board and the GKMI representatives. The 1989–92 PIPKA Main Board is as follows: chairman, Eddy Sutjipto; vice chairman, Stephen Chandra; secretary, Firnoyoso Sabdono; vice secretary, Gabriel Mangunsong; treasurer, Stevanus Haryono; vice treasurer, Bambang Handoyo; executive secretary, Yahya Chrismanto.

The Board meets once a year; the Main Board meets every three months. The Board's duties are to make and maintain long-range and short-range programs, to set policies, and to appoint a director or an executive secretary to carry out the programs. The executive secretary, who appoints the workers, is fully responsible to the Board.

Challenges

The PIPKA vision is to reach the whole of Indonesia for Christ. Indonesia is the greatest archipelago in the world with a total of 13,667 islands and 180 million people, the fifth largest population in the world. Could it be reached by PIPKA, such a small mission body, supported by a small Mennonite conference with limited personnel and finances? Praise the Lord, since the owner of this church and the mission body is not a small God. Really, he is great and powerful. Nothing is impossible for those who believe in him. He has stirred many Mennonite brothers and sisters and other Christian agencies to help PIPKA realize her vision. In the last fifteen years, Mennonite Brethren Missions/Services, Mennonite Central Committee, Eastern Mennonite Board of Missions and Charities, and World Vision International have joined with PIPKA to reap the Lord's harvest in Indonesia. As a result, within twenty-five years PIPKA has gone out far beyond her original area and has reached nine provinces in four big islands, namely Kalimantan, Sumatra, Java, and Bali. In church planting, PIPKA has planted fifty churches with 2,000 members and established four churches. Those four churches, especially two in Jakarta, have grown rapidly and have planted twenty other churches in the surrounding area with total membership of 1,500. In

Jakarta now there are five established churches and fourteen outposts with a total of 1,350 members. Their vision for the year 2000 is to have at least fifty churches with membership amounting to a minimum of ten thousand. This urban program is known as "The Jakarta Vision." So, altogether PIPKA has shared seven established Mennonite churches with 3,500 members, scattered in nine provinces. Those are about one-third of the total members of the Indonesian Muria Synod. Are they enough?

According to the latest census, 86 percent of the Indonesian people are Muslim, 7 percent Protestant, 4 percent Catholic, 3 percent Buddhist and Hindu, and 1 percent others. By knowing this fact, we can see that the achievements reached by PIPKA are relatively small and that the projections to be reached are still far ahead. Can PIPKA really do it by herself? These are the challenges PIPKA is facing. PIPKA knows that the participation of the brothers and sisters from abroad has its own place and limitations and, of course, will not be forever. On the other hand, as a mission body owned by GKMI, PIPKA has to be more mature, being able to stand on her own feet and living interdependently with others, but how and when? To reach this, the cooperation with the GKMI has to be maintained and increased. The PIPKA leadership has to be improved as well, so that PIPKA will be able to offer the best for Jesus, the head of the church, when he comes again—and his coming is very near.

"Open your eyes and look at the fields! They are ripe for harvest."
"The harvest is plentiful but the workers are few."
"Whom shall I send? And who will go for us?"

Yahya Chrismanto Gandawijaya, Indonesia, b. 1943, M.Div., executive secretary of PIPKA.

Clyde Shenk, American missionary, greeting Pastor Nashon Nyambok at Shirati, Tanzania. (EMBMC photo by David W. Shenk)

Stop and plant—mission outreach to London

by Elias Mc. Moyo

This account of the Brethren in Christ (BIC) mission outreach to London, England, is not intended as a critical and exhaustive history but a careful, simple explanation of how the work came into being, its growth, struggles, and future projections. I claim no originality beyond interpretative narration. Many have contributed to the inception of this mission.

Background

The Brethren in Christ communities in the United States and Africa, in a joint venture of faith, responded to the call from the Macedonia of their day in cooperation with the few BIC people already living in London. Through consultation they agreed that a researcher be sent to London to conduct a church planting feasibility study. The idea for a London mission arose in response to the BIC London residents who were noted to have said, "Come and help; London needs Christ, and the time has come that you stop flying over London to the USA or to Africa. Stop and plant." The response was also accelerated by the vision of the BIC/USA mission task force on new fields, which met in October 1976 to discuss the issues relating to new opportunities for missions. To carry out God's purpose for the church effectively, BIC churches sought God's guidance in setting forth a plan of action on how they would fulfill the vision. In 1979 Kenneth B. Hoover—under the administration of Dr. Roy Sider, overseas secretary of Brethren in Christ World Missions—was assigned to do research in London.

Dr. K.B. Hoover's three months in London

In February 1979 Dr. Hoover arrived in London with his conviction that Christians must join hands as a witness of the kingdom wherever they are. He contacted many Christian organizations and people from different cultures who were already ministering to the souls in London. His arrival was greeted by some students with echoes of anxiety, because some of the students from Africa thought this would add to their problems. Unfortunately, the BIC with their limited resources could not scratch the students where they were itching. This was evidenced by a letter that Roy Sider wrote to me saying, "The BIC is interested in the welfare of all who contact the ministry for any purposes whatsoever … but regret that the BIC in London is unable to provide financial help." The views of the people of London generated ideas from which the untiring Dr. Hoover formed his opinion and recommendations. When he went back to the United States in April of 1979, he recommended that the Christian ministry be made a priority and that a full-time pastoral consultant was necessary. On April

13 to 14, 1979, the BIC Board for World Missions USA met and adopted the proposal in consultation with the BIC communities in Zimbabwe and Zambia, who also adopted the proposal.

The inception of the BIC International Fellowship UK in East London

February 24, 1980, my wife, Fadzai Moyo, our three children (Tha, Patience, and Faith), and I arrived in London after being approved by the BIC communities in the USA and Africa to pioneer the work. We lived in three different hotels. The problem of accommodation caused a serious stress to us. I had to ask the question, "Did God separate us from our people so that we die in London?" To my amazement, a small voice continued to give us the thought that it is an obedient servant who believes, and it takes belief to be an obedient servant. Our first ministry started from Lancaster Gate Hotel before we were settled at 22 Russell Road, Buckhurst Hill, Essex, where we lived for six months and continued conducting prayer meetings with individual families as we visited them in their homes.

On April 6, 1980, at 2:30 p.m. the first fellowship service was conducted at the London Mennonite Centre. After introductions I, the newly posted pastor, gave greetings with three points: "If the London ministry is to succeed, each member must be (1) committed to Christ, (2) committed to people—God's creations, and (3) committed to the Great Commission." After that, Dr. Henry Ginder, who was visiting London, gave a forceful Easter message and encouraged participation in the ministry by every soul. Twenty people attended the service. That June, the Reverend Curtis Book and his family arrived to replace us as we left London for further studies at Fuller Theological Seminary and Asuza Pacific University in the United States. We were pleased and thanked the Lord for allowing us to share in fellowship with the Books.

In June of the same year, the BIC churches in Zambia, Zimbabwe, North America, and the London support group formed an Executive Council, which became the decision-making body. Since this was a four-partner ministry, each supporting country had a representative. In July 1980 we left for the US, and the Book family took over the leadership with the understanding that we were returning in 1982. They remained in the same house for a year, continuing with contacts and Bible studies. Curtis Book, who was also assigned to research church planting, met Roger Forster, pastor and founder of Ichthus Christian Fellowship. Forster unequivocally encouraged the expansion of the BIC ministry in London. On April 13, 1981, a purchase of a residence for the pastoral couple was completed. In August 1982 we came back, and the Books returned to the US. It was during this year that we formed the first congregation. After one year the attendance started to grow, and we introduced a weekly Bible study as well. For one year the activities continued in the house.

Growth and struggles

On October 3, 1983, we secured a venue, Durning Hall Community Centre (with a beautiful sanctuary, conference rooms, kitchen, etc.) on a contribution basis. The sanctuary was used for worship, Bible study, Sunday school for children, Christmas parties, and church meetings. The following year an office was granted to me for use two days a week for both counseling and administration. In 1984 the fellowship started a visitation program, which involved the members in door-to-door witnessing. It is here that we experienced God's love, which developed our vision and started to turn the members inside out for missions. Excellent rapport was established with other churches throughout the community. By the end of 1984 our average attendance went up from twenty-one in 1983 to twenty-six. In 1985 a Sunday school committee was formed with Fadzai Moyo as the superintendent. Mthabisi Moyo (my son) and Mr. Jabulani Moyo were the first baptismal candidates. In 1986 Mr. Kabomeka Pupe was baptized and Mrs. Sinanzeni Ncube installed as the first deaconess.

The contacts made by the fellowship resulted in few British nationals worshiping with us. In 1984 the council put forward a closure of Forest Gate Fellowship (the first BIC congregation) in favor of church planting. That proposal created an unpleasant climate. Praise God, after deep consideration and prayer all those concerned approved that Forest Gate cease to function in its present form but that it become an extension point from the hub of the proposed BIC church planting project in the northwest part of London. It is here that the Executive Council was dismantled, and the whole of the London work fell under Roy Sider. My wife and I became members of the church planting team with Mr. and Mrs. Curtis Byers. Curtis Byers and family arrived in October 1985 and conducted research in a new area where the BIC would plant a second congregation. Brother Byers and family remained with that project for thirteen months. At the end of that time, he recommended that a new area in Brent, Kensal Rise, had spiritual needs.

In January of 1987 the services continued at the Durning Hall Centre, East London, under the leadership of Curtis Byers as a part-time pastor and a church planter in the northwest. At the beginning of 1987 both the Moyo and the Byers families moved to the north part of London. Mr. Byers continued serving the church for fourteen months until May 1988, when he was relieved by missionary Bryan Sollenberger and went home for a furlough. When he returned after four months, he was assigned to work with Brentwater Church. From January 1987 to September 1989 Forest Gate Church witnessed the decline of membership, church activities, and offering contributions. Under the leadership of Mr. Byers, the committee met in April 1987 to discuss the lack of progress. After a long and serious discussion, it was agreed that a full-time pastor was needed. As it now stands, Forest Gate is run under the chairmanship of Mr. Willie Ncube and Mr. Kabombeka Pupe as lay pastor. There are nine church members today.

Brethren in Christ ministries begin in the northwest

Under the name North West London Christian Ministries, the work began in Kensal Rise. Because of the racial mixture in the area, my family was assigned to plant a multiracial congregation in Kensal Rise, and Curtis Byers served as assistant pastor to Norman Savine and was also assigned as pastor of extension ministries with the overall responsibility for church planting in an adjoining neighborhood. The Brentwater Church, an existing congregation that applied for recognition as a Brethren in Christ church, has been received as an associate church of the denomination while they study the BIC statement of doctrine. Curtis Byers continues his ministry with Brentwater.

In 1988 Bryan Sollenberger arrived from the USA to join the Moyos in Kensal Rise, and Norman Kase arrived in August of the following year. The team concentrates on door-to-door street ministry and friendship evangelism, which are the caring methods at the heart of evangelism. March 25, 1989, we began the first house group Bible study at the home of Ms. Marlene Blore. Seven people were present. Although it took a longer time than expected, we are delighted that we have believers in Christ; and several Christians in the community have offered to host Bible studies in their homes. On January 28, 1990, in addition to our Friday Bible study, the Kensal Ministry Team (Norman Kase, Bryan Sollenberger, Fadzai Moyo, and I) started a house worship service with the new believers. On that first day, fifteen people were in attendance. We hope in the future to transfer the worship service from a house to a nearby school.

Conclusion

The vision of the above congregations and all the missionaries is to see more BIC churches in the United Kingdom and in the whole of Europe in the future. For Kensal Rise I have made a plea before the Lord that we will have succeeded if we fulfill three basic aims in church planting: (1) bring people to Christ, (2) nurture them for Christ, and (3) send them out for Christ in accordance with 2 Tim. 2:2. The urgency of the task is that souls are dying without Christ. Every effort is made by missionaries to make Christ known through the vision of the Brethren in Christ Missions. The Brethren in Christ in London believe that God is delighted to use small beginnings to bring into being work of wide-ranging spiritual influence for his glory and the extension of his kingdom. You can join us in this fight of faith by your daily prayer as you think of our Master's words, "As my father has sent me, so send I you." This is our vision, which is God's agenda for every Christian church. The challenges of the 1990s make us press on. Let us not fail, for this is not the time for missionary servants to lose their nerve.

Elias Mc. Moyo, Zimbabwe, b. 1947, M.A. in missiology, Brethren in Christ missionary to London, England.

Radio mission in the multicultural Gran Chaco

by Marvin Duerksen

In 1975 the Mennonites, who are inclined to withdraw from the world, began mission work from Paraguay into the Gran Chaco with the help of modern mass communication media. The first large streams of Mennonite refugees from Canada and the Soviet Union had penetrated this uninhabited area, which is the size of the Federal Republic of Germany, between 1927 and 1930. A mission union, Licht den Indianern (Light to the Indians), had been founded in 1935 with the consent of the government. Although at the time there were only a couple hundred Lengua Indians living in the settlement area comprising the present Mennonite colonies, the close contact with the natives aroused in both individuals and congregations the idea of mission work. From the beginning there was concern for the physical as well as the spiritual needs of the Indian. For this reason, mission work and counseling always ran parallel in such important areas as public health, agriculture, and education. All this was influenced by the common struggle of the two groups for survival in the hot, dry Chaco.

The situation led to the development of its own set of rules, which may be unique. As Sieghart Schartner and Wilmar Stahl wrote in the 1986 publication *Wer ist mein Nächster*, "Efforts to maintain the culture, regional incorporation, and national integration are simultaneously noticeable." In the midst of the struggle for economic survival, overcome successfully by the Mennonites at least, approximately fifteen thousand Indians have gathered among the thirteen thousand settlers of German origin in the Gran Chaco. This has made mission activity possible right at their doorstep for years. After the founding of Licht den Indianern, however, ten years passed before the first baptismal service took place among the Lenguas on February 24, 1946. The Indian culture, characterized by shamanism, defended itself against the penetration of the good news. But the early missionaries were convinced that the gospel would meet the needs of the Indians: "Inspired by this faith, they went to work. And this faith could overcome all obstacles resulting from personal poverty, the Chaco War, and the struggle for one's own existence during the pioneering days, and obstacles resulting from the clashing of two very different cultures, where there was confrontation without understanding each other" (Hans J. Wiens, *Daß die Heiden Miterben seien*, 1989).

In 1960 Mennonite radio amateurs were the first to develop the idea of constructing a missionary radio station. Subsequently, Frank Kroeker, a missionary, assumed the initiative under the auspices of the Evangelical Mennonite Conference of Canada (EMCC). Thus, a noncommercial, Christian multilingual radio station was put into operation in Filadelfia on the AM band under his leadership in 1975. The Paraguayan government issued the license, and the EMCC together with the Menno, Fernheim, and Neuland colonies were the contract partners.

At first the station broadcast only four hours a day. Today it broadcasts fourteen hours a day in Spanish (60 percent), German (26 percent), Lengua and Chulupí (9 percent), Guaraní (3 percent), Ayoreo (1 percent), and English (1 percent). The actual producers of the programs are almost exclusively from the respective cultural and linguistic group. The area reached by the broadcasts includes all of the Chaco and the marginal areas of Argentina, Bolivia, and Brazil as well as parts of East Paraguay. Radio station ZP-30, La Voz del Chaco Paraguayo, is a constant companion at home, during a trip by car, in the office, or during the tereré break, in the hospital, or on an isolated cattle ranch. The station offers a popular free-message service, broadcasting about 2,500 messages a month in the various languages of the area. This is the only way in which the inhabitants of this area of underdeveloped infrastructure—where regular mail and telephone service are available only in the colonies—can maintain contact with each other. In addition to the local message service, there is a national and an international news service in the two main languages, Spanish and German. Informational programs on agriculture and animal husbandry, health advice, and general education and music programs complete the cultural part of the presentation.

The pride of the Indians is obvious as they report on the life and activities in their settlements. They are also very proud of their own musical productions recorded in the large studio at the radio headquarters. A total of twenty such recordings by Indian groups, presenting songs with Christian content, were made in 1987 and 1988 alone. Some five thousand cassettes of Indian music were produced in this manner between 1984 and 1988, amounting to at least 25 percent of the total production of music cassettes during this period. Additionally, there are ten thousand cassettes of sermons and evangelization recordings, mainly in German. In early 1989, in response to the development of modern entertainment technology, a lending service of uplifting video tapes in German and Spanish was begun.

The enthusiasm of the inhabitants of the area was great when, in 1975, the first programs aired. They also began to produce programs of music and the spoken word in Lengua and Chulupí. In the same way that Henry Buchagard, missionary to the Ayoreos, began to produce programs in that language at the mission station at El Faro Moro in 1976, the missionaries Gerhard Hein and Dietrich Lepp began to work at the tiring details of producing programs in Chulupí and Lengua. From the beginning the Indians attached great significance to having moderators and speakers who had a good reputation. The first programs for these language groups had a simple content, their technology corresponding to the open fields in which they were recorded. It was an enormous help to have a radio as a means of proclaiming the Word, for in this way the majority of the ten thousand Lengua and Chulupí could be reached. Today special groups such as children, mothers, whole families, or the individual believer are targeted with corresponding programs. Although certain programs specializing in sending greetings are well received, other programs are characterized by monotony. Brief contributions and lively dialogues are lacking, as are qualified technologists who could train the Indian moderators. The programs are, indeed, a valuable opportunity to address the Indians personally, for hardly a family is without a radio receiver. Letters from listeners indicate that the programs for Indians actually are heard in the remote regions of the Argentine Chaco.

There is also a large audience in a wide radius among speakers of Spanish and Guaraní. As opposed to the Indians in the area settled by the Mennonites, who are in constant contact with counseling services and missionaries or with the local congregations, these radio listeners are often confronted with the word of God in their loneliness and helplessness. In this context radio programs can attract attention to the word of God. They can invite and they can accompany the life of those who are already firmly committed to the faith; but in the decisive process of conversion and what follows, listeners require direct human contact, someone to talk to who will help them and pray with them.

Radio mission work cannot serve as a substitute for life in a congregation, but it can lead to a beginning and a continuation of congregational life. With this in mind, the need to visit listeners in the remote areas has become more and more evident in the course of time. For this reason the Chaco Radio Mission, which is responsible for the specifically spiritual programs of the station, has begun to organize such visitation trips during the last two years. These trips through lonely steppe landscapes and uninhabited forest regions demand great endurance and faith in God. That, however, makes the experience of meeting with field workers, soldiers at isolated bases, or mothers at home with their children all the more worthwhile. These people appreciate a friendly word, an intercessory prayer, or a word of encouragement. They are happy to learn to know people who work at the station and who, in 1988, drove more than 9,000 miles to evangelize, to distribute testaments, or to present films. This has resulted in many decisions for Christ and in winning new listeners for the station.

In the future this work among the Latino Paraguayans will gain in significance if the government attracts more settlers into the Chaco. The radio programs for the different Indian communities will remain an indispensable part of the broadly based mission work in the Chaco, because again and again in recent years the natives have confessed to faith in shamanism. Fortunetellers, sorcerers, and exorcists are again in demand. As a March 1989 information sheet from Licht den Indianern noted, "They frequently incorporate Christian elements into their practice, so that even the faithful are led astray." The task of the local congregation to carry the gospel into all the world thus remains of significance, as well as the responsibility to call to service those qualified workers who understand this as the work of the Lord.

Marvin Duerksen, Paraguay, b. 1959, MA, journalist, member of Fernheim Mennonite Church. Translated by Gerhard Reimer.

Tent evangelism in Paraguay. (MBM/S photo by Gerald Falk, 1985)

A call to peacemaking

by Gene Stoltzfus

> We ask our conferences and congregations to envision Christian
> Peacemaker Teams as a witness to Jesus Christ by identifying
> with suffering people, reducing violence, mediating conflicts,
> and fostering justice through peaceful, caring direct challenge of
> evil. This may include biblical study and reflection, document-
> ing and reporting on injustice and violation of human rights,
> nonviolent direct action, education, mediation, and advocacy. To
> be authentic, such peacemaking should be rooted in and sup-
> ported by congregations and churchwide agencies. We will
> begin in North America but will be open to invitations to
> support initiatives in other places. (Techny call ... from the
> meeting at Techny Towers in Illinois, USA, where the statement
> for Christian Peacemaker Teams was formulated in 1986.)

We live in nations that are robbing the poor of our world and squandering
treasuries on monuments of destruction. The blood of the victims may be on our
hands. We are living in special times when we are called from our separate
nations to stand strong with each other against the sin of violence and for justice.
The vision of Christian Peacemaker Teams was launched at the Mennonite
World Conference Assembly at Strasbourg in 1984. Many of us studied the
vision for stronger peacemaking. Representatives from many of our churches
agreed that our times cry out for a strengthened biblical peace witness that
includes active peacemaking. This means that new efforts in public witness and
creative experiments in nonviolent direct action will be a part of our congregational life. In some cases this will mean Peacemaker Teams. The mandate for
Christian Peacemaker Teams (CPT) calls for action first at home to roll back the
tide of militarization that has infected our corporate life, robbed our children of
nutrition and education, and buried our souls in cynicism. Then it calls for
Peacemaker Teams to follow the fires of militarism around the globe.

In North America and Europe, CPT committees have sponsored conferences and
initiated Bible study/nonviolence training in several areas. There is wide interest
for international and domestic peacemaking teams but not yet a financial component to support it. However, without money we cannot do much to realize our
peacemaking vision.

The global Mennonite family is invited to become part of the peacemaking
harvest. It is hard work. We can begin by learning about bases, military production facilities, and national defense information campaigns in our own communities. During the week of Assembly 12 in Winnipeg, some of us will visit a
missile site in North Dakota. If we were to stay longer in Winnipeg, we might

try to learn more about the mission of the Canadian Air Force, which is head-quartered in Winnipeg. Our prayer and reflections in North Dakota will send a message around the world that we follow Christ by standing for life. We will announce that the Minuteman III weapons under the ground there bring fear, cost money that should go elsewhere, and erode our spiritual wholeness. In our study of the locations of congregations in the Americas and Europe, we have found an unexpected correlation between the location of military bases and arms production with our church communities. We believe that witness against these death-producing centers is necessary to announce the new life and new mind of Christ in our age. If our peacemaking ministry is to be complete, we need the active participation of Mennonites on all continents.

We call on Mennonites to speak out as people who have witnessed the light of the Bible. We are called to act boldly in prayer, written and spoken words, dialogue, negotiations, and by direct action or civil disobedience. Consider offering one day each month, two weeks each year, to this effort. We can live as people who are washed in the blood of the Lamb. Some of us are invited to careers as volunteer peacemakers, part-time or full-time volunteers in God's peace movement. The world would be a new place if every Mennonite congregation worldwide had an active peacemaking mission devoted to public witness.

There are rewards, but there is also a cost in peacemaking. Controversy, the normal result of confrontation of evil, brings painful change for all parties. The Holy Roman Empire shook in the face of an Anabaptist critique that was followed up with action. We need not fear controversy. Second, we will learn to read the Bible with new eyes, through the eyes of victims and the poor. Third, some new people will join our congregations because they see the gospel in action; others will dislike us and say bad things about us.

We honor the blood of our ancestors by boldly anchoring our commitment to peace. We honor those from our communion who stood with slaves to draft the earliest abolitionist documents at Germantown, Pennsylvania. We honor those who faithfully refused to take up arms in the revolutionary wars or to salute the flag. We honor the sacrifices of those who would not purchase war bonds or pay war taxes. We honor our own Mennonite sisters and brothers everywhere who pay the price of militarization. We honor future generations of Mennonites by providing a legacy of peacemaking. And we honor God by pointing to the fulfillment of the earth rather than resigning ourselves to its destruction.

Let us be purified by the blood that is flowing before us through the generations and around us in our own time. Let this blood, the blood of the cross, not be a source of guilt. Let it be an instrument of grace to sustain and to make all things new. Amen!

Gene Stoltzfus, USA, b. 1940, M.A. in Southeast Asian studies, M.Div., Christian Peacemaker Teams staff person, Mennonite Voluntary Service volunteer.

Asia International Reconciliation Work Camp

by Carl C. Beck

Spirit founded

"God has done a great thing for us here. We must have another one." Thus declared Chang Kyung Seuk at the close of our first attempt at work camps in August of 1965. The place was Taegu, Korea. That first camp had come about as a clear work of the Spirit himself. Neither it nor the ensuing series of camps was consciously planned or institutionalized. They happened to fill a need in our Asian brotherhood and kept growing, one camp at a time.

The 1965 camp came to be within a Christian Youth Seminar held in Tokyo in the spring of 1964. We had invited several Korean students who were residing in Japan to that seminar. There, for the first time, Christian Japanese university students met Christian Korean students and heard from their mouths the suffering and persecution they and their parents had endured during the Japanese occupation and annexation of their homeland. The Japanese were mortified. "We must somehow make amends to our brothers and sisters in Korea," was their reaction. The first work camp in Korea sponsored by Mennonite Central Committee (MCC) was the result. Thirteen Christian young people from Japan, mostly Mennonite and Brethren in Christ, joined seventeen from Korea to work at terracing rice paddies at the MCC Vocational School at Kyung Sang, Korea. This was at a time, twenty years after the war's end, when Japanese and Korean Christians were not yet talking with each other and Korean students were rioting in Seoul's streets against a proposed Japan-Korea peace treaty, which was conceived to be anti-Korean. On the third evening of the work camp, there were tense moments as long pent-up feelings broke loose. But then the spirit of Jesus took over and deep, tearful reconciliation began to happen. Two weeks later, when Korean campers saw the Japanese off at Pusan's wharf, there was not a dry eye on either side. A direct result of this first camp (after Korean churchmen had observed reconciliation happening among the youth) was a series of annual MCC-sponsored Reconciliation Seminars by Korean and Japanese churchmen. The seminars continued alternately in Korea and Japan for the next twelve years.

Spirit-moved expansion

Korean youth begged for another camp. MCC consented. In August of 1966 a second camp was held at Obirin University near Tokyo. We built a memorial chapel on campus. "Just one more," they begged. Again MCC agreed to sponsor. The foundation for a health facility at a Christian hospital in Taegu, Korea, was the result of the third camp. By this time the Taiwan Mennonite churches had heard of these reconciliation efforts. "We, too, were involved in the suffering and persecution of a Japanese occupation," they said. "We, too, want to be part of the reconciliation." So they sent two young men (now senior pastors in Taichung, Taiwan, ROC) to the third camp. Impressed, they begged, "Our young people must have this kind of experience. Could we not have one more camp hosted by the Taiwan churches?" So the fourth camp took place in Taiwan in 1968. A road up a mountain to a new farming community and a number of inter-Mennonite romances leading to happy, fruitful homes and the budding of several church leaders were left as visible results. Mennonite young people from Indonesia and India joined this fourth camp.

By the fifth camp, held in Sapporo, Japan, in 1969, all the Mennonite and Brethren in Christ churches in Asia except the Philippines were represented. We felt that our original purpose of reconciliation was pretty well completed and the camps could well discontinue. But Hong Kong had already invited us for a fifth camp, and again MCC acquiesced. When the suggestion was made that the word "reconciliation" could perhaps now be dropped from our title, the response was: "Perhaps we are no longer 'reconcilees,' but now we should become reconcilers in an Asia of many tensions." The word "reconciliation" remained in our name.

Asia Mennonite Conference is born

By the sixth camp at Faith-Love Home in Fanling, Hong Kong, in 1970, where we leveled and drained a playground area, it was felt that the graces the youth were experiencing should be shared more widely. So the camp director invited a representative church leader from each national church to join the Hong Kong camp with the express purpose of exploring the possibility of founding an Asian Mennonite conference. By the time the camp closed, complete plans for the first Asia Mennonite Conference to be held at Dhamtari, India, in fall 1971 together with detailed program, financing, hosting, and travel subsidies were in place.

The seventh MCC-sponsored work camp was hosted by the combined Mennonite, Brethren in Christ, and Missionary churches at a new hospital at Shamnagar, near Calcutta, India. It was scheduled for the two weeks preceding Asia Mennonite Conference at Dhamtari so campers might be able to join the conference. They did, and made a memorable contribution. During the conference the work camp director offered the mother organization (work camp) to the daughter (Asia Conference) and resigned. The conference rose boldly to the challenge, accepted the work camp as an integral part of itself, and called the director back to serve under the conference now instead of MCC.

Conference-sponsored camps

The eighth camp, and first one sponsored by Asia Mennonite Conference, took place at Nha Trang, Vietnam, in 1972. A sea wall was built along the coast facing our MCC hospital complex to hold back an encroaching ocean threatening the hospital and surrounding community. For this camp Sammy Sacapaño from the Philippines was finally able to secure a visa and completed our Asian Mennonite family.

Up to this point camps had been annual affairs. Now that the conference was in place, it was felt that the pace of camps could slow down. So the ninth and tenth camps were not held until 1974 in Bangladesh and 1977 in the Philippines. In Bangladesh our project was putting in foundations for a large school complex for homeless boys in the rural town of Brahmanbaria, about five hours out of Dacca. It was MCC hosted and conference sponsored. In the Philippines our project was in the relocated mountain town of Pantabagan, nearly a day's journey from Manila. Here we repaired washed-out roads and terraced hillsides to stop erosion. Our Philippine brothers and sisters proved to be very warm hosts, and here was granted perhaps our highest point in fellowship and spiritual response. Two more camps have been held: one in Hong Kong in 1982, and a twentieth anniversary camp returned to what had been Mennonite Vocational School near Taegu, Korea.

Another result of these camps was a series of three all-India work camps. Indian young people from our six conferences in India remained largely unaware of each other. So in the fall of 1977, MCSFI (Mennonite Christian Service Fellowship of India) sponsored a work camp in the Missionary Church area at Balarampur, near Calcutta, where we spent nearly two weeks putting in the foundation for a new building on the church-sponsored school campus. This camp was for five conferences in central and eastern India. A second camp was opened for the South India Mennonite Brethren conference at their hospital at Jadcherla, where we painted buildings and leveled fields for rice paddies. The third camp occurred in 1987 in Rhaghunathpur mission school, where youths from all six India conferences gathered for a week of work camp followed by another five days of youth retreat. Nearly two hundred participated in these meetings. By the end of the week, we had pretty well enclosed a one-and-one-half acre neglected Mennonite cemetery with a 24-inch-wide, 4-foot-high brick wall.

Camp routine varies by climate, but ordinarily the work project occupies the camper's time from early morning to mid-afternoon. Anabaptist seminars, peace studies, and discussions of youth needs fill late afternoon and evening hours. Camp numbers have varied from the thirty at the first camp to the two hundred at Rhaghunathpur, but forty-five to fifty seems to be an ideal number.

A continuation of periodic camps would seem advisable for some time yet. Asia Conference needs these fellowship opportunities. Our young people need to find their spiritual identity. Asian churches need this added stimulus to Anabaptist and peace studies. The camp should continue to act as a catalyst for finding and encouraging future church leaders in the warmth of their Anabaptist heritage.

Carl C. Beck, Japan, b. 1919, retired missionary under Mennonite Board of Missions.

These children have gathered fish for the family meal from a pond that was installed by MCC.
(MCC photo by Kevin Stout, 1987)

Interethnic cooperation in the Chaco

by Wilmar Stahl

Hunting grounds

"Chaco" refers to a semiarid region, covered with scrub forests and grass savannas, extending between the Rio Paraguay in the east and the Rio Izozog in the west, including parts of what today is Argentina in the south and portions of Bolivia in the north. In prehistoric days a dozen different Indian tribes, with the help of a rather diversified foraging economy, had adapted their cultural systems to this particular environment. Socially organized in hunting bands numbering thirty to fifty individuals, they covered areas of approximately 300 square miles each, gathering a variety of some fifty different roots, grasses, stems or fruits of plants, wild honeys, insects, fish, plus a wide spectrum of animals from turtles to peccaries. Although the peripheral groups had been involved in colonial wars ever since the Spaniards arrived, the Lengua Indians of the Central Chaco started to make their first contacts with Western goods and ways toward the end of the nineteenth century. This encounter started with trade, proceeded to cattle ranch invasion, and culminated with the systematic colonization of the area by German Mennonites. In all of this process of cultural contact, the Lengua lived with a peaceful attitude toward the newcomers, entering a process of selective cultural change whereby material innovations were eagerly accepted but hunting and gathering remained as a way of life. Ranches, agricultural colonies, and mission stations were considered to be an expansion of the hunting grounds and exploited for what occasional benefits they could yield in trade, sporadic labor contracts, or charity.

Cultural change

Since those first contacts a hundred years ago, the environment of the Lengua Indians has changed extensively. Parallel to the native "distribution economy," the white immigrants have set up an elaborate "production economy" based on farming and cattle raising. This development set off a widespread immigration of other native groups of the Chaco, resulting in a relatively high population density. In an area where in prehistoric times 1,000 Lengua might have lived, today 5,500 Lengua, 8,000 natives of other tribes, 11,000 German Mennonites, and 1,500 nationals of Latin origin are sharing the habitat.

A changed environment for the Chaco foragers has meant adapting their cultural system in many ways. New artifacts soon changed the material aspects of native cultures. Labor contracts replaced hunting and gathering, but income continued to be managed according to the traditional "distribution economy." Groups became more sedentary and tended to increase rapidly in numbers. Where villages used to have fifty members, they now grew to five hundred and more.

The deepest cultural changes, however, may have occurred in the area of religion. As before, social and spiritual harmony still constitute the highest ideal of Chaco natives. However, its realization no longer depends on shamanistic rituals but rather is sought in the communion of Christian believers. Today, in more than twenty church groupings of evangelical orientation, some 4,500 adult members led by lay pastors are practicing Christian discipleship.

Starting development cooperation

How did these religious changes come about? Generally speaking, they can be considered a consequence of the immigration of German Mennonites who, starting in 1927, were making the Chaco their new home. Living in daily exposure to their hunting neighbors, the German Mennonites organized an interest group in 1932 in order to evangelize the aborigines. In 1946 a Lengua church grew out of this effort, igniting an accelerated conversion process among the natives and a generalized interest for mission work in the local Mennonite churches. Upon their conversion, the native Christians started their conquest for a new identity. Parting from an integrated understanding of culture, they judged that acceptance of Mennonite faith also would have to imply an acceptance of the Mennonite way of life. So the mission committees were confronted with more and more requests for assistance in agricultural resettlement and primary education. Local Mennonite churches and North American mission boards cooperated in this process of adaptation, but they increasingly felt more uncomfortable with their role and finally negotiated with Mennonite Central Committee (MCC) for it to assume the socioeconomic aspects of the assistance. The outcome of these deliberations was that in 1962 a new agency in charge of the social ministries was founded, joining with the representation of MCC, mission boards, and the local Mennonite colony administrations. The new organization eventually grew into what today is known as "ASCIM" (Asociación de Servicios de Cooperación Indígena-Menonita or, in English, Association of Ministries for Indian-Mennonite Cooperation).

ASCIM, according to its bylaws, pursues the goal of accompanying the native churches in their process of socioeconomic adaptation, meeting needs in cooperation with the communities on the basis of the principle of "help for self-help." This process is being supervised by an officially accredited association, presently composed of fifty-six Indian and German Mennonite church and settlement leaders. Finances for the ongoing program activities are contributed by MCC, Internationale Mennonitische Organisation (IMO), the national government, Indian communities, and local German Mennonite churches and colonies. Funds for special projects also come from international development agencies.

ASCIM ministries

First contacts between ASCIM and Indian groups usually are made when these latter live as migrant laborers in some workers' village in a German Mennonite colony, where they are employed in agriculture, agrarian industries, construction, etc. Their aspirations for their own piece of land are mostly explained on the basis of needs related to "social disharmony." Cooperation begins with a process whereby potential land purchases are reviewed, group expectations are elaborated, and a plan for socioeconomic community life is worked out. The group then can be resettled, establishing a new colony, where usually approximately one hundred families will find a new home. For this new beginning, ASCIM provides, besides land, a basic set of agricultural equipment and the necessary infrastructure, such as roads, water supply, and buildings for social services. Today in the Central Chaco there are twelve such agricultural settlements, where on 100,000 hectares more than eight thousand aborigines are living on legally secured land plots. Families will arrange their economic subsistence in different ways, but usually it amounts to a combination of gardening, farming, cattle raising, and wage earning. Favorite cash crops are cotton and castor beans. Average cattle ownership amounts to three head per family.

In order to accompany the native farmers in their new economy, ASCIM assigns an extension agent to each one of the settlements. The agent gives agricultural advice and raises general socioeconomic awareness. Production credits are made available in order to promote farming and cattle raising. Marketing of agricultural products is managed through a cooperative system, as is the commercialization of consumer goods. A further service offered by ASCIM is a comprehensive program of primary health care. The most frequent diseases in the native population are tuberculosis, intestinal parasites, and malnutrition among infants. The attention to these "social" illnesses is given from a central hospital in Yalve Sanga and in ten health posts located in Indian communities. Health education is provided through radio programs in Indian languages, home visits of native health promoters, pregnancy clubs, and mother-infant clinics.

In the absence of government services, ASCIM also has started and maintains a primary education program from preschool through junior high. The first three years are taught in native languages, and then the curriculum changes to Spanish and the national school plans. About 90 percent of all children participate in the first stage, but only 40 percent enroll in the higher grades (Spanish curriculum). In the area of nonformal education, a program for training in home economics is offered for teenage girls, and an agricultural training center accepts most male youngsters who do not find their way into higher school grades. In a rather informal program, ASCIM is promoting the encounter of Indian and German women, who together organize special events of sharing and learning skills of sewing, baking, and various crafts. Another program of nonformal education has to do with the promotion of community organization and leadership training, aiming to discover ways to harmonize traditional Indian norms with national laws in such a way that functional communities can be the result.

Search for partnership

When the first contacts were made between Lengua Indians and German Mennonites sixty years ago, "paternalism" was the internationally accepted model for
mission work. This also became the guiding pattern in the Chaco, the more so
since the aborigines, following culture-specific methods of foragers, presented
themselves as "needy" and apparently eager to enter "dependency relationships."
Following this model through the years, the German Mennonite settler community developed a conviction that the mission committees at first, and ASCIM at a
later stage, were the responsible boards to provide social welfare to their native
neighbors. As far as the native community was concerned, this "soft attitude"
was considered a welcomed expansion of their hunting grounds. Meanwhile,
much has changed in and around the Indian communities. Many are owners of
their land, are constantly exposed to the ways of the national society, and have
entered direct relations with government institutions. A special law, issued in
1981, defines native communities as autonomous social units, allowing them to
register as such, obtaining a legal corporate identity. Besides, natives of the
Central Chaco by now are living in a second generation of steady contacts with
white man's ways and, as such, can be considered to be well informed about
their new social environment. These developments have meant a clear challenge
for ASCIM to reevaluate traditional forms of cooperation, aiming to move from
"paternalism" to "fraternalism," the more so since "dependency" is increasingly
recognized as a threat to Christian brotherhood. Partnership, therefore, has
become the official model for interethnic cooperation in ASCIM-related projects. This implies that the initiative for community development has to be
generated by the native groups, that a high degree of identification in the form of
community effort is expected, and that projects are jointly planned, executed,
and evaluated. Obligations on both sides are jointly negotiated and contractually
committed.

Viewed from a cross-cultural perspective, the partnership model has some
serious implications. It presupposes, for instance, a high degree of cultural
tolerance with regard to the other groups. This circumstance is severely tested
whenever suffering is observed cross culturally, but standards to measure it are
based on a Western-defined threshold of suffering. A second area of testing can
be experienced in the confrontation of different economic systems, where a
hunting and gathering methodology runs head on with objectives in the area of
developing a production economy. In this ASCIM is challenged to define its
position with regard to cultural change in the native societies, avoiding cultural
imperialism on the one side, but on the other side recognizing the dynamic
nature of culture, which never can be seen as an end in itself but as a changing
instrument to master a changing environment.

Wilmar Stahl, Paraguay, b. 1946, M.A. in development anthropology, coordinator of formal and informal
education for Asociación de Servicios de Cooperación Indígena-Menonita.

Native American Mennonites

by Malcolm Wenger

In a colorful and solemn ceremony marked by tears of joy, Amelia Two Bulls Old Crow and Newton Old Crow were ordained in April of this year for Christian ministry in the Zion Mennonite Church (Arapaho) of Canton, Oklahoma, and the Mennonite Indian Church (Southern Cheyenne) of Seiling, Oklahoma. Newton is a member of the Crow tribe and Amelia of the Northern Cheyenne. Wearing blankets of bright red and dark blue, some of the chiefs and headmen of the Cheyenne and Arapaho tribes attended. On Newton's invitation most people had come in traditional garb. Ribbon shirts, fringed shawls, moccasins, deer skin clothing, beadwork, and feathers were worn with pride. Because the church building was too small, a tent had been pitched beside it to accommodate the group. A tepee in front of the church also helped make it clear that these were Native American Christians celebrating a very important event in the life of their churches.

The ordination was also an interdenominational and intertribal gathering. Representing the churches that had been most involved with the couple, both Mennonites and American Baptists participated in the ceremony. In addition to English, songs of worship were sung to traditional tunes in the Crow, Cheyenne, Arapaho, and Kiowa languages.

These small churches had been longing for strong Indian leadership, and it was one of God's unexpected gifts, beyond human planning and programming, that brought them these leaders. Both came out of years of dependency on alcohol, which prepared them in a special way to minister to the needs of the communities in which they serve. Three years of training for Christian ministry at interdenominational Cook Christian Training School further sharpened their gifts.

The startling burst of mission activity on the part of the early Anabaptists had already cooled when their Mennonite descendants came to North America. The first tentative steps to break out of the resulting isolation and again "… go … make disciples … baptize … teach" as Christ had commanded were taken when the General Conference Mennonites reached out in 1880 to the Southern Arapaho and Cheyenne in "Indian Territory" (now the state of Oklahoma). The Mennonite Brethren soon followed with a mission to the Comanche in 1895, while the General Conference expanded to the Hopi in 1893 and the Northern Cheyenne in 1904.

From the late 1940s to the 1980s, Mennonites and Brethren in Christ added to these early efforts twenty or more new missions to the Native peoples of North America. Added to the tribes mentioned above were the Blackfeet, Choctaw, Cree, Creek, Navajo, Ojibway (Saulteaux Chippewa), Sioux, and Metis (mixed bloods). In 1986 all Mennonite and Brethren in Christ missions in the United States and Canada together budgeted over $2.5 million and had staffs of over three hundred including many volunteers. Alongside the expansion there has been attrition with about a half dozen Indian churches or mission efforts closed in recent years.

These efforts to share the gospel with Native Americans have turned out to be far more complicated and difficult than Mennonites expected. Not only were very different cultures being brought together, but unfortunately it was often assumed that the white man's culture was an integral part of the Christian faith. The Indian flavor of the recent ordination, the continuing work on translations of the Bible where needed, and the development of indigenous hymnody are small signs of developing sensitivity in the area of expressing the Christian faith in culturally appropriate ways.

There is also a growing realization that injustices to Indian people have a bearing on the response to the Christian message. The Hopi have not forgotten the bitter first taste they had of Christianity when the Spanish church, supported by the military, was planted in 1629 and finally uprooted in the tragic event when the Hopi killed some of their own people in 1700.

Mennonites coming from Europe often moved onto land that had just been taken by governments from Indians by methods that often left Indians with little choice. A minister friend said that the title on the land on which his Indiana home was built went back to Indian ownership even though no tribal group lives in that area anymore.

Lawrence Hart, Southern Cheyenne chief, told a Mennonite conference of the experience of some of his relatives in making an agreement with the United States military that they would remain at peace and fly the American flag in their camp on Sand Creek in Colorado. Feeling secure, the men went hunting only to have a Colorado militia, led by a Christian minister, attack the camp and kill men, women, and children. He closed his presentation with the question, "Why am I a Christian?"

In Canada, where comparatively little military violence was used against the Native Canadians, churches still have to live down the times when they operated Indian boarding schools and attempted to replace Indian culture with that of the white man. People still living remember being punished for speaking their own language and being allowed to visit their homes only a few times during the year.

Even now whites in Wisconsin are protesting fishing rights given to Indians by treaty in exchange for their lands. In Canada the North Atlantic Treaty Organization (NATO) is more and more using Labrador for low-level training flights by military jets in spite of the protests of those who have lived there for generations that this is disrupting their lives and disturbing the wildlife of that area.

So it is no small miracle that there are now in the Mennonite family brothers and sisters, committed Christians, from many tribes of Native Americans. Their churches are small, and the Christians often form a small minority of the people of their tribe. But they are increasingly becoming a part of Mennonite conferences and sharing positions of leadership on boards and committees, this in spite of the fact that the focus of missions has shifted to work overseas.

Cheyenne pastor Joe Walks Along tells of attending the triennial sessions of the General Conference Mennonite Church at Fresno, California, in 1971. When he returned home, his father asked him about the other Indians he had met there, and he had to tell him that he was the only one at the conference. In 1989 at the joint conference of the Mennonite Church and the General Conference Mennonite Church in Normal, Illinois, a whole stage full of Native people led a morning devotional hour.

Mennonite Central Committee (MCC) has often taken the lead in standing by Indian peoples who have experienced injustice, sometimes with surprising results. The Huma, a Choctaw group, were once said to be extinct. MCC U.S. discovered communities of Huma living in the swamplands of the Mississippi Delta in Louisiana. Despised by their neighbors and excluded from schools, they were not recognized as Indians by the American government. MCC was able to record the history of the communities and trace family lineage, thus proving Indian ancestry and gaining federal recognition. Because of this Mennonite ministry, a leader of the Huma community is now pastor in a Northern Cheyenne Mennonite church.

The formal programs of missions are just one of the ways in which the lives of Mennonites have intersected with the Native people. Families have given foster or adoptive care to Native children. Health workers and teachers and other professionals have worked in Native communities. For a short time even the Minister for Indian Affairs and Northern Development in the Canadian government was a Mennonite, although the ambiguities of such a position are clear from the title.

Non-Indian Mennonites are discovering that they have things to learn from their Native brothers and sisters. At the installation of Arapaho Chief Arthur Sutton as pastor, his church celebrated with a feast. As people lined up for food, Arthur was urged to get in line. "No," he said, "chiefs always eat last." Servanthood as a mark of leadership has been taught for generations in many Indian groups.

Malcolm Wenger, USA, b. 1919, served in missions to Native Americans from 1944–85 in various capacities through the General Conference Mennonite Church and the Conference of Mennonites in Canada.

Agricultural work in Kenya. (MCC photo by Mark Beach, 1985)

Council of Anabaptists in Los Angeles (CAL)

by Allan Yoder

Los Angeles is an international city. The Mennonite churches reflect the multi-cultural composition of the city both in their membership and in their leadership from around the globe. The Council of Anabaptists in Los Angeles (CAL) is composed of the Mennonite Church (MC), General Conference Mennonite Church (GC), and Mennonite Brethren (MB) congregations in Southern California. The growth of the CAL-related churches is indebted to the international community. These groups have grown during the last ten years, increasing from seven churches in 1980 to thirty churches in 1990.

The Southwest Mennonite Conference (MC) was the first to focus attention on Los Angeles for church development. They decided to target their resources in developing new churches among a variety of people groups in Southern California. The first step was calling Hector Muñoz (Puerto Rico) to start Spanish-language churches in 1980. Three churches were developed, including a Salvadoran church led by Salvador Arana, a Mexican-American church led by Justo Moreno, and a Guatemalan church led by Eliseo Franco. The second step was the formation of a Belizian congregation by a small group that had been a part of Los Angeles Mennonite Fellowship. They became known as Family Mennonite Church and are now the largest Mennonite congregation in Southern California. The third step was receiving missionary assistance from one of the newer members of Mennonite World Conference, the Jemaat Kristen Indonesia (JKI). The JKI, under the leadership of Sutanto Adi, called Herman Tan to establish new Indonesian churches in Los Angeles and provided financial assistance for this endeavor. The fourth step was to appoint an area minister for Southern California to oversee the new churches and provide direction for continued church development. Allan Yoder, a son of missionaries to Cuba, was called in 1985.

During the past five years, additional congregations have developed and existing congregations strengthened. A few of the new congregations include a second Indonesian church led by Sutanto Adi, a fourth Hispanic church (MC/GC) led by Eliseo Franco (Guatemala), an Asian-Indian outreach being established by Ananda Sairsingh (Trinidad), and an International Student church being organized by Virgo Handoyo (Indonesia). Other congregations have also developed, including the counties surrounding Los Angeles, as churches have felt a vision to reach out. Some of the newer congregations have developed with the purpose of sending out church workers and focusing service and ministry on the hurts around them.

The Mennonite Brethren decided to expand in Southern California and began to experience growth after placing Juan Martinez (Mexican-American), director of

Hispanic Ministries, in Los Angeles. During the past four years, four new congregations have been added. These include a South American church led by Juan Martinez, a Central American church led by Juan Montes (Venezuela), and two Mexican churches led by Luis Colon (Puerto Rico) and Franklin Flores (Costa Rica). A Chinese church (Cantonese/Mandarin) has also been started, led by Luke Liu.

The General Conference has also been active in establishing a Chinese congregation, led by Mark Chen, and working together with the Mennonite Church in various of the efforts named above, including a new group in San Bernardino County led by Jeannie and Dennis Rempel, former missionaries in Burkina Faso.

The new congregations have joined the existing congregations, such as a Mexican-American (MB) congregation with an outreach to the gangs in East Los Angeles, an African-American (MC) congregation with a 280-student elementary school, and several other long-established churches such as Faith (MC), led by Stanley Green (South Africa).

With the growth of the Mennonite churches in Southern California, many needs have been uncovered as people become a part of our worshiping community. The ministries that CAL has developed have been in response to those needs.

CAL was organized in 1986 as a result of the need of the area leaders to have fellowship with each other, to share with one another, and to pray for one another. During these times together, a vision for service and justice ministries developed. The first ministry to develop was in the area of immigration. Southern California has one of the greatest refugee populations in the Americas. The churches that were being established were sometimes composed entirely of newly arrived refugees. The greatest need was to provide assistance for these brothers and sisters in dealing with the complexities of the immigration system in the United States. CAL established a committee to assist individuals in dealing with their immigration problems. Together with West Coast Mennonite Central Committee, CAL was able to call a part-time immigration worker, Rebeca Jiménez Yoder (Costa Rica).

A related issue has been that of employment for our church members. CAL is working at creating an economic development program to help provide assistance in starting small businesses and in receiving training. Under the direction of Barbara and Kent Besson (Belize), CAL currently operates a lawn route, which provides employment for two people while at the same time giving affordable lawn care to the elderly. Another ministry outreach is a group home for abused children. Janis and Stuart Mallory provided the vision for this ministry and, with the financial assistance of many of the CAL churches, have been able to establish the first group home.

To help keep our Anabaptist understandings clear, CAL has been involved in providing educational opportunities for church leaders through occasional seminars and courses. Pasadena Mennonite has also established a "Peace and Justice Lectureship," which has helped clarify Anabaptist issues in relation to the church and society. Other congregations have given leadership in establishing service and justice ministries. Some of those include feeding the hungry, Victim-Offender Reconciliation, and aiding the homeless.

The Anabaptist community in Southern California is growing and maturing. One of the issues that will need to be considered is the relationship between the various international groups in Southern California and their Anabaptist brothers and sisters in their country of origin. Another issue that would be useful to consider is how to build bridges between CAL and Anabaptist groups in other parts of the world with the intention of church development in both locations. The experiences to date have been very positive, but more could be done.

Los Angeles is an expensive city in which to live and work. Congregations and ministries are continually faced with the challenge of the high cost for facilities. New options for how and when and where churches meet need to be explored. Already, many churches do not meet on Sunday morning as a result of the cost of meeting space.

The Mennonite community in Southern California believes that Anabaptist theology is the most credible urban theology. We have noticed that as we practice and teach peace, our churches grow. We have seen our Anabaptist theology take root in the city and have seen it prosper. Leaders have embraced these understandings, and people from many languages and cultures have united in this effort. We pray that what has begun during the past decade will be but a shadow of what is to come.

Allan Yoder, USA, b. 1952, president of the Council of Anabaptists in Los Angeles, director of extension and evangelism for the Southwest Mennonite Conference.

These five Native American women are among those whose singing is heard on Navajo Gospel Hour. (MBM photo by Naswood Burbank, 1988)

Subsistence farming in Haiti

by Gordon Hunsberger

To understand farming in Haiti, it is necessary to know something of the history of the country and its people. Haiti was a French colony for about two hundred years. The majority of Haitians are the descendants of Africans brought by the French as slaves. In 1800 or so, while the French were fighting the Napoleonic wars in Europe, the slaves rebelled and drove the French out. Haiti became an independent country—the second country in the Western Hemisphere to gain its independence, preceded only by the United States. At the time of independence, the slave population was roughly 300,000 to 400,000. The French had established a plantation system, and at first some of the Haitian leaders tried to carry it on. But the slaves wanted their freedom. Many scattered throughout the valleys and mountains, where they claimed plots of land and grew their food. Since the total population was fairly small, there was plenty of land available.

The French had taught the slaves little other than to be obedient. But the slash-and-burn method of agriculture that their African ancestors used had not been lost, so they continued it and included some of the things they had learned by observation from the French. Slash-and-burn agriculture works reasonably well in subsistence farming as long as there is plenty of land available. The secret of success is to allow land to lie idle for a long enough time, up to ten or twelve years after having taken off a few crops. During the idle time the land is soon covered with grass, then shrubs, followed by trees. The dead grass, dying shrubs, and fallen leaves build up a mulch that restores fertility to the soil. After the idle period, the grass, shrubs, and trees are cut and burned and a crop is planted.

Problems of overpopulation

Since independence, however, the population of Haiti has increased from 350,000 to about 6 million. Land holdings were divided and subdivided. The idle periods between crops decreased from ten years to five, then four or three or two. Trees were cut to provide more cropland. Humus and soil fertility decreased, and soil erosion increased by leaps and bounds. Haiti is about 80 percent mountains and 20 percent plains land. Haitians have a saying, "Behind the mountains are mountains." Much of the fertile plains land is owned by the wealthy or controlled by the government. Most of the poorer people are peasant farmers, and much of their land is mountainous. Even those fortunate enough to have employment often need land to grow some food, because their pay is low.

A combination of overpopulation, reduction of forest cover, overworked land, and poor soil conservation practices has resulted in massive soil erosion throughout the mountainous areas. Once-productive mountainsides have lost most of their fertile topsoil and no longer produce enough food to feed the family.

Ways of helping

Various aid and development organizations, including Mennonite Central Committee, are working at the problem of soil erosion by helping with reforestation and teaching better soil conservation practices. Effective soil conservation can be achieved by planting trees, digging ditches to catch water, making ridges, or building rock wall terraces, all on the contour, on cultivated mountainsides. Trees can be a valuable crop in a country like Haiti with a year-round warm climate and usually abundant rainfall. In as little as ten or twelve years, valuable hardwoods can be grown to a usable size of 10 or 12 inches in diameter. This is an especially important resource in a world that is rapidly being deforested. Some Haitian peasants are beginning to understand the importance of trees as a source of income as well as a means of soil conservation.

Subsistence farming

Most Haitian farmers are subsistence farmers because they do not have enough land to do otherwise. The first priority is always to grow enough to feed yourself and your family. But one or two hectares of eroded mountain land is often not enough to do that adequately, much less have anything left to sell for cash income, which everyone needs as well.

The most common cash crop is coffee. Space can usually be found for a few coffee bushes. Cocoa is also a useful cash crop. Both are exported and dependent on world prices, which fluctuate widely. Sugar cane is grown as a cash crop, mostly in the plains and by larger landowners. Major food crops in mountain areas are corn and beans. In the valleys where there is irrigation, rice is grown. In areas with less rainfall, sorghum is useful. Bananas are important for domestic consumption, especially plantains, which are harvested green and cooked. Other important foods are root crops such as cassava or manioc, sweet potatoes, and yams. Fruits such as mangoes, citrus, pineapples, and papaya grow well and are an important source of food for the family and for sale within the country.

Since most families are very poor and have no cash reserves—in fact, many are constantly in debt—the goal is to have food available in the garden as much of the time as possible. A good manager can do this, barring unforeseen weather conditions such as drought, floods, or tropical storms. Crops are usually interplanted. Beans may be planted first, followed by corn and later by cassava. Beans will be harvested first, then corn a few months later. Cassava takes a full season of ten to twelve months to mature and is often harvested during the dry season, as are sweet potatoes and yams. Root crops can be left in the ground during the dry season and harvested as needed for consumption.

Rodents and insects frequently damage stored grain. Because of storage problems and the need for cash, producers often sell much of their corn, beans, sorghum, or rice at harvest time, but must then buy grain later for food and seed at much higher prices. Improving storage facilities and methods is a way that aid organizations help provide more food. Many families try to have a reserve food supply in the form of a few breadfruit or coconut trees. Trees, being deep rooted, will usually produce a crop even during dry periods.

Livestock on Haitian farms

Most Haitian farmers have livestock, but only in small numbers. Since feeding grain to livestock is a less efficient way to produce food, and since food is usually in short supply, most livestock are fed on things that are unfit for humans. Few peasant farmers will have a cow; most cows produce little more milk than what a calf needs because of unproductive strains and poor feed. Where sugar cane is grown, cattle are often fed the refuse from the cane crop. Goats are more common than cattle because they require less feed. They are usually thin and almost never milked. They are kept to produce offspring, which are used for meat. Goats are destructive of tree seedlings and a hindrance to reforestation. Most families in the rural areas and villages keep a few chickens. They are usually small bantam breeds and forage for themselves. Donkeys, mules, and small horses are used as pack animals.

Pigs are a valued livestock. They usually forage for themselves along paths and in ravines, where they consume whatever waste they can find. They are often fitted with yokes to make it more difficult for them to get through the cactus fences and into gardens. Pigs grow slowly since they are fed little, often taking 24 to 30 months to market size. To fatten them in the last few months, they are fed wormy mangoes, surplus avocados, or palm oil seeds. In the late 1970s and early 1980s, Haiti's pig population was wiped out by African swine flu. After several years, repopulation took place with stock imported from the United States. Banks are nonexistent in rural Haiti, so pigs sometimes serve as a bank. When a little money becomes available, a pig is bought. Later, when the money is needed, the pig is sold in the hope of receiving more than the purchase price.

Most Haitians have little opportunity to improve their farming skills and are unaware of the need to maintain soil fertility and control erosion. Help from government agricultural services is very limited. Young people frequently move to the city in search of employment. Even those who find work often receive too little pay to support themselves, so they return to the rural communities where they might at least have access to some land on which to grow food. Many Haitians want to emigrate in search of a better place to make a living. Often they are environmental refugees, fleeing from a land where population growth has outstripped the available natural resources. It is not a pretty picture.

Gordon Hunsberger, Canada, b. 1914, Mennonite Central Committee volunteer in Haiti and Ontario from 1975–89, retired farmer.

Job creation program

by Charmayne Denlinger Brubaker

Bangladesh, a country bordered by Burma and India, sits on a river delta. Most of its 55,598 square miles of land is flat and fertile soil. The country's farmers are able to produce enough food to feed its 110 million citizens, but many of its people cannot afford to buy the food produced. Those who do not have land on which to grow food seek employment in cities and factories or hire themselves out as day laborers to other farmers. But about 40 percent of Bangladesh's work force is unemployed or underemployed. MCC started its ministry in Bangladesh in 1970 after a devastating cyclone. A costly war for freedom in 1971 added to the country's problems. MCC's first workers provided relief food aid and started agricultural programs. In Saidpur they opened a clinic for severely and mildly malnourished children in refugee camps. At the clinic they distributed emergency rations and taught nutrition to the parents of the children. But they quickly saw that parents did not have the money needed to buy enough food for their children. Nor could the parents purify families' drinking water by boiling it; they did not have enough money to buy the kerosene or firewood needed to do this. Farmers whose crops barely fed their families were not able to risk growing new "foreign" crops that were more nutritious. The same parents and children came repeatedly to the clinic, because they did not have the money needed to improve their health. MCC workers also learned that the people of Bangladesh were ready and willing to work to improve their living conditions, but jobs were scarce. They started the job creation program in 1975 in response to poverty in Mirpur, a refugee camp north of the capital city of Dhaka, and in Saidpur, a town in the north where refugees from the 1971 war had settled.

Current program

Today, in 1990, more than five thousand people work directly in enterprises that were started through MCC's job creation program and that have now "graduated" from MCC ownership. Another twenty thousand people work in occupations created by "links with suppliers or customers of those projects," says Rollin Rheinheimer, Mennonite Central Committee worker from Akron, Pennsylvania, who directs the job creation work. About 1,300 people work in projects that MCC currently owns. They make paper, soap, cloth, mats, rope, twine, solar-dried soybeans and coconut, wooden skipping rope handles, and crafts. The management staff of the job creation program involves four expatriate staff and twenty-five Bangladeshi staff who work alongside the project leaders.

About 50 percent of the items produced are sold within Bangladesh, rather than exported, and the twenty-five MCC-owned or MCC-assisted projects are located in six districts, rather than only near refugee camps. The target group, though, is more narrowly focused than it was in the early years. The program aims to develop new projects that provide jobs particularly for "landless, rural, unemployed, heads of household women." MCC also aims to establish projects that (1) can be replicated within the country and (2) can eventually be producer owned and operated.

Today's problems

Establishing projects that will eventually be owned and operated by the producers is difficult when the producers are landless, rural women. Most landless, rural women in Bangladesh are illiterate and lack the business skills needed to own and operate the microenterprises MCC has traditionally established. "How does MCC teach landless, rural women—who live from hand to mouth—about cash flow, long-range planning, inventory control, record keeping, and accounting?" asks Rheinheimer. Another problem comes from local competition. MCC's solar-dried coconut project, Surjosnato, has been expanding ever since its start in 1980. It has worked diligently and successfully at locating local buyers for its product. Biscuit factories in Dhaka buy 80 percent of the dried coconut produced. Producers in the project have been receiving a monthly wage of 875 taka (US $26), the monthly wage earned by a farm worker. MCC has worked deliberately at paying people wages that enable them to feed their families. MCC job creation staff calculate that a family of five needs a monthly income of 1,000 taka for its rice, lentils, vegetables, and oil. This amount of money does not buy the family any meat or fish. But this policy makes MCC projects vulnerable to local competition; local entrepreneurs do not, and often cannot, pay producers a fair living wage. "Now that we have developed a market," reports Rheinheimer, "a local business person is threatening to start a factory and 'take the market' away." This local entrepreneur aims to produce solar-dried coconut and sell it for less than Surjosnato does. He can do this because he will pay producers only 300 taka a month. "When people do not have a job, 300 taka a month is better than zero taka a month," Rheinheimer notes.

MCC's choice to work with rural, landless women has also made it difficult to establish quality control standards. People who live in poverty are more conscious of price than of quality, observes Rheinheimer. They do not have the luxury of buying quality items, so convincing poor producers of the need to produce quality items is difficult. They work to produce low-cost items. Investing more time and resources into a product to make it higher quality, and therefore more expensive, is foreign to their way of thinking, Rheinheimer notes. Yet poor quality items do not sell in North American and European markets.

MCC's choice to work with rural, landless women also means that MCC needs to invest time and money into training these producers about design and marketing. MCC has periodically had artists and designers go to Bangladesh, for example, to work with the producers making wheat straw cards. If the wheat straw producers are going to sell wheat straw cards in Europe and North America, they need to design cards that are attractive to North American and European buyers. The producers also need to change designs periodically. MCC has also asked MCC volunteers with specific technical training to work within the job creation program designing the equipment. An MCC expatriate worker, for example, has designed a pulp beater for the MCC paper factory in Feni. People trained to do this type of research are few in Bangladesh at this time.

MCC, as a nongovernmental agency, does not plan to stay forever in Bangladesh. Therefore, existing options are (1) total MCC ownership of a project; (2) starting a project, paying for the initial research and development of a product, forming a management committee, and then turning the project over to a local nongovernmental organization; or (3) same as option 2, but turning the project over to private ownership—ideally to the producers themselves. None of these options is easily accomplished.

Future directions for the program

The program will continue to develop new enterprises. New areas of concentration are low-cost techniques for food processing, food preservation, and low-cost but durable building materials and crafts. Food is plentiful at harvest time, but methods of preservation are either too sophisticated or too costly for the rural poor. The job creation program is now studying the feasibility of fruit and vegetable canning or processing that will provide new job opportunities and, at the same time, help provide more nutritious food for the country's people. Bangladesh is subject to periodic cyclones and floods. The job creation program is looking for ways to help poorer Bangladeshis with materials and methods of home and building construction that will withstand these disasters. The goal again is not only to provide new jobs but also to produce products or processes useful to the poor in the country. Experimentation continues with forms of ownership. Employee ownership, or at least control, is desirable, since the intent is to benefit the producers as much as possible. The job creation program staff continues to give increasing emphasis to management training for producers so that project workers have a basic understanding of how to make a product profitably and how to get that product to market. Increasingly the job creation program is working on training Bangladeshis rather than doing things with expatriates. Three Bangladeshi women have been hired to work in women's development. They teach project personnel the skills necessary to work, how to manage their projects, and they help them develop a better awareness of their worth and value to their family and community.

Jobs continue to be a priority in this country. The people want employment, and MCC's job creation program will continue to create that employment by assisting with technical and managerial skills and by training people to help themselves.

Charmayne Denlinger Brubaker, USA, b. 1951, Secretary of Mennonite Central Committee Information Services, MCC worker in Bangladesh from 1978–81, writer and editor for MCC Information Services from 1982–89.

The work of AMAS with children

by Anita Dyck

In Brazil, the largest country of South America with an area of 8,511,965 square kilometers and 150 million inhabitants, the development in the large cities is taking giant strides and is approaching that of the modern metropolises. However, the poverty on the periphery of these cities and in the interior of the country is deplorable. It is a country of disturbing contrasts. A downright chaotic economic policy and galloping inflation encourage the gap between the poor and the rich to widen. Supposedly 80 percent of the population belongs to the poorest stratum of society. In the slums of the cities and in the country, the children and young people make up the majority and are the ones most affected by this great poverty. There is no structure or basis for a healthy development for them. Our country has 28 million street children. They grow up without any of the most basic necessities such as adequate food, clothing, education, health care, security, and love. They become antisocial or societal outsiders.

After the German-speaking Mennonite congregations had overcome the difficult beginning years, they turned to their immediate surroundings. What they saw challenged them to help after they themselves had been helped. They began to spread the message of the gospel but soon saw that the needs of the whole person had to be met, spiritual as well as physical, and that the children suffered the most from this poverty. Through the initiative of individuals who were moved by the missionary spirit, they began to gather children around themselves. Soon a small children's home was established in the small city of Palmeira close to Witmarsum Colony. As a result of this beginning, a wide field opened up that could no longer be managed by a few individuals. The support of the congregations was essential.

At the suggestion of the ninth Mennonite World Conference assembly in Curitiba, the daring step of organizing a Mennonite relief agency, Associação Menonita de Assistência Social (AMAS), was undertaken in September 1972. The goal was to help suffering children and families, care for them both spiritually and physically, and present to them the love of God in word and deed. The goal was organization of child care in day-care centers and schools. Support for the establishment of this organization came from the three Mennonite congregations in Curitiba and the vicinity: Witmarsum, Vila Guaira, and Boqueirão. These are only small congregations, but very quickly they found support for the work of their relief agency from their friends, congregations, and organizations both at home and abroad. Thanks to this help, especially financial help, it was possible for this work to spread, grow, and serve the neighbor in need.

Now, as I write in 1989, this organization daily cares for 565 children and members of their families in day-care centers and schools. This aid reaches approximately three thousand people in six different projects in Curitiba and in the neighboring localities of Porto Amazonas, Palmeira, Cercado, and Lapa. The latter project is new this year and the first one undertaken jointly with the Mennonite Brethren of that city. Additionally, there is cooperation with the Associação Evangélica Menonita (AEM) in the Araguacema project. AEM maintains two schools there with a total of approximately 450 children and a clinic in which an AMAS-appointed nurse carries the responsibility. The assistance of AMAS is indirect in this project; AMAS helps with finances and serves in an advisory capacity. Additionally, there is the cooperation with Mennonite Central Committee in Recife, which works with AMAS in Brazil.

What does the work of AMAS look like in real life? Let us accompany one of the children. Adão is from Porto Amazonas, a city of four thousand. He lives in a two-room hut with his mother and four brothers and sisters. The father, an alcoholic, left the family. Adão, all of eight years old, has to take care of the two smaller children because his mother and older brother have to leave for work at a tree nursery before dawn. The three children would be left by themselves unattended all day if the day-care center would not take them. So Adão wakes up the small children, helps them get dressed, and puts a diaper on the smallest one. Then, whether it is sunny, raining, or cold, they walk the 3 kilometers to the center. The youngest one needs to be carried again and again. There is little strength for this, for they have had no breakfast because there was nothing in the house.

When they finally arrive at the center, Adão can let go of his responsibilities and be a child among other children. Kind and loving "aunties" care for him and the two smaller children of his family. After receiving a warm breakfast and a bath and being properly dressed, they hear of God's love during the daily devotion. They sing and play until the nourishing noon meal. In between, on hot days, there is also some fruit or juice. After a nap, which the children need badly because they have very low reserves of energy, there is a small lunch followed by all kinds of interesting activities as they work at handicrafts and learn according to their age level. Before they go home at night, they are fed a nourishing soup. Then Adão with his two charges, as well as all the other children, head for home. When the mother comes home tired, the children have at least been taken care of and she can occupy herself a bit with the small household and laundry.

What results does AMAS expect from this program? This effort is an act of dedicated service and is not based on measurable success. The Lord of the harvest is God himself. If, however, neglected and undernourished children grow up to be independent, strong young people and responsible parents, that is simultaneously a reward and a challenge not to get weary but to continue.

Ten years ago Adriano came to the day-care center in Palmeira with his younger brother. His parents were divorced. His father was an alcoholic, and his mother took care of the children herself. Because she knew that her boys were cared for at the center, she took a job where she worked very hard and earned enough money to care for her family. She was also able to save a little and, with the help of the family care, acquired a small building plot. Today her own three-room house is located on this plot. She will continue to make improvements on it. Adriano, now fifteen years old, took a course in typing and office work in the AMAS vocational school while staying at the day-care center and attending regular school classes in the city. He is currently working as an office assistant in the state bank, receives his own salary, and is even able to help his mother. Paulo, a friend his same age at the center, received the same chances to enter a vocation. After a few months he was dismissed; he had not been reliable and was not accepted by society. Success and failure go side by side.

Benicio, sixteen years old, also came from a broken family. He practically grew up at the center. Here he was raised, educated, and trained as a cabinetmaker in the vocational school. Now he is a legitimate employee in a furniture factory, earns his own livelihood, and additionally is able to help his four brothers and sisters. He has found his place and finds satisfaction in his vocation.

There are a number of employees in this relief organization who themselves were once children in the day-care centers. Rosane, for example, is now a child-care worker and passes on to other children the love and care she herself experienced. Or Jacira, who works in the kitchen, now prepares meals for the group of children to which she herself belonged at one time. And the young man who coordinates the training program in Palmeira, a reliable coworker in his congregation, happily passes on his testimony through faithful work. No one would guess he was once one of the boys who lacked the most basic necessities of life.

The work is well worthwhile. Through this service we want to point to God's never-ending grace, which alleviates suffering through activated love and takes care of spiritual suffering with compassion. Thus we try to demonstrate to the poorest of the poor the essence and purpose of existence: to honor God with our lives.

All of the conditions for "service in the love of Christ," the motto of AMAS, are present. Without the undergirding of contributions and sponsorships from many friends in the affluent countries and without the intercessory prayers of brothers and sisters in the faith, it would be impossible to do justice to the demands. AMAS is thankful for all the prayers, gifts, and help and continues to offer many the opportunity to participate in service in the love of Christ.

Anita Dyck, Brazil, b. 1934, member of the Mennonite church of Boqueirão, editor of the periodical *Bibel und Pflug*, and administrator of the German section of AMAS.
Translated by Gerhard Reimer.

Indian women and children. (MBM/S photo, 1984)

Child nutrition in Nepal

by Miriam E. Krantz

Bringing the known and the new together was a real learning experience during my first assignment in Nepal in 1964 as head of the dietary department of Shanta Bhawan Hospital (SBH) in the Kathmandu Valley. I had studied about child nutrition, but never had I seen such malnourished children. It was understandable that the few abandoned children could be in such a condition, but what about those with seemingly well-nourished parents? Obviously food was needed. But what kinds of food would be most helpful for the present and a help to the mother in the future? There were limitations on what the hospital could provide. And the usual struggle to get any food inside the child's mouth, let alone the stomach, took a lot of energy on the part of the child, mother, and staff. What foods the children would be given when they got home was largely an unanswerable question—unless we went to the home to see what resources were available.

Community exposure

It was a fruitful experience in the early 1970s when as community nutritionist I could spend more time out in the Community Health Program (CHP). During home visiting some families even permitted me to go into their kitchen areas—usually forbidden to outsiders. (Some kitchens had to be purified later.) Meal schedules, types and amounts of food consumed daily, food and water sources, who tends the children, views on sanitation and food hygiene—what a wealth of information to process. As time went on, I discovered that this was a complex world—one full of possibilities—often with very caring grandparents, even plenty of food in most of the homes. But there were other homes that seemed at first glance to be very poor. The malnourished children came from both kinds of home situations. Yet so did the well-nourished children! How could this be?

The CHP clinics concentrated on maternal and children's health. Reports stated that 50 percent of children died before they reached age five. Treatment of diarrhea, other infections, and malnutrition left little time for staff to talk with and learn from mothers. Donations of skim milk powder were available for mothers of malnourished children. Clinic activities were sometimes disrupted by the other mothers demanding milk powder. Much of the milk that was distributed was not fed to children, but was consumed by other family members or sold to teashops. What was given sometimes caused acute diarrhea leading to further undernourishment. Perhaps even worse, mothers were developing a dependency on imported foods rather than learning what they could do for themselves.

Searching for and building relationships

In 1973 a year-long nutrition study was done in two ethnically different villages to identify foods available in the homes and current infant feeding practices. The children studied were all between the ages of 8 to 12 months and 1.5 to 2 years at the beginning of the study and included children who were malnourished, borderline, and well nourished. We learned that good foods were readily available but that children were not able to digest the coarse foods they were given, that the mealtimes were too few to provide an adequate amount of calories and other nutrients, and that no one was really sure if the child ate the food he or she was given since there was very little meal supervision. There seemed to be a knowledge gap about the relationship of food to health rather than a lack of food. It was during this time with mothers that we learned they would be willing to act on their own suggestion that grinding the roasted soybeans, corn, and wheat would make a more digestible and acceptable supplementary food for their young children. This discovery was a real answer to prayer, for now we could introduce this idea for child feeding in the area where milk distribution was preventing the clinics from carrying out their aim of participating in curative and preventive care by discussing with mothers what they could do by themselves to provide foods adequate in both calories and protein. Samples of the roasted flour of soybeans, corn, and wheat (2:1:1) were sent for analysis in mid-1973. This flour became known as super flour (Sarbottam Pitho), because it contains complete protein and because it is so versatile. Other combinations of pulse and cereal grains can be used. Imported foods were phased out of the CHP completely. By this time nutrition was beginning to be recognized as an important health component. Also in 1973 nutrition, with a strong maternal-child emphasis, was included in the public health curriculum at the government nursing campus for the first time.

A nutrition rehabilitation center (NRC), the first in Nepal, was established in June 1974 in a rural village served by the SBH Community Health Program. The primary objective was to train mothers (or other caretakers) in the appropriate use of local foods and good feeding methods and to develop the ability to teach other mothers when they returned home. An expected benefit was the recovered children, but the families were also amazed that "food with love," not medicine, is the treatment for most malnourished children. The mothers shared with us a wealth of information about food customs, beliefs, and practices, which in turn has been used to make the content of a variety of teaching materials more relevant to the situation in Nepal. Trainees from the government Women's Affairs Training Center spent time at the center. Students from campuses of the Institute of Medicine came to observe and went away with a new appreciation for mothers' abilities to rehabilitate their own children and for what can be done with simple, local foods. Super flour preparations (porridge or flat breads made without sugar and milk) and green leaves (usually puréed) were the only additions to what the child ate with his or her mother, and oral rehydration solution plus food was given to children with diarrhea—yet many of these very malnourished children were back to their normal weight-for-height within two to four weeks! For example, eighteen-month-old Suku, irritable, thin, with swollen feet and peeling skin, weighed 7.5 kilograms. Eleven days later his father hardly recognized his son, now smiling, with nicely filled-out body, smooth skin, and weighing 8.1 kilograms. After being home one month, where he continued to eat the super flour his father made, he weighed 10.0 kilograms. Suku's brother, born later, was given super flour porridge in addition to breast milk from the fifth month and remained a healthy child. The parents had learned important lessons. There are now two home-based rehabilitation programs and another NRC.

In 1973 the first annual seminar for volunteers was held. Nutrition was an important aspect of the training. Several of the early volunteers are now in management positions in health and nutrition. Volunteers continue to be valuable resource people and interpreters of their communities. In 1974 we held the first annual seminar for traditional birth attendants. Nutrition was considered too sensitive a subject for such traditional individuals; we had to wait until 1975 to include nutrition, and then only by having a one-part skit. Five years later they presented their own nutrition drama! Most of these women are illiterate but professionals in their own right. We also held a seminar for witch doctors (shamans) in order to get acquainted with each other's aims. After that a couple of witch doctors sent their wives and malnourished children to the NRC when they were unable to treat them.

The first national nutrition planning meeting, the Project Formulation on Nutrition and Goiter, was held in October 1975. From then on, nutrition began to be included in government planning, with UNICEF taking a strong role. There were many opportunities to cooperate. Requests for writing nutrition materials and for participation in nutrition training programs increased and continue to come in.

Problems and assets

Nepal, a small country between India and China (Tibet), supports 17.8 million people on 147,181 square kilometers. More than seven hundred people depend on one square kilometer of arable land for their main food supply. Climate irregularities, steep terrain, pressures of population growth, deforestation, erosion, and food supply distribution constraints have had an adverse effect on the nutrition of mothers and children. The daily per capita calorie supply is 88 percent of requirements, although the average index of food production is 97 percent. Fifty percent of the pregnant women and 80 percent of lactating mothers are nutritionally anemic. The annual number of deaths of infants under one year of age per one thousand live births is 129; the rate for those under five years of age is 200. The annual number of births is 723,000, and infant and child deaths come to 145,000. Twenty-seven percent of children age 12 to 23 months are wasted, i.e., less than 77 percent of the median weight-for-height; and 72 percent of the children age 24 to 59 months are stunted, i.e., less than 77 percent of the median height-for-age. It is reported that every thirteen minutes a child dies of a diarrhea-related illness; nutritional blindness claims one child each day.

Some of the problems of malnutrition are due to poverty of material resources, but most are related to poverty of knowledge. Most homes have or could have enough food to prevent malnutrition, but when a child is ill and does not want to eat, the parents give in and do not continue to encourage him or her to eat. There are many food and liquid restrictions according to the age or condition of the child. Advice is usually first sought from traditional healers or witch doctors. Much time is lost while parents take the child from one shrine to another. Much money is spent on mantras and animal sacrifices. By the time a health worker sees the child, it may be too late. In recent years with the increase of biscuit factories, white bread bakeries, and forceful advertising, nutritious traditional foods are being replaced by those poor substitutes. Good practices such as jwaano-seed soup to increase breast milk production are being disregarded. Bottle feeding is increasing. Much money is spent on infant formula, commercial infant foods, soft drinks, and other luxury items—money that could provide adequate, wholesome food for the whole family. Smoking, which can cause low birth weight infants and respiratory problems, is widespread. Nepal is near the top in the number of women smokers. A couple of years ago the per capita spending on cigarettes was twice that of the per capita health budget.

Into the future

Awareness campaigns need to continue to pick up momentum, or else purely commercial or selfish interests will continue to erode the good food traditions. Nationals engaged in health and nutrition, agriculture, forestry, water resources, rural technology, education, etc., need to do their homework. They need to find out what the good traditional practices were or are and revive/encourage such, always asking the question, What are the present and long-term implications of what we are doing? It is a privilege to work with nationals on these issues.

The mother and developing infant need to be thought of as a single unit. In some situations, the mother-in-law also needs to be added. There are good, neutral, and harmful customs, practices, and attitudes in every culture. It is wise to search for the positive to find solutions to many problems. Mothers will give oral rehydration solution to children with diarrhea. They will make and give cereal/pulse-based supplementary foods to infants after the fifth month. They will even add puréed green leaves to foods. They do quickly learn new feeding techniques for ill, malnourished, or simply irritable children. They can and do share information with other mothers. Traditional healers are sometimes open to listen and to learn. God is asking us to be present—to give support and encouragement to the caretakers of children just as he has done on behalf of our total nourishment.

Miriam E. Krantz, Nepal, b. 1937, B.S. and postgraduate work in home economics education, nutrition consultant with the United Mission to Nepal, member of the New Providence Mennonite Church in Lancaster (Pennsylvania) Conference.

Sponsorship program of IMO

by Volker Horsch

A few years ago a young couple visiting relatives in the vicinity of Neuwied, West Germany, dropped by the office of IMO, the relief organization of European Mennonites. The young woman came from the Menno Colony in Paraguay. During the course of the conversation, the sponsorship program of IMO became the main topic. "I, too, am one of the sponsored persons," said my guest, "and thankfully I remember how I had the opportunity to go to Central School in Menno. I would not be what I am today if I had not had the opportunity to get an education. At that time it was so difficult to meet the requirements of the program. School itself was not the problem; we took part in everything that was offered and required. The relationship of teachers and students was first class, and I managed my studies, although I had to apply myself. We were encouraged to write letters to our sponsors, to those from whom the money for our education came. But what could be of interest to our sponsors? We could not think of anything to write! When the letter was finally written, the waiting for an answer began. And I did not receive one. I wrote again, and a third time, but an answer never came. I would so much like to thank my patrons personally, but how do I find them?" So a searching through our records began, and we were all very satisfied when the names and address finally lay before us.

This incident is an exception. It demonstrates in a clear-cut way the difficulties and, at the same time, the prospects and the fruits of this program. Sponsorships in the Menno Colony were among the first that IMO supported from the late 1960s to the early 1970s. At the same time Mennonite Central Committee (MCC), the sister organization in North America, took over sponsorships in India and Indonesia. In Menno Colony, Paraguay, Central School looked after the program, which was upheld as long as seemed necessary. Then sponsorships for pupils from the native population of Paraguay took its place because Menno Colony could now provide the school fees for its own growing generation. So pupils in Villa Hayes and Cambyreta as well as Colegio Albert Schweitzer received support. For sponsorship of Indians, ASCIM, an organization for the promotion and settlement of Indians in the Chaco, was entrusted with the program. In the mid-1970s the program was extended to Brazil, where AMAS, the relief program of the German-speaking Mennonites, became a partner. Again the sponsored were pupils—as in Araguacema, Central Brazil—and, since 1987, children in day-care centers in the southern part of the country. Quite soon, in the early 1970s, a program partnership was formed with a committee called PAKKRI from the young Javanese Church of Pati. The unique part of this program is that orphans, or half-orphans whose living parent cannot provide sufficient means, receive the support.

In later years the sponsorship program was expanded to include career training. In Paraguay young people of German-Mennonite background participated first, but soon the participants came largely from the native population. For them a concerns committee was formed, with representatives from the Mennonite Brethren and General Conference, from German-speaking as well as from missionary congregations. Unfortunately, the number of sponsored individuals must remain low because the cost of sponsorship is quite high. Twenty-one adults could receive scholarships in recent years, whereas more than five hundred pupils at various schools are supported regularly.

An essential element of the sponsorship program is that the donor knows who the beneficiary is. Sponsors donate not only for general relief work or a merely functional purpose but for an individual who needs help and who, with that help, can better approach life. The latter pins down the second point of emphasis: the program is aimed at the education and training of young people. They must be prepared for the life that awaits them. They must receive the qualifications to give shape, with their own contribution, to the society into which they grow. And so this program is seed for the future. The incident described in the intro-duction depicts something out of the life of this program. Because the program was intentionally structured in such a way that both donor and recipient should know there is a person with a face and name, with a particular environment and a story at the other end, it is important that at least a minimum of contact take place. The emphasis is not on thank-you's or intense communication—these are unnecessary, for the people concerned are spatially and culturally too far apart. Yet both donor and receiver feel that something is missing without some sign of life. If answers to letters, for example, do take place, something of the person at the other end becomes discernible, something that enriches.

IMO's contribution to the program is modest. It only attends to the negotiation between the individuals to be sponsored and their donors, and it forwards the re-ceived monies. It also sets the framework within which the program can operate. Much more important is the task that falls to the program partners overseas. They must not only choose the beneficiaries, who should be the most needy and worthy of being sponsored, but must also accompany them and observe their progress. IMO remains in contact with its program partners and gives the sponsors an annual report to keep them up to date. Of course, all these efforts stand and fall with the sponsors. They must supply the means through which the program remains effective. Some of them have remained faithful to the program for many years. They deserve thanks. The sponsored children, too, generally have not disappointed the hopes that were set for them. Nothing is left but to wish that the program can also be a blessing in the future.

Volker Horsch, Federal Republic of Germany, b. 1933, general secretary of Internationale Mennonitische Organisation (IMO), a relief organization of European Mennonites.
Translated by Anita Lichti.

Mennonite refugee work in Miami

by Walter W. Sawatzky

"Will the last American to leave Miami please bring the flag."

This was a popular bumper sticker around Miami in the early 1980s, when this rapidly changing metropolitan community at the southern tip of Florida (United States) was knocked out of any sense of social equilibrium by the mass immigration of 125,000 Cubans and 7,000 Haitians within a four-month period.

The past twenty-five years of immigration have remade Miami. Perhaps no other American city has experienced such dramatic ethnic transformation. It has strained the fibers of community institutions to their absolute limit. Early in 1989, when thousands of Nicaraguans crossed the Texas border and turned eastward to Miami, the city sent emissaries to the West in an effort to discourage them from coming to Miami. There are no jobs and no places to sleep, they said. Nearly five out of ten Miamians are foreign born. No other major urban area in North America, including New York (two out of ten) contains this kind of demographic. While the various ethnic groups in Miami must yet learn to coexist, most of the city's current residents have accepted and, to some degree, have begun to appreciate the community's cultural diversity.

Mennonites arrived in Miami with the first large wave of Cubans in the early 1960s. They came from Pennsylvania to establish an alternative service program while the refugees from Castro's Cuba sought economic and political freedom. Over the next twenty years Mennonites trickled in and out. In fact, by 1985 Miami still showed only one small Mennonite church of twenty-two members. Meanwhile, Cubans had exploded onto the South Florida scene in numbers exceeding three-quarters of a million. By 1990 the number of Haitian refugees living in Greater Miami has risen to 85,000, and Central Americans from El Salvador, Nicaragua, and Guatemala are arriving in significant numbers.

Mennonites did not become overtly involved in refugee-related ministries until 1980, when local church leaders sent a plea to Mennonite Central Committee (MCC) for assistance with the huge influx of Caribbean boat people from Cuba and Haiti. MCC's early work in Miami related primarily to the physical and social needs of Haitian immigrants. In contrast to other refugees arriving in Miami around 1980, Haitians had few places to turn for assistance. The tiny, poor Haitian community in South Florida had no means to support newcomers.

Typically, the first people to flee a dictatorship or censorship in their native land are the business and civic leaders. Only much later, when the situation becomes truly unbearable for the anonymous workers, do they follow the upper middle classes into exile. Castro's communist regime and "Papa Doc" Duvalier's dictatorship sent thousands of leaders from Cuba and Haiti into American exile in the early 1960s. Cubans went to Miami, Haitians to New York and Montreal.

Mennonite Disaster Service (MDS), the local Association of Mennonite Ministries (AMM), and MCC all joined the generous Christian response to needs in the Haitian community. MDS sent units to Miami in the early 1980s to repair and renovate church buildings in Little Haiti. AMM, meanwhile, helped several congregations buy their own facilities through loans and by taking co-responsibility in signing for mortgages.

MCC sent Creole-speaking workers to refugee camps to interpret and to process immigration applications. MCC workers also taught English and assisted at community social service agencies. Currently MCC has four workers whose primary assignments are with Haitian programs in South Florida:

1.   Little Haiti Housing Association is a church-based community development corporation initiated in 1987 through the efforts of an MCC worker. MCC provides a temporary staff person to help Haitian churches achieve their vision of providing affordable, adequate housing to low-income Haitian-American families. The story of housing woes in South Florida's Haitian community is also the story of Presendieu Colas, who paid more each month to the Belle Glade Water Department than he paid to his landlord because he did not know plumbing could leak and no one wondered why a one-room tenement apartment would have a $260 water bill. Many, like Presendieu, are unwilling to make a fuss over deficient housing for fear of jeopardizing their fragile claim to be in America.

2.   Haitian Catholic Center (HCC) offers emergency food and shelter assistance to the needy in Belle Glade. The MCC worker at HCC is a nurse who attempts to provide and facilitate minimal health care to those who cannot gain access to the community health-care system. Home visits provide the opportunity to learn about other social and spiritual needs the person may have. For many among the more than eighty thousand Haitians in South Florida, the "promised land" has fallen far short of their dreams. Marie Bernadette is a single mother with three children. She had a daytime job as a cleaning maid last summer. Unable to afford a baby-sitter, she left the nine-year-old in charge of the three- and five-year-olds. Now that school has started, she is at home with the youngest, but is unable to pay her rent or feed her family. "I cannot pay all my bills making $3.35 per hour," she says softly, her head bowed. "I hear they pay $5 [per hour] for motel maids in Orlando, so I am going up there soon."

3.   A Haitian-American pastor is seconded to several Haitian churches in Miami to help facilitate youth programs. This work involves regular meetings with pastors, parents, and youths to begin to bridge a generation gap accentuated by the rapid assimilation of Haitian young people into American culture. In addition, this MCC worker is building a network of Haitian pastors, which will serve

as a springboard for cooperative community projects. One such program is a Haitian Leadership Institute currently in formation. The institute will offer theological, biblical, and community development courses to enhance the ministry of Haitian congregations in their neighborhoods.

4.   Another worker who formerly served with MCC in Haiti is seconded to Southeast Mennonite Conference as a liaison to the Haitian community. The first task was to assist in the birth of a Haitian Mennonite congregation in Miami's Little Haiti. MCC continues to be a partner with the conference in providing a local facilitator for Mennonite work among Haitians.

In its four years of ministry, the Eglise du Nouveau Testament (Church of the New Testament) has been a blessing to many who had just arrived from Haiti. It has been a place where lives have stabilized after the traumatic departure and voyage to Miami. Mondes and Laude Mondesir tell such a story. Not long before they joined this Haitian Mennonite church, they arrived on United States shores by boat. Like thousands of fellow Haitians, Mondes and Laude risked their lives for a chance to start this new life. They boarded a 40-foot wooden boat with 113 others in Haiti and set sail for Miami. They decided that they had nothing to lose on this precarious 800-mile voyage. They could see no future for themselves in Haiti. Food is scarce, the soil has been eroded, jobs are nonexistent, and education is meager but, above all, useless. Ten days without fresh water and in the teeth of a howling storm on the eleventh, many in the boat were ready to go back. These were overruled. "It is better to die than to return," they repeated. A day later the waves threw them ashore on Miami Beach. Somehow, by God's grace, they had dodged all the potential dangers. Most importantly, the US Coast Guard had not spotted them on the water.

Between 1981 and 1989, 21,406 Haitian refugees on over three hundred boats were stopped by the Coast Guard, most of them in international waters, and returned to Haiti as illegal "economic migrants." Fewer than 150 have been permitted into the United States, most of these for medical treatment of dehydration or sunstroke. Only five have been allowed to pursue asylum claims in the United States. The Reverend Thomas Wenski, director of the Haitian Resettlement Program in Miami, says, "The unavoidable perception is that Haitians are being denied entry to the US because they are poor and because they are black."

Mennonite Christians in Miami, though few in number, continue to play an important role in calling for a just immigration policy and in walking with our Haitian brothers and sisters toward a spiritual and social wholeness. The future of the Mennonite church in Miami clearly lies in its ability to befriend and evangelize the refugee populations of this Caribbean city.

Walter W. Sawatzky, USA, b. 1952, Mennonite Central Committee program coordinator and assistant moderator of the Southeast Mennonite Conference.

Two Bangladesh women sift through the rubble after a tornado ripped through great parts of their country. MCC responded to the disaster by providing kerosene lamps and food. (MCC photo by Mark Nord, 1989)

Asylum in Germany

by Theo Landes

> "For my thoughts are not your thoughts, neither are your ways
> my ways," declares the Lord. "As the heavens are higher than
> the earth, so are my ways higher than your ways and my
> thoughts than your thoughts." (Isaiah 55:8,9)

Asylum seekers have a legal right to come as refugees to West Germany. The borders are open for everyone. Because of the experience of the past, there are currently many strong humanistic streams of thought in West Germany which insist that the dignity of unprotected, helpless refugees must be guaranteed by inviolable rights anchored in the constitution. A basic point of departure is "The Refugee Convention of Geneva." An explanation of this guideline is contained in Article 16 of the constitution: "Politically persecuted people enjoy the right to asylum."

Acceptance of refugees in West Germany

The refugees who come across the borders are first housed in camps. At some places the different nationalities live separately in several smaller camps. In Neuburg on the Danube, according to the housing situation, there is a big camp. On fenced-in grounds of about 3 acres there are five buildings, each with thirty-eight rooms. Each room has living space of 5.5 x 4 meters. In such a room three people live, sometimes different nationalities. Here they do their cooking, sleep, and do everything else. About four hundred to five hundred people live in the entire camp, sometimes more, representing more than twenty nationalities.

The physical care in the camp

Every person in Germany, whether foreigner or German, regardless of nationality or social standing, has the right to that which is necessary for living. It is the concern of the government and its social service that no one must go hungry or freeze. Every asylum seeker will have a warm room. In other camps they receive enough money to purchase groceries. Here in the camp in Neuburg they receive a package of groceries two times each week. Each one receives DM 80,- a month as pocket money and DM 300,- clothing money each for summer and winter clothing. Travel costs, for example to the offices in Ansbach, Zirndorf, or Munich, to process their request for asylum are paid by a welfare program. In case of refusal of asylum, they have the right within a certain period of time to hire a lawyer to help them make an appeal. The government pays the costs for the lawyer in working on the case.

The bureaucratic road to asylum

A written request for asylum must be made. The politically persecuted receive asylum. Each case is individually investigated (sometimes taking years) and follows its course through different judicial offices. After rejection, appeal can be made and a lawyer will find out if the case really fits with Article 16, paragraph 1.

Most people who come from Eastern bloc countries and from the Third World are economic refugees. They want to escape the poverty of their country. Some of them are here for adventure.

Expectation, reality, and disappointment of the refugees

In Germany they expect political solidarity and democratic freedom. But in many cases, especially if they do not speak good German, they suffer psychologically. They expect economic security, but they are not allowed to get a work permit to earn any money for five years. They have social security, but socially they live in isolation from the German people. The foreigners expect warmth, hospitality, and love. The Germans offer coldness, solidarity, discipline, work pressure, the pressure of success, authority, underestimation of their worth, and fear of being disturbed. Even German Mennonites do not find foreigners in Germany so very pleasant.

The great mission opportunity for the German Christians

God so loved the world that he sent his Son. We the Christians have received his love, are redeemed, and ought to see and love the people like Jesus does. We as Mennonite Christians at Mennonite World Conference Assembly 12 should not be so much concerned about the good activities of a few Mennonites around the world. But we should and must have a burden for so many lost people around the world, especially the many coming to Germany. It is not the fulfillment of life or the thoughts or way of God for the refugees here to achieve as quickly as possible the high standard of living in Germany. It is our task to obey the command of Jesus to bring his kingdom among these people, not only in the form of social help but also the spiritual help of the word of Jesus with the promises of the Bible.

My work

It is to pass on God's love six days a week. I make visits in the camp. Most of the people are friendly and hospitable. Many times I sit down with them in their room and we have a cup of coffee or tea together. Thus conversations develop. Some of them have a lot to tell about the problems of their past and their hopes for the future.

The first thing I have to do is just to listen for a long time. Their special thinking always revolves around themselves and around their problems and how they can find help to succeed in life. But that is not the thinking of God. God's thoughts and ways come from above and are higher than our ways and thoughts. I try to get them to think in the historical and biblical way, how the prophets foretold the future and it happened, for example, Isaiah 7:14 and Matt. 1:23. Jesus, the greatest prophet, foretold what we read in Matt. 24:30 and 24:36–42, and it will and must be fulfilled.

At the beginning of my work two years ago, I had a group of about six Polish people whom I taught German. At the end I opened my German Bible and explained to them that God's plans were not just made today, but were made a long time in advance. Isaiah 53:7,8 is an illustration. Six hundred years after this was written it was fulfilled in John 1:29, where we read: "Look, the Lamb of God, who takes away the sin of the world!" I showed them the same verses in the Polish Bible, and they understood the meaning of it.

My social service

I also have many practical things to do to help. If someone receives a letter from the state administrative court or from another office, it is always written in bureaucratic German. Then I may translate that which is written into understandable English or into simple German. I frequently write letters to lawyers or to other offices in order to speed up the request for asylum. Sometimes I am able to help people by giving them articles of clothing. I accompany people to an office in order to help them with speaking German. There are also telephone calls to be made. If someone receives toleration or temporary residence permission or asylum, then he must find a place to live and I help with the moving. I attempt to be helpful in every kind of situation. Frequently I teach German, although I am not a trained teacher. People also come to our home with their requests. So we have guests for a meal in our home, and sometimes we have them living with us for a short period of time. The help of my wife and family is also included. My wife visits women and families in the camp. Not the least of our concerns is to invite people to our Sunday worship service. Because God, who has called the light to shine in the darkness, has shone in our hearts, the knowledge of the glory of God in the face of Christ might be made known through us.

We sense that my life and the life of my family is a life of fulfillment. Nowhere can it be more fulfilling than in the service of the Lord. In the lives of two young men, one an Iranian and another an Egyptian, we see that the fulfillment of their lives has been found in following Jesus.

Theo Landes, Federal Republic of Germany, b. 1927, farmer by profession, served as a missionary in Europe and Africa, and currently works with refugees through Mennonitische Heimatmission.
Translated by Omar Stahl.

Tutoring program within the Urban Community Development in Philadelphia, Pennsylvania. (MCC photo)

Trying to restore unity

by Dorcas Horst Cyster

South Africa, a country of great beauty and human tragedy. A land of desperate greed and abject poverty. A country of contradiction and vast polarization: in society, economics, education, and, sadly, within the church. Into this context of division, God has brought a ministry of just and meaningful reconciliation. The Broken Wall Community of Reconciliation Ministry (a name taken from Eph. 2:14) was started in 1986 with the establishment of a legal trust. This trust is made up of Christian leaders from various denominational and social backgrounds. They give pastoral care and practical leadership to the developing "lifestyle community" and wider ministry. The founding directors of this ministry are Dr. Graham Cyster, a so-called "colored" from Cape Town, and his wife, Dorcas Horst Cyster, from the United States. Graham did religious studies in the United States and Great Britain. He was involved with the Post Green Community in England for six and one-half years. Dorcas is a registered nurse and was involved with the Mennonite church and Voice of Calvary Ministries in Jackson, Mississippi, for seven years. Their experiences in cross-cultural communities and social development gave them a vision for the healing power of a community ministry in the extremely divided country of South Africa.

The people of South Africa live in emotional fear, anger, and resentment, all of which affects virtually every aspect of their lives. For many, these emotions are a conscious reality of their being for which they feel no regret. For others, the emotions lie deeply buried and only surface when these individuals become intimately involved with people of other races. Most agree that things need to change, but they lack the experience and personal commitment to get it started. The Broken Wall Community is a ministry committed to assisting individuals to find healing from the hurts of apartheid. We believe the scars of our society can only be erased by submission to one another in developing Christ-centered relationships. These relationships must include repentance, vulnerability, and confrontation for the purpose of healing and restoring justice. They must cross boundaries that historically and socially have never been crossed. The building of community can be seen in several ways. The ideal and center of our vision is the actual "lifestyle community." Presently our community is made up of two families and one single person from various racial groups living together and sharing meals, finances, and cultures. We have a process of application for those interested in joining this lifestyle. It has become evident to us that many are not yet at the place where they can freely open their lives to the extent of living together. Part of the ministry is developing a process to gradually introduce and teach steps to reconciliation and cross-racial relationships. We are involved with an evangelical youth organization in developing this process and already have about fifty young people interested.

An important goal of our ministry of reconciliation is to encourage the emergence of black leadership. People of color have been oppressed in this society for so long that they have little self-confidence and, usually, an inferior attitude about themselves. They have been so dominated by white leaders that many do not believe they have the capacity to lead their own people. Through racial reconciliation this subservient attitude will be exposed and they will be assisted in overcoming it, thus giving them new confidence and dignity. This will also help the Christian church provide leaders in a post-apartheid South Africa.

In addition, we are involved with the social needs of the black community through preschools. We do not run the preschools, because we feel the leaders of the respective communities can do this more adequately. We raise money for food, play equipment, and other needs. We also assist the leaders in drawing up proposals and in decision making and, most importantly, by providing emotional support for this very difficult task. The children who attend these preschools are very poor and sometimes eat three meals a day at the preschool because there is no food for them at home. The teachers sometimes go for weeks without pay because of the insufficient funds and only take their salary after the children's needs have been met.

The obstacles to our task become more evident the deeper we involve ourselves with the ministry of true reconciliation. Apartheid has been successful in a negative way. The church tends to be very superficial in its approach to reconciliation, with a blithe we're-all-saved-so-we're-all-brothers-and-sisters attitude. A "racially integrated" church usually means a white church where a few black, colored, or Indian people attend. The evangelical church teaches that one can either be a Christian or involved in politics, not both. Any stand taken against injustice by opposing government policies is considered "political." Part of our ministry is to enlighten Christians to the fact that one's faith can be made practical in the struggle for justice and freedom. Ironically, participation in the present structures of government is not condemned, but approved. This is the type of contradiction we face. Our commitment to follow biblical principles of nonviolence and love for all people tends to separate us from the more popular ecumenical movement. We do participate in mass marches and rallies organized by these groups and, in this way, try to break down these barriers.

Within the "lifestyle community" we face many cultural, social, and emotional barriers. We have lived together about two years now, and it has been a constant challenge for all of us. Differences in the way we raise our children, the way we spend money, the value we place on material things, the openness with which we communicate, the degree of trust we have, the role of men and women and singles—and the list goes on—become part of our everyday life. For this reason it has become important for us to have weekly meetings of the community for practical and worship purposes and to have a pastoral team from the trust to assist in sorting things out.

As pioneers of this type of ministry in South Africa, we face much skepticism and criticism. The new is often not understood, and we are perceived as being ahead of the times. As a result, we find it difficult to get financial support from within the country and have to rely on support from overseas. This means we have to do considerable traveling and ministry abroad. Although this is difficult at times, we count it a privilege to extend our ministry by keeping people informed and burdened for what is going on within South Africa.

To facilitate the previously mentioned reconciliation program, we are planning to build a multipurpose center with dormitories in 1990. The facilities now available to all races are limited and often inadequate to accommodate such a program. It is essential that the young people have the opportunity to share living quarters. The center will also be used for church retreats, especially for people from the black townships who need a respite from the pace and squalor of the township life. Another exciting dimension of our involvement is the "Community Church Movement," with one hundred members. We are working with a black pastor who has asked us to assist him in developing nonracial, peace churches that are committed to the needs of society. There are three churches affiliated with this movement, and we hope to expand. The existing denominations have proved very unsympathetic to such a grassroots church, and so we have ventured out on our own. We believe strongly that this church movement must originate from the people at the grassroots who have been oppressed. They must be the leaders, and we see ourselves as assisting as servants. We are now taking steps to affiliate with Mennonite World Conference.

We relate to many people. Our goal of reconciliation among the people of South Africa demands that we attempt to reach both Afrikaner and the most radical freedom fighter. In our community we have six adults and four children. Our four preschools are all located in nearby black townships. We employ a farm worker to maintain our vegetable garden, and that garden supplies both the community and preschools. We have bimonthly rallies, which incorporate worship, social tea time, and a challenging teaching. These have been attended by groups of 150 to 200 people of all racial groups. Our overseas offices are affiliated with Voice of Calvary Ministry in Jackson, Mississippi, Post Green Community in Poole, England, and Arbeitskreis Versöhnung für Südafrika in Germany.

We feel we work so hard with few visible results. We often feel so powerless against the forces of evil in this land. Yet we remain here, sometimes with little faith but firm in the commitment that the truth of the gospel of Jesus demands us to follow him and serve, to be a ministry of justice and peace in a land that knows much oppression and turmoil.

Dorcas Horst Cyster, South Africa, b. 1956, registered nurse, co-director of the Broken Wall Community and Ministry.

Three children in the Transkei (a South African homeland) join together in a joyous spirit. (MCC photo by Harvey Harman, 1988)

Ministry to drug addicts in Amsterdam

by Georgine Boiten-du Rieu

Motto: "If the child was Father to the Man, then Society was undoubtedly the Mother." (Eugène Heimler, *A Link in the Chain*)

The largest percentage of the population of Western Europe is now living in the big cities, but that has not always been the case. In the early Middle Ages the towns, although representing freedom and independence from the lords, did not house the majority as they do in the postindustrial period. The attraction of the city today is not as logical as many arguments pretend when they suggest the profit of urban work, school, cultural life, luxury, amusement, and freedom. In reality, a growing percentage of the working population prefers to commute and live in a village. All over the world philosophers, psychologists, theologians, sociologists, lawyers, even authors and poets have written about their vision and feelings concerning increasing urban criminality. Nowhere is unemployment as frightening as in the big, old cities, and nowhere is criminality so common on every level of society. The cultural activities are mainly for tourists, who do not see the excessive lifestyles and suffering behind the façade. Amusement and freedom become boring, developing into lack of morality.

More than anywhere else, the city dweller is part of a group that determines one's "personality." No parents, no teachers, no youth leaders teach youngsters to develop their personalities. The city increasingly denies the relationship of place and time, value and meaning. The person becomes a meaningless individual, if not an object, an island. No, the arguments to move to the city are usually more excuses than truth. I wonder whether a death wish is a more basic motivation than anything else. Surely city life for very many people means mental, moral, and physical death, a last escape from the meeting with oneself.

That is not new. Both the Old and New Testaments are full of this kind of experience: Sodom, Babel, Rome, Ephesus, etc. That is why Jerusalem will be built as a village, not as a Babylon. Men and cattle will be numerous. This message Zechariah gives to humanity as a sign of hope for the future.

A last escape ... a death wish ... that is the real reason why so many youngsters go to the big cities. Feeling themselves objects in the hands of others, called society, they are neither saved nor beloved, without niche, without security, unemployed, useless. They choose the city as the beginning of a way out. Their internal psychological "chemistry" will choose one of three possibilities for escape: insanity, self-destruction, or antisocial behavior. Together they comprise the same hated establishment of the modern city population. They lack relationships and are materialistic, egocentric, amoral.

In 1954 when Rolf (my future husband) and I came to Amsterdam, we had to be in the city to finish our university studies in theology and psychology after having completed our general theological formation and a year of practical experience in the suburbs of Paris. (The Mennonite seminary is in Amsterdam.) Our lifestyle became that of Amsterdam. We lived in a run-down house in the red-light district. Our intention was to live among the post-World War II citizens (Jews after the persecution, refugees, those on the periphery). We hoped to support the city churches we belonged to—Presbyterian and Mennonite—by modern evangelization, that is, in solidarity. So we held jobs, just as everybody was supposed to do. We lived on the level of the ordinary person. We helped one another and were helped by our neighbors in little things such as the many reparations of houses, sharing meetings and clubs, and bringing in a clear Christian foundation in daily life. We received many people.

We worked with a five-year plan, maximum 2 x 5 years! After ten years Rolf and I had increased our household with our own four children as well as many other people living with us: students, interns, artists, families, and youngsters, all suffering from postwar problems (World War II, colonial wars, Korea, Vietnam, etc.). More important than anything else was the engagement of seven people living together to the extent possible. Four of us are still together after twenty-five years. Others joined the community "Spe Gaudentes" (those who rejoice in the hope). The place of living was no longer romantic idealism and self-assessment but a common vocation.

We live together in the old downtown area of Amsterdam, center of crime, alcohol, drugs, smuggling, gambling, and prostitution, center for society's dropouts through insanity, self-destruction, and antisocial behavior. We try to be a sign of hope by our daily lives, our security in our relationship by the water of baptism, and our creation of a little society within the big society as a sign of hope of Jerusalem, of heaven. Many Christians from all over the world join our community for a time. All bring into the community their love, their gifts, their skills, their faith, their strength and weakness, their abilities. Only by being one, one body of Christ, reading, praying and celebrating together, being one community sharing our gifts, being one in many nationalities, can we witness of God's oneness, his shalom, his purpose of wholeness for everybody. Only by being one before the Lord have we found the strength for thirty-five years in a dropout society.

As said, we have different professions: doctors, nurses, ministers, social workers, artists, carpenters, psychologists, cooks, teachers, lawyers, etc. So people joining or visiting us in an informal manner find us as friend, student, and teacher, as specialists but always part of the community, a not-so-easy balance between professional and friend. This relaxed approach is not a trick or method but part of our principle of belonging together in a dropout world with one God. We have different professions in our community, but our tasks can be many:

cleaning, employment agency, counselor, etc. Of course, there are limits in what we accept, but we are determined never to really let someone down. No one is a closed case. So we have no clients, but we all belong to "God's funny people." If one lives with us, then he shares our life in prayer (regular meetings in the chapel), in normative behavior (drug free, and relationships after the Ten Commandments). He shares our work according to his abilities. So work therapy is not a pastime but community building. Living with us means living in relationships that underline the spoken word, whether that be the professional spoken word during the meal, doing the dishes together, or having a long talk before the open fire. We have to give "the patients" the basic framework to help them analyze their life situation, make up their mind, and make a new start.

We ourselves need the community every time a patient tests us to see if we will let him down, not realizing that often he lets himself down, and so it goes. Is then all for nothing? In God's creation nothing is for nothing. All are one! Too late? Too late for the AIDS patient? How Greek we are! The Bible knows about only one time—eternity. The devil divides (although this should not be confused with discernment). He divides people by war or schism. We divide into mine and yours, places here and places there, times past and future. We can only be a healing community—as a community with Christ as the foundation must be—if we believe what unity (not equality) means: to be one, whole, perfect, eternal, that is, shalom.

Listen Israel, your God is one.

Jantine Georgine Boiten-du Rieu, The Netherlands, b. 1930, educated in theology and social psychology, minister of religion for the Mennonite church.

Craftsmanship helps the Hutterian Brethren at the Woodcrest Bruderhof to earn their livelihood by manufacturing Community Playthings, educational equipment, and furniture. (Woodcrest Archives photo)

Establishing a new Bruderhof in Germany

by Derek Wardle

A Hutterian Bruderhof is a Christian community of families, single brothers and sisters, and children who live, work, and worship together at one place called a Bruderhof, or "place of the brothers." This word was used by the Hutterian Brethren of Reformation times who held all things in common just as is done on a Bruderhof today. The inner motivating force is Christian love. Its outward expression is that of a living organism where each serves the other in daily life.

How does a new Bruderhof come into being? Let us take as an example the new Michaelshof near Bonn in the Federal Republic of Germany.

The need for a new community may be twofold. The growth of the existing Bruderhofs through new members joining and through the birth of children into the families makes it necessary to establish a new place. Another reason, and in the case of the Michaelshof, the predominant one, was to respond to the interest and desire of people to visit and seek ways of radical discipleship. Over the past decade many guests from Europe, and especially Germany, had visited the Darvell Bruderhof in England or even the communities in the United States, and some had joined. Many more sought contact but could not undertake these journeys. In response to this interest, the brotherhoods in the United States and England decided in 1988 to establish a house in Germany as a "mission post." This decision had the enthusiastic support of the Hutterian colonies of Manitoba and the Dakotas.

Members from the English Bruderhof went to Germany to find possible properties: a house to accommodate a small group, with extra room for guests and a space for a workshop in an area easily accessible to visitors. After the choices had been narrowed down to three, the elders of the western, or Schmiedeleut, communities (Manitoba and Dakota) and the eastern (US and England) communities visited these possibilities along with several brothers and sisters with practical experience in the needs of communal living. No decision was made; no one place seemed "right." The elders returned home. Only then was a further remote possibility remembered and investigated. Haus Waldfrieden, some 40 kilometers southeast of Bonn, proved to be the place. It was purchased with funds mainly provided by the Schmiedeleut colonies and was cleaned, renovated, and staffed by brothers and sisters from many different communities. Furniture and equipment came from the other Bruderhofs as well as from friends in Germany. A small sewing shop was set up in the basement where guests could be included in the communal work, sewing parts for Rifton Equipment for People with Disabilities on industrial sewing machines.

Visitors came, beginning on the first day. The Hutterites have become increasingly well known in Germany since the publication of Holzach's book, *Das vergessene Volk*. Several books by Eberhard and Emmy Arnold and others were also published in German in the 1980s. The media were immediately interested, and newspaper, radio, and television all carried reports on the return of the Hutterites to Germany after their expulsion by the Nazis in 1937 as "undesirable." Journeys were also made from Waldfrieden to speak with groups, attend conferences, or visit individuals who had expressed an interest. Longer journeys were made into Eastern Europe (before the new freedom of movement). The unexpected response soon showed that this house was too small and that it would be necessary to look for a larger place.

From the beginning considerable effort was put into establishing friendly relations with the immediate neighborhood. And so it was neighbors who pointed to the Michaelshof, a former boys' home that had been empty for five years. It is one mile away from Haus Waldfrieden. Again, the purchase of this property was a joint east-west Hutterian venture. In early November 1988 almost all the young people from the English Bruderhof spent a week cleaning and repairing the buildings. By Christmas brothers and sisters from five communities in Manitoba and the Dakotas and from five eastern communities were living there. In January the first container with machinery, furniture, workshop material, and household furnishings arrived from the Bruderhofs in the United States.

Michaelshof was to become a full-fledged Bruderhof. It needed a core of families who could carry out the task of building up a new community. These came from existing Bruderhofs in the United States, where everyone has pledged himself to serve where needed and in whatever capacity is required. So a servant of the Word (minister), a steward or business manager, a school teacher, and brothers and sisters able to set up the communal work-departments—kitchen, laundry, offices, workshops, children's nursery—were proposed, agreed to, and sent over with the support of all, and with the backing of several families who moved with them. The majority of these needed to be German speaking. At the time of writing (May 1990), there are seventy members in the household at the Michaelshof.

The new shop for Rifton equipment was moved to larger quarters on the Michaelshof. Foam, vinyl, and other materials were sent over from England and the United States to be sewn and assembled. Other finished items were also shipped in to be sold in the European market. Community Playthings—educational equipment for kindergartens—found a ready market as brothers and sisters went out on the road daily to promote sales or attended educational exhibits. These sales efforts, which took much-needed strength away from home in the early days of building up, have resulted in the community already being able to pay for its daily running costs. Capital expenditures will continue to come for some time from the English and North American communities. The sewing shop provides work opportunities also for visitors. This is such an essential part of sharing life together, work as well as talk!

The Michaelshof hopes to have its own community school from first to eighth grade as in the eastern communities. In anticipation of this, a German couple with experience in education has spent hours preparing curricula to obtain permission from the authorities. At present the children all attend public school. When they return from school each day, they meet with a brother and sister appointed to help them with their school work and to undertake work and other activities with them. The younger children spend most of the day in the community nursery, which is staffed by the sisters and equipped largely with Community Playthings.

Rooms in the large main house and in the smaller buildings had to be adapted for these different needs. Already the community has outgrown the dining and meeting rooms. Possibilities of further expansion are being explored.

The Michaelshof is experiencing a never-ending stream of visitors from all over Europe, including the German Democratic Republic. Certainly the media continue to make the Bruderhof known. Whitsunday this year is the seventieth anniversary of the little community that began at Sannerz in Germany, leading to the new Bruderhof movement. The Michaelshof is arranging a conference for this anniversary. The West German television wishes to make a documentary of the occasion. But perhaps it is rather the turmoil in Europe, the seeking for life's purpose beyond material prosperity, that draws people to explore an alternative way of living and causes some to commit themselves to it for life.

So a new Bruderhof is not "organized" but grows organically in the same way that a child is nurtured by its parents until it can become an entity, still remaining part of the greater family of the brotherhood. Wherever there is the earnest desire to establish a society that will be a living witness to the kingdom of God, God himself will lead and guide it to fulfillment.

At the time of writing, the brotherhoods in the United States have purchased another property in the Catskill Mountains of New York. Again its building up will be a joint effort of eastern and western communities in financing, cleaning, renovating, and staffing. Already eighty sisters have come from the western colonies for a major clean-up! It will grow like the Michaelshof with the support of all and according to the particular needs of a community in North America.

To all who long for a new life in Christian love and community, we wish joy and courage. It is possible!

Derek Wardle, UK, b. 1922, member of the Bruderhof communities since 1943, teacher in the Bruderhof schools for forty years, currently working in publishing for the Hutterian Brethren in Ulster Park, New York.

Child in a refugee camp in Costa Rica. (MCC photo by John Paul Lederach, 1987)

Church and society

by Ovidio Flores

The idea of "church and society" should be a subject discussed daily by believers. Although some prefer to ignore it, they cannot escape the challenge in that way. The church is immersed in society and has a fundamental role: to communicate God's plan of salvation to all humanity. The church can never avoid its principal task. In any country or region where there are churches, society is waiting to see the church's views on daily problems. Whether the church supports or denounces the unjust structures of society, a common recognition of the function of the church exists. We Mennonites live in a world with social, political, and economic changes that directly affect how we carry out our faith, and we need to be ready to understand the signs of the times (present and future) and to interpret God's work in the course of history.

The following account provides an example of the social changes that the church faces and will confront in several parts of the world. In Central America, we have a country that is going through a social revolution (Nicaragua) and the remaining countries where there is a strong military orientation under the tutelage of the United States. Evangelical missions in the United States were instructing the pastors in Nicaragua to ask their young church members not to collaborate with the compulsory military service as a Christian testimony of not bearing arms. Yet, at the same time, these same evangelical missions were asking their leaders in countries such as El Salvador and Guatemala to collaborate with the government, which was established by God. What a contradiction!

This shows us how the church can be used as a political instrument to support political systems and to justify the struggle between different ideologies. The church that does not take seriously the social changes that are taking place will be easily deceived by error and will not be able to discern its function in society. The various aspects that I share in this document with the international Mennonite community are meant to help us explore and reflect together on the task of being witnesses within this changing society. God has placed us in this world to assume responsibility as a church while we walk as a pilgrim people in search of the kingdom.

Social justice and prophetic commitment

The basic preoccupation of the gospel is social justice. For that reason Jesus established several principles in the Sermon on the Mount as ways of practicing social justice, such as loving one's neighbor. These teachings of Jesus are for the church to live out here on earth and within our society and have no value for the life in eternal glory. What happens in our societies, however, is that those who think differently than we do are not valued and become our enemy.

The prophetic commitment of the church should be a permanent stance in society to denounce everything that adversely affects life, everything that dehumanizes and brings chaos, violence, and misery. There are various opportunities for the prophetic witness, from the local level where rivers are being contaminated, to the national level where expenditures for war are robbing children of the opportunity for an education, to the international level where the external debt subjects poor countries to external exploitation and supports the affluence of the rich countries. How can the church meet its social responsibility?

Discipleship and the human rights movement

The concept of discipleship in the Bible is more than a personal confession to God. Jesus himself said, "By this they will know that you are my disciples ...." Immediately one can recall many examples of Jesus being in favor of human rights. We must understand Jesus' miracles within this context, his compassion for the lepers, his solidarity with the sinful woman, the priority of the common good above any religious tradition—all are examples for the practice of discipleship. Christian discipleship implicitly carries with it concern for defending and respecting the life of every person, regardless of that person's culture, religion, ideology, or political orientation.

Because of the church's accommodation within the system, it has neglected to protect life and has dedicated itself to protecting its own interests (false patriotism), occupying itself with a program of activities for Sundays. This results in reluctance to deal with human rights and leads to thinking that this is work only for politicians of the opposition. Another stance is to limit the work for human rights only to the political desaparecidos, or "disappeared ones."

Christian discipleship should have a much broader vision of what human rights means, which is equivalent to supporting life. It must begin with the basic necessities, food and housing, and move to other levels of responsibility to express our Christian faith. Areas to explore and participate in favor of human rights are as follows:

• Protecting the environment for all.
• Working for better conditions for prisoners.
• Sharing experiences and nonviolent alternatives relating to the struggles of different countries.
• Offering ourselves as a resource for reconciliation and consolation.

- Supporting projects or alternative solutions to the problems of the poor, groups of oppressed women, minorities, refugees, and others.
- The churches in the rich countries should take more responsibility for addressing the centers of power in their own countries.
- The external debt is limiting the rights of the people to the extent that they are repressed for demanding a just negotiation.

As Mennonite communities we have the challenge to understand the moments of history critically in order to be promoters of life, a responsibility that transcends the sociopolitical level.

Community groups

The formation of Christian community groups is only a means and not an end in itself. Since the Abrahamic story, God has called a group of people to be the carriers of the message of salvation, to communicate to society the intention of God's plan for the world. We can see this in the people of Israel as well as in the community of the disciples; we learn about it in the witness of the early church; it is restated in the Middle Ages when groups of Christians became aware of God's call and questioned the dominant religious structures, which were distancing themselves from God's plan to "be a blessing to all peoples." Our early Anabaptist brothers and sisters understood that plan of being faithful to God's purpose. At a certain juncture they became a community of resistance, of protest, including a profound sense of social justice. Those communities were themselves expressions of their nonconformity. In the book *Christian Mission and Social Justice*, John Driver and Samuel Escobar point out some areas in which Anabaptists shared with other nonconformist groups of that time:

- The Anabaptists insisted that the gospel was pertinent to the social and economic reality.
- The Anabaptist option was a call to human freedom so we could act and believe according to our own conscience without coercion.
- The Anabaptist option was a group of resistance to the established authorities (church-state).
- The Anabaptist option was nonviolent, understanding that there is a struggle between the two kingdoms and their different ways of operating, one using violence and the other practicing nonviolence.

The previous points give us a base to see the function of the church in changing times, past or future, and point out that we cannot escape the historical moment. In community life we experience forgiveness and reconciliation among individuals. Then the community members, reconciled with God and with their brothers and sisters, become instruments of peace for the world. For that reason, the formation of community groups has a spiritual, moral, and social value within society. In societies that are oriented to the realization of the individual, to economic competition, where human values are secondary, Christians with more responsibility are called to look for and develop community initiatives that can become instruments of holistic evangelization. We cannot be Christians by ourselves. The community shapes our Christian character, for it is within the community, and only there, that we learn to be brothers and sisters and children of God. How can Mennonites return to this community vision in an individualistic society?

Separation and integration within society

The church cannot avoid being part of society. When we try to escape from it, we show our irresponsibility and become objects of suspicion. Historically, the church has wanted to explain this escapism by separating the material from the spiritual, the secular from the sacred. The prolife plan presented in the Bible does not emphasize such separation. Instead, it calls for conversion of all human relations. These include the economic, political, and social domains. In consequence, the church as a divine-human institution is called to be the presence of God in the world and to understand with Christ's mind the signs of the times (Luke 12:54–56). Julio de Santa Ana, in his book entitled *Por las sendas del mundo caminando hacia el Reino*, says a very central thing:

> The human sciences do not have the possibility of perceiving
> God in a given situation or to discover the fundamental purpose
> of events. Faith, however, starting with the situation, returns to it
> by seeing how the "theological" agents respond in this context
> (what can be perceived by faith). Elements of our everyday
> reality in our situation thus take on a theological density that
> permits us to better understand them. Starting with current
> reality, the community of believers returns to it in order to
> indicate how God is manifested in it, and also to point out those
> events that are mediating the presence of the kingdom.

The church will always have a conflict of separation from and integration to society. We believe that only a clear understanding of the mission of the church and the constant struggle for the values of the kingdom will allow the church to maintain a faithful testimony in each social context. The church, especially we Mennonites, in the remaining years of this century will have great influence amid the materialistic values of a godless society and the prevailing apathy of not wanting to know what is happening in the political, economic, and social world, not so that we become activists in these areas but rather so we can read the signs of the times and become useful salt and light to society.

Subcultures and subgroups

The Mennonite church can easily understand what it means to be part of a subculture because of our tradition. In fact, for this reason we have "Mennonite" colonies in several Latin American countries that have become "exclusive" with their own language, schools, and special favors from the government. (For example, they do not have to do military service, but the native people do in order to protect their properties.) I think that these communities are in danger of losing the fundamental aspects of their faith in Christ because they have put too much emphasis on defending cultural aspects. The coming years will bring social, political, economic, and agricultural changes that will no doubt affect the lives of these brothers and sisters. What can the international Mennonite community do to share with them (colonies) what we see from the outside?

The minority and diverse groups living among a dominant culture can be evangelizing elements for the Mennonite churches. For instance, the Central American refugees living in Kitchener, Ontario (Canada), contribute to the practice of the Mennonite faith; and the work with Vietnamese refugees and the evangelizing work among Chinese communities in the United States will bring renewal to the church. To the extent that the Mennonite church participates with different cultures, groups, and subgroups, including different confessions, the church will be renewed, will have better criteria for valuing the vision of the first Anabaptists, and will have the capacity to spell out the evangelizing task for the rest of the century.

Mission and service

What is mission? Many times we think it is something extra that the churches do, a short-term project, a trip outside one's country of origin, a visit to explore or trace territories. I think that these concepts have been assimilated by the church within an expansionist society. The expression "going in mission" is very similar to the one used when military personnel are sent to intervene in another country, or when geologists are sent by their mining company to look for ore. The church has a different mission, and if it does not it is no longer the Lord's church. The Bible is clear: "... that you may declare the praises of him who called you out of darkness into his wonderful light" (1 Pet. 2:9). In other words, continuing to announce the values of God's reign and calling for a life commitment continue to be the motive of Jesus' mission expressed on the cross.

We could think of future mission in the following ways:

- Mission with ourselves.
- Mission with our family.
- Mission with our neighbors.
- Mission with our local congregation and conference.
- Mission with our country (structures).
- Mission of solidarity with all brothers and sisters in Christ in the world.
- Mission with all humanity.

In reality, a church that does not perform acts of service becomes useless and a religious entertainment devoid of faith and hope. From its origins the Mennonite church had a profound concern for service as the practice of faith and a preoccupation for the social dimensions of people's lives that contribute to peace with justice. The work of service cannot be separated from the mission of the church. To serve is the central mission, just as Jesus did it. Biblical service is the concern for better relationships among men and women, looking for opportunities for all to be beneficiaries of God's creation and its resources, caring for one another, and supporting the underprivileged. Christian service is not something that we do so that people become Christians. The church's Christian responsibility does not expect that the motivation for service will be to proselytize for our group. Service should be an expression of God's love, the divine compassion manifested by the church (the body of Christ) in favor of those who suffer spiritually as well as socially and economically.

This service can be translated into concrete actions in society through the following:

• Centers for the care of children and the elderly.
• Protection of refugees.
• Assistance during emergencies.
• Productive projects for subsistence.
• Educational projects for the community.
• Pastoral work of consolation, reconciliation, mediation, and others.

In the coming years there will be an increase of poverty, the problem of refugees for political and economic reasons, ideological wars, the destruction of the atmosphere, and racial segregation. In the coming years, the international Mennonite community should continue to explore new ways of serving in the name of Christ and ways to fulfill the church's mission here on earth.

Conclusion

The church will have significance to the extent that it fulfills God's mission in society and not on the basis of how large it is. In the coming years humanity will experience even greater social changes, which will raise the expectations of society about the church because the prevailing models in the economic and political realms will not correlate with peaceful living together. Humanity will continue to lose all hope in the current leaders in power. As a profound expression of desperation, the peoples will ask: Where is the church? What do Christians say? and the Mennonites? May God help us to be faithful.

Ovidio Flores, Honduras, b. 1947, agronomist specializing in rural development, currently Mennonite Central Committee consultant for Central America for development programs.
Translated by Daniel and Margaret Schipani.

From the edge to the center

by Hans-Jürgen Goertz

The relationship of the Mennonites to the ecumenical movement is not easy to determine, for there is no such thing as *the* Mennonites or *the* ecumenical movement. Though we speak of the "worldwide brotherhood" in which all Mennonites are united, basically the cord that holds us together is rather thin. It consists of a series of denominational peculiarities that have preserved themselves throughout the centuries: believer's baptism, separation of church and state, nonresistance, and the denial of oath. But the spiritual vitality of this brotherhood is not capable of encompassing this cord anymore. The Spirit blows elsewhere, perhaps in a little church along the Zaire River, in a meetinghouse on the outskirts of Chicago, in a mission station on Java. Very little connects one place with the other; little do the people of one know of the other. A Mennonite Indian in the Chaco and a Mennonite businessman in Krefeld, a Mennonite woman in Tanzania and a Mennonite housewife in Siberia—worlds separate them. Perhaps they all refer back to a mutual confessional source, especially to their nominal patron Menno Simons of Witmarsum. But what they believe and how they believe separate them no less from each other than Catholics, Lutherans, and Mennonites in Europe and North America.

The "worldwide brotherhood" is an illusion, and therefore it is difficult to speak accurately of the relationship of the Mennonites to the ecumenical movement. There are Mennonites who, from the beginning, have worked enthusiastically in this movement and are trying gradually to overcome the denominational barriers of Christianity. There are others who see in this movement nothing other than a satanic temptation and who fight it wherever they can. There are also Mennonites who waited with initial skepticism and then found ways to approach and join this movement at one place or another: in consultations and dialogues, in joint social welfare ventures, and in reconciliation service in areas of tension.

The ecumenical movement is not unified either. This statement follows from a look at its sources: the missionary, the dogmatic (Faith and Order), and the ethical (Life and Work). Also varied are the organizational forms of the movement. Most of the churches of the world have joined together in the World Council of Churches (WCC), which was founded in 1948. Founding members were, among others, the Algemene Doopsgezinde Sociëteit (General Anabaptist Society) and the Vereinigung der Deutschen Mennonitengemeinden (United German Mennonite Congregations). But the movement cannot be absorbed entirely in this organization. It covers more. For example, for years various churches have made contacts with the Roman Catholic church, which does not belong to the WCC. Also for years churches that do not work with the WCC and are still skeptical about it have cooperated on national, regional, and local levels in various ways. This is also true for numerous Mennonite conferences in

various countries. The situation has become complex. In addition, the fear that
the denominational identity of individual churches must be given up in favor of a
"super church" is retreating more and more into the background, and more and
more clearly into the foreground moves the experience that forms must be found
to portray the unity of the church of Jesus Christ in the multiplicity of its denominations—as an answer to Jesus' promise that we shall all be one (John 17).

Among the churches the experience has grown that faith in Jesus Christ in our
various political and social situations must be witnessed to and lived in varying
ways: differently in a democratically governed, affluent society than under a
dictatorial regime, differently in solidarity with a revolutionary liberation
movement than in a society that is destroying its environment. In our world,
which has become essentially more complicated than at the time of Christ and
the apostles, it is not possible to express faith and the resulting ethical obligation
uniformly. The love-thy-neighbor commandment will have to find different
expressions in San Salvador than in the Bernese Jura; the faint and helpless read
Scripture differently than the mighty. There are situations in which people feel
admonished by the Christian message to bear patiently the injustice that befalls
them, and there are situations where the same gospel summons up action against
the injustice that has been done against them. Both actions can be correct. It can
be right to protest at the top of one's voice and to organize opposition. It can be
just as right to be silent and to wait. The "truth" of Jesus Christ cannot be
perfectly represented in its totality by any one church anymore. A leftover will
always remain, one that is not inconsiderable. As the sociologist Peter Berger
expressed it, we stand today under a "compulsion to be heretical." And although
heresy, i.e., the one-sided, distorted choosing from a comprehensive truth, has
become our fate, this fate must not lull us into a false sense of security. We see
before us the task—if not ours alone anymore, then at least jointly striving—to
bring this "truth" in whatever forms are possible for us within a spirit of mutual
respect and mutual trust, as inclusively as possible, to expression.

What I have just described can be pictured with an illustration which most
probably originates from the writings of church fathers and which has, in the
meantime, frequently been used to refer to the ecumenical movement. It is the
picture of a wagon wheel with spokes that run toward and are firmly anchored in
the hub at the center. The wagon wheel symbolizes the globe on which we find
the numerous churches. The hub symbolizes Jesus Christ, Lord of the world.
When the churches are summoned to draw closer to the Lord, they follow the
spokes and move toward the center. The closer they come to the center, the
nearer they come to each other, until they will finally all be one "in Christ."

It is immensely clear that no one church can now already claim to be the central
point of Christian unity in this world. In view of the center, all churches—
without exception—are outsiders, the small churches, which have always been
pushed to the edge, as well as the big churches, who set the tone and did not

make life easy for the outsiders to fulfill their spiritual task in this world. Today all churches are outsiders and are beginning to recognize how difficult the position is for those who do not stand in the center of public life and general interest. They are also beginning to see how promising this position on the edge can be, how helpful for all who are weary and heavy laden and must receive help with spiritual and material solidarity. Suddenly they see with the eyes of the Samaritan, who was also an outsider and perceived the distress at the roadside while the priest and Levite officially overlooked it on their way to Jerusalem. The mutual road to the center has opened the eyes of the churches to the miserable reality in this world and has strengthened the knowledge that there is only one possible way to refer the "world" to the center in Jesus Christ; namely, they do not exhibit themselves or demonstrate their denominational indispensability, but rather they give a hand where the need for help is great, just as Jesus did not come to rule but to serve. This means a moving toward him who has become a symbol for the ill-treated and driven. The ecumenical movement has helped us to rediscover the nature of the servant in Christianity. And that is not a new idea for us. No one can truly know Christ, the Anabaptist Hans Denk wrote, "unless he follows him with his life." Christ is recognizable in an ecumenical life.

In the ecumenical movement we also learn that we can win more than we lose. Perhaps we will stop fearing loss of our denominational face if the needs of others teach us to think differently than our fathers did or our brothers still think. The tradition of those who did not defy the national-socialistic spirit of the Third Reich can hardly allow us to expect that they will approve the antiracial program of the WCC. But they that hear the sighs of those who suffer because of the color of their skin even today will have no other choice than to give up all denominational-theological qualms and support this program with all their might. Perhaps the ecumenical movement will also allow us to lose those inhibitions that often befall us when we deal with bishops and cardinals, priests and nuns. The time of clerical triumphalism is over. We now have the opportunity to let our rather brittle and spiritually shallow layman's piety be enriched by the spirituality of an "elite" who draw from a rich spiritual tradition. We discover that the symbols of a ritualistic piety begin again to speak in our mass societies. Perhaps we will also lose the arrogance that occasionally plagues us when we meet people who satisfy their spiritual needs in an infantile manner or who lead a life as if there were no God. Perhaps we will lose ourselves and win others.

The ecumenical movement is a spiritual movement, a movement that the Holy Spirit keeps in motion. It emanates impulses that renew and enrich us. It helps us to walk the road from the edge to the center more determinedly, more courageously, and with a greater sense of responsibility than before.

Hans-Jürgen Goertz, Federal Republic of Germany, b. 1937, Dr. theol., professor of social and economic history at Hamburg University.
Translated by Anita Lichti.

Man from Bhuapur, Bangladesh, carries home food that he received in a relief food distribution program of Service Civil International, an MCC partner. (MCC photo by Shahidul Alam, 1988)

The Mennonite peace witness tomorrow

by Dorothy Friesen

"He [the king] shall seduce with flattery those who violate the covenant; but the people who know their God shall stand firm and take action. And those among the people who are wise shall make many understand, though they shall fall by sword and flame, by captivity and plunder, for some days." (Daniel 11:32–33)

"We must obey God rather than men." (Acts 5:29b)

"True evangelical faith does not lie dormant ..." (Menno Simons)

Introduction

We live in an exciting and precarious era. Now, more than ever, the peace witness of the Mennonites worldwide is vitally necessary to global well-being and survival. Through peacemaking, the church can touch the wounds of modern civilization and become part of a historic reconciling effort. Participation may change the character of the church, but active, faithful peacemaking will attract many new believers to the community of faith. Our historic peace witness over the centuries was forged in the crucible of experience—of direct encounters with the powers and principalities. Now, as we build our vision and work for the 1990s, there are several questions to consider. What is the current world situation in which we live and in which we are called to pursue peace? What are our special gifts as a worldwide Mennonite community of faith? What are the obstacles to overcome? How can we equip ourselves for the challenge?

Context

A year ago who could have predicted the changes that swept across the world in late 1989 and 1990: the remarkable shifts in the Soviet Union, the change in governments in Eastern Europe, the unbanning of the African National Congress in South Africa. Peoples' movements for human rights have also been trampled in Burma, China, and the United States (where the poor have been struggling nonviolently for a just share for two hundred years). The institutions of the military have been either ignored, as in Eastern Europe, or used to turn back history, as in Burma. The role of the armed forces, especially in the United States, has been enlarged to include ever greater assignments in counterinsurgency. The dualistic world system, already changing because of the economic rise of Japan, the Pacific, and Western Europe, has fallen apart with Soviet President Mikhail Gorbachev's declaration of a unilateral ideological cease-fire. However, the thaw in the Cold War and the accompanying possibilities for a decrease in East-West tensions may not be good news for the Third World. Now, more than ever, small nations will be pressured to say "uncle" at the whim of the

US, the sole remaining military superpower. Panama was invaded with impunity; the people of Nicaragua were worn down by the economic embargo and the civil war fueled by the United States. At the time of this writing, it remains to be seen where the United States government will move its armies next.

A "guidance" document sent by US President George Bush to the US military (and leaked to the press in February 1990) warns that defenses must be kept up because the fight against the Soviet Union will now shift to the Third World. Why can the United States not join Gorbachev's "era of new thinking"? The military-industrial complex is hard to dismantle when the few making money from building bombs and fighter planes are so entwined with the political power. But the unwillingness to consider turning "swords into plowshares," even when your enemy is doing it, reveals not only economic and political problems but a deeply spiritual problem in the United States and other Western countries.

The spiritual problem is also manifested in the massive environmental problems: the destruction of the air, the water, the soil, and the forests, which has occurred in both capitalist and socialist countries. It is no accident that the greatest ecological damage is being done in formerly colonized countries where people of color reside. Part of the ease with which tractors were sent into the Amazon and gigantic logging operations were set up in Southeast Asian nations is connected to a (sometimes covert, but nevertheless real) white notion of supremacy and a devaluation of people of color.

The historic and continuing pattern between the nations of the North and South has resulted in a vast and growing economic gap. Even within a rich country like the United States, the gap between rich and poor is increasing. A two-tier system of health care, education, and services exists—technologically sophisticated medical care for those who can afford it and closed hospitals and clinics in poor, often black or Latino urban neighborhoods. Forty million people in the United States, for example, live under the poverty level. Weapons help to defend the unequal sharing of resources. The development and building of sophisticated weapons systems lines the pockets of a few influential companies and their stockholders. Weapons production and the willingness to consider deployment on such a massively destructive scale are the result of the intellect gone wild, with no emotional input to balance such decisions. The nuclear weapons industry and the political decision makers who call for the weapons dismiss the relational question, "What impact will this have on my neighbor?" Ignoring Jesus' command to "Love your neighbor as yourself" deepens our spiritual poverty.

Despite the East-West thaw in relationships, we are still hovering at the point from which the world could move toward destruction or ecological wholeness. A small group of thoughtful, committed citizens can tip the balance. What ordinary people decide to do will make a difference—even a small minority like the worldwide body of Mennonites. A happy outcome is not guaranteed even if all

Mennonites worldwide pursue peace actively. We cannot predict the effect of our sacred intention to follow the Prince of Peace even to the point of a contemporary cross. But we also know that there is much less of a chance for peace and ecological wholeness if a historic peace church decides to sit at the sidelines of history, even when we think we may have the best of reasons to do so.

Our history as a source of strength and insight

War, the gap between rich and poor, environmental destruction, and white supremacy notions are intimately interrelated. To pursue peace means confronting economic inequity and racism, which in turn requires us to deal with questions of power and control. As Mennonites, we have a unique history with both strengths to draw on and temptations to overcome in living out our commitment to peacemaking today. Our most authentic contribution will draw from our historical experience and strengths. The formation period of any group sets the tone for future generations. As Anabaptist Hans Denk asserted, we know God truly by following God daily—a step-by-step, risky journey of faith. Our heritage is not one of liberal thought; rather it is set in commitment to radical action and in recognition that change comes from the bottom up. Whether we as individual Mennonites are from northern European stock or not is irrelevant. We draw inspiration and strength from the courage and commitment of the hardy band of sixteenth-century revolutionaries who are our spiritual forebears.

The Holy Roman Empire, splitting at the seams by the sixteenth century, was further undermined by the stubborn, naive action of the motley group of peasants, artisans, and dissident clergy through their acts of provocation like baptism. The story that many of us learned at home or in Sunday school about Anabaptist Dirk Willems is still instructive for us. Dirk, fleeing from soldiers, crossed a partially frozen river safely. The soldiers, in hot pursuit, fell through the ice. Dirk rescued them, and then they arrested him. The story is usually told to emphasize nonresistance and "turning the other cheek" even if it results in harm to ourselves. But a prior question is, What did Dirk do that was so threatening to the state that soldiers chased him across half-frozen rivers? Dirk and his comrades were not simply an annoyance to the political establishment. They were perceived as an obstacle to a new realignment of forces in Europe. As the Empire crumbled and the main ideology, Roman Catholicism, lost its hegemony in Europe, the smaller political powers maneuvered to fill the vacuum. A new deal was struck, which brought a few new members into the ruling club. By allowing a few lesser princes and dukes to join the circle of power, the basic social class order would not be entirely disrupted. A peasant revolt was aborted. The Anabaptists, by ignoring the state's power to determine their religious expression, threatened this attempt at political accommodation to new realities.

When an empire crumbles or redefines itself, whether it is the Holy Roman Empire, the Soviet Empire, or the Liberal Democratic Empire, new alternatives present themselves in the vacuum created. There are new opportunities to press for peace, for justice, for care of the earth, for a new basis of relationship. The openings must be taken quickly, because these opportunities are fleeting. The forces buttressing a system (under whatever ideological name) that benefits a few to the detriment of the majority will close ranks quickly to prevent a change.

The simple, faithful commitment of the sixteenth-century Anabaptists was not enough to complete the process of change. But neither did the Anabaptists' testimony return empty. God promised that words spoken in truth would not return empty, and the Anabaptists' testimony to truth has reverberated down the centuries to keep hope alive. The refusal to accommodate even when it looked like the sensible thing to do at the moment has held up better over the generations as a source of inspiration than a short-term, "more realistic" strategy. That fact can help us with decisions we have to make now about how to position ourselves in the world. Our words, action, and strategy need to keep pointing to the vision, however dimly it may shine and however slim the possibility for its fulfillment or completion in our lifetime.

Another contribution from our heritage is the emphasis on corporate life. Dirk Willems was a heroic individual, but he was also part of a movement of people whose commitment and sacrifice no doubt strengthened each member to continue what may have seemed like a suicidal mission. The Anabaptists had a support system, which empowered Dirk to take risks and removed the usual rationales for caution. For example, hiding behind the excuse that no risks can be taken in order to protect one's children was not possible. Children of a martyr would be taken care of by others in the movement.

It was inspiring to see that the face of Europe was redrawn basically through nonviolent protest. The armies were irrelevant in most places. It is also instructive for a peace church to note that the masses of determined people standing in the streets of Eastern Europe this past year did not materialize overnight. In the German Democratic Republic, for example, cell groups and small prayer meetings in church basements preceded mass street demonstrations. Formerly marginalized dissidents now lecture the US Congress on morality in politics. As Jesus told the Pharisees: If the disciples were silent, "the very stones would cry out" (Luke 19:40b). Mennonite communities around the world today continue to point, however weakly, to the values of nonviolence, service, and community. Though the values may be dimmed somewhat, this is a base from which to build an appropriate peace witness for our time. Most importantly, we need to find a way to bring that witness to bear upon the political and economic decisions that mean life and death to people around the world.

A foundation for peacemaking—facing our temptations

If our peace witness is to bear fruit, we must identify and face our temptations.

We know Jesus said that the tree that does not bear fruit will be cut down and thrown in the fire. In preparation for our peace witness in the twenty-first century, our branches must be pruned and our roots dug deeper so that the world can benefit from our blossoms and fruit.

In our eagerness to be reconcilers, Mennonites face a special temptation to view ourselves a-historically, above history, unaligned with any side. Mennonites in North America and Europe may still have a minority, if not a persecuted, mentality. However, in reality we are part of a relatively affluent, educated, predominantly white culture in countries that wield economic control and, in the case of the United States, military dominance around the world. There is a dissonance created between our mentality and our actual circumstances. As we gain more access to the goodies of our society, we locate ourselves in, and willingly adopt, the dominant thought patterns. The temptation is to disengage from our uncomfortable radical past, dismissing it as no longer relevant. As we slip farther in time from our forebears, the Anabaptists, we share some common temptations or doubts with other Christians in our century. We doubt that God resides and sides with the poor. We doubt that God has used the foolishness of this world to confound the mighty. We doubt that our security is in God and not in weapons or material possessions. We are on a side, whether we chose it consciously or unconsciously. Instead of being the pure arbiters, we are the ones who need to be reconciled with the poor. This is where the testimony of Mennonite sisters and brothers who are in the struggle in Asia, Africa, and Latin America is absolutely crucial. If we are engaged with each other, those of us in the rich North may be able to overcome the temptation to theologize or evangelize from the "locus imperium." To develop a friendship with victims of our national policies means having to confront those policies for the sake of our friendship. It pushes us to ask relational questions and not only realpolitik questions.

Another temptation we face is the easy way we slip into equating "niceness" with the gospel. This is perhaps based on a fear of anger or conflict. But the full power available to us to confront the powers and principalities is muted unless we throw ourselves into the fray with the complete range of our emotions. Education, Bible study, and spiritual foundation are good preparation, but they are only germane when they are completed by engagement with the world. By its nature, action for peace suggests change. It is disturbing. The Anabaptist believes that faith is only completed in action. Understanding comes from direct involvement. Action sparks the questions, and that moment of engagement is the teachable moment. It may be messy sometimes, but grace can only abound where people sin boldly.

A related temptation for Mennonites with our traditional emphasis on community is to view community as a means to perfection or as an end in itself. Thinking of community in itself as being enough because it points toward the kingdom of God has serious pitfalls. Members focus on each other and do not take as seriously the fact that God is God of all the world and is concerned about social and political relations, the environment, etc. People concerned about inequity and violence detour into spiritual navel-gazing with a few others, promising themselves that when they "get it together" they will reach out beyond their immediate circle. No one will be completely healthy; we all carry the scars of psychological struggles and wounds from childhood. Acknowledging that we are wounded peacemakers can save us from arrogance. Rather than relying on our perfection or emotional omniscience to guide us, we are forced to act and take risks without a security net—to live by faith.

Foundation for peacemaking—utilizing our strengths

Our strength has been at the grassroots local level, whether in the solid rural communities in the West or the relief, service, and development work done around the world, often in rural communities. Now more than ever we live in an age where what happens locally is intimately connected with global events because of the intertwining of trade and production around the world and the satellite systems for transfer of information. What faces our global village— pollution; rape of the earth; continued testing, building, and storing and threat of use of nuclear weapons—is really a local problem with global implications. These monsters of death are not in some far-off place. The nuclear production, storage sites, and waste dumps are in local communities, often near Mennonite congregations. The US bases are dotted across the world in local communities.

To make a clear peace witness, we do not have to go far away; we can confront evil and violence at our doorstep. We can sit in Strasbourg or Harrisonburg or Winnipeg and know there is a coup in the Philippines or that six Jesuits and their housekeeper in El Salvador are shot and killed almost as soon as it happens, and yet we do not know that the factory one-half mile from our house is producing bullets or sensors or cluster bombs for those actions. We can deny that death production goes on near us. But then we do not have the luxury of asking, Why did good Germans not stop Nazi atrocities, or why do people in Third World countries allow torture? Our peace witness requires active curiosity. We need to ask: How does this industry, which supplies jobs in my community, affect my neighbor? In this age of instant communication, my neighbor is South African, Honduran, and Palestinian. As more radioactive wastes are buried in local communities, the question of how this affects my neighbor literally becomes a local issue. Based on past Mennonite efforts, I identify three tendencies for implementing our peace witness: (1) movement, (2) manure, (3) joint ventures.

The "Mennonite Movement" in the US includes organizations like the Mennonite Disaster Service (MDS) or SELFHELP Crafts and the recently authorized Christian Peacemaker Teams. The genius of MDS and SELFHELP lies in the way they were established through the vision of individuals within the constituency and the way in which they continue through the active participation of grassroots volunteers who join the cause. It is important to note that existing Mennonite institutions served as foster parents for these movements, and they are Mennonite at the core—both in value and style.

"Mennonite Manure," the second tendency, is harder to recognize or measure. Manure does its job when it is spread around the field. Individual Mennonites, schooled in the historic peace church community values, have often joined other denominations for a variety of reasons (often because there is no Mennonite church geographically close to where their work has taken them). These individuals "fertilize" their local congregation with peace concerns. In travels around Canada and the United States in the past years, I have been amazed by the number of people who approach me after a community or university talk to identify themselves as Mennonites, no longer in Mennonite congregations but still concerned about peace. One professor at a state school in Wisconsin put it succinctly, "My job is to tell the church I belong to now to stop support for warmongering. You would be surprised how many people are listening."

Another tendency, which has aspects of both movement and manure, is the "Joint Venture." Philippine Protestant theologian Feliciano Carino describes this phenomenon in the Philippines as an "ecumenism of the streets." For example, a local Mennonite congregation joins with other denominations in a city or town to work on peace concerns. It might be a temporary alliance focusing on a specific issue or a more permanent partnership to establish a peace center with an office and staff. As in most joint ventures, there is a varying degree of control and participation by the partners. The joint venture does not mean church mergers or theological discussions. It is a grassroots phenomenon observable around the world. Christians from every denomination who are concerned about justice, equity, and human rights are finding each other and working together. Mennonites can be an important component of this new mix.

When we talk about the peace witness of the future, the various configurations of movement, manure, and joint venture all have a place and need to be recognized as growing out of the Mennonite community of values and faith commitments. They do not, however, replace the need for strong Mennonite institutional action on peace. Though Mennonites are locally based with a congregational polity, we have also created strong central institutions and means of communication. These official organizations could have a tremendous role to play in supporting a vibrant peace witness. They can especially play a role in linking Mennonites with similar concerns internationally.

Equipping ourselves for the challenge

To move toward a dynamic peace witness in the midst of world changes, we need to equip ourselves, making sure we are both internally empowered and externally supported. We need to develop a "spirituality on the run." The mobile lifestyles of urban industrialized society in the West erodes some of the strengths found in rooted rural communities. Grinding poverty and displacement due to war can undercut community building in other countries as well. What we need is a conscious rooting, appropriate in the modern context—clusters of people committed to prophetic Christian ministry within a disciplined support structure, which can continue to function even when people are dispersed. The point of organizing groups that can function in dispersion is to build an empowerment structure to sustain people through longer periods of ministry, even when they move. These peace clusters are not communal. Prophetic peace ministry by its very nature requires fairly intense commitment of emotion, time, and energy. So does communitarian life. The two frequently fail to empower one another. The threads of spirituality, biblical study, analysis, and action for justice provide a context for discernment for those who often find themselves almost alone in the search for faithful, effective action. Working on these threads with a group can lead to an ongoing, interwoven corporate life of challenge and support.

While Mennonites do have a history of service, that service has often meant an interim experience for young people before they move into a mainstream vocation. The bulk of international service work is done by volunteers from North America and Europe in Third World countries. Volunteers have tended to carry models for community development from home and college without first engaging in rigorous criticism of the chaotic and often ecologically destructive development that Western civilization has promoted. Often the nature and quality of that service carries within it a certain elitism that assumes that the Germanic "servant," who comes from a position of power, can help and that the recipient of the service, often a person of color, needs what is offered. It is not appropriate for middle-class outsiders to prescribe solutions for the oppressed in any country. And good intentions to help the poor will not be enough unless those intentions are accompanied by a hard-nosed critique of the system that creates poverty and a critique of why arms, including nuclear weapons, are needed to protect the economic interests.

Conclusion

Mennonites have an opportunity for a vital peace witness in the future. Preparation for the challenge of peacemaking in a new arena will include deeper spiritual formation, biblical discernment, social analysis, and, above all, commitment to direct engagement with the powers that be. A key component of the witness of this traditionally Germanic church is genuinely listening to the Third World Mennonite sisters and brothers who are engaged in the struggle for justice and peace.

Dorothy Friesen, USA, b. 1949, M.A. in peace studies, Mennonite Central Committee worker in Southeast Asia from 1976–79, long-term volunteer with Mennonite Voluntary Service, and co-founder and current director of Synapses, a worldwide peace and justice action network located in Chicago, Illinois.

Integrity of creation—reconciliation with nature

by Dorothea Ruthsatz

When reflecting on the integrity of creation, we are participating in a worldwide interconfessional dialogue. The General Assembly of the World Council of Churches (WCC) called upon all churches to participate in a conciliatory process of mutual responsibility for justice, peace, and the integrity of creation in Vancouver in 1983. Many churches in many countries of the world have engaged in this process. By the time this article is published, the World Convocation on Justice, Peace, and the Integrity of Creation in Seoul, Korea, will have come to an end. Will the Mennonites know its results and live up to them?

We have been familiar with the notions of justice and peace for a long time. They have a rich tradition in church history. The notion of integrity of creation, however, is new. It is the churches' response to a completely new situation: the human race will possibly or is likely to completely destroy itself and the world as a whole, both vegetable and animal life. Due to this situation, we are forced to talk about God in a different way and to understand our Christian life in a different way than we did until now. The idea "integrity of creation" is meant to encourage this changed attitude. It does, however, also entail certain difficulties, especially as far as its translation into other languages is concerned. The wording of the WCC intends to emphasize that the earth and everything living on it form a unity and are intended and loved by God, the creator. The German and French translations are "Bewahrung der Schöpfung" and "sauvegarde de la création," with the focus on a loving and preserving attitude of men and women toward nature. In the German language, "integrity" implies "inviolability." Yet the claim of "inviolability of nature" would immediately be disproved by reality. Nature is, of course, violated by the human race and its culture. The limits between a constructive and a destructive attitude toward nature are, however, fluid.

"Integrity of creation" entails another difficulty of interpretation. There is no "creation by itself." There is actually only a given—in the final analysis a historically incidental condition of the environment—which presently arouses our concern. The Christians cannot be interested in maintaining this condition. A correct description of the political task concerned is the aim to preserve the fundamental natural conditions of life. This kind of description does, however, not include the profession of God, which is always implied when we speak about "creation" rather than "nature." It is not easy to define what is really meant by "integrity of creation." It is, however, necessary if we intend to act efficiently and change something, striving for a common goal. Or is it questionable that theologians and Christians must exert a stronger and more direct influence on the current worldwide crisis than they did in the past?

The problems of nature and its destruction are virulent all over the world. They do not stop at national frontiers or religious borders. This difficult situation affects men and women of any social class and any conviction. Therefore, I would first like to describe the problems and possible approaches to a solution in a not specifically Christian language. Thereafter, I will deal with several questions which, due to the subject, any Christian and especially any Mennonite has to respond to.

The problem

In 1984 the World Commission for Environment and Development started its work at the request of the United Nations (U.N.) General Assembly. The members of the commission came from twenty-two countries with completely different political systems and completely different cultural and religious background. The work was presided over by Mrs. G. Harlem Brundtland, the Norwegian prime minister. The report of the commission, which was unanimously submitted to the U.N. General Assembly in 1987, is titled "Our Common Future." Rather than submitting another assessment of the international situation, the commission primarily gave recommendations for action. Nevertheless, I would like to quote some remarks on the international situation from this report. We will not be able to comprehend today's world, which was the appeal of the preparatory study book for Assembly 12—and to act adequately until we know at least the basic facts.

The destruction of our environment is similar to a cancerous tumor, which is gradually and apparently irresistibly spreading over the earth. During this century alone, the world population increased from 1.6 to 5 billion, and this figure will duplicate in the future generation. The use of fossil fuel multiplied by almost thirty, and industrial production rose by more than fifty times during this century. In this period, more land was cleared for agricultural settlements than in the entire previous history of humanity. All over the world, about 15 million acres of arable land fall victim to the continuous expansion of deserts every year. In the meantime, the area covered by tropical rain forests, which was originally 16 million square kilometers, has diminished to 9 million square kilometers. Fifty percent, according to some estimations even up to 90 percent, of all plant and animal species of the earth are living in the rain forests. Inconsiderate deforestation results in a massive extinction of species, which will turn out to be the most serious setback for life on earth since its beginning. Between 1940 and 1980, international water consumption increased by 100 percent and will once again duplicate by the year 2000. At least partly due to the combustion of fossil fuel and deforestation, the carbon dioxide ratio contained in the air has increased by about 30 percent during the last one hundred years, with the trend still climbing sharply upward. This development entails the risk of climatic changes, which might lead to a rise of the sea level and thus to the flooding of coastal towns and river areas. In 1986 experts drew our attention to the reduction of the ozone layer in the atmosphere. The consequences of the overacidification of woods, land, and water are becoming more and more obvious in Europe, Canada, and the United States. At the same time, it is to be supposed that the inappropriate storage of toxic waste has meanwhile led to a contamination of numerous waters and soils and thus the human food chain. On the other hand, international military expenses already exceed the sum of the gross national products of China, India, and southern Africa.

The current global threats to our world mainly originate from the industrial countries. Nuclear disasters, the destruction of the ozone layer, the greenhouse effect, the arms race, and the unfair allocation of resources have their beginning in these countries. On the other hand, poverty is one of the main causes and main consequences for the destruction of the environment in the developing countries. Poor people often do not destroy their environment because they are ignorant, but in order to survive. Therefore, it is useless to try to tackle the problems of environmental protection without a broad perspective, which takes note of the causes of poverty in the world as well as the injustice in international relations. Taking account of these considerations, and after listening to those affected in all parts of the world, the Brundtland report defines "continuous development" as the goal of development of both the industrialized and the developing countries. "Continuous development" is a development that satisfies today's needs without taking the risk that future generations will not be able to satisfy their own needs. Responsibility for social justice between the generations logically also implies justice within each generation. When summarizing the political and economic, the technical, social, and institutional proposals of the U.N. Commission, "continuous development" means an evolutionary process harmonizing the use of resources, the aim of investments, and the direction of technological progress and institutional change and enlarging the present and future potential for fulfilling human needs and desires. Although this requires economic growth, the developing countries have to play a decisive role in this process and achieve successes, and we have to change our ideas of the quality of growth. Growth must be less material- and energy-consuming than in the past, and its consequences must be more equitable. The path to continuous development requires foresight and internationalism. Concepts of the future must no longer be shaped primarily by national interests. Mutual understanding and a sense of mutual responsibility are urgently required in our still-divided world. The progress of the human race depends to a large extent on our ability to recognize that we are neighbors on a small and vulnerable planet and that our obligation to care for each other is a mutual obligation.

A Christian response

If a "reconciliation with nature" in the sense of the Brundtland report is to be achieved, which special tasks will then have to be fulfilled by the faithful, by Christians of any distinction, and especially the Mennonites?

1.   If Christians take the situation seriously that the human race is able and has already begun to annihilate itself and the whole world, this must inevitably lead to a new idea of God: God's almightiness is questioned by the destructive power in the hands of men and women. Like the Jewish religious philosopher H. Jonas, the theologian G. Kaufman of Mennonite tradition also decides to renounce the claim of God's sovereignty over the world. Kaufman may still symbolically speak of God as the creator and of us and our world as creation. To this end, he renounces a personal idea of God, understanding God as a symbol uniting those forces and dimensions of the ecologically and historically retroactive network that create and preserve life and further its development. God is to be understood in the sense of the physical, biological, historical, and cultural preconditions of human life, which also maintain it and lead to a more perfect humanity. According to Kaufman, this paves the way for holding men and women personally responsible for their fate on earth and, furthermore, even to claim that our fate on earth has become God's fate on earth. It is in this claim emphasizing human responsibility that the thoughts of the Christian theologian and the Jewish philosopher coincide, directly joining the appeal of the Brundtland report.

Many faithful people will be reluctant to sacrifice the traditional idea of an almighty God for the sake of their own sense of responsibility. They actually do not have to do so—if for God's sake they do not sacrifice their sense of responsibility as well. There may consequently be different argumentations for an ecologically beneficial ethic, i.e., an ethic that is in accordance with creation. But, in my opinion, they cannot do without the idea of responsibility.

2.   A prerequisite of responsibility is causal power: the author is answerable for his act; he is held responsible and possibly held liable for its consequences. Besides this, there is another idea of responsibility that does not refer to the liability for the act done but to the determination of the action to be taken; according to which I consequently do not feel responsible primarily for my behavior and its consequences but for the matter that asserts a claim to my action. This is the kind of responsibility and sense of responsibility that Jonas means when he speaks about the ethic of responsibility for the future required today. This ethic must put an end to the thoughtless and joyous feast celebrated by the human race during several industrial centuries and curb the galloping pace. Can people only be forced by necessity to listen to reason and assume responsibility? Or can people change their perception, even if this requires an extraordinary moral effort, before the limits of nature are reached? The former would mean to agree with the apostle Paul when, in Romans 7, he concedes to men and women the will to be good and not the accomplishment of the good. The hope for an insight and one's own possibilities, however, is witnessed by a woman mentioned in the New Testament: the poor widow mentioned in Mark 12:44. She gives everything she has, her whole possession—and is declared by Jesus to be an ideal for us. This woman shows how we have to understand our power: in the final analysis, it may be small and insignificant, but it is not to be

despised. Power will perhaps make those advocating a religious attitude for which defenselessness plays or has played an important role feel a little bit uncomfortable. But the Mennonites will not escape from becoming aware of their power and making use of it if they want to participate in the preservation of the natural conditions of life. I do not intend to list what the individual or individual congregations can contribute. This must be elaborated in small groups depending on the location and the situation. I would, however, like to point out that everybody sets great expectations on international organizations and that our Mennonite World Conference is such an international organization as well. How can it contribute to the change of perception that is necessary for the integrity of creation? Regrettably, provisions may not be made for interconfessional or inter-religious discussion at Assembly 12. In any case, our worldwide brother/sister-hood may succeed in overcoming national interest: within the framework of Assembly 12, rich and poor people of all kinds of cultural and social identity will meet and become friends. Against the background of the requested universal sense of responsibility and the necessary global thinking, this is a success of extraordinary significance. Assembly 12 will be a forum to experience solidarity with all men and women.

Integrity of creation, however, encompasses more than just the human race. This could also be considered more closely at Assembly 12 by taking the example of a traditional Mennonite subject. We often discuss the subject of violence only under the aspect of the relationships between men and women and among different peoples. The new philosophical dimension, which we have to take into consideration when striving for the integrity of creation, requires an extension of this anthropocentric discussion. Especially our way of life in the industrialized countries and the structures of our technological culture are characterized by violence against nonhuman life. In this context, meat consumption in the Federal Republic of Germany may serve as a small but rather typical example. On the average, each citizen there eats 100 kilograms of meat every year. According to the standards of the U.N. World Nutrition Council, a quantity of 8 or 9 kilograms of meat per year is sufficient to meet the human demand for animal protein. By eating eleven times as much, we exert violence against nature. If the Germans would not eat more meat than necessary, the grain produced by German farmers would be sufficient, and we would not have to import feed at dumping prices from the Third World, where food for domestic consumption could then be produced more reasonably than grain for export purposes. Moreover, factory farming, which produces the excessive meat quantities, in most cases entails cruelty to animals and is extremely harmful to the water, the air, and the soil due to the large quantities of liquid manure produced. There are numerous examples of our often unconscious violence against nature. This applies to driving a car, especially at high speed, as well as to the construction of nuclear power plants. To put it in a nutshell, a measure for our violence against nature is our energy consumption. Energy supply is vital to the industrial system, which still is so violent against nature. Besides this, the availability of energy shows the unfair allocation of what is taken from nonhuman nature among the men and women living on this earth. In countries with an industrial market economy, the average per capita energy consumption today exceeds the per capita consumption in the African states south of the Sahara by more than eighty times.

If the Mennonites are interested in the reduction of violence in any field of life, especially the Mennonites in Europe and North America have to change their way of life by reducing their energy consumption. Apart from the development of softer technologies and more efficient use of energy, we will probably also have to save energy and pay a higher price for energy consumption—as well as for many other consumer goods. Prices must tell the truth about production costs. Everything that is expensive to produce must be expensive in the market. In former times, production costs were the costs for labor, capital, land, raw materials, ancillary goods, and charges. The environment was for free. Nature paid the price. Since the 1970s, there have at least been ecolaws. They entail costs for the manufacturer. For the sake of us all, the manufacturer usually passes these costs on to the consumer. Since then, prices have also begun to reflect ecological truth. But this is only a beginning. The prices for irrecoverable raw materials and the investments for ecologically beneficial production are still much too low. Otherwise there would not be such a devastating exploitation. We will consequently have to learn to renounce and boycott consumption or, in other words, modify our needs. The philosopher and natural scientist C.F. v. Weiz-säcker even raises the question of whether we are moving toward an international ascetic culture. Our survival might depend on whether it will be possible for us to exercise a democratic asceticism, a deliberate renunciation of the whole society of goods that are apparently available from an economic point of view.

3.   Only the caring life reveals a holistic nature, not the analyzed, decomposed, dissected life. The living being is vulnerable and mortal. The human has the ability to suffer and feel pain in common with the animal, and we are already compared with dried grass in Psalm 90. The dispute as to which position the human being may claim among the other creatures has been decided. We will cease to be the lords of creation unless we know that we are not the lords of creation. This paradoxical sentence by C. Amery implies the recognition that everything in the world is a fellow creature, that the human being shares a common fate with nature, and that we either have to live in harmony with nature as a part of it or else will not survive.

In spite of this, the opposite, the mechanistic conception of the world and its comprehension of nature, is still in force. There are still many people believing in an objective, merely instrumental reasoning of natural sciences. The perception that by means of the rationality of the exact sciences nature itself, a powerless object in the hands of the self-defining human subject, can be perceived is still widely accepted. This theory, based on timeless rational ideas, tries to pretend an abstract eternity by seizing control over nature to avoid its threat, thus also avoiding the threat of death. The Greek word "physis" always implies the rise and decline of a living being, birth and death. The notion of nature, which stems from the Latin word "nasci," to be born, only comprises half of the meaning of physis, i.e., only the rise—and this has become an essential aspect of the individualistic way of thinking and acting of the Occident; one's own death, one's own dying, and one's own finiteness were and are suppressed. Whereas the death of millions of other living beings is not only willingly accepted, but also was and is often caused in an awful way by making best use of one's knowledge and imagination. I am thinking here of war and torture, of experiments on animals or research work with embryos, which are left over from insemination in test tubes, of genetic engineering or of the annihilation of tons of food in the European Community—there are numerous examples. If, therefore, the suppression of death is the cause and consequence of our civilization's hostility to life, it would be time to recover a good relationship to natural death. Genuine religious practice must resist the shock caused by the awareness of the fact of death. Christian faith in creation does not have to perceive the invisible God through creation; it can recognize God in the life and death of Jesus. The words of Jesus are recorded, "In truth, in very truth, I tell you, a grain of wheat remains a solitary grain unless it falls into the ground and dies; but if it dies, it bears a rich harvest" (John 12:24). Jesus means that the promise of experienced and admitted weakness is the ability to live and bear fruit. Only if death is admitted and painfully tasted in such an admission does the consciousness of being a creature reveal itself. This consciousness makes it possible for us to perceive nature in a different way than just scientifically rational terms. The feeling of being a creature makes it easy to feel compassion for the fellow creature. This compassion corresponds to life for other human beings and things. We will only seriously testify to Christ in our world if we are capable of living and dying for our world and its integrity—as he did.

Dorothea Ruthsatz, Federal Republic of Germany, b. 1957, minister of the Mennonite congregation in Krefeld.

Note
I want to acknowledge particular references, among others, to whom I am indebted for new insights: G.D. Kaufman, *Theologie für das Nuklearzeitalter*, München 1987; Volker Hauff, editor, *Unsere gemeinsame Zukunft – Der Brundtland-Bericht der Weltkommission für Umwelt und Entwicklung*, Greven 1987; H. Jonas, *Das Prinzip Verantwortung*, Frankfurt am Main 1979; U. Duchrow/G. Liedke, *Shalom – Der Schöpfung Befreiung*, den Menschen Gerechtigkeit, den Völkern Frieden, Stuttgart 1987; G. Altner, *Die Überlebenskrise in der Gegenwart*, Darmstadt 1987.

Amish men, plowing with many horses instead of heavy tractors, help to preserve the soil in Lancaster County. (The People's Place photo)

New directions in mission

by Nancy R. Heisey

In the 1990s, Christians around the world are taking special note of the fact that the church has gone on for two thousand years since the time when Jesus was in the world. The close of the twentieth century provides an opportunity for reflection about the history of the church, and the advent of the twenty-first stirs believers to plans, dreams, and visions, as well as to some fears, about the future of the church. Since the time of Jesus, the gathering of his followers known as the church has spread from a small group in Palestine to a multiplicity of groups found in every continent of the world. That geographical reality, together with the issues of this historical moment, can lead Christians to new ideas about directions for the church in mission.

Looking again at the Bible

Christians throughout history have maintained the centrality of the Scripture in defining and determining our work, especially the task of reaching out beyond our own communities. Often mission movements have been informed and motivated by particular passages of Scripture. But we have seldom taken the time to relate the whole of the Bible to the whole task of mission. Doing so now is an essential new direction in mission.

The Old Testament is rich in images of God's people as a light to the nations. The New Testament foundations for mission can be found as Jesus still sends his followers out in pairs to proclaim God's kingdom and to heal. After Jesus' death and resurrection, the Gospel accounts give further guidance on mission models: John underlines that Jesus sends his followers out in the same way as God sent him into the world; Matthew emphasizes the task of teaching all of what Jesus taught and making disciples of all the world's peoples; the record in Acts emphasizes the geographical spreading out of the word, as Jesus' followers are pushed by persecution and impelled by the Holy Spirit. Paul's model of starting in the worship centers of his own people, being willing to discuss the difficult issues of his time, connecting many new bodies of believers through letters, and paying his own way, offers a clear picture of how mission tasks might be undertaken.

Restating definitions

Mission, service, evangelism, church formation, relief, development, justice advocacy, and peace witness are all terms that can be included in the definition of mission. There continue to be debates among Christians about which words should be included. This paper begins with the assumption that "mission" is the broadest of all terms used to describe the church being sent out beyond its own community. This community of faith must never forget that its essential nature is to proclaim God's kingdom and call outsiders in to enlarge the community. Any task that sends believers into the world as a sign of God's kingdom is mission.

Mennonites and Brethren in Christ have traditionally given a large place to service as a central part of reaching out beyond ourselves. However, we have usually defined service as one piece of the task, as one half of a whole of which mission is the other half; and often we have acted as if service is the lesser half of our task. A redefinition that makes sense to our worldwide fellowship is to see service as whole and meaningful in and of itself, the essential style for all mission tasks. The key to this understanding can be found in Jesus' own words: Here I am among you—preaching, healing, teaching, speaking to the authorities—as a servant.

Broader understanding of where Christians should be in mission

Too often Christians have defined mission as proclaiming the gospel somewhere far away to people who are very different from us. Another new direction in mission is the understanding that God is at work everywhere in the world. Missionaries do not bring God to any place or people. They bring their own knowledge of and experience of God to share, and a desire to find how God is at work in the setting that is new to them. It may be that they will be able to point to God's work in this setting in a way that enlightens what local people have seen but not understood.

The twenty-first century world will contain a variety of environments where the gospel message must continue to be heard. There will still be places where the gospel has not been heard at all. There will be many more places where the gospel requires a new hearing. Some settings labeled "closed" to the gospel have responded in that way to outside mission workers because of a poor Christian witness or because of the linking of Christian witness to unsavory Western/Northern political and economic policies. In other settings the traditional message of the churches has been heard in the past and discarded as irrelevant to modern realities. Finally, in places where the church is alive and growing, the gospel will still need to be preached. The community of believers must always be aware that the good news is richer and bigger than human efforts to define it.

Christians called into mission must first evaluate our own settings as we decide where to begin our work. Because Western/Northern society is familiar with Christian ideals but has largely discarded active faith, Western/Northern Christians need to take very seriously the call to proclaim good news where we are. We may want to call missionaries from those places where the church is active and growing to teach us anew what is good news. Christians everywhere need to reflect on what forms of mission might most honestly and winsomely bring the good news to those environments that have not heard the good news or have heard it badly. Quite likely the witness in those settings will take some very untraditional and un-Western forms.

Shifting power and control

Currently most of the monetary and institutional resources used in mission are in the hands of Western/Northern churches. In parts of the world where the churches are growing rapidly there are other models of mission, although those engaged in such mission are unlikely to define what they are doing in structural terms. Most mission models take seriously the need for people and the importance of call. However, Western/Northern models place people and call in the context of organizations, finances, plans, and objectives. Christians in other places connect people and call with a sense of the Holy Spirit's leading and the assumption that the missionaries will depend on the societal structures of those to whom they go.

Two critical needs for the church in mission in the twenty-first century are (1) for Western/Northern mission structures to take seriously, respect, and refrain from co-opting these other mission models when we encounter them and (2) for Western/Northern mission church structures to work hard to find ways to put our financial and material resources at the disposition of churches in mission elsewhere. Perhaps the most critical mission challenge for wealthy churches is the challenge to give up some of our wealth so that we can become more honest and equal partners with the worldwide church seeking to live out the good news in our world.

Renewing our identity

An important task for Mennonites and Brethren in Christ people in North America in the twentieth century has been the search for our roots as a faith community. Excitement about our sixteenth-century heritage has led to calls to new faithfulness, which have been heard by other churches around the world. These brothers and sisters urge us to continue to share our discoveries widely and freely among all God's people. As we have learned about our past, some of us have returned to the communities that emerged from our earlier mission efforts to share with them the faith traditions that we have rediscovered.

As people in mission in the twenty-first century, we need to renew our identity in several ways: (1) We must seek to see how the biblical message that challenged our forebears challenges us at this time; (2) we must allow sisters and brothers around the world to explore their own heritage as well as helping them to use that of our heritage which is useful to them; (3) we must be free in continuing to share our faith understandings with the broad fellowship of believers; and (4) we must allow new communities of faith to take shape in a way that fits their context, offering our fellowship but not insisting on our specific identity in order for them to participate with us.

Conclusion

Mennonite and Brethren in Christ in mission have much to be thankful for as we enter the 1990s and beyond. We can be thankful for what we have learned from our history and how our family has been enriched as people from around the world have joined us. As we continue to explore new directions in mission for the next century, we can go beyond reacting against our own and others' interpretations of the mistakes of the past. Rather, we take heart in the belief that God is working all things out according to God's purpose. We can rejoice in the fact that the worldwide church helps us to better understand the mission challenges of our rapidly changing future. Together we commit ourselves to continue to bear witness to God's kingdom among us while we wait for its complete coming. Even so, come, Lord Jesus.

Nancy R. Heisey, USA, b. 1952, associate executive secretary of Mennonite Central Committee (Akron, Pennsylvania).

Realizing true partnership among our churches

by Donald R. Jacobs

Community, an Anabaptist/Mennonite theme

When the Anabaptist movement began in 1525, the believers addressed one another simply as "brethren." They used the language of the family. For many it was indeed their new family. As they witnessed to their newly found faith in Christ, they encountered stiff resistance. Many lost their lives. Widows, widowers, and orphans were left behind. The way they supported and assisted one another in very high-risk evangelism welded them together even more solidly. What happened to them is reminiscent of that memorable Pentecost in Jerusalem when the Holy Spirit was poured out. Being in Christ meant being in a new family.

The "brethren" lived their beliefs. They truly cared for one another. Many of them believed that the Lord was about to return in any case, so why hold on to this world's possessions? As early as 1527 Hans Hut and his group were practicing a common purse. Historian C.J. Dyck notes, "They also studied carefully the example of the early church ... and, while not taking it as a legal command in every detail, came to see it as a powerful demonstration of the truth that economic sharing and vital apostolic obedience belong together."[1] One of the outstanding features of the Anabaptists was their belief in the visible church. It was not just a spiritual unity but a true unity of community. Many of the leaders, including Menno Simons himself, stressed the use of church discipline, including the ban, to reinforce the concept of a loving, caring community of believers. Article 8 of the Dordrecht Confession (1632) stated, "We believe in and confess a visible Church of God, consisting of those who ... have truly repented, and rightly believed; who are rightly baptized, united with God in heaven, and incorporated into the communion of the saints on the earth (1 Cor. 12:13)."[2]

The sense of brotherhood was further strengthened by the restrictions under which Mennonites found themselves in the seventeenth century. They needed one another in order to survive. Unable to participate in the normal commercial and industrial life of their nations, they lived on the margins of society, normally in agricultural communities. In these communities they put into practice their belief that the church is in fact a living, growing community in which love for one another marked their common life. There were exceptions, of course, but the idea of building a caring, sharing community as an expression of the love of Christ was never abandoned among the Mennonites. Slowly doors opened for some Mennonites to move to Russia, North America, and to nations in Europe that were more tolerant of Mennonites. But wherever they went, they deliberately established communities, mostly rural ones.

It should be noted that through all those years the Mennonites shared a common culture to a greater or lesser degree. Their culture was basically German or Dutch even though they were scattered from Russia to Canada. It is safe to say that by 1875, 350 years after the movement began, all members could still speak either Dutch or German or a blend of the two (Low German). A great outpouring of Mennonite mutual aid occurred when German-speaking Mennonites passed through Holland, where they boarded ships to cross the Atlantic Ocean in search of a new home. The Dutch Mennonites were extremely liberal toward their "brothers in Christ." And when German-speaking Mennonites began their emigration from Russia in 1873, over $100,000 was raised in the United States and Canada to help.[3] In this century Mennonite Central Committee (MCC) was formed as an agency to help German-speaking Mennonites to settle in Latin America and Canada particularly. It has since broadened its scope significantly to provide assistance wherever it is needed in the world. But MCC was born to help fellow ethnic Mennonites.

In summary, the Mennonite church has always placed high priority on practical sharing of goods among the brotherhood. This was not only a theory but an action. Whether the needy brother or sister was a near neighbor or was from the Ukraine in Russia, Jesus taught them to share; and that is what they did. But the major portion of their sharing was with the Mennonites with whom they shared a common culture.

Community and mission endeavors

Then the picture changed. Its scope got broader. Mennonites[4] gradually became involved in active cross-cultural missions. These developed slowly at first. Some of the first missionaries simply "went." Then the churches, here and there, took official action to send missionaries into other cultures for the purpose of bringing the gospel to them so that they, too, could declare their loyalty to Jesus Christ. This transition from a "colony"-minded church to a "missions"-minded church set the Mennonites on a new course. Not all of the Mennonites launched out in missions, some no doubt fearful that it might be troublesome to bring non-Germanic believers into the church. By becoming a missionary church the Mennonite church was destined to lose its mono-cultural nature, which it had enjoyed for several centuries.

The decades 1890 to 1910 saw a burst of activity as North American Mennonite missionaries entered India, Zimbabwe, China, Nigeria, and Zambia.[5] This provided a basis for increased activity, which eventually placed missionaries in over fifty nations. It is interesting to note how the first missionaries put into practice their belief in the sanctity of the Christian community. Pieter Jansz and his young wife sailed from Holland in July 1851 to Java in Indonesia. They were the first Mennonite foreign missionaries. By the year 1890, several dozen Javanese believers had come to Christ and formed themselves into a church.

Because of the hostile nature of their Islamic environment, they established a colony. In their colony they shared with one another as a new family. As all Mennonites, they shared the joys and disciplines of life in community. Then in 1889 to 1891 a few North American missionaries sailed for India, and in 1911 some went to Zaire. Many followed this missionary example into more than fifty nations on all continents. Wherever they went, the missionaries carried a burden for mutual assistance.

Each culture expressed the commitment to authentic community in a great variety of ways. Normally in the first years of a mission, believers gravitated to the "mission stations" where they could live in proximity to other believers. They were often a harassed minority. By living in these tight communities, they put into practice their vision of Christian community. These communities did not have only a spiritual unity, but they shared all of life. This phenomenon of believers clustering around mission stations was not peculiar to Mennonites. Almost all missions were experiencing it, but for the Mennonites it had a biblical basis as well as a practical one.

The writer's own experience in Tanzania was rather typical. Mennonite congregations formed on the eastern shores of Lake Victoria just south of Kenya among at least ten distinct language groupings. Through the years the church discovered the grace of unity that was outstanding in the eyes of believers and nonbelievers alike. One of the strongest expressions of their new life in Christ was their love for one another across tribal and racial lines. This unity was tested time and time again, and it will certainly be tried in the future as well. Nevertheless, even though it was not a perfect fellowship, it was a new experience in community because prior to the coming of Christianity local and even regional bodies were usually tribal in character. So in the Mennonite Church of Tanzania the believers had as their daily agenda the demands of living in harmony with brothers and sisters from a great variety of cultures.

The most rapid expansion of churches around the world has occurred within the past fifty years. The Mennonite church entered a new language area, a nation, or another tribe on the average of one every eight or so months. This was not just the work of Western mission boards, but the believers themselves carried the gospel to their neighbors even though those neighbors were of another culture entirely. The church spread spontaneously through evangelism.

Mutuality in the present day

This expansion of the church by including believers from over one hundred cultures has radically changed the face of Mennonitism around the world. At this meeting of Mennonite World Conference Assembly 12 in 1990, the Germanic and Dutch cultures are no longer the only or even the dominant cultures in the church. This article addresses the issue of mutuality in the church. The Mennonite church today is culturally pluralistic, and that trend is probably fixed. The churches are still moving into new language and people groups around the world. There is every reason to believe that each year a new "culture" will be entered through normal evangelism. The question is whether Mennonite commitment to mutuality will transcend cultural differences or not. Social scientists have discovered that mutuality works best within cultures and rarely between cultures. That may be true, but the New Testament teaches that the love of Jesus Christ rises above loyalty to tribe or clan. The gospel of Jesus Christ brings into being churches in which all are to be received as true brothers and sisters no matter what their culture or race.

This is not a theoretical issue for world Mennonites but a very practical and urgent one. Ideally each church or fellowship, whether large or small, new or old, should make available to all other parts of the family its spiritual, historical, cultural, personnel, and financial resources for the strengthening and extension of the kingdom of God. Solidarity in Christ requires that it should be a true family in which the needy are assisted in a Christlike manner. No decision should be made on any basis other than to build the great body of Christ in the world.

Considering partnership in solidarity does in no way diminish the freedom of the local churches or conferences. Partnership is simply an enabling method to be more effective in the ministry to which the Lord has called the whole church. When partnerships are formed, there is a mutual self-giving, which is always necessary in true brotherhood; but true partnership in Christ protects the dignity and integrity of all of the partners. It could well be that some local Mennonite churches will wish to establish partnership arrangements with non-Mennonite churches or agencies. Each local church or conference should have freedom under the headship of Christ to determine which partnerships are mutually compatible and which are not. No church should choose the partners that another church should have.

There are several areas in which partnership is called for:

Evangelism and cross-cultural mission—A new feature in our time is the vast network of Mennonite churches all over the world. They exist in over one hundred cultures. They are there. And that is good news as far as evangelization is concerned. Of course, there are thousands of cultures in which they are not, but they are scattered strategically all over the world. The future of missions will be an exercise of forming new partnerships for the further evangelization of our globe.

The Mennonite churches around the world are just beginning to form their own sending agencies or, to use the more traditional term, mission boards. This trend will certainly accelerate in the years ahead. A full tenth of all missionaries are now being sent by sending agencies in the newer churches around the world. Is it possible that mission groups across the church could link arms in a new, Spirit-led movement of evangelism? The need for such a brave new step is apparent when the future of missions is examined. The churches should work in true partnership as they move into the future. Much work has yet to be done. The missionary task is as yet unfinished:

1. Instead of one mission agency taking the initiative to enter a new frontier area alone, it is much wiser to form multicultural teams to demonstrate as they evangelize what the new kingdom of God looks like. By blending resources, much more can be done. This method would also decentralize the power somewhat. It would underline that the church of Jesus Christ is both at home in every culture and, at the same time, not completely at home in any.

2. Much of the world is now closed or closing to traditional missionaries from the West. But doors are open for non-Western Christians to move freely in those nations with limited access. This will probably require some new approaches, but with God's grace it is possible.

3. Many churches in the West have lost some of their enthusiasm for the gospel. Here is one way that the newer churches could be of great help, by bringing revival to the churches which, after expending themselves in missions, are often weary and confused.

Meeting human need both within the church body and beyond—The first call upon the resources of the international body of Christ is to help brothers and sisters within the fellowships who do need help. To refuse this kind of charity is to misunderstand the obligations of membership in the church. This was a fundamental part of the Pauline understanding of mission and solidarity in Christ. Each Mennonite community will also help its neighbors. This is built into the Mennonite understanding of the love of Christ. This same burden for the needs of all needy people anywhere in the world is just as central to the full understanding of the gospel. Every church in the world should have the joy and blessing of helping needy people in communities beyond its own.

Strengthening the faith commitment of all members everywhere—The Western churches have been known as the great givers. This grace should be shared with all members of the body. Those with little should give their little, but those with much should give much. As these resources are mixed and used, all get the blessing.

Assisting one another in areas of education, leadership training, development enterprises, and economic growth—A huge disparity between the churches in the more industrialized nations and those who are caught in the jaws of poverty persists. Where churches reach out to their brothers and sisters in Christ for help in education, leadership training, and development, they should have some assurance that they will indeed have partners who care.

Hindrances to partnership

It is important to recognize the factors that militate against true partnership and mutuality between cultures:

1.   The Mennonite churches and denominations never did have a unified mission witness. Over a dozen mission boards emerged in North America alone. Each worked hard at world missions and each, in a sense, extended its own denomination or conference. There were some exceptions to this, such as the Congo Inland Mission, which combined several denominational interests. However, by and large the churches pursued mission in isolation from one another. They often did confer, but the structures were bilateral. Very few resources flowed back and forth among the mission agencies. This served to keep the newer Mennonite churches separate. Emerging churches knew only their mission partners. The pressing need for the years ahead is to establish a climate for broad sharing. The Mennonite structures will be tested, certainly, as the imperative of mutuality gains strength.

2.   Modern missions carried a dual mandate: a spiritual one, which constrained them to invite men and women to follow Jesus Christ with all their hearts, and a cultural mandate, which required them, in love, to share what they had and what they knew with the emerging churches. Therefore, a high priority was also given to education, health, and economic development. The mission societies assumed that as people became Christian they would automatically view life as Western cultures did. For many years this cultural expectation was strong even though it was not articulated. Most missionary agencies have dropped the cultural mandate that marked Western missions for many years. Some mission agencies have withdrawn from any interchurch aid at all in reaction to the cultural imperialism of the past. However, the Mennonite churches do not believe that just because a conference becomes autonomous it no longer is a part of the worldwide mutuality system.

3.   The rapid expansion of the worldwide Mennonite church took place when Western cultural expansion was on the increase. The Mennonite missions also carried some burden for the material as well as physical aspects of life. As decolonization runs its historical and rightful course, it is becoming more evident that the Mennonite churches were influenced by the historical colonization movement. That understanding calls for a change of attitude.

4.   Because the Western churches had financial resources and highly developed administrative structures, great tensions often resulted between the "mission" and the emerging churches. The disparity in wealth and education was often so

great that communication almost broke down, particularly when the churches attempted to establish their independence. The colonial powers solved this problem by simply leaving, allowing their former colonies to fend for themselves as they were able. On the contrary, because of the spiritual bonds in Christ, mission agencies and the local churches continued to relate to one another long after the colonial era. But the gap between rich and poor has grown steadily, which further exacerbates this problem.

5.   Even though Mennonite missionaries held to a doctrine of church that assumed mutual sharing, they were also influenced by Western culture, which is very individualistic, self-protective, and ethnocentric. This was true not only of the missionaries but of the mission agencies themselves. The problem was further complicated by the fact that in many cultures where the missions were at work, the local churches had a more profound understanding of what it meant to be a member of the family of Christ because of their own cultural conditioning in the context of solidarity.

6.   A structural issue will need to be faced if true mutuality is to gain in strength. The problem arises from the fact that the linkages between what might be termed the "sending" churches and the newer churches were mission boards. These mission boards acted on behalf of the churches. The mission boards, therefore, had the primary contact with the emerging churches around the world. When the newer churches become fully independent, it is often difficult for them to connect in a meaningful way with the churches that gave birth to the mission boards. So in many cases the newer churches experience frustration in their attempt to relate church to church. Ways must be found to weld meaningful relationships between newer and older churches.

Why is this an urgent issue?

1.   It is the key to the future of missions. Every church, every conference, no matter how rich or poor, is responsible for world mission, beginning locally and progressing to the ends of the earth. Many of the churches in the poorer areas of the world have vision and spiritual zeal but lack finance to propel them into world mission. By blending resources, the Mennonite churches around the world today could usher in a new wave of evangelization unlike any seen in the denomination until now.

2.   The African, Latin American, and Asian Mennonite churches are growing about four times faster, on average, than the churches in Europe and North America. The spiritual vitality that enables this rapid growth is sorely needed in the "Western" churches. This would be reason enough to pursue the mutuality in relationships that is inherent in our solidarity in Christ.

3.   It is the will of God that all of the local churches within the unity of the global body of Christ express their love for one another both in spiritual and tangible ways. This is especially important if there are many cultures in the church. Even non-Christians help their "own." Agape, which creates solidarity in the church, is much more radical; it shares with all.

The underlying motivation for mutuality among churches is not simply to get work done but to clarify for all the world what the nature of the kingdom of God really is. It is not a human institution based on cultural affinity but a universal brotherhood that includes people from every tribe and nation. It is a bold announcement that Jesus Christ is already establishing a new kingdom on the earth. It is made up of humble, thankful believers who have committed themselves to their Lord and to one another in love. They are in the world yet not of it. They live on the earth, yet their loyalty is to the King who inhabits eternity, the Lord Jesus Christ. The worldwide Mennonite church is included in the prayer of our Lord Jesus Christ, as recorded in John 17, "I have given them the glory that you gave me, that they may be one as we are one: I in them and you in me. May they be brought to complete unity to let the world know that you sent me and have loved them even as you have loved me."

"May the God who gives endurance and encouragement give you a spirit of unity among yourselves as you follow Christ Jesus, so that with one heart and mouth you may glorify the God and Father of our Lord Jesus Christ" (Rom. 15:5–6). That admonition to the Roman church by the apostle Paul is a fitting challenge for the Mennonite churches around the world today.

Christ reveals his kingship first of all in his worldwide church as the local churches and conferences remain faithful to each other in the essential solidarity that Jesus has created in them—over and above all relative cultural, linguistic, national, historical, and religious contexts in which they witness.

Donald R. Jacobs, USA, b. 1928, Ph.D., executive director of Mennonite Christian Leadership Foundation, ordained pastor.

Notes
1.   Cornelius J. Dyck, *An Introduction to Mennonite History*, Herald Press, Scottdale, Pennsylvania, 1981, p. 144.
2.   Howard John Loewen, *One Lord, One Church, One Hope, and One God: Mennonite Confessions of Faith*, Institute of Mennonite Studies, Elkhart, Indiana, 1985, p. 65.
3.   Dyck, p. 203.
4.   The Brethren in Christ church is included from this point.
5.   Wilbert Shenk, "Growth Through Mission," *Mennonite World Handbook*, Mennonite World Conference, Lombard, Illinois, 1978, pp. 20–31.

Minati Rani Mundul, mother of four children, at work in the Bagdha Wooden Crafts project in Agailjhara, Bangladesh, where she makes skipping rope handles. (MCC photo by Charmayne Brubaker, 1990)

Konferenzen

(Seite 335-417)

1	Anschrift und Gründungsjahr
2	Sprache
	Vorstand
3	Vorsitzender/Präsident
4	Kassenführer
5	Schriftführer
6	Postanschrift
	Publikationen
7	Name und Anschrift
8	Verlag
	Friedensbelange
9	a) Kriegsdienst; b) Kriegsdienstverweigerung; c) Unterstützung für KDV; d) Ersatzdienst; e) Kriegssteuerverweigerung
	Mission
10	Missionswerke
11	Zahl der Mitarbeiter
12	Jahreshaushalt
	Diakonie
13	Hilfswerk(e)
14	Zahl der Mitarbeiter
15	Jahreshaushalt
	Mitgliedschaft und Organisation
16	Zahl der Gemeinden
17	Zahl der Predigtplätze
18	Zahl der Glieder und Gäste
19	Zahl der Glieder
20	Taufe durch: a) Besprengen; b) Begießen; c) Untertauchen
21	Glaubensbekenntnis?: a) Ja; b) Nein
22	Zahl der Gottesdienste je Gemeinde und Woche
23	Gottesdienstbesuch in % der Gliederzahl
24	Konferenzstruktur: a) kongregational; b) synodal; c) bischöflich
	Mitarbeiterschaft
25	Zahl der Prediger/Ältesten
26	Evangelisten/Gemeindebauer
27	angestellte Pastoren
28	Bibelschulen/Seminare
29	andere Ausbildungsmöglichkeiten: a) Fernstudium; b) gelegentliche Seminare; c) sonstiges
30	interkonfessionelle Beziehungen

Convenciones

(Páginas 335-417)

1	Dirección y año establecido
2	Idioma usado por miembros
	Oficiales
3	Presidente
4	Tesorero
5	Secretario ejecutivo
6	Enviar correspondencia a
	Publicaciones
7	Nombre y dir. de publicación oficial
8	Agencia publicadora
	Asuntos relacionados con la paz
9	a) Servicio militar obligatorio; b) Provisión gubernamental para la objeción por conciencia (OC); c) La iglesia apoya oficialmente la OC; d) Opciones aprobadas por el gobierno para servicio alternativo; e) Algunos miembros rechazan los impuestos militares
	Misión
10	Organización(es) misionera(s)
11	Número total de obreros
12	Presupuesto anual total
	Servicio
13	Organizaciones de servicio
14	Número total de obreros
15	Presupuesto anual total
	Membresía y organización
16	Número de congregaciones
17	Número de lugares de adoración
18	Comunidad cristiana total
19	Número de miembros bautizados
20	Bautismo: a) aspersión; b) derramamiento de agua; c) inmersión
21	¿Confesión de fe?: a) sí; b) no
22	Frecuencia de reuniones por semana
23	Asistencia promedio (porcentaje de la membresía)
24	Gobierno eclesial: a) congregacional; b) sinodal; c) episcopal
	Liderato
25	Pastores/diáconos ordenados
26	Evangelistas/personas que plantan iglesias
27	Pastores con salario
28	Institutos bíblicos/seminarios
29	Otro entrenamiento de líderes: a) educación teológica por extensión; b) seminarios ocasionales; c) otro
30	Familia denominacional mundial

Agencias/Facilitación

(Páginas 418-436)

	El primer párrafo de la columna describe el propósito, objetivo, o visión de la organización.
1	Nombre alternativo o iniciales por las cuales se conoce a la organización
2	Dirección
3	Número telefónico
4	Número de télex
5	Número de máquina de telefax/facsímil
6	Código de cable
7	Año establecida
	Oficiales
8	Persona que preside
9	Oficial ejecutivo principal
10	Tesorero
	Auspiciadores
11	Grupo o grupos que auspician esta organización
	Presupuesto
12	Moneda de las cantidades señaladas abajo
13	Entrada anual total
14	Entrada anual recibida de convenciones y congregaciones Menonitas/Hermanos en Cristo
15	Entrada anual recibida de individuos y compañías privadas
16	Entrada anual recibida de individuos y organizaciones no Menonitas/Hermanos en Cristo
17	Gasto anual total
18	Gasto anual para personal
19	Gasto anual para materiales (mercadería)
	Empleados/obreros
20	Número de empleados a tiempo completo
21	Número de empleados a tiempo parcial
22	Número de voluntarios

Werke/Handreichung

(Seite 418-436)

	Zweck, Ziel und Vision
1	Name/Abkürzung
2	Anschrift
3	Telephon
4	Telex
5	Telefax
6	Telegrammadresse
7	Gründungsjahr
	Leitung
8	Vorsitzender
9	Geschäftsführer
10	Kassenführer
	Sponsoren
11	Träger
	Jahreshaushalt
12	Währungseinheit
13	jährliche Einnahmen
14	… von Konferenzen/Gemeinden
15	… von Personen/Firmen
16	… von nichtmennonitischen Gebern
17	jährliche Ausgaben
18	davon Personalkosten
19	davon Sachkosten
	Mitarbeiter (nach Köpfen)
20	davon vollzeitig
21	davon teilzeitig
22	davon Freiwillige

Conferences

(Pages 335-417)

1	Address and year established
2	Languages used by members
	Officers
3	Moderator
4	Treasurer
5	Executive secretary
6	Send mail to
	Publications
7	Official periodical name and address
8	Publishing agency
	Peace concerns
9	a) Compulsory military service; b) Government provision for conscientious objection (CO); c) Church officially supports CO; d) Government-approved alternative service options; e) Some church members reject war taxes
	Mission
10	Mission organization(s)
11	Total number of workers
12	Total annual budget
	Service
13	Service organization(s)
14	Total number of workers
15	Total annual budget
	Membership and organization
16	Number of congregations
17	Number of places of worship
18	Total Christian community
19	Number of baptized members
20	Baptism: a) sprinkling; b) pouring; c) immersion
21	Confession of faith?: a) yes; b) no
22	Worship services per week
23	Average attendance as percentage of membership
24	Church government: a) congregational; b) synodal; c) episcopal
	Leadership
25	Ordained preachers/elders
26	Evangelists/church planters
27	Salaried ministers
28	Number of Bible schools/seminaries
29	Other leadership training: a) theological education by extension; b) occasional seminars; c) other
30	Global denominational family

Conférences

(Page 335-417)

1	Adresse et année de fondation
2	Langues utilisées par les membres
	Responsables
3	Président/e
4	Trésorièr/e
5	Secrétaire
6	Adresse de contact
	Publications
7	Périodique officiel—nom et adresse
8	Editeur
	Questions concernant la paix
9	a) Service militaire obligatoire; b) Statut d'objecteur de conscience reconnu par l'Etat; c) Soutien officiel des objecteurs de conscience par l'Eglise; d) Service civil reconnu par l'Etat; e) Membres d'Eglises refusant de payer les impôts militaires
	Mission
10	Organismes missionnaires
11	Nombre total des collaborateurs
12	Budget annuel total
	Diaconie
13	Organismes de service
14	Nombre total des collaborateurs
15	Budget annuel total
	Membres et organisation
16	Nombre d'assemblées
17	Nombre de lieux de culte
18	Nombre total de la communauté
19	Nombre de personnes baptisées
20	Forme du baptême: a) aspersion; b) effusion; c) immersion
21	Confession de foi?: a) oui; b) non
22	Fréquence des cultes par semaine
23	Pourcentage de participation par rapport au nombre total de membres
24	Direction de l'Eglise: a) congrégationelle; b) synodale; c) épiscopale
	Responsables
25	Prédicateurs et anciens consacrés
26	Evangélistes/implanteurs d'églises
27	Responsables salariés
28	Nombre d'écoles bibli./séminaires
29	Autres formations des responsables: a) formation théologique décentrée; b) séminaires occasionnels; c) autres
30	Orientation la plus proche dans la famille mennonite

Oeuvres/Coordination

(Page 418-436)

Le premier paragraphe de la colonne désigne l'objet, le but ou la vision de l'organisation.

1 Autre nom ou sigle de l'organisation
2 Adresse
3 Numéro de téléphone
4 Numéro de télex
5 Numéro du téléfax
6 Adresse télégraphique
7 Année de fondation

Responsables

8 Président/e
9 Fondé de pouvoir
10 Trésorièr/e

Patronage

11 Groupe(s) patronnant l'organisation

Budget

12 Monnaie utilisée dans les chiffres ci-dessous
13 Revenu annuel total
14 Revenus annuels reçus des conférences et assemblées mennonites et des Frères en Christ
15 Revenus annuels reçus de particuliers ou de compagnies privées
16 Revenus annuels reçus de particuliers ou d'organisations non-mennonites/Frères en Christ
17 Dépenses totales annuelles
18 Dépenses annuelles pour le personnel
19 Dépenses annuelles pour les biens (marchandises)

Employé(e)s/ Collaborateurs(trices)

20 Nombre d'employés à plein temps
21 Nombres d'employés à temps partiel
22 Nombre de volontaires

Agencies/Facilitation

(Pages 418-436)

The first paragraph of the column describes the purpose, goal, or vision of the organization.

1 Alternative name or initials by which the organization is known
2 Address
3 Telephone number
4 Telex number
5 Facsimile machine number
6 Cable code
7 Year established

Officers

8 Chairperson
9 Chief executive officer
10 Treasurer

Sponsors

11 Group or groups that sponsor this organization

Budget

12 Currency for amounts shown below
13 Total annual income
14 Annual income received from Mennonite/Brethren in Christ conferences and congregations
15 Annual income received from private individuals or companies
16 Annual income received from non-Mennonite/Brethren in Christ individuals and organizations
17 Total annual expense
18 Annual expense for personnel
19 Annual expense for material (merchandise)

Employees/workers

20 Number of full-time employees
21 Number of part-time employees
22 Number of volunteers

Directory 1990

Commentary

by Diether Götz Lichdi, Editor

There are people who are reluctant to collect statistical information. Some very thoughtful believers view this as a temptation of human pride: They point to the megalomania of David and its punishment (2 Sam. 24). Counting God's people is considered a sign of distrust or arrogance, taking human fate into our hands rather than leaving it to God's grace. There is, however, another approach to statistics: They can praise the Lord's precious gifts and his never-ending mercies (Lam. 3:22). With this in mind, the computation of figures can be seen as a desire to understand the ways in which God has led us and to realize our needs as a Mennonite faith community. You may interpret the statistical section as a collection that teaches us about meeting challenges with humility and obedience.

The Directory provides data collected by MWC in a three-step procedure: (1) In the spring of 1989 we mailed a questionnaire asking for general information to 162 conferences and a separate questionnaire to 34 agencies/organizations. We requested that information be correct as of June 30, 1989. We received 106 questionnaires from conferences and 32 from agencies/organizations. In some cases more recent information was supplied due to a later return. Through experience with the 1978 edition of *Mennonite World Handbook*, the *MWH 1984 Supplement*, the biennial MWC *Mennonite and Brethren in Christ World Directory*, consultation with mission boards, and continuous contacts with churches and church leaders around the world, MWC knew of the existence of the majority of organized groups. Missions were not considered in this survey of conferences. (2) In the fall of 1989 we mailed a follow-up questionnaire to 158 conferences asking for membership data and confirming names of officers as of December 31, 1989. Of those questionnaires, 92 were returned. (3) In cases where we lacked sufficient information after sending reminder letters and additional questionnaires, we vigorously pursued all other possible sources: knowledgeable resource people, news articles, conference yearbooks, past experience. We also made numerous phone calls and sent faxes around the world to try to reach conference leaders themselves.

The result is a four-part Directory (Conferences, Agencies, Facilitation, and Training) using "statistics" and "topics" as frames of reference. Statistics include names and addresses, membership, congregations, number of ministers, leadership training, budget figures, and number of workers. Topics include languages, peace concerns, baptism, church government, meeting patterns and attendance, publications, confessions of faith, and interdenominational contacts. Some figures are followed by a sign (±) to indicate that the number is an estimate. The estimate was made by the group itself or by an MWC source.

The reader will notice some inconsistent information that may be misleading. For reasons of time and space we did not annotate. Although some of the figures may not meet statistical standards, it is our conviction that this material approximates accurate information. The findings, of course, are not definitive and may stimulate further research. We aimed to condense material sufficiently to be readable at first glance in a workable format. To make the section accessible in four languages (English, French, German, Spanish), we inserted guides to explain the coded numbers. Tear off the guide for your language—one side for the Conference Section and another for the Agency and Facilitation Sections—and use it to interpret the book as you read. The guides are reprinted on pages 331 to 334. For an explanation of frequently used abbreviations, see page 6.

Membership—Uncertainty about definitions still exists. The questionnaire asked for the number of baptized members and, separately, the total Christian community to clarify that point. The latter was intended to include baptized members, children, catechumens, and adherents. (See Charts A through I.)

The membership figure for the USSR came down from 55,000 to 26,200, but this decrease is not truly reflected by an increase in the Federal Republic of Germany because not all Aussiedler with a traditional "Mennonite name" joined one of the existing or newly established congregations. A correct number for the Soviet Mennonites was not previously and cannot now be established. We do have detailed estimates for known congregations (53 with 6,615 members), many of whose members emigrated during the last month. For more information, see *Mennonitisches Jahrbuch 1990* and *Mennonite Encyclopedia V*.

Languages—The days when Mennonites around the world could converse only in German passed away one hundred years ago. Due to the acculturation in North America and to the missionary outreach, particularly after World War II, the Mennonites of the world use 78 languages. The majority of the conferences (76) use more than one language; eight conferences exercise five languages. A slight minority of 69 conferences live with one language.

The most common language is English (listed by 57 conferences, including 36 conferences reporting English as a first language), followed by Spanish (52/39) and German (49/34). French use is much less (14/2). The combination English/German (14) is the most used, ahead of Spanish/German (11). It is not possible to explore how many Mennonites use one of the four languages of MWC (English, French, German, Spanish) as the primary, or first, language; but the guess would be English ahead of German, with the prediction that Spanish will outnumber German before the next assembly.

Other than the Germans themselves, the conferences that still use German as their first or only language are the conservative groups in the Americas (Old Colony, Old Order Amish, Hutterites, and Mennonites in the Chaco). Conferences in North America and West Africa are among the most multilingual, with the General Conference listing as many as 16 languages. Of the 53 out of 145 conferences that list one of the four languages as their only language, Spanish leads (30), followed by English (12) and German (9). The Spanish lead is primarily due to the multitude of conferences and countries in Latin America.

Our responses indicate that the following languages are used by our members:

Adangbe	Ewe	Kuaniama	Serbo-Croatian
Amharic	Français	Kurya	Shai
Annang	Ga	Lao	Sindebele
Arapaho	Guaraní	Lengua	Sioux
Bengali	Hindi	Lingala	Sotho
Blackfeet	Hmong	Luo	Swahili
Cantonese	Hopi	Mandarin	Tagalog
Chatisgarhi	Ibibio	Mayan	Taiwanese
Cheyenne	Igbo	Navajo	Tigrinya
Chichewa	Ilocano	Nederlands	Tonga
Choctaw	Indonesian	Nivaclé	Tschocué
Comanche	Italiano	Ojibway	Tshiluba
Cree	Japanese	Oriya	Twi
Creek	Javanese	Orominga	Umbundu
Creole	Kekchi	Pilipino	Uraon
Deutsch	Khmu	Português	Vietnamese
Dioula	Kikongo	Punjabi	Xhosa
Efik	Kimbundu	Russian	Zulu
English	Kituba	Santali	
Español	Krobo	Saulteaux	Total 78

Peace concerns—Of those conferences from which we received questionnaires, 22 countries, accounting for 55 conferences, have no compulsory military service. Among them are the United States, Canada, India, and Japan. Of the 13 European countries listed, 11 have compulsory service, as do the majority of countries in Latin America (13 out of 24). At least eight conferences in countries with compulsory service clearly do not support conscientious objection. This figure is derived from the 106 questionnaires that were returned, citing only those that responded with a definite "no" to that question. Of those eight, some were recently established and some are in countries that have experienced war. Most conferences whose members are drafted support their members (at least ideally). Twenty-seven conferences indicated that they have members who reject war taxes.

Baptism—All but seven conferences who returned the first questionnaire answered this question, thus creating the most comprehensive account on the questionnaire. In all, 121 conferences exercise a single mode of baptism and 24 conferences practice two or three modes. Immersion turned out to be the most popular mode (73), widely used among Mennonite Brethren and Brethren in Christ groups and younger conferences as well. Next to immersion is pouring (67) ahead of sprinkling (29). It might be assumed that some conferences do not differentiate between sprinkling and pouring; therefore, both should be seen as one (96). Although the conference figures do not give information as to the number of baptisms applied to each mode, it seems to be a safe statement that baptism by immersion is gaining prominence and that the sprinkling mode is diminishing.

Confessions of faith—Mennonites are a creedal people. The overwhelming majority of 104 out of 126 conferences answering the question indicated that they have a written confession. The number and variety of confessions disclosed to *MWH* cannot be elaborated here. Their explanation and evaluation would be a challenging task for future research.

Worship—There seems to be a tendency to more worship services and meetings during the week than was customary in earlier times. Only three (conservative) groups meet regularly every two weeks. In 34 conferences a weekly service is customary, but 98 groups report that they meet at least twice a week—even five times (Cuba). Besides the Sunday worship, there are many occasions oriented toward particular subgroups within the church (young people, parents, women, etc.) or subjects of common interest (Bible study, peace, environment, etc.). Mennonites in older congregations do not seem to meet as frequently as others.

Church government—The first Anabaptist congregations 465 years ago were formed under strong anticlerical sentiment. This conviction led to a structure that we would call "congregational" today. Because Mennonites have been guided by tradition, it is not astounding that 76 conferences out of 129 report a congregational structure, i.e., independent congregations not subject to the regulations of the conference. Less than one-third of the conferences (45) use a synodal church government, i.e., sending representatives to a governing body that makes binding decisions. Only 21 conferences, including the Old Colony Mennonites to some extent, maintain episcopal structures, i.e., part of a hierarchy with leadership exerted by a bishop or governing body. (Included more than once are those groups that describe their church government as a combination of styles.) Both the synodal and episcopal patterns have their roots in Anabaptist history, the synodal with the Swiss brethren and the episcopal with the Mennonites.

Training—The survey reveals that conferences see a need to provide training for their leaders. The possibilities, however, differ depending on the size of the conference and their finances. Most of the institutions are in Canada and the

United States (see Training Section). The survey displayed in the Training Section is not complete, but it gives insight as to (1) Bible Schools, (2) Seminaries, (3) Theological Education by Extension (TEE), and (4) Liberal Arts Colleges. In the Conference Section, 103 conferences out of 145 gave 175 indications of some form of continuing education. TEE was indicated by 61 conferences, while 92 reported occasional seminars. Thirty-eight conferences use other tools for training their preachers, evangelists, and workers.

Interdenominational connections—Although Mennonites are reticent about outside relationships—especially with the World Council of Churches (WCC), in which two European conferences are members—there are many links to other denominations. Fifty-seven conferences report some connection to other denominations, mostly to evangelical groups or to various National Councils of Churches and their equivalent. The breakdown by continent may be significant: Only 3 in Canada/USA but 23 in Latin America, 13 in Europe, 11 in Africa, and 7 in Asia maintain connections to some degree.

Names—Twenty-one conferences out of 135 do not use the designation "Mennonite" in their conference name (excluding the two Hutterian groups and the 11 Brethren in Christ conferences). The oldest of these is the Algemene Doopsgezinde Sociëteit. Others include several conservative groups and conferences in Asia (4), Africa (1), and Latin America (7). One respondent voiced his concern: "… one wonders what the name 'Mennonite' really signifies … [it] does not mean such things as the aim, purpose, and teaching of that worthy leader …."

Agencies and Facilitation—The Dutch Doopsgezinde collected funds to help fellow believers in Danzig, Bern, and the Palatinate as early as 1660. They formed the first Mennonite relief agency, Fonds voor Buitenlandsche Nooden. Today numerous Mennonite agencies serve in mission (25), relief (23), or peace concerns (2). Some of these are listed in the Conference Section. The Agency Section and Facilitation Section display further examples.

With respect to figures for MCC (combined, about US $54 million), note that some revenue is obtained from non-Mennonite people and institutions. MCC employs more than 1,000 individuals, primarily of Mennonite background. Whereas most North American Mennonites support just one relief organization, MCC, they maintain various mission boards relating to different conferences. Combined budgets are lower than MCC (US $29.5 million), but the personnel is more numerous (1,600). Please read the statements of each organization's vision.

Diether Götz Lichdi, editor.

A. Conference Section Summary

Continent Continent Kontinent Continente	Country Pays Land País	Baptized Members Personnes baptisées Getaufte Glieder Miembros bautizados			Organized Bodies or Groups Organismes Organisierte Körperschaften Cuerpos o grupos organizados		
		1978	1984	1990	1978	1984	1990
Africa Afrique Afrika Africa	Angola*		192	1,250		1	1
	Burkina Faso		13	57		1	1
	Ethiopia	5,000	7,200	10,000	1	1	1
	Ghana	607	854	1,200	1	1	1
	Kenya*	1,200	2,700	4,900	1	1	2
	Malawi			420			1
	Nigeria	3,333	5,000	6,873	1	1	2
	Somalia*	100	100		1	1	1
	South Africa			107			2
	Tanzania	10,045	13,616	20,078	1	2	2
	Zaire*	59,548	66,408	112,906	3	3	3
	Zambia	2,455	6,000	6,632	1	1	1
	Zimbabwe	3,583	5,184	12,039	1	1	1
	Total	85,900	107,300	176,500	11	14	19
Asia/Australia Asie/Australie Asien/Australien Asia/Australia	Australia*	500	12	33	0	1	1
	Hong Kong		35	59		1	1
	India*	35,040	44,048	76,670	6	6	7
	Indonesia*	34,700	62,911	65,660	2	2	3
	Nippon	1,955	2,710	2,962	5	5	5
	Philippines	1,005	2,500	666	1	1	2
	Taiwan, ROC	907	1,200	1,493	1	1	1
	Vietnam*	150	150		1	1	1
	Total	74,300	113,600	147,600	16	18	21
Caribbean, Central & South America Caraïbes, Amérique Centrale et Sud Karibik, Zentral- und Südamerika Caribe, América Central y del Sur	Antigua**			725			1
	Argentina*	1,230	1,516	2,100	1	2	2
	Belize*	1,522	1,660	1,592	3	6	6
	Bolivia*	8,000	6,203	6,763	4	6	6
	Brasil*	3,462	4,785	6,209	4	4	5
	Chile		390			1	
	Colombia*	1,325	2,633	1,800	2	2	2
	Costa Rica	303	850	1,218	1	1	2
	Cuba			45		1	1
	Ecuador		15	140		1	1
	El Salvador		75	257		1	2
	Guatemala*	320	1,789	4,295	1	4	4
	Haïti*		900	914		3	3
	Honduras*	750	2,850	8,020	1	2	4
	Jamaica	300	385	422	1	1	1
	México*	13,800	31,161	19,626	6	8	9
	Nicaragua*	290	1,732	3,917	2	3	3
	Panamá	700	400	700	1	1	1

**(Barbados, Barbuda, Dominica, French St. Martin, Grenada, Guyana, Jamaica, St. Vincent, Tobago, Trinidad, US Virgin Islands)

Continent Continent Kontinent Continente	Country Pays Land País	Baptized Members Personnes baptisées Getaufte Glieder Miembros bautizados			Organized Bodies or Groups Organismes Organisierte Körperschaften Cuerpos o grupos organizados		
		1978	1984	1990	1978	1984	1990
Caribbean, Central & South America Caraïbes, Amérique Centrale et Sud Karibik, Zentral- und Südamerika Caribe, América Central y del Sur	Paraguay*	9,700	14,076	19,898	9	15	16
	Perú*			150			1
	Puerto Rico	765	909	868	1	1	1
	República Dominicana*	975	1,800	2,600	1	2	2
	Trinidad and Tobago*		44	110		1	1
	Uruguay*	769	971	877	1	3	3
	Venezuela*		85	120		1	2
	Total	44,300	75,300	83,400	39	70	79
Europe Europe Europa Europa	Belgique*	100	85	40	(1)	1	1
	BRD*	9,783	11,125	18,348	3	5	7
	DDR	285	244	168	1	1	1
	Eire		10	10		1	1
	España		28	214		2	2
	France	2,300	2,000	2,000	2	1	1
	Great Britain		30	27		1	1
	Italia	46	66	129	1	1	1
	Luxembourg*	100	105	100	(1)	1	1
	Nederland	25,589	20,200	18,000	1	1	1
	Österreich	182	1,050	300	(1)	1	1
	Schweiz*	2,626	2,750	3,000	1	1	1
	USSR*	55,000	55,000	26,200	4	4	4
	Total	96,100	92,700	68,600	13	21	23
North America Amérique du Nord Nordamerika América del Norte	Canada*	88,500	101,197	114,400**	7(10)	8	14(10)**
	United States*	224,500	238,794	266,100**	14	12	15**
	Total	313,000	340,000	380,500	21	20	29
	Grand Total	613,600	728,900	856,600	100	143	171

*Includes membership estimates. Nombres estimés inclus. Enthält geschätzte Mitgliedschaft. Incluye membresía estimada.
Continental totals rounded upward to the nearest 100. Total par continent, arrondi à la centaine supérieure. Total per Kontinent aufs nächste 100 aufgerundet. Los totales continentales han sido redondeados hacia arriba a la próxima centena.
( ) Counted in another country. Inclu dans le nombre d'un autre pays. Unter einem anderen Land gezählt. Incluído junto con otro país.

**For purposes of comparison with previous years, these figures were deduced from MWC sources and the help of Margaret Loewen Reimer. Figures from MWC questionnaires were as follows:

	Baptized Members	Organized Bodies or Groups
Canada*	55,316	14
Canada/USA*	276,316	10
USA*	48,826	5
Total	380,500	29

B. Christian community and baptized members

Continent	Christian Community	Baptized Members	Percentage of Christian Community to Members
Africa	229,914	176,500	130
Asia/Australia	356,581	147,600	240
CCSA*	124,236	83,400	150
Europe	82,505	68,600	120
North America	573,913	380,500	150
Total	1,367,149	856,600	160

*Caribbean, Central and South America.

C. Growth

Continent	Baptized Members (in thousands)			Increase 1978–90 per annum, rounded	Yearly Increase as %	Increase 1978–90 as %	Countries			Organized Bodies/ Groups		
	1990	1984	1978				1990	1984	1978	1990	1984	1978
Africa	176.5	107.3	85.9	7,550	8.8	105.5	13	11	9	19	14	11
Asia/Aust.	147.6	113.6	74.3	6,108	8.2	98.7	8	8	7	21	18	16
CCSA*	83.4	75.3	44.3	3,258	7.4	88.3	24	23	16	79	70	39
Europe	68.6	92.7	96.1	(2,292)	(2.4)	(28.9)	13	13	10	23	21	13
North Am.	380.5	340.0	313.0	5,625	1.8	21.6	2	2	2	29	20	21
Total	856.6	728.9	613.6	20,250	3.3	39.6	60	57	44	171	143	100

*Caribbean, Central and South America.

D. Countries with the most members

1	United States of America	266,100	7	Tanzania	20,078
2	Canada*	114,400	8	Paraguay*	19,898
3	Zaire*	112,906	9	México*	19,626
4	India	76,670	10	Federal Republic of Germany	18,348
5	Indonesia	65,660			
6	Soviet Union	26,200			

*Due to estimations, it is possible that relative positions should actually be reversed.

E. Ten conferences with most members

1 Mennonite Church General Assembly 102,276
2 Mennonite Savodara Sangam   63,250
3 Communauté Mennonite au Zaire   50,000
4 Gereja Injili di Tanah Jawa   47,000
5 Communauté des Eglises
    de Frères Mennonites au Zaire   46,906
6 General Conference of the
    Mennonite Brethren Churches   43,452
7 General Conference Mennonite
    Church (USA)   33,812
8 Conference of Mennonites in Canada   28,994
9 Brethren in Christ General Conference
    (North America)   19,853
10 Algemene Doopsgezinde Sociëteit   18,000

F. Ten conferences with fewest members

1 Soshanguve Brethren in Christ Church   7
2 Irish Mennonite Movement   10
3 Comunidad Cristiana de los Hermanos
    Menonitas de España   24
4 British Conference of Mennonites   27
5 Australian Conference of Evangelical
    Mennonites   33
6 Conseil Mennonite Belge   40
7 Iglesia Menonita (Amish—Honduras)   40
8 Sociedad Misionera Cubana
    Hermanos en Cristo   45
9 Mission et Eglise Mennonite
    au Burkina Faso   57
10 Conference of Mennonite Churches
    in Hong Kong   59

G. Conservative groups

	Membership (Estimated)	Christian Community (Estimated)
Hutterian Brethren*	14,000	35,000
Old Order Amish	56,200	127,800
Old Order Mennonite**	10,000	15,000
Old Colony/related, N. America	14,600	30,000
Old Colony/related, Latin America	30,100	70,000
Total	124,900	277,800 (182%)

*Not including Society of Brothers. **United States.

H. Size of congregations

Continent	Congregations*	Conferences	Members in thousands	Members per Congregation
Africa	1,230 (18)	19	176.5	143
Asia/Australia	1,212 (20)	21	147.6	122
CCSA**	810 (57)	79	83.4	103
Europe	310 (19)	23	68.6	221
North America	3,974 (29)	29	380.5	96
Total	7,536 (143)	171	856.6	114

*Figure in parenthesis indicates the number of conferences reporting. **Caribbean, Central and South America.
Mennonite congregations are small because (1) it is felt that community (fellowship) can best be maintained in a small congregation where all can share their concerns and joys, and (2) most Mennonites still live in scattered locations and are a gathered church. Our responses for congregations included 10 estimates out of 143 responses, or 510 congregations out of 7,536. This means that only 6.8 percent of the number of congregations were estimated, whereas 31.3 percent of membership figures were estimated (268,000 members out of 856,600).

I. Conferences with the most congregations

	Congregations	Members	Members per Congregation
1 Mennonite Church General Assembly	1,055	102,276	97
2 Mennonite Savodara Sangam	810	63,250	78
3 Hutterian Brethren	353	14,000	40
4 CMZ Zaire	350	50,000	143
5 General Conference of the MB Churches	317	43,452	137
6 General Conference Mennonite Church*	258	33,812	131
7 CEFMZ Zaire	228	46,906	206
8 Brethren in Christ General Conference	225	19,853	88
9 Ibandla Labazalwane ku Kristu e Zimbabwe	173	12,039	70
10 Conference of Mennonites in Canada	156	28,994	186
11 Algemene Doopsgezinde Sociëteit	139	18,000	129
12 KMT, Dayosisi ya Mara Kusini	130	13,078	101
13 Brethren in Christ Church (Zambia)	116	6,632	57
14 Church of God in Christ, Mennonite	111	12,694	114
15 Beachy Amish	105	7,238	69
Total	4,526	472,224	104

*Figures for the General Conference Mennonite Church include the United States only. The General Conference has member congregations in Canada and South America, but those congregations also belong to their respective national conferences and are counted with those conferences in this Directory.

J. Oldest conferences

Old Order River Brethren	c. 1780
Algemene Doopsgezinde Societeit	1811
Old Order Mennonites	1845
Verband deutscher Mennonitengemeinden	1854
Church of God in Christ, Mennonite	1859
General Conference Mennonite Church	1860
Evangelical Mennonite Church	1865
Old Order Amish	c. 1870
Brethren in Christ General Conference	1871
Hutterian Brethren	1874
General Conference of the Mennonite Brethren Churches	1879
Vereinigung der Deutschen Mennonitengemeinden	1886
Chortitzer Mennonite Conference	c. 1890
Konferenz der Mennoniten der Schweiz	c. 1890
Sommerfeld Mennonite Church	1894
Old Colony Mennonite Church—Saskatchewan	c. 1897
Mennonite Church	1898
Conference of Mennonites in Canada	1902
Brethren in Christ Church (Zambia)	1906
Communauté Mennonite au Zaire	1912
Mennonite Church in India	1912

Summary

Established	
Before 1920	19
1920–45	8
1946–60	24
1961–70	24
1971–80	27
1981–90	30
Total	132

K. Publications

Continent	Conferences With Periodicals	Conferences Without Periodicals	Publishing Houses
Africa	5	13	0
Asia/Australia	8	13	0
CCSA*	19	61	2
Europe	13	7	2
North America	13	16	7
Total	58	110	11

*Caribbean, Central and South America.
Some publications serve more than one conference. A few conferences publish more than one periodical, pushing the number of magazines and newspapers applying to Mennonites to 70–80.

L. Mennonite World Conference Assemblies 1925–1990

Year	City	Theme	President
1925	Basel	400th Anniversary of the Founding of Anabaptism	Christian Neff
1930	Danzig	Mennonite World Relief Work, Mennonites in the USSR	Christian Neff
1936	Amsterdam	400th Anniversary of Menno Simons	Christian Neff
1948	Goshen/ Newton	Brotherhood and Reconciliation	P.C. Hiebert
1952	Basel	The Church of Christ and Her Commission	H.S. Bender
1957	Karlsruhe	The Gospel of Jesus Christ in the World	H.S. Bender
1962	Kitchener	The Lordship of Christ	H.S. Bender
1967	Amsterdam	The Witness of the Holy Spirit	Erland Waltner
1972	Curitiba	Jesus Christ Reconciles	Erland Waltner
1978	Wichita	The Kingdom of God in a Changing World	Million Belete
1984	Strasbourg	God's People Serve in Hope	Charles Christano
1990	Winnipeg	Witnessing to Christ in Today's World	Ross T. Bender

Conferences

(Pages 335-417)

1	Address and year established
2	Languages used by members
	Officers
3	Moderator
4	Treasurer
5	Executive secretary
6	Send mail to
	Publications
7	Official periodical name and address
8	Publishing agency
	Peace concerns
9	a) Compulsory military service; b) Government provision for conscientious objection (CO); c) Church officially supports CO; d) Government-approved alternative service options; e) Some church members reject war taxes
	Mission
10	Mission organization(s)
11	Total number of workers
12	Total annual budget
	Service
13	Service organization(s)
14	Total number of workers
15	Total annual budget
	Membership and organization
16	Number of congregations
17	Number of places of worship
18	Total Christian community
19	Number of baptized members
20	Baptism: a) sprinkling; b) pouring; c) immersion
21	Confession of faith?: a) yes; b) no
22	Worship services per week
23	Average attendance as percentage of membership
24	Church government: a) congregational; b) synodal; c) episcopal
	Leadership
25	Ordained preachers/elders
26	Evangelists/church planters
27	Salaried ministers
28	Number of Bible schools/seminaries
29	Other leadership training: a) theological education by extension; b) occasional seminars; c) other
30	Global denominational family

Conférences

(Page 335-417)

1	Adresse et année de fondation
2	Langues utilisées par les membres
	Responsables
3	Président/e
4	Trésorièr/e
5	Secrétaire
6	Adresse de contact
	Publications
7	Périodique officiel—nom et adresse
8	Editeur
	Questions concernant la paix
9	a) Service militaire obligatoire; b) Statut d'objecteur de conscience reconnu par l'Etat; c) Soutien officiel des objecteurs de conscience par l'Eglise; d) Service civil reconnu par l'Etat; e) Membres d'Eglises refusant de payer les impôts militaires
	Mission
10	Organismes missionnaires
11	Nombre total des collaborateurs
12	Budget annuel total
	Diaconie
13	Organismes de service
14	Nombre total des collaborateurs
15	Budget annuel total
	Membres et organisation
16	Nombre d'assemblées
17	Nombre de lieux de culte
18	Nombre total de la communauté
19	Nombre de personnes baptisées
20	Forme du baptême: a) aspersion; b) effusion; c) immersion
21	Confession de foi?: a) oui; b) non
22	Fréquence des cultes par semaine
23	Pourcentage de participation par rapport au nombre total de membres
24	Direction de l'Eglise: a) congrégationelle; b) synodale; c) épiscopale
	Responsables
25	Prédicateurs et anciens consacrés
26	Evangélistes/implanteurs d'églises
27	Responsables salariés
28	Nombre d'écoles bibli./séminaires
29	Autres formations des responsables: a) formation théologique décentrée; b) séminaires occasionnels; c) autres
30	Orientation la plus proche dans la famille mennonite

Konferenzen

(Seite 335-417)

Convenciones

(Páginas 335-417)

	Konferenzen		Convenciones
1	Anschrift und Gründungsjahr	1	Dirección y año establecido
2	Sprache	2	Idioma usado por miembros
	Vorstand		**Oficiales**
3	Vorsitzender/Präsident	3	Presidente
4	Kassenführer	4	Tesorero
5	Schriftführer	5	Secretario ejecutivo
6	Postanschrift	6	Enviar correspondencia a
	Publikationen		**Publicaciones**
7	Name und Anschrift	7	Nombre y dir. de publicación oficial
8	Verlag	8	Agencia publicadora
	Friedensbelange		**Asuntos relacionados con la paz**
9	a) Kriegsdienst; b) Kriegsdienstverweigerung; c) Unterstützung für KDV; d) Ersatzdienst; e) Kriegssteuerverweigerung	9	a) Servicio militar obligatorio; b) Provisión gubernamental para la objeción por conciencia (OC); c) La iglesia apoya oficialmente la OC; d) Opciones aprobadas por el gobierno para servicio alternativo; e) Algunos miembros rechazan los impuestos militares
	Mission		**Misión**
10	Missionswerke	10	Organización(es) misionera(s)
11	Zahl der Mitarbeiter	11	Número total de obreros
12	Jahreshaushalt	12	Presupuesto anual total
	Diakonie		**Servicio**
13	Hilfswerk(e)	13	Organizaciones de servicio
14	Zahl der Mitarbeiter	14	Número total de obreros
15	Jahreshaushalt	15	Presupuesto anual total
	Mitgliedschaft und Organisation		**Membresía y organización**
16	Zahl der Gemeinden	16	Número de congregaciones
17	Zahl der Predigtplätze	17	Número de lugares de adoración
18	Zahl der Glieder und Gäste	18	Comunidad cristiana total
19	Zahl der Glieder	19	Número de miembros bautizados
20	Taufe durch: a) Besprengen; b) Begießen; c) Untertauchen	20	Bautismo: a) aspersión; b) derramamiento de agua; c) inmersión
21	Glaubensbekenntnis?: a) Ja; b) Nein	21	¿Confesión de fe?: a) sí; b) no
22	Zahl der Gottesdienste je Gemeinde und Woche	22	Frecuencia de reuniones por semana
23	Gottesdienstbesuch in % der Gliederzahl	23	Asistencia promedio (porcentaje de la membresía)
24	Konferenzstruktur: a) kongregational; b) synodal; c) bischöflich	24	Gobierno eclesial: a) congregacional; b) sinodal; c) episcopal
	Mitarbeiterschaft		**Liderato**
25	Zahl der Prediger/Ältesten	25	Pastores/diáconos ordenados
26	Evangelisten/Gemeindebauer	26	Evangelistas/personas que plantan iglesias
27	angestellte Pastoren	27	Pastores con salario
28	Bibelschulen/Seminare	28	Institutos bíblicos/seminarios
29	andere Ausbildungsmöglichkeiten: a) Fernstudium; b) gelegentliche Seminare; c) sonstiges	29	Otro entrenamiento de líderes: a) educación teológica por extensión; b) seminarios ocasionales; c) otro
30	interkonfessionelle Beziehungen	30	Familia denominacional mundial

Agencies/Facilitation

(Pages 418-436)

Oeuvres/Coordination

(Page 418-436)

The first paragraph of the column describes the purpose, goal, or vision of the organization.

Le premier paragraphe de la colonne désigne l'objet, le but ou la vision de l'organisation.

1	Alternative name or initials by which the organization is known
2	Address
3	Telephone number
4	Telex number
5	Facsimile machine number
6	Cable code
7	Year established
	Officers
8	Chairperson
9	Chief executive officer
10	Treasurer
	Sponsors
11	Group or groups that sponsor this organization
	Budget
12	Currency for amounts shown below
13	Total annual income
14	Annual income received from Mennonite/Brethren in Christ conferences and congregations
15	Annual income received from private individuals or companies
16	Annual income received from non-Mennonite/Brethren in Christ individuals and organizations
17	Total annual expense
18	Annual expense for personnel
19	Annual expense for material (merchandise)
	Employees/workers
20	Number of full-time employees
21	Number of part-time employees
22	Number of volunteers

1	Autre nom ou sigle de l'organisation
2	Adresse
3	Numéro de téléphone
4	Numéro de télex
5	Numéro du téléfax
6	Adresse télégraphique
7	Année de fondation
	Responsables
8	Président/e
9	Fondé de pouvoir
10	Trésorièr/e
	Patronage
11	Groupe(s) patronnant l'organisation
	Budget
12	Monnaie utilisée dans les chiffres ci-dessous
13	Revenu annuel total
14	Revenus annuels reçus des conférences et assemblées mennonites et des Frères en Christ
15	Revenus annuels reçus de particuliers ou de compagnies privées
16	Revenus annuels reçus de particuliers ou d'organisations non-mennonites/Frères en Christ
17	Dépenses totales annuelles
18	Dépenses annuelles pour le personnel
19	Dépenses annuelles pour les biens (marchandises)
	Employé(e)s/ Collaborateurs(trices)
20	Nombre d'employés à plein temps
21	Nombres d'employés à temps partiel
22	Nombre de volontaires

Werke/Handreichung
(Seite 418-436)

Agencias/Facilitación
(Páginas 418-436)

Werke/Handreichung	Agencias/Facilitación
Zweck, Ziel und Vision	El primer párrafo de la columna describe el propósito, objetivo, o visión de la organización.
1 Name/Abkürzung	
2 Anschrift	
3 Telephon	1 Nombre alternativo o iniciales por las cuales se conoce a la organi- zación
4 Telex	
5 Telefax	
6 Telegrammadresse	2 Dirección
7 Gründungsjahr	3 Número telefónico
Leitung	4 Número de télex
8 Vorsitzender	5 Número de máquina de telefax/ facsímil
9 Geschäftsführer	
10 Kassenführer	6 Código de cable
Sponsoren	7 Año establecida
11 Träger	**Oficiales**
Jahreshaushalt	8 Persona que preside
12 Währungseinheit	9 Oficial ejecutivo principal
13 jährliche Einnahmen	10 Tesorero
14 … von Konferenzen/Gemeinden	**Auspiciadores**
15 … von Personen/Firmen	11 Grupo o grupos que auspician esta organización
16 … von nichtmennonitischen Gebern	
17 jährliche Ausgaben	**Presupuesto**
18 davon Personalkosten	12 Moneda de las cantidades señaladas abajo
19 davon Sachkosten	
Mitarbeiter (nach Köpfen)	13 Entrada anual total
20 davon vollzeitig	14 Entrada anual recibida de con- venciones y congregaciones Menonitas/Hermanos en Cristo
21 davon teilzeitig	
22 davon Freiwillige	
	15 Entrada anual recibida de individuos y compañías privadas
	16 Entrada anual recibida de individuos y organizaciones no Menonitas/ Hermanos en Cristo
	17 Gasto anual total
	18 Gasto anual para personal
	19 Gasto anual para materiales (mercadería)
	Empleados/obreros
	20 Número de empleados a tiempo completo
	21 Número de empleados a tiempo parcial
	22 Número de voluntarios

Conferences

Angola, Burkina Faso
Angola, Burkina Faso
Angola, Burkina Faso
Angola, Burkina Faso

Igreja Evangélica Irmãos Mennonitas Renovada em Angola	Mission et Eglise Mennonite au Burkina Faso

	Igreja Evangélica Irmãos Mennonitas Renovada em Angola		Mission et Eglise Mennonite au Burkina Faso
1	C.P. 6764, Luanda, Angola (1980)	1	B.P. 40, Orodara, Burkina Faso (1980)
2	Português, Français, Kikongo, Kimbundu, Kuaniama, Tshocué, Umbundu	2	Français, Dioula
		3	Siaka Traore *Comité Directeur*
3	Domingos Lukato za-Kindakisa *Président*	4	
4	Francisco Suama *Trésorier-Financier*	5	
5	Bozo David Mabeia *Représentant Légal*	6	Ouedraogo P. Paul
6	Bozo David Mabeia		
7		7	
8		8	
		9	
9	a, c	10	
		11	
10		12	
11			
12		13	
		14	
13	c/o Domingos Lukato za-Kindakisa, C.P. 3819, Luanda	15	
14	7		
15	240.000 Kuanzas (US $8,000)		

16	13	21	a	26	17
17		22	3	27	46
18		23	69.5	28	0
19	1,250 ±	24	b	29	b, c
20	c	25	58	30	MB

16	1	21	a	26	
17	4	22	2	27	
18	110	23		28	0
19	57	24	b	29	a, b
20	c	25		30	

Africa
Afrique
Afrika
Africa

Ethiopia, Ghana
Ethiopie, Ghana
Äthiopien, Ghana
Etiopía, Ghana

<table>
<tr><td colspan="2">

Meserete Kristos Church

</td><td colspan="2">

Ghana Mennonite Church

</td></tr>
</table>

	Meserete Kristos Church		Ghana Mennonite Church
1	P.O. Box 24227, Addis Ababa, Ethiopia ☎ [251] (1) 112387 (1959)	1	P.O. Box 5485, Accra-North, Ghana (1962)
2	Amharic, Orominga, Tigrinya	2	English, Adangbe, Ewe, Ga, Shai, Twi, Krobo
3	Soloman Kebete *Moderator*	3	Samuel Tetteh Okrah *Moderator*
4		4	Edmund Bannerman *Conference Treasurer*
5	Yohannes Germamo *Administrative Secretary*	5	Prince Asilevi *Conference Secretary*
6	Yohannes Germamo	6	Prince Asilevi
7		7	
8		8	
9	a	9	c
10		10	
11		11	
12		12	
13		13	
14		14	
15		15	

Meserete Kristos Church

16	31	21		26	56
17	1,484	22		27	
18	19,320	23		28	
19	10,000	24	b	29	
20		25	180	30	MC

Ghana Mennonite Church

16	17	21	a	26	1
17	20	22	2	27	3
18	1,800	23	80	28	0
19	1,200	24	b	29	a, b
20	a (70%), c	25	25	30	MC

Africa
Afrique
Afrika
Africa

Kenya
Kénya
Kenia
Kenya

Kenya Mennonite Church, Kisumu Diocese

1	P.O. Box 4351, Kondele, Kisumu, Kenya (1988)
2	English, Swahili, Luo
3	Musa Adongo *Bishop and Chairman*
4	Moses Otieno *Treasurer*
5	Samuel Adongo *Secretary*
6	Musa Adongo
7	
8	
9	c, e
10	
11	
12	
13	
14	
15	

16	20 ±	21	a	26	30 ±
17	20 ±	22	2	27	0
18	3,600 ±	23	80	28	0
19	900 ±	24	c	29	a, b, c
20	b	25	10 ±	30	MC

Kenya Mennonite Church, Southern Diocese

1	P.O. Box 39, Suna, Migori, Kenya (1988)
2	English, Swahili, Luo
3	Joshua Okello Ouma *Bishop*
4	Peter N. Oruongo *Treasurer*
5	Philip E. Okeyo *General Secretary*
6	Joshua Okello Ouma
7	
8	
9	c, e
10	Ogwedhi Sigawa Community Development Project, P.O. Box 512, Suna
11	
12	
13	
14	
15	

16	46	21	a	26	11
17	50	22	1	27	0
18	4,500	23	80	28	0
19	4,000	24	c	29	a, b, c
20	b (98%), c	25	14	30	MC

Africa
Afrique
Afrika
Africa

Malawi
Malawi
Malawi
Malawi

Mpingo Wa Abale
Mwa Yesu

1	P.O. Box 2544, Blantyre, Malawi (1986)
2	English, Chichewa
3	Selemani Chibwana *Wapampando*
4	Ephraim Bainet Disi *Msungichuma*
5	Ephraim Bainet Disi *Mlembi*
6	Ephraim Bainet Disi
7	
8	
9	
10	
11	
12	
13	
14	
15	

16	25	21		26	1
17	15	22	2	27	1
18	800	23	80	28	0
19	420	24	b	29	
20	c	25	0	30	BIC

Africa
Afrique
Afrika
Africa

Nigeria
Nigéria
Nigeria
Nigeria

Church of God in Christ, Mennonite (Nigeria)

Mennonite Church (Nigeria)

	Church of God in Christ, Mennonite (Nigeria)		Mennonite Church (Nigeria)
1	P.O. Box 129, Ile-Ife, Oyo State, Nigeria	1	P.O. Box 123, Uyo, Akwa Ibom State, Nigeria
2	English		(1959)
		2	English, Efik, Ibibio, Annang, Igbo
3		3	Ime Udo Nsasak *Bishop/Moderator*
4		4	Bassey Peter Amadak *Treasurer*
5		5	Nseobong Francis Uko *National Secretary*
6		6	Nseobong Francis Uko
7			
8			
9	c	7	
		8	
10		9	
11			
12		10	
13		11	
14		12	
15		13	
		14	
		15	

	Church of God in Christ, Mennonite						Mennonite Church					
16	10	21	a	26		16	57	21	a	26	18
17		22	2	27		17	60	22	2	27	60
18		23		28		18	10,008	23	80	28	
19	239	24	b	29		19	6,634	24	c	29	a, b
20	b	25		30	CGC	20	c	25	102	30	MC

Africa
Afrique
Afrika
Africa

South Africa
Afrique du Sud
Südafrika
Africa del Sur

Community Church Movement

Soshanguve Brethren in Christ Church

	Community Church Movement		Soshanguve Brethren in Christ Church
1	P.O. Box 96, Lotus River, 7805 Cape Town, South Africa ☎ [27] (21) 62-1367 (1989)	1	P.O. Box 8276, Pretoria 0001, South Africa (1987)
2	Xhosa, English	2	Sotho, Zulu
3	F. Norawana	3	S.M. Maloka *Moruti*
4	Graham Cyster	4	A.P. Nkuna
5	Peter Fuba	5	K.H. Madlabane *Mfundisi*
6	Graham Cyster	6	K.H. Madlabane
7		7	
8		8	
9	a, b, c, d	9	a, b, d
10		10	
11		11	
12		12	
13		13	
14		14	
15		15	

Community Church Movement:

16	3	21	a	26	5
17	5	22	2	27	1
18	300	23	70	28	0
19	100	24	b	29	a, b, c
20	c	25	0	30	

Soshanguve Brethren in Christ Church:

16	2	21	a	26	3
17	2	22	2	27	2
18	70	23	70	28	0
19	7	24	b, c	29	c
20	c	25	5	30	BIC

Africa
Afrique
Afrika
Africa

Tanzania
Tanzanie
Tansania
Tanzania

Kanisa la Mennonite Tanzania, Dayosisi ya Mara Kaskazini

Kanisa la Mennonite Tanzania, Dayosisi ya Mara Kusini

	Mara Kaskazini		Mara Kusini
1	Shirati Hospital, Private Bag, Musoma, Tanzania (1979)	1	P.O. Box 7, Musoma, Tanzania; P.O. Box 120, Musoma, Tanzania (1980)
2	Swahili, Kurya, Luo	2	Swahili, English
3	Zedekia Marwa Kisare *Askofu*	3	Salmon S. Buteng'e *Makamu Mwenyekiti*
4	John O. Nyagwegwe *Mtunza Hazina*		
5	Lawrence Makonyu *Katibu Msaidizi*	4	Koreni S. Togoro *Mtunza Hazina*
6	Zedekia Marwa Kisare	5	Joram M. Mbeba *Katibu Mkuu*
		6	Joram M. Mbeba
7		7	*Maendeleo Matawin*, Box 7, Musoma
8		8	Musoma Mennonite Press
9	c	9	c
10		10	
11		11	
12		12	
13		13	
14		14	
15		15	

	Mara Kaskazini							Mara Kusini					
16	7	21	b	26	21		16	130	21	a	26	146
17	66	22	1	27	17		17	130	22	1	27	35
18	12,056	23	75	28	0		18	14,500	23	70	28	1
19	7,000	24	b, c	29	a, b		19	13,078	24	b, c	29	a, b, c
20	b	25	49	30	MC		20	a, b	25	181	30	MC

Zaire
Zaire
Zaire
Zaire

Communauté des Egl. de Frères Mennonites au Zaire (CEFMZ)	Communauté Evangélique Mennonite (CEM)

#	CEFMZ	#	CEM
1	B.P. 81, Kikwit, Zaire (1945)	1	B.P. 440, Mbuji Mayi/Kasai Oriental, Zaire (1962)
2	Kituba, Français	2	Français, Lingala, Swahili, Tshiluba
3	Kusangila Mwemba Kitondo *Président et Représentant Légal*	3	Mukengeshayi Lukasu *Président*
4	Ngunza *Secrétaire Financier*	4	Nsumbu Mulunda *Trésorier Général*
5	Mumbimba *Secrétaire Comptable*	5	Nkumbi Mudiayi Shambuyi *Secrétaire Général et Représentant Légal*
6	Kusangila Mwemba Kitondo	6	Nkumbi Mudiayi Shambuyi
7	*Mwinda*, B.P. 4714, Kinshasa II	7	*Kilisto Ehele*, B.P. 440, Mbuji Mayi/ Kasai Oriental
8		8	
9		9	c, e
10	Frères Mennonites à Bangui, B.P. 988, Bangui (République Centrafricaine); Bureau de la Mission, B.P. 81, Kikwit	10	
11	8	11	
12	US $7,500	12	
13		13	
14		14	
15		15	

#		#		#		#		#		#	
16	228	21	a	26	4	16	1	21	b	26	40
17		22	1–2	27	16	17	145	22	4	27	120
18		23	62	28	0	18	17,600	23	80	28	1
19	46,906	24	b	29	a	19	16,000	24	b	29	b
20	c	25	97	30	MB	20	c	25	110	30	

Africa
Afrique
Afrika
Africa

Zaire
Zaire
Zaire
Zaire

Egl. du Christ au Zaire, Communauté Mennonite au Zaire (CMZ)

1	B.P. 18, Tshikapa, Zaire; B.P. 4081, Kinshasa 2, Zaire (1912)
2	Français, Kituba, Lingala, Swahili, Tshiluba
3	Cibulenu Sakayimbo *Président et Représentant Légal*
4	Kabeya Kanda Mwana
5	
6	Cibulenu Sakayimbo
7	
8	
9	
10	
11	
12	
13	
14	
15	

16	350 ±	21	a	26	8
17	350 ±	22	2	27	
18	62,500 ±	23	90	28	1
19	50,000 ±	24	b	29	a, b
20	c	25	821	30	

Africa
Afrique
Afrika
Africa

Zambia, Zimbabwe
Zambie, Zimbabwe
Sambia, Simbabwe
Zambia, Zimbabwe

Brethren in Christ Church (Zambia)

Ibandla Labazalwane ku Kristu e Zimbabwe

1	Box 630115, Choma, Zambia (1906)	1	P.O. Box 711, Bulawayo, Zimbabwe (1963)
2	English, Tonga	2	English, Sindebele
3	Enock Shamapani *Bishop*	3	Stephen N. Ndlovu *Umfundisi Omkhulu*
4	Mukuwa Kalambo *Muyobozi we-Nkomo ya-Mali*	4	Jake Shenk *Umphathisikhwama*
5	D.C. Hamulumbu *Mulembi*	5	Leslie Khumalo *Umabhalane*
6	Enock Shamapani	6	Stephen N. Ndlovu
7	*Monthly Newsletter*, Brethren in Christ Church, Box 630115, Choma	7	*Amazwi Amahle*, P.O. Box 711, Bulawayo
8		8	
9	a	9	a, c
10	Nahumba Mission, Box 630115, Choma ☎ [260] (32) 20278	10	Brethren in Christ Church, 92 Jameson Street, Bulawayo ☎ [263] (9) 62839
11	2	11	40
12	Kwacha 35,000 (US $1,700)	12	US $8,000
13		13	
14		14	
15		15	

16	116	21	a	26	0	16	173	21	a	26	9
17	123	22	2	27	8	17	196	22	2	27	13
18	10,000	23		28	1	18		23	69	28	1
19	6,632	24	b	29	a, b, c	19	12,039	24	c	29	b
20	c	25	11	30	BIC	20	c	25	21	30	BIC

Asia/Australia
Asie/Australie
Asien/Australien
Asia/Australia

Australia, Hong Kong
Australie, Hong-Kong
Australien, Hongkong
Australia, Hong Kong

Australian Conference of Evangelical Mennonites	Conference of Mennonite Churches in Hong Kong

	Australian Conference of Evangelical Mennonites		Conference of Mennonite Churches in Hong Kong
1	9 Brougham Ave., Fennell Bay, N.S.W. 2283, Australia (1980)	1	Hong Kong Mennonite Centre, 76 Waterloo Road 1/F, Kowloon, Hong Kong (1985)
2	English	2	Cantonese
3	Foppe Brouwer *Chairperson*	3	Wong Wing-Sang (Paul)
4	A. McQueen *Treasurer*	4	Chan Ling (Peggy)
5	Pam Rouse *Secretary*	5	Tang Roden
6	Foppe Brouwer	6	Wong Wing-Sang (Paul)
7	*Yearly Newsletter*, 9 Brougham Ave., Fennell Bay, N.S.W. 2283	7	
8		8	
9	c	9	c
10		10	
11		11	
12		12	
13	Care and Share, 9 Brougham Ave., Fennell Bay, N.S.W. 2283 ☎ [61] (49) 593847	13	
14	4	14	
15	Australian $3,000 (US $2,370)	15	

16	3	21	a	26	3
17	3	22	2	27	0
18	70	23	85	28	0
19	33	24	a	29	b
20	a, b, c	25	3	30	MC

16	3	21	a	26	1
17	3	22	2	27	1 1/2
18	85	23	75–100	28	0
19	59	24	b	29	b, c
20	a (90%), c	25	4	30	GC/MC

India
Inde
Indien
India

Bharatiya General Conference Mennonite Kalisiya

Bharatiya Jukta Christa Prachar Mandali

1	P.O. Jagdeeshpur, Dist: Raipur MP 493 555, India (1926)
2	Hindi, Chatisgarhi, Oriya
3	B.J. Kumar *Sabhapati*
4	Z.B. Gardia *Khajanchi*
5	S. Benn *Sachiv*
6	B.J. Kumar, Z.B. Gardia, S. Benn
7	*Mennonite Darpan*, P.O. Jagdeeshpur, Dist: Raipur MP 493 555
8	BGCMC
9	c, e
10	
11	
12	
13	P.R.E.A.C.H. Board, P.O. Jagdeeshpur, Dist: Raipur MP 493 555
14	7
15	

1	Hastings Chapel, 10 St. Georges Gate Road, Calcutta 700 022, India (1958)
2	Bengali, English
3	Pronoy Sarkar *Chairman*
4	
5	Srinath Marandi *General Secretary*
6	Pronoy Sarkar
7	
8	
9	
10	
11	
12	
13	
14	
15	

16	22	21	a	26	34
17	55	22	2	27	34
18	12,000	23	50	28	3
19	6,000	24	b, c	29	a, b
20	a	25	34	30	GC

16	30 ±	21		26	
17		22		27	
18		23		28	
19	2,500 ±	24		29	
20		25		30	

Asia/Australia
Asie/Australie
Asien/Australien
Asia/Australia

India
Inde
Indien
India

Bihar Mennonite Mandli

1	Mennonite Mission Compound, P.O. Chandwa, Dist. Palamau, Bihar 829 203, India (1948)
2	Hindi
3	Danial Tirkey
4	Walter Khakha
5	Sushil Kumar Topno
6	Sushil Kumar Topno
7	
8	
9	
10	
11	
12	
13	Mennonite Service Agency, Chandwa, Palamau, Bihar
14	5
15	535,000 Rupees (US $31,800)

16	16	21	a	26	1
17		22	1	27	
18		23		28	0
19	700 ±	24	a	29	
20		25	7	30	MC

Brethren in Christ Church Orissa

1	Bank Colony, P.O. Medical College, Berhampur, Orissa 760004, India (1981)
2	English, Oriya
3	Manoranjan Roul *Chairman*
4	Sudhansu Das *Treasurer*
5	Pramod Kumar Roul *Secretary*
6	Pramod Kumar Roul
7	
8	
9	e
10	
11	
12	
13	
14	
15	

16	14	21	a	26	10
17	20	22	2	27	12
18	2,000	23	95	28	0
19	240	24	a	29	b
20	c	25	2	30	BIC

**India
Inde
Indien
India**

Brethren in Christ Church Society

Mennonite Church in India

	Brethren in Christ Church Society		Mennonite Church in India
1	Box 6, Purnea, Bihar 854 301, India (1968)	1	P.O. Gurur, Durg (MP) 4, India (1912)
2	Hindi, Santali, Uraon	2	English, Hindi
3	Samuel Hembrom *General Director*	3	O.P. Lall *Moderator*
4	Hem K. Paul *Treasurer*	4	J. Das *Treasurer*
5	Patras Das *Secretary*	5	G.C. Paul *Executive Secretary*
6	Samuel Hembrom	6	G.C. Paul
7		7	
8		8	
9	e	9	e
10		10	
11		11	
12		12	
13	Brethren in Christ Development Society, Mission Compound, P.O. Banmankhi, Purnea, Bihar	13	CASA, Rachna Building, 2 Rajendra Place, New Delhi 110008
14	6	14	
15	135,000 Rupees (US $8,000)	15	

16	42	21	b	26	10	16	15	21	a	26	2
17		22	1	27	8	17	18	22	2	27	3
18		23	60	28	0	18	2,980	23	50	28	0
19	1,920	24	b	29	b	19	2,060	24	c	29	a, b
20	c	25	8	30	BIC	20	b	25	20	30	MC

**India
Inde
Indien
India**

Mennonite Savodara Sangam

1	MB Medical Centre, Jadcherla 509302 AP, India (1958)
2	

3	P.B. Arnold *Adyakksudu*
4	D.S. Krupadanm *Koshadikari*
5	M.B. Devadass *Kariyadarsi*
6	P.B. Arnold

7	
8	
9	
10	
11	
12	
13	
14	
15	

16	810	21		26	
17	820	22		27	
18	240,000	23		28	
19	63,250	24		29	
20		25		30	MB

**Indonesia
Indonésie
Indonesien
Indonesia**

Gereja Injili di Tanah Jawa (GITJ)

Persatuan Gereja-Gereja Kristen Muria Indonesia (GKMI)

	Gereja Injili di Tanah Jawa (GITJ)		Persatuan Gereja-Gereja Kristen Muria Indonesia (GKMI)
1	Jl. Penjawi 48, Pati 59111, Jateng, Indonesia (1940)	1	Jl. Sompok Lama 60, Semarang 50249, Jateng, Indonesia (1920)
2	Javanese, Indonesian	2	Indonesian
3	Drie Sutantyo Brotosudarmo *General Chairman*	3	Agus Suwantoro
4	H. Manurung *Treasurer*	4	Adi Gunawan
5	Soesanto Harso *General Secretary*	5	Yesaya Abdi K.J.
6	Soesanto Harso	6	Yesaya Abdi K.J.
7		7	*Berita GKMI*, Jl. Sompok Lama 60, Semarang 50249, Jateng
8		8	
9		9	
10		10	PIPKA
11		11	
12		12	
13		13	Yayasan Pembinaan Dan Pengembangan Swadaya (YPPS), Jl. K.H. Wahid Hasyim 76–78, Kudus 59317 ☎ [62] (291) 21524
14		14	
15		15	

	GITJ						GKMI				
16	60	21		26		16	26	21	b	26	23
17	171	22		27		17	26	22	1	27	14
18	60,000 ±	23		28	1	18	19,679	23	76–86	28	0
19	47,000 ±	24		29		19	16,160	24	a, b	29	a
20		25		30	ADS	20	a	25	63	30	

Indonesia
Indonésie
Indonesien
Indonesia

Sinode Jemaat Kristen Indonesia (JKI)

1	Jl. Brigjen Sudiarto 20, Ungaran, Jawa Tengah 50511, Indonesia
	(1985)
2	Indonesian
3	Lukas F. Susiloputro *Ketua Umum*
4	Mrs. Timotius Sugiarto *Bendahara*
5	S. Hadi Suwignjo *Sekretaris*
6	Lukas F. Susiloputro
7	*Suara Pelayanan* (Surya), Brigjen Sudiarto 20, Ungaran, Jateng 50511
8	
9	
10	
11	
12	
13	
14	
15	

16	45	21	a	26	0		
17	45	22	1	27	2		
18	4,000	23	85	28	1		
19	2,500	24	a	29	a, b		
20	c	25	15	30			

**Japan
Japon
Japan
Japón**

Japan Mennonite Christian Church Conference

Nihon Kirisuto Keiteidan

1	NTT Apt. 213, Minami-12 Nishi-12, Chuo-ku, Sapporo 064, Nippon (1956)
2	Japanese

3	Tetsuo Maruyama *Shikkōiinchō*
4	Kazuko Kanaya *Kaikeikakari*
5	Toshihiko Sakabe *Shoki*
6	Tetsuo Maruyama

7	*Michi*, T. Nashimoto, 3-jo 6-chome Suehiro, Asahigawa 071; *Kakehashi*, Y. Kobayashi, 2-6, 3-chome Azabu-cho, Kita-ku, Sapporo 001; *Izumi*, T. Igarashi, 3-ban 16, Sono-cho Oasa, Ebetsu 069
8	

9	e

10	
11	
12	
13	
14	
15	

16	19	21	b	26	0
17	20	22	1–2	27	6
18		23	82	28	1
19	410	24	a	29	a, b, c
20	b (95%), c	25	2	30	MC

1	1179 Higashi Fukagawa, Nagato, Yamaguchi 759-41, Nippon (1971)
2	Japanese

3	Asao Nishimura *Iincho*
4	Hidetane Sugata *Kaikei*
5	
6	Asao Nishimura

7	
8	
9	
10	
11	
12	
13	
14	
15	

16	6	21	a	26	3
17	6	22	2	27	2
18		23	95	28	0
19	97	24	b	29	b
20	c	25	3	30	BIC

Japan
Japon
Japan
Japón

Nihon Menonaito Kirisuto Kyokai Kaigi

Nippon Menonaito Burezaren Kyodan

Nihon Menonaito Kirisuto Kyokai Kaigi	Nippon Menonaito Burezaren Kyodan
1 2-20 Kirishima, Miyazaki-shi 880, Nippon (1964)	1 1-12, 2 chome, Ikeda, Osaka 563, Nippon (1964)
2 Japanese	2 Japanese
3 Masafumi Shibahara *Gicho*	3 Toshihiko Etoh *Gicho*
4 Tsuguo Matoba *Shuji (Kaikei)*	4 Kiyotaka Kunisue *Kaikei*
5 Yoshiaki Maekawa *Shoki*	5 Yuzo Takatani *Syoki*
6 Masafumi Shibahara	6 Toshihiko Etoh
7 *Menonaito*, 2-7-1 Nakatsuru, Oita-shi 870	7 *Yokz. Otozure*, 1-12, 2 chome, Ikeda, Osaka 563
8	8
9 e	9 c
10	10 Foreign Mission Committee Meeting, 1-12, 2 chome, Ikeda, Osaka 563 ☎ [81] (6) 727-61-1397
11	11 5
12	12 ¥ 4.635.000 (US $32,250)
13	13 Welfare Committee Meeting, 1-12, 2 chome, Ikeda, Osaka 563
14	14 5
15	15 ¥ 150.000 (US $1,000)

16	18	21	a	26	9
17	24	22	1	27	4
18		23	50	28	0
19	763	24	a	29	
20	b (90%), c	25	8	30	GC

16	25	21	a	26	3
17	25	22	2	27	22
18	3,000	23	85	28	1
19	1,619	24	b	29	b
20	a, c (99%)	25	22	30	MB

Asia/Australia
Asie/Australie
Asien/Australien
Asia/Australia

Japan
Japon
Japan
Japón

Tokyo Chiku Menonaito Kyokai Rengo

1	c/o Japan Anabaptist Center, 2-1-17 Honan, Suginami-ku, Tokyo 168, Nippon (1964)
2	Japanese

3	Michio Ohno *Gicho*
4	Hiroko Yamasaki *Kaikei*
5	Takio Tanase *Shoki*
6	Michio Ohno

7	
8	

9	e

10	
11	
12	
13	
14	
15	

16	5	21	b	26	1
17	5	22	1	27	3
18	164	23	75	28	0
19	73	24	a	29	b
20	b (50%), c	25	5	30	GC/MC

Asia/Australia
Asie/Australie
Asien/Australien
Asia/Australia

Philippines
Philippines
Philippinen
Filipinas

Church of God in Christ, Mennonite

Mennonite Missions Now

	Church of God in Christ, Mennonite		Mennonite Missions Now
1	P.O. Box 186, MCPO, 1299 Makati, Metro Manila, Philippines	1	177 Tabia Street, Barangay Salac, Lumban, Laguna 4014, Philippines (1974)
2		2	Pilipino, English, Tagalog, Ilocano
3		3	Edgardo B. Docuyanan *Chairman*
4		4	Gervacio D. Balucas *Treasurer*
5		5	Ambrocio L. Porcincula *Secretary*
6		6	Ambrocio L. Porcincula
7		7	
8		8	
9	c	9	a, c, e
10		10	Mennonite Missions Now, Inc., 177 Tabia Street, Barangay Salac, Lumban, Laguna
11		11	26
12		12	Peso 10,000 (US $460) + US $20,000
13		13	Calamity and Disaster Committee, 177 Tabia Street, Barangay Salac, Lumban, Laguna
14		14	5
15		15	Peso 3,000 (US $138) + US $2,500

	Church of God in Christ, Mennonite							Mennonite Missions Now					
16	21	21	a	26			16	13	21	a	26	5
17		22	2	27			17	13	22	2	27	0
18		23		28			18	1,003	23	90	28	0
19	235	24	b	29			19	431	24	a	29	a, b
20	b	25		30	CGC		20	c	25	7	30	MC

Taiwan ROC, Vietnam
Taiwan R de C, Vietnam
Taiwan ROC, Vietnam
Taiwan R de C, Vietnam

Fellowship of Mennonite Churches in Taiwan (FOMCIT)

Mennonites in Vietnam

(participating in the Evangelical Church of Vietnam)

	Fellowship of Mennonite Churches in Taiwan (FOMCIT)		Mennonites in Vietnam
1	Box 27-050, Taipei, Taiwan 10490, ROC (1959)	1	
2	Mandarin, Taiwanese	2	Vietnamese
3	Benjamin Tsai *Chú-sek*	3	
4	Wu Chia-Shih *Hōe-kè*	4	
5	Chang Ying Sheng (Joshua) *Su-kì*	5	
6	Benjamin Tsai	6	Nguyen Quang Trung, 67/107 Bui Dinh Tuy, Phuong 12, Quan Binh Thanh, Ho Chi Minh City, Vietnam
7	*Manna*, Box 27-050, Taipei 10490	7	
8		8	
9	a	9	
10		10	
11		11	
12		12	
13		13	
14		14	
15		15	

16	19	21	a	26	9	16		21		26	
17	19	22	2	27	20	17		22		27	
18	4,500	23	70	28	0	18		23		28	
19	1,493	24	a	29	b	19		24		29	
20	a	25	16	30	GC	20		25		30	

**Antigua, Argentina
Antigua, Argentine
Antigua, Argentinien
Antigua, Argentina**

Global Missions Inc.

(Antigua, Barbados, Barbuda, Dominica,
French St. Martin, Grenada, Guyana, Jamaica,
St. Vincent, Tobago, Trinidad,
US Virgin Islands)

Iglesia Evangélica Menonita Argentina

	Global Missions Inc.
1	P.O. Box 1077, St. John's, Antigua and Barbuda
	(1973)
2	English, Français
3	Terry Miller *Director*
4	Lilian Joseph *Secretary/Treasurer*
5	Crafton Lewis *Director*
6	Terry Miller
7	*Sharon Star*, P.O. Box 1077, St. John's
8	
9	c
10	
11	
12	
13	
14	
15	

	Iglesia Evangélica Menonita Argentina
1	Mercedes 149, Buenos Aires 1407, Argentina
	(1919)
2	Español
3	Lucio Casas *Presidente de la Junta Directiva*
4	Abel Comas *Tesorero de la Junta Directiva*
5	Mario Snyder *Secretario de la Junta Directiva*
6	Lucio Casas
7	*Perspectiva*, Mercedes 149, Buenos Aires 1407
8	
9	a, c
10	
11	
12	
13	
14	
15	

16	17	21	b	26	3
17	17	22	2	27	3
18	1,060	23	90	28	0
19	725	24	c	29	a, b
20	c	25	27	30	

16	30	21	a	26	0
17	30	22	2	27	2
18	2,000	23	75	28	0
19	1,600	24	b	29	a, b
20	b (60%), c	25	30 ±	30	MC

Belize
Bélize
Belize
Belice

Belize Evangelical Mennonite Church

1	P.O. Box 30, Orange Walk Town, Belize (1975)
2	English, Español
3	Teodoro Torres *President*
4	Albert Codd *Treasurer*
5	Pastor Romero *Secretary*
6	Pastor Romero
7	
8	
9	
10	
11	
12	
13	
14	
15	

16	13	21	b	26	11
17	13	22	2	27	0
18	669	23	80	28	1
19	247	24	a	29	b
20	b (25%), c	25	1	30	MC

Caribbean Light and Truth

1	Box 35, Punta Gorda, Belize (1974)
2	English, Mayan, Kekchi
3	Daniel Stutzman *Bishop*
4	Paul Stutzman
5	Walter Beachy
6	Daniel Stutzman
7	*Caribbean Light and Truth Newsletter*, Rural Route 2, Kalona, IA 52247 (USA)
8	
9	c
10	
11	
12	
13	
14	
15	

16	10	21	a	26	8
17	12	22	2	27	0
18	240	23	98	28	2
19	156	24	a	29	
20	b	25	4	30	

Caribbean, Central & South America
Caraïbes, Amérique Centrale et Sud
Karibik, Zentral- und Südamerika
Caribe, América Central y del Sur

Belize
Bélize
Belize
Belice

Evangelical Mennonite Mission Conference, Blue Creek

Kleingemeinde

	Evangelical Mennonite Mission Conference, Blue Creek		Kleingemeinde
1	Box 2, Orange Walk Town, Belize (1981)	1	P.O. Box 427, Belize City, Belize (1959)
2	Deutsch, English	2	English, Deutsch, Español
3	George B. Dyck	3	Heinrich R. Penner/Jakob K. Barkman/ Johan B. Loewen *Aelteste*
4		4	Walter P. Kornelsen/Klaas B. Reimer/ Menno L. Dueck/Eddy M. Reimer *Diakonen*
5	Ben D. Wiebe *Pastor*		
6	Ben D. Wiebe		
7		5	Heinrich M. Reimer *Schreiber*
8		6	A.K. Reimer
9	c	7	*Leserfreund*, P.O. Box 427, Belize City
10		8	
11		9	
12		10	
13		11	
14		12	
15		13	Auswärtige Hilfe
		14	2
		15	

16	1	21	a	26	0	16	4	21	a	26	
17	1	22	2	27	1	17		22	1–2	27	
18	225	23	200	28		18		23	95	28	0
19	118	24	a	29	b	19	500 ±	24		29	
20	b	25	2	30	EMMC	20	b	25	21	30	

Caribbean, Central & South America
Caraïbes, Amérique Centrale et Sud
Karibik, Zentral- und Südamerika
Caribe, América Central y del Sur

Bolivia
Bolivie
Bolivien
Bolivia

Conferencia de Iglesias Evangélicas Anabautistas

Iglesia Evangélica Menonita Boliviana

	Conferencia de Iglesias Evangélicas Anabautistas
1	Cajón 2487, Santa Cruz, Bolivia (1973)
2	Español, Deutsch
3	Daniel Gomez *Presidente*
4	Maria Klassen *Tesorera*
5	Juan Klassen *Secretario*
6	Juan Klassen
7	
8	
9	a

	Iglesia Evangélica Menonita Boliviana
1	Casilla 3086, Santa Cruz, Bolivia (1970)
2	Español
3	Leónidas Saucedo R. *Coordinador*
4	Roberto Sequeira M. *Tesorero*
5	Nelly Salas S. *Secretaria*
6	Leónidas Saucedo R.
7	Boletín *El Puente*, Casilla 3086, Santa Cruz
8	
9	a, c

Conferencia de Iglesias Evangélicas Anabautistas

16		21	b	26	2		
17	3	22	2	27	3		
18	240	23	130	28	0		
19	153	24	a	29	a, b, c		
20	c	25	14	30	EMMC		

Iglesia Evangélica Menonita Boliviana

16	5	21	a	26	0		
17	5	22	2	27	1		
18	325	23	75	28	0		
19	120	24	b	29	a, b		
20	a, b, c	25	18	30	GC		

Brazil
Brésil
Brasilien
Brasil

Associação das Igrejas Irmãos Menonitas do Brasil	Associação das Igrejas Menonitas do Brasil (AIMB)

1   Av. Comendador Franco 7770, 81.500
    Curitiba, PR, Brasil
    (1960)
2   Deutsch, Português
	1 Rua Cristiano Strobel 23, 81.500
	    Curitiba, Brasil
	    (1973)
	2 Deutsch, Português

3 Ernesto Wiens 4 Norbert Wieler 5 Jacob August 6 Ernesto Wiens	3 Jakob Isaak *Presidente* 4 Hans Braun *Tesoureiro* 5 Rudolf Arno Heinrichs *Secretário* 6 Jakob Isaak
7 *Informativo* 8	7 *Bibel und Pflug*, Rua Francisco Derosso 2660, 81.500 Curitiba 8
9 a, b, c, d	9 a, b, c, d
10 Missionskomitee 11 10 ± 12 US $100,000 ±	10 11 12
13 14 15	13 AMAS 14 15

16	5	21	a	26	2 ±	16	3	21	a	26	27
17	15	22	2	27		17	8	22	2	27	4
18	3,500 ±	23	90	28	1	18	1,400 ±	23	70	28	1
19	2,100 ±	24	a	29	a, b	19	898	24	a	29	a, b
20	c	25		30	MB	20	b, c	25	11	30	GC

Brazil
Brésil
Brasilien
Brasil

Associação Evangélica Menonita (AEM)

Church of God in Christ, Mennonite

	Associação Evangélica Menonita (AEM)
1	Rua Venezuela 318, Jardim Nova Eurõpa, 13035 Campinas, São Paulo, Brasil (1957)
2	Português
3	Hans Gerhard Peters *Presidente*
4	Amadeu José Coimbra *Tesoureiro*
5	Teodoro Penner *Secretário Executivo*
6	Teodoro Penner
7	*Intercâmbio Menonita*, Rua Venezuela 318, 13035 Campinas, São Paulo
8	AEM Edições
9	a, b, c, d
10	
11	
12	
13	
14	
15	

	Church of God in Christ, Mennonite
1	c/o Charles Becker, C.P. 35, 76200 Rio Verde, Goiás, Brasil
2	Português
3	
4	
5	
6	
7	
8	
9	a, b, c, d
10	
11	
12	
13	
14	
15	

Associação Evangélica Menonita (AEM):

16	25	21	a	26	13
17	32	22	2	27	16
18	2,400	23	80	28	1
19	1,200	24	a	29	a, b, c
20	a, b, c	25	26	30	GC

Church of God in Christ, Mennonite:

16	3	21	a	26	
17		22	2	27	
18		23		28	
19	211	24	b	29	
20	b	25		30	CGC

Brazil
Brésil
Brasilien
Brasil

Convenção Brasileira das Igrejas Irmãos Menonitas

1	Rua Ubaldino do Amaral 480, 80.060 Curitiba, PR, Brasil (1966)
2	Português
3	Paulo Quentino *Presidente*
4	Almir Goulart *Tesoureiro*
5	Almir Goulart *Secretário Executivo*
6	Almir Goulart
7	*Informativo*
8	
9	a, b, c, d
10	
11	
12	
13	
14	
15	

16	23	21	a	26	3 ±
17	23	22	3	27	
18	2,500 ±	23	90	28	1
19	1,800 ±	24	a	29	a, b
20	c	25		30	MB

Colombia
Colombie
Kolumbien
Colombia

Asociación de Iglesias Hermanos Menonitas de Colombia

Iglesia Evangélica Menonita de Colombia

1	Avenida Guadalupe No. 1B-71, A.A. 4172, Cali-Valle, Colombia (1969)
2	Español
3	Diego Martínez Muños *Presidente*
4	William Valencia Caicedo *Administrador Nacional*
5	Pedro Pablo Daza Triana *Secretario*
6	William Valencia C.
7	
8	
9	a, c
10	
11	
12	
13	Fundación Menonita Colombiana para el Desarrollo, A.A. 26640, Bogotá ☎ [57] (1) 2452256
14	21
15	

16	30 ±	21	a	26	18
17		22	2	27	12
18		23		28	0
19	1,000 ±	24	a, b	29	b, c
20	c	25	3	30	MB

1	Apartado Aéreo 53-024, Bogotá 2, Colombia ☎ [57] (1) 287-3660 (1952)
2	Español
3	José Chuquin *Presidente*
4	Gustavo Angulo *Tesorero*
5	Peter Stucky *Secretario Ejecutivo*
6	Peter Stucky
7	*Menoticias*, Apartado Aéreo 53-024, Bogotá 2
8	
9	a, c
10	
11	
12	
13	MENCOLDES, Apartado Aéreo 26640, Bogotá ☎ [57] (1) 245-2256
14	20
15	

16	11	21	a	26	1
17	15	22	2–3	27	8
18	2,000 ±	23		28	2
19	800 ±	24	a	29	a, b
20	a, b, c	25	7	30	GC

Caribbean, Central & South America
Caraïbes, Amérique Centrale et Sud
Karibik, Zentral- und Südamerika
Caribe, América Central y del Sur

Costa Rica, Cuba
Costa-Rica, Cuba
Costa Rica, Kuba
Costa Rica, Cuba

Asociación Convención de Iglesias Evangélicas Menonitas de C.R.

Sociedad Misionera Cubana Hermanos en Cristo

	Asociación Convención de Iglesias Evangélicas Menonitas de C.R.		Sociedad Misionera Cubana Hermanos en Cristo
1	Apartado 116–3000, Heredia, Costa Rica (1974)	1	Calle 102 No. 10710, Entre 107 y 109, C.P. 19340, Cuatro Caminos Ciudad Habana, Cuba (1954)
2	Español	2	Español
3	Adrián González Cruz *Sobreveedor Nacional*	3	Juana M. García *Presidente*
4	Ana Victoria Rivera Chavéz *Tesorera*	4	Felix Rafael Curbelo *Tesorero*
5	Fabio López *Secretario*	5	José Francisco Rodríguez *Secretario*
6	Adrián González Cruz	6	Juana M. García
7	*Mensajero Menonita*, Apartado 116–3000, Heredia	7	
8		8	
9	c, e	9	a, c
10		10	
11		11	
12		12	
13	Comité de Servicio Social—Convención Menonita, Apartado 116–3000, Heredia	13	
14		14	
15		15	

16	17	21	a	26	1		16	2	21	a	26	0
17	17	22	2	27			17	2	22	5	27	2
18	1,415	23	85	28	1		18	150	23	75	28	0
19	1,050	24	b	29	a, b		19	45	24	b	29	
20	c	25	8	30	MC		20	c	25	2	30	BIC

Caribbean, Central & South America
Caraïbes, Amérique Centrale et Sud
Karibik, Zentral- und Südamerika
Caribe, América Central y del Sur

Dominican Republic
République Dominicaine
Dominikanische Republik
República Dominicana

Concilio Nacional Menonita Faro Divino

Conferencias de las Iglesias Evangélicas Menonitas, Inc.

1	Apartado 3, Bonao, República Dominicana
	(1976)
2	Español

3	Hilario de Jesús *Presidente*
4	Luis S. Inoa *Tesorero*
5	Carlos Barranco *Secretario*
6	Carlos Barranco

7	
8	
9	
10	
11	
12	
13	
14	
15	

16	20	21		26	
17	20	22		27	
18	1,500	23		28	
19	1,200	24		29	
20		25		30	MC

1	Apartado 21408, Santo Domingo, República Dominicana
	(1951)
2	Español

3	Reynoso Merán *Presidente*
4	Firo Cuello Baez *Tesorero*
5	
6	Reynoso Merán

7	
8	
9	
10	
11	
12	
13	
14	
15	

16	25 ±	21	a	26	10 ±
17	35 ±	22	3	27	25 ±
18	1,600 ±	23	125	28	0
19	1,400 ±	24	a	29	a, b
20	c	25	5 ±	30	EMC

Ecuador, El Salvador
Equateur, Salvador
Ecuador, El Salvador
Ecuador, El Salvador

Iglesia Evangélica Menonita del Ecuador

1	Casilla 10936, Guayaquil, Ecuador (1983)
2	Español
3	Ricardo Herrera *Presidente*
4	Gilma Zambrano
5	Martha Moreno
6	Ricardo Herrera
7	
8	
9	a, c
10	
11	
12	
13	
14	
15	

16	3	21	a	26	2
17	8	22	4	27	0
18	320	23	75	28	0
19	140	24	a	29	a, b
20	b (10%), c	25	0	30	MC

Iglesia Evangélica "Menonita" de El Salvador

1	Calle 15 de Septiembre, 4a Ave. Sur, Metapán, Santa Ana, El Salvador (1980)
2	Español
3	Adelso Landaverde A. *Presidente*
4	Adelso Landaverde M. *Tesorero*
5	Juan Pablo Linares *Secretario*
6	Adelso Landaverde A., Adelso Landaverde M.
7	
8	
9	a, c
10	
11	
12	
13	
14	
15	

16	3	21		26	4
17	3	22	Ev. 2	27	3
18	170	23	50	28	0
19	125	24	c	29	c
20	c	25	1	30	

Guatemala
Guatémala
Guatemala
Guatemala

Iglesia Menonita de Guatemala

Iglesia Nacional Evangélica Menonita Guatemalteca

	Iglesia Menonita de Guatemala		Iglesia Nacional Evangélica Menonita Guatemalteca
1	Apartado 1779, Ciudad de Guatemala, Guatemala (1977)	1	Apartado 1, 16909 San Pedro Carchá, Alta Verapáz, Guatemala (1980)
2	Español	2	Kekchi, Español
3	Chester H. Pérez L. *Presidente*	3	Tomás Cuc Tot *Naxjolomi*
4	Fidelina de Véliz *Director de Finanzas*	4	Francisco Sacul Tún *Aj ilol tumin*
5	Nancy Rivera *Secretaria*	5	Javier Xol *Laj Tzib*
6	Chester H. Pérez L.	6	Javier Xol
7		7	
8		8	
9	a, c	9	a
10		10	
11		11	
12		12	
13		13	
14		14	
15		15	

16	7 ±	21	a	26	0
17		22	4	27	
18	750 ±	23		28	
19	500 ±	24	a	29	a, b
20	c	25		30	MC

16	54	21	a	26	3
17	54	22	3	27	1
18	5,000 ±	23	85	28	1
19	3,500 ±	24	b	29	a, b, c
20	b	25	54	30	MC

Haiti
Haïti
Haiti
Haití

L'Eglise de Dieu en Christ Mennonite

1	Box 1400, Port-au-Prince, Haïti
2	Français

3	
4	
5	
6	
7	
8	

9	c

10	
11	
12	
13	
14	
15	

16	18	21	a	26	
17		22	2	27	
18		23		28	
19	354	24	b	29	
20	b	25		30	CGC

Honduras
Honduras
Honduras
Honduras

Iglesia Menonita

1	Colonia Menonita, Guaimaca, F.M., Honduras (c. 1982)
2	Español, Deutsch, English
3	David Peachey
4	
5	
6	David Peachey
7	
8	
9	a, c
10	
11	
12	
13	
14	
15	

16	3 ±	21	a	26	
17		22	2–3	27	
18		23		28	
19	40 ±	24		29	
20	b	25		30	A

Iglesia Menonita
Baluarte de la Verdad

1	Colonia Menonita, Guaimaca, F.M., Honduras (c. 1986)
2	Español, Deutsch, English
3	Ernest Schmucker *Presidente*
4	Paul Schmucker *Tesorero*
5	Oscar Gonzales *Secretario*
6	Ernest Schmucker
7	
8	
9	a, c
10	
11	
12	
13	
14	
15	

16	2	21	a	26	0
17	3	22	3–4	27	0
18	300 ±	23		28	0
19	100 ±	24	c	29	
20	b	25	3	30	BA

Caribbean, Central & South America
Caraïbes, Amérique Centrale et Sud
Karibik, Zentral- und Südamerika
Caribe, América Central y del Sur

Honduras
Honduras
Honduras
Honduras

Iglesia Menonita Hondureña

Organización Cristiana Amor Viviente

1	Apartado 77, La Ceiba, Honduras (1965)
2	Español

3	José Isaías Flores *Presidente*
4	Armando Maldonado *Tesorero*
5	Manuel Izaguirre *Secretario*
6	José Isaías Flores

7	*Noti Menon*, Apartado 77, La Ceiba
8	Oficina Central I.M.H.

9	a, c, e

10	
11	
12	

13	Comisión de Acción Social, Apartado 340, San Pedro Sula; MAMA, Apartado 340, San Pedro Sula ☎ [504] 57-2250; 53-2760
14	19
15	Lempira 252,623 (US $125,000)

16	85	21	a	26	5
17	92	22	2	27	30
18	3,500	23	90	28	2
19	3,000	24	a	29	a, b
20	c (95%)	25	3	30	

1	Apartado 978, Tegucigalpa, Honduras (1976)
2	Español

3	René Peñalva *Presidente de Junta Directiva*
4	Javier O. Soler *Administrador Nacional*
5	Osmán A. Peñalva *Secretario*
6	Osmán A. Peñalva

7	
8	

9	a

10	
11	
12	

13	Hogar Vida Nueva, Centro de Educación Cristiana, Difusora Cristiana de Radio, Apartado 978, Tegucigalpa ☎ [504] 22-2031; 34-0052; 34-0049
14	51
15	US $78,000

16	16	21	a	26	
17	16	22	2	27	19
18	8,834	23		28	0
19	4,880	24	b	29	b
20	c	25	11	30	

**Jamaica
Jamaïque
Jamaika
Jamaica**

Jamaica Mennonite Church

1	28 Upper Waterloo Road, P.O. Box 358, Kingston 10, Jamaica (1959)
2	English
3	Robert Henry *Moderator*
4	Myrtle Ffrench *Treasurer*
5	Lloyd Moore *Secretary*
6	Robert Henry
7	
8	
9	c
10	Evangelism Committee, P.O. Box 358, Kingston 10
11	4
12	US $1,500
13	
14	
15	

16	11	21	a	26	0
17	11	22	3	27	9
18	600	23	90	28	0
19	422	24	a	29	b
20	a, c	25	1	30	MC

Caribbean, Central & South America
Caraïbes, Amérique Centrale et Sud
Karibik, Zentral- und Südamerika
Caribe, América Central y del Sur

Mexico
Mexique
Mexiko
México

Church of God in Christ, Mennonite

Consejo de las Iglesias Hermanos Menonitas

	Church of God in Christ, Mennonite		Consejo de las Iglesias Hermanos Menonitas
1	Apartado 374, 25000 Saltillo, Coahuila, México	1	Monte Atlas 14–54, Colonia Independencia 44902, Guadalajara, Jalisco, México (1987)
2	Español	2	Español
3		3	Hugo Hernandez *Presidente*
4		4	
5		5	Felipe Avila *Secretario*
6		6	Hugo Hernandez
7		7	
8		8	
9	a, c	9	a, c
10		10	
11		11	
12		12	
13		13	
14		14	
15		15	

#	CGC	#		#		#			#	MB	#		#		#	
16	40	21	a	26			16	9	21	a	26	1
17		22	2	27			17	10	22	3	27	4
18		23		28			18	350 ±	23	200	28	0
19	366	24	b	29			19	150 ±	24		29	a, b
20	b	25		30	CGC		20	c	25	3	30	MB

Mexico
Mexique
Mexiko
México

Iglesia Evangélica Menonita

1	c/o Manuel Barragan, C.P. 31968, Oscar Soto Maynez, Chihuahua, México (c. 1968)
2	Español
3	Manuel Barragan *Presidente*
4	
5	Umberto Borjorquez *Vice Presidente*
6	Manuel Barragan
7	
8	
9	a
10	
11	
12	
13	
14	
15	

16	12	21	b	26	
17	12	22	2–3	27	1
18	400 ±	23		28	0
19	150 ±	24	a	29	a, b, c
20	b	25	0	30	EMCC

Iglesia Evangélica Menonita de la Mesa Central de México

1	c/o Avemaría 60-2, Coyoacan 04000, México D.F., México (1964)
2	Español
3	Ruben Zuniga *Coordinador*
4	
5	Victor Pedroza *Coordinador*
6	Ruben Zuniga, Calle Ovaciones 883, Col. Prensa Nacional, C.P. 54170, Tlalnepautla, Edo. de México
7	
8	
9	a, c
10	Comité Unido de Misiones, c/o Avemaría 60-2, Coyoacan 04000, México D.F.
11	10
12	
13	
14	
15	

16	7	21	b	26	5
17	7	22	1–4	27	3
18	300 ±	23	100	28	0
19	200 ±	24	a, b	29	a, b, c
20	a, c	25	14	30	MC

Caribbean, Central & South America
Caraïbes, Amérique Centrale et Sud
Karibik, Zentral- und Südamerika
Caribe, América Central y del Sur

Mexico
Mexique
Mexiko
México

Iglesia Evangélica Menonita del Noroeste de México

1	Apartado 38, Ahome, Sinaloa, México (1961)
2	Español
3	Isaac Cota *Presidente*
4	Martin Bojorquez *Tesorero*
5	Augustin Suarez *Secretario*
6	Martin Bojorquez
7	
8	
9	a
10	
11	
12	
13	
14	
15	

16	12	21	a	26	1		
17	15	22	2	27	1		
18	300	23	80	28			
19	200	24	a	29			
20	b (50%), c	25	12	30	MC		

Kleingemeinde in Mexiko

1	Apartado 502, Cuauhtémoc, Chihuahua, México 31500 (1948)
2	Deutsch, English, Español
3	Levi L. Dueck
4	Menno B. Dueck
5	Menno B. Dueck
6	Menno B. Dueck
7	
8	
9	a
10	
11	
12	
13	
14	
15	

16	7	21		26	0		
17	7	22	1	27	4		
18	2,000 ±	23	95	28	0		
19	960 ±	24	a	29			
20	b	25	26	30			

Caribbean, Central & South America
Caraïbes, Amérique Centrale et Sud
Karibik, Zentral- und Südamerika
Caribe, América Central y del Sur

Mexico
Mexique
Mexiko
México

Mennonitengemeinde zu Mexiko

1	Apartado 681, Cuauhtémoc, Chihuahua 31500, México
	(1963)
2	Deutsch, Español
3	Peter Rempel
4	
5	Philip Dyck
6	Philip Dyck
7	
8	
9	a, c
10	Missionskomitee, c/o Isaac Bergen, Apartado 329, Cuauhtémoc, Chihuahua 31500
11	3
12	
13	Hilfskomitee, Apartado 681, Cuauhtémoc, Chihuahua 31500
14	
15	

16	4	21	b	26	1
17	5	22	2–3	27	3
18	800 ±	23		28	1
19	400 ±	24	a	29	
20		25	4	30	GC

Caribbean, Central & South America
Caraïbes, Amérique Centrale et Sud
Karibik, Zentral- und Südamerika
Caribe, América Central y del Sur

Nicaragua
Nicaragua
Nicaragua
Nicaragua

Convención de Iglesias Evangélicas Menonitas de Nicaragua (CIEMN)

1	Apartado 3305, Managua, Nicaragua (1977)
2	Español
3	Marcos A. Orozco *Presidente*
4	Pedro Ocon *Tesorero*
5	Israel Mora *Secretario*
6	Marcos A. Orozco
7	
8	
9	c
10	
11	
12	
13	
14	
15	

16	53	21	a	26	50
17	83	22	4	27	0
18	2,916	23	80	28	1
19	1,749	24	b	29	a, b
20	b (20%), c	25	4	30	MC

Fraternidad de Iglesias Evangélicas Menonitas de Nicaragua

1	Apartado 3163, Managua, Nicaragua (1974)
2	Español
3	Bayardo Antonio Blandón Mejía *Presidente*
4	
5	
6	Bayardo Antonio Blandón Mejía
7	
8	
9	c
10	
11	
12	
13	
14	
15	

16	8 ±	21	a	26	
17	8 ±	22	3–4	27	5 ±
18	400 ±	23		28	0
19	150 ±	24	a	29	a, b
20	b	25	5 ±	30	EMCC

Nicaragua
Nicaragua
Nicaragua
Nicaragua

Iglesia Hermanos en Cristo (Nicaragua)

1	Apartado 1044, Managua, Nicaragua (1977)
2	Español
3	Agustin Monge Flores *Presidente*
4	
5	Rosendo Perez Silva
6	Rosendo Perez Silva
7	
8	
9	c
10	
11	
12	
13	
14	
15	

16	55	21	a	26		
17		22		27	0	
18		23		28	0	
19	2,018	24		29	c	
20	c	25	6	30	BIC	

Caribbean, Central & South America
Caraïbes, Amérique Centrale et Sud
Karibik, Zentral- und Südamerika
Caribe, América Central y del Sur

Panama
Panama
Panama
Panamá

Iglesia Evangélica Unida (Hermanos Menonitas)

1	Apartado 87-1901, Panamá 7, Panamá (1971)
2	Español

3	Tonny Mémbora *Presidente*
4	Obdulio Isaramá A. *Tesorero*
5	Yerson Caísamo A. *Secretario General*
6	Obdulio Isaramá

7
8

9

10
11
12

13
14
15

16	16	21	a	26	1
17	16	22	3	27	0
18		23	50	28	2
19	700	24	b	29	b
20	c	25	9	30	MB

Caribbean, Central & South America
Caraïbes, Amérique Centrale et Sud
Karibik, Zentral- und Südamerika
Caribe, América Central y del Sur

Paraguay
Paraguay
Paraguay
Paraguay

Beachy Amish Mennonite Fellowships

Convención Evangélica de Iglesias Paraguayas Hermanos Menonitas

	Beachy Amish Mennonite Fellowships	Convención Evangélica de Iglesias Paraguayas Hermanos Menonitas
1	c.d.c. 166, Asunción, Paraguay (1967, 1977, 1986)	c.d.c. 1154, Asunción, Paraguay (1971)
2	Español, English, Deutsch, Guaraní	Español, Guaraní
3		Juan Silverio Veron Aquino *Presidente*
4		Ricardo Jimenez *Tesorero*
5		Tito Pastor *Secretario*
6	Philip Eichorn (Iglesia Luz y Esperanza; Iglesia Primera Línea), John H. Myers/ Eli H. Schlabauch (Iglesia Florida)	Juan Silverio Veron Aquino
7	*Calvary Messenger*, Route 2, Box 182, Seymour, MO 65746 (USA)	*La Voz del Rebaño*, c.d.c. 1154, Asunción
8		Comité Ejecutivo
9	a, c	a, c
10		Comité de Evangelismo y Misiones, c.d.c. 1154, Asunción ☎ [595] (21) 83-891
11		5
12		US $57,000
13		
14		
15		

	Beachy Amish					Convención Evangélica				
16	3	21	a	26		31	21	a	26	1
17		22	2	27		35	22	2	27	7
18	250 ±	23	100	28		3,000	23	80	28	1
19	91	24	a	29		1,500	24	a	29	a, b, c
20	b	25	6	30	BA	c	25	11	30	MB

Caribbean, Central & South America
Caraïbes, Amérique Centrale et Sud
Karibik, Zentral- und Südamerika
Caribe, América Central y del Sur

Paraguay
Paraguay
Paraguay
Paraguay

Convención de los Hermanos Evangélicos Lengua

Convención de las Iglesias Evangélicas Nivaclé

	Convención de los Hermanos Evangélicos Lengua		Convención de las Iglesias Evangélicas Nivaclé
1	Luz a los Indígenas, c.d.c. 984, Filadelfia, Chaco, Paraguay (1978)	1	Oficina ASCIM, Filadelfia, c.d.c. 984, Asunción, Paraguay (1975)
2	Español, Lengua	2	Nivaclé
3	Ernesto Unruh *Presidente*	3	Victor Dias *Presidente*
4	Cecilio Alfonzo *Tesorero*	4	Andres Rivas *Tesorero*
5	Enrique Mendoza *Secretario*	5	Basilio Torres *Secretario*
6	Ernesto Unruh	6	Basilio Torres
7		7	
8		8	
9	a, c	9	a, c
10		10	
11		11	
12		12	
13		13	
14		14	
15		15	

Convención de los Hermanos Evangélicos Lengua:

16	8	21	b	26	7
17		22	2	27	0
18		23	50	28	1
19	1,300 ±	24	a	29	a, b
20	c	25	8	30	

Convención de las Iglesias Evangélicas Nivaclé:

16	7	21	b	26	4
17	27	22	2	27	0
18	6,000	23	30	28	1
19	1,400	24	a	29	a, b
20	c	25	42	30	

Paraguay
Paraguay
Paraguay
Paraguay

Convención de las Iglesias Evangélicas Unidas

1	Oficina ASCIM, Filadelfia, c.d.c. 984, Asunción, Paraguay (1978)
2	Lengua
3	Ditrich Pana *Presidente*
4	Jorge Ramírez *Tesorero*
5	Jorge Ramírez *Secretario*
6	Ditrich Pana
7	
8	
9	a, c
10	
11	
12	
13	
14	
15	

16		21	a	26	5
17	11	22	2	27	0
18	4,600	23	80	28	1
19	3,300	24	c	29	a, b, c
20	a (80%), c	25	17	30	

Evangelische Mennonitische Gemeinde

1	Kolonia Tres Palmas, c.d.c. 166, Asunción, Paraguay
2	Deutsch
3	Herbert Siemens *Gemeindeleiter*
4	
5	
6	Herbert Siemens
7	
8	
9	a
10	
11	
12	
13	
14	
15	

16	1	21	a	26	1
17	1	22	2–3	27	2
18	200 ±	23		28	0
19	75 ±	24	a	29	a, b
20	b	25	2	30	EMCC

Caribbean, Central & South America
Caraïbes, Amérique Centrale et Sud
Karibik, Zentral- und Südamerika
Caribe, América Central y del Sur

Paraguay
Paraguay
Paraguay
Paraguay

Iglesia Evangélica Menonita del Paraguay

Konferenz der Evangelischen Mennonitischen Brüderschaft von S.A.

	Iglesia Evangélica Menonita del Paraguay		Konferenz der Evangelischen Mennonitischen Brüderschaft von S.A.
1	c.d.c. 2475, Asunción, Paraguay (1988)	1	Filadelfia, Chaco, Paraguay (1967)
2	Español, Guaraní	2	Deutsch, Español
3	Julio César Melgarejo *Presidente*	3	Abram Boschmann *Vorsitzender*
4	Mario Ramón Téllez *Tesorero*	4	Abram Klassen *Kassierer*
5	Carlos Altenburger *Secretario*	5	Abram Klassen *Schreiber*
6	Carlos Altenburger	6	Abram Boschmann
7		7	
8		8	
9	a, c, e	9	a, c
10	COMAESP, c.d.c. 166, Asunción ☎ [595] (21) 293-054	10	
11		11	
12		12	
13		13	
14		14	
15		15	

16	16	21	a	26	0	16	2	21	a	26	15
17	20	22	2	27	10	17	3	22	1	27	4
18	2,050	23	90	28	1	18	520	23	80	28	0
19	1,000	24	b	29	a, b, c	19	480	24	a	29	b, c
20	c	25	14	30	GC	20	c	25	10	30	

Caribbean, Central & South America
Caraïbes, Amérique Centrale et Sud
Karibik, Zentral- und Südamerika
Caribe, América Central y del Sur

Paraguay
Paraguay
Paraguay
Paraguay

Konferenz der Mennonitischen Brüdergemeinden von Paraguay

1	c.d.c. 166, Asunción, Paraguay (1961)
2	Deutsch, Español
3	Gerhard Ratzlaff *Konferenzleiter*
4	Jacob Klassen *Kassierer*
5	Heinz Wölk *Schreiber*
6	Gerhard Ratzlaff
7	*Konferenzblatt*, c/o Konferenz der M.B.G. von Paraguay, c.d.c. 166, Asunción
8	
9	a, c
10	Licht den Indianern; Chaco Radio Mission, Filadelfia, Asunción
11	
12	
13	Christlicher Dienst; ASCIM
14	
15	

16	7	21	a	26	21
17	7	22	1	27	3
18	2,025	23	60	28	1
19	1,355	24	a	29	c
20	c	25	29	30	MB

Mennonite Christian Brotherhood (Agua Azul & Rio Corriente)

1	Colonia Agua Azul, c.d.c. 166, Asunción, Paraguay
2	Español, English
3	Paul Hollingshead *Bishop*
4	
5	
6	Paul Hollingshead
7	
8	
9	a, c
10	
11	
12	
13	
14	
15	

16		21		26	
17		22		27	
18		23		28	
19	155	24		29	
20		25	7	30	

Caribbean, Central & South America
Caraïbes, Amérique Centrale et Sud
Karibik, Zentral- und Südamerika
Caribe, América Central y del Sur

Paraguay
Paraguay
Paraguay
Paraguay

Misión Evangélica Mennonita

Vereinigung der Mennonitengemeinden von Paraguay

	Misión Evangélica Mennonita		Vereinigung der Mennonitengemeinden von Paraguay
1	c.d.c. 166, Asunción, Paraguay (1959)	1	Colonia Friesland, c.d.c. 166, Asunción, Paraguay (1967)
2	Español, Deutsch, Guaraní, Lengua	2	Deutsch, English, Español
3	Fred Buhler *Director*	3	Erwin Rempel *Konferenzleiter*
4	Fred Buhler	4	Heinrich Pätkau
5	Ken Zacharias *Secretario*	5	Heinrich Pätkau
6	Ken Zacharias	6	Erwin Rempel
7		7	
8		8	
9	a, c	9	a, c
10		10	Comité Mennonita de Acción Evangélica y Social, Venezuela 1464, c.d.c. 166, Asunción ☎ [595] (21) 293-054
11		11	
12		12	
13		13	Servicio Voluntario Mennonita ☎ [595] (21) 293-650
14		14	
15		15	

16	9	21	a	26	6	16	16	21	a	26	597
17	9	22	2	27	4	17	40	22	1–2	27	16
18	400	23	80	28	0	18	10,176	23	70–80	28	2
19	200	24	a	29	a	19	5,746	24	a, b	29	a, b, c
20	b (50%), c	25	1	30	EMCC	20	b	25	87	30	GC

Peru, Puerto Rico
Pérou, Porto-Rico
Peru, Puerto Rico
Perú, Puerto Rico

Iglesia Hermanos Menonitas (Perú)

1	(1985)
2	Español
3	Valerio Ramos *Pastor*
4	
5	
6	Valerio Ramos, Apartado de Correo 610, Piura, Perú
7	
8	
9	a
10	
11	
12	
13	
14	
15	

16	4	21		26			
17	5	22	3–4	27	1		
18	300 ±	23		28	0		
19	150 ±	24	a	29	a, b, c		
20	c	25	1	30	MB		

Convención Iglesias Evangélicas Menonitas de Puerto Rico, Inc.

1	Apartado 2016, Aibonito, PR 00609 (1948)
2	Español
3	José Luis Vázquez *Presidente*
4	Maribel Colón Ortiz *Tesorera*
5	José Enrique Jiménez *Secretario Ejecutivo*
6	José Enrique Jiménez
7	*Alcance Menonita*, Apartado 2016, Aibonito, PR 00609
8	
9	c
10	
11	
12	
13	Comité Menonita de Emergencia, Apartado 2016, Aibonito, PR 00609 ☎ [1] (809) 735-8841
14	
15	

16	14	21	a	26	0		
17	14	22	2	27	10		
18	950	23	80	28	1		
19	868	24	b	29	b		
20	a (25%), c	25	8	30	MC		

Trinidad and Tobago
Trinité et Tobago
Trinidad und Tobago
Trinidad-Tobago

Mennonite Church of Trinidad and Tobago

1	P.O. Box 300, Port-of-Spain, Trinidad (1984)
2	English
3	Hubert Doodnauth *President*
4	Russell Thomas *Vice President/Treasurer*
5	Lorna Granger *Secretary*
6	Hubert Doodnauth
7	
8	
9	c
10	
11	
12	
13	
14	
15	

16	2	21	a	26	
17	2	22	3	27	
18	130 ±	23	70	28	
19	110 ±	24	a	29	a, b
20	a, c	25	0	30	MC

Caribbean, Central & South America
Caraïbes, Amérique Centrale et Sud
Karibik, Zentral- und Südamerika
Caribe, América Central y del Sur

Uruguay
Uruguay
Uruguay
Uruguay

Consejo de las Congregaciones de los Hermanos Menonitas

Convención de Iglesias Menonitas en Uruguay

	Consejo de las Congregaciones de los Hermanos Menonitas
1	Av. Instrucciones 1659, Peñarol, Montevideo, Uruguay (1963)
2	Español
3	Jorge Velázquez *Presidente*
4	Herbert Bitancort *Tesorero*
5	Hector Magis *Secretario*
6	Jorge Velázquez
7	
8	
9	
10	
11	
12	
13	
14	
15	

	Convención de Iglesias Menonitas en Uruguay
1	3 de Febrero 4381, Montevideo, Uruguay (1972)
2	Español
3	Nirio Nelson Colina *Presidente*
4	Herman Woelke *Tesorero*
5	Alicia Cabrera *Secretaria*
6	Nirio Nelson Colina
7	*Compartiendo*, 3 de Febrero 4381, Montevideo
8	
9	c
10	
11	
12	
13	
14	
15	

Consejo de las Congregaciones de los Hermanos Menonitas:

16	6	21		26	
17	7	22	3	27	
18	200 ±	23	80	28	
19	160 ±	24	a	29	a, b, c
20	c	25		30	MB

Convención de Iglesias Menonitas en Uruguay:

16	6	21		26	0
17	9	22	3	27	5
18	400 ±	23		28	1
19	200 ±	24	a	29	b
20	a, b, c	25	4	30	GC

Caribbean, Central & South America
Caraïbes, Amérique Centrale et Sud
Karibik, Zentral- und Südamerika
Caribe, América Central y del Sur

Uruguay
Uruguay
Uruguay
Uruguay

Konferenz der Mennonitengemeinden in Uruguay

1	c.d.c. 400, Montevideo, Uruguay (1951)
2	Deutsch, Español
3	Reinhard Fast *Vorsitzender*
4	H.-U. Goertz/B. Penner *Kassenführer*
5	Klaus Dück *Schriftführer*
6	Klaus Dück
7	*Konferenznachrichten*
8	
9	
10	Missionskomitee, 3 de Febrero 4381, Montevideo ☎ [598] (2) 39-32-74
11	12
12	US $16,000
13	Consejo Inter-Menonita de Servicio Social, Ariel 4573, Montevideo ☎ [598] (2) 39-32-74; Mennonitisches Kinderheim "Siquem"
14	7
15	

16	4	21	a	26	96
17	5	22	1	27	0
18	691	23	60	28	1
19	517	24	a	29	a, b, c
20	a (20%), b	25	18	30	GC

Venezuela
Vénézuela
Venezuela
Venezuela

Concilio de las Iglesias Evangélicas Menonitas en Venezuela

Iglesia Evangélica Hermanos en Cristo de Venezuela

	Concilio de las Iglesias Evangélicas Menonitas en Venezuela
1	Apartado 5137–1010A, Carmelitas, Caracas, Venezuela (1979)
2	Español
3	Juan Victor Montes Consuegra *Presidente*
4	Gustavo Rene Jara Matus *Tesorero*
5	Manuel Enrique Pena Valladares *Secretario de Actas*
6	Manuel Enrique Pena Valladares
7	*El Portavoz Menonita*, Apartado 5137–1010A, Carmelitas, Caracas
8	
9	a, c, e
10	
11	
12	
13	
14	
15	

16	2	21	a	26	12
17	4	22	2	27	2
18	120 ±	23	90	28	1
19	60 ±	24	b	29	a, b, c
20	c	25	12	30	MC

	Iglesia Evangélica Hermanos en Cristo de Venezuela
1	Apartado 29056, Montalban 1021, Caracas, Venezuela (1989)
2	Español
3	Gordon Gilmore *Contact*
4	
5	
6	Gordon Gilmore
7	
8	
9	a
10	
11	
12	
13	
14	
15	

16	3	21	a	26	
17	3	22		27	
18	160 ±	23	270	28	
19	60	24		29	
20	c	25		30	BIC

Caribbean, Central & South America
Caraïbes, Amérique Centrale et Sud
Karibik, Zentral- und Südamerika
Caribe, América Central y del Sur

Country Pays Land País	Organized Bodies or Groups Organismes Organisierte Körperschaften Cuerpos o grupos organizados	Baptized Members Personnes baptisées Getaufte Glieder Miembros bautizados
Argentina	Alianza Evangélica Menonita (Affiliated with Konferenz der Evangelischen Mennonitischen Brüderschaft von Südamerika)	
	Altkolonier Mennonitengemeinde	500 ±
Belize	Altkolonier Mennonitengemeinde (Little Belize and Shipyard)	450 ±
	Beachy Amish Mennonite Fellowships	121
Bolivia	Altkolonier Mennonitengemeinde	5,700 ±
	Bergthaler Mennonitengemeinde	130 ±
	Reinländer Mennonitengemeinde	160 ±
	Sommerfelder Mennonitengemeinde	500 ±
Costa Rica	Beachy Amish Mennonite Fellowships	168
El Salvador	Iglesia Evangélica Menonita (Beachy Amish)	132
Guatemala	Conservative Mennonite Fellowship, Inc.	125 ±
	Mennonite Air Missions	170 ±
Haïti	Communion Mennonite d'Haïti	400 ±
	Mennonite Son Light Missions	160 ±
México	Altkolonier Mennonitengemeinde	16,500 ±
	Sommerfelder Mennonitengemeinde	700 ±
Paraguay	Altkolonier Mennonitengemeinde	
	Colonia Durango	700 ±
	Colonia Manitoba	159
	Colonia Rio Verde	909
	Bergthaler Mennonitengemeinde	625 ±
	Reinfeld Mennonitengemeinde	64
	Sommerfelder Mennonitengemeinde	
	Colonia Santa Clara	89
	Colonia Sommerfeld	750 ±

Europe
Europe
Europa
Europa

Austria, Belgium
Autriche, Belgique
Österreich, Belgien
Austria, Bélgica

Arbeitsgemeinschaft Mennonitischer Brüder-gemeinden (AMBÖ)

Conseil Mennonite Belge

1	Aigen 28, A-4843 Ampflwang, Österreich ☎ [43] (7675) 3192 (1970)
2	Deutsch, Serbo-Croatian
3	Franz Rathmair *Vorsitzender*
4	Georg Reischl *Kassier*
5	Artur Baerg *Schriftführer*
6	Franz Rathmair
7	*Quelle des Lebens*, c/o A. Baerg, Sepp-Stöger-Str. 7, A-4400 Steyr
8	
9	a, b, c, d
10	
11	
12	
13	
14	
15	

16	7	21	a	26	6
17	8	22	1	27	5
18	450	23	130	28	0
19	300	24	a, b	29	b
20	c	25	25	30	MB

1	c/o Centre Mennonite de Bruxelles, rue Franklin 102, B-1040 Bruxelles, Belgique ☎ [32] (2) 734-8107 (1972)
2	Français, Nederlands
3	Willy Hubinont *Président*
4	Samuël Gosset *Trésorier*
5	Steve Shank *Secrétaire*
6	Willy Hubinont, 13 rue Haute, B-1338 Lasne, Belgique
7	*Connexe*, rue Franklin 102, B-1040 Bruxelles
8	
9	a, b, c, d
10	
11	
12	
13	
14	
15	

16	4	21	b	26	2
17	4	22	1	27	0
18	85	23	50–70	28	0
19	40 ±	24	a	29	a, b
20	a (50%), c	25	12	30	MC

Europe
Europe
Europa
Europa

Federal Republic of Germany
République Fédérale d'Allemagne
Bundesrepublik Deutschland
República Federal de Alemania

Arbeitsgem. zur geistl. Unterstützung in Mennonitengem. (AGUM)

1	Wacholderweg 5, D-4800 Bielefeld 1, Bundesrepublik Deutschland (1978)
2	Deutsch
3	Erwin Sawatzky *Vorsitzender*
4	Peter Rempel *Kassier*
5	Ignaz Kapetschny *Schriftführer*
6	Erwin Sawatzky
7	
8	
9	a, b, c, d
10	
11	
12	
13	
14	
15	

16	12	21	b	26	8		
17	18	22	2	27			
18		23	50–75	28	0		
19	3,850	24	a	29			
20	a	25	39	30	GC		

Arbeitsgem. Mennonitischer Brüdergem. in Deutschland (AMBD)

1	c/o Alexander Neufeld, Osterkamp 10, D-4800 Bielefeld 1, Bundesrepublik Deutschland ☎ [49] (521) 296746 (1966)
2	Deutsch
3	Alexander Neufeld *1. Vorsitzender*
4	Abram Pankratz *Kassierer*
5	Thomas Jenne *Schriftführer*
6	Alexander Neufeld
7	*Quelle des Lebens*, c/o A. Baerg, Sepp-Stöger-Str. 7, A-4400 Steyr (Österreich)
8	
9	a, b, c, d
10	
11	
12	
13	IMO
14	
15	

16	7	21	a	26	5		
17	12	22	2	27	14		
18	1,700	23	130	28	0		
19	1,044	24	a, b	29	b, c		
20	c	25	50	30	MB		

Europe
Europe
Europa
Europa

Federal Republic of Germany
République Fédérale d'Allemagne
Bundesrepublik Deutschland
República Federal de Alemania

Bund Taufgesinnter Gemeinden e.V. (BTG)

Mennonitenbrüdergemeinden (Independent Congregations)

	Bund Taufgesinnter Gemeinden e.V. (BTG)		Mennonitenbrüdergemeinden (Independent Congregations)
1	Steinbült 27, D-4811 Oerlinghausen, Bundesrepublik Deutschland (1989)	1	c/o Hans von Niessen, Langendorfer Str. 29, D-5450 Neuwied 1, Bundesrepublik Deutschland ☎ [49] (2631) 31871
2	Deutsch	2	Deutsch, Russian
3	Heinrich Löwen *Vorsitzender*	3	
4	Andreas Beuth *Kassierer*	4	
5	Johann Richert *Schriftführer*	5	
6	Heinrich Löwen	6	Hans von Niessen *Contact*
7	*Jünger & Meister*, Steinbült 27, D-4811 Oerlinghausen; *Evangl'skaja Vera* (Russian)	7	
8		8	
		9	
9	a, b, c, d		
		10	
10		11	
11		12	
12			
		13	
13		14	
14		15	
15			

16	7	21	a	26	8		16	8	21		26	
17	7	22	2	27	14		17	8	22		27	
18	6,000 ±	23	100	28	0		18		23		28	
19	2,500 ±	24	a	29	a, b, c		19	2,000 ±	24		29	
20	c	25	50	30	MB		20		25		30	MB

Europe
Europe
Europa
Europa

Federal Republic of Germany
République Fédérale d'Allemagne
Bundesrepublik Deutschland
República Federal de Alemania

<table>
<tr><td colspan="2">

Mennonitische Heimatmission (MHM)
</td><td colspan="2">

Verband deutscher Mennonitengemeinden (VdM)
</td></tr>
</table>

	Mennonitische Heimatmission (MHM)		Verband deutscher Mennonitengemeinden (VdM)
1	Ludwig-Thoma-Str. 6, D-8061 Vierkirchen, Bundesrepublik Deutschland ☎ [49] (8139) 1015 (1969)	1	Augrund 39, D-6920 Sinsheim-Dühren, Bundesrepublik Deutschland ☎ [49] (7261) 5653 (1854)
2	Deutsch	2	Deutsch
3	Wolfgang Schmutz *Vorsitzender*	3	Heinrich Funck *1. Vorsitzender*
4	Peter Russek *Kassier*	4	Ernst Landes *Rechnungsführer*
5	Wilfried Gundlach *Schriftführer*	5	Elfriede Lichdi *Schriftführerin*
6	Wolfgang Schmutz	6	Heinrich Funck
7	*Brennpunkt Gemeinde*, Ludwig-Thoma-Str. 6, D-8061 Vierkirchen	7	*Brücke Mennonitisches Gemeindeblatt*
8		8	Agape-Verlag
9	a, b, c, d, e	9	a, b, c, d, e
10		10	Deutsches Mennon. Missionskomitee ☎ [49] (7641) 7509
11		11	16
12		12	DM 280.000 (US $165,000)
13		13	"Christenpflicht", Schönbrunn, D-8071 Post Denkendorf/Mfr ☎ [49] (8466) 242
14		14	5
15		15	DM 200.000 (US $120,000)

16	13	21	a	26	7	16	22	21	a	26	3
17	13	22	2	27	9	17	22	22	1–2	27	9
18	500	23	100	28	0	18	1,700	23	60	28	1
19	310	24	c	29	b	19	1,610	24	b	29	b, c
20	c	25	9	30		20	a (70%), c	25	65	30	

Federal Republic of Germany
République Fédérale d'Allemagne
Bundesrepublik Deutschland
República Federal de Alemania

Vereinigung der Deutschen Mennonitengemeinden (VDM)

1	Agnetendorfer Straße 55, D-5300 Bonn 1, Bundesrepublik Deutschland ☎ [49] (228) 666225 (1886)
2	Deutsch
3	Heinold Fast *Vorsitzender des Vorstands*
4	Hans-Günter Mekelburger *Kassenführer*
5	Rainer Wiebe *Geschäftsführung*
6	Heinold Fast, Brückstraße 74, D-2970 Emden
7	*Brücke Mennonitisches Gemeindeblatt*
8	Agape-Verlag
9	a, b, c, d
10	Deutsches Mennon. Missions-Komitee ☎ [49] (7641) 7509
11	6
12	
13	Hilfswerk der Vereinigung der Deutschen Mennonitengemeinden; IMO
14	
15	

16	34	21	b	26	
17	50 ±	22	1–2	27	18
18		23	10–100	28	0
19	7,034	24	a	29	b
20	a, b, c	25		30	

Europe
Europe
Europa
Europa

France, German Democratic Rep.
France, Rép. Démocrat. Allemande
Frankreich, DDR
Francia, Rep. Democrática Alemana

Association des Eglises Evangéliques Mennonites de France (AEEMF)

Mennonitengemeinde in der DDR

1	Place du marché, F-68580 Seppois le Bas, France ☎ [33] (89) 256034 (1925)
2	Français
3	Jacques Graber
4	René Eyer
5	Pierre Sommer
6	Jacques Graber
7	*Christ Seul*, 3 route de Grand-Charmont, F-25200 Montbeliard
8	Editions mennonites
9	a, b, d
10	Comite de Mission Mennonite Français ☎ [33] (89) 714301; Assn. Mission. Mennonite de Lorraine
11	12
12	1.054.000 FF (US $182,500)
13	Caisse de Secours
14	
15	393.000 FF (US $68,000)

16	27	21	a	26	6
17	33	22	2	27	10
18	3,000	23	70	28	1
19	2,000	24	a	29	a, b
20	a, c (60%)	25	71	30	

1	Schwedter Str. 262, DDR-1054 Berlin, Deutschen Demokratischen Republik (1961)
2	Deutsch
3	Knuth Hansen *Gemeindeleiter*
4	Bärbel Schultz *Kassenwart*
5	Ronald Koch *Stellvertreter des Vorstandes*
6	Ronald Koch, Knuth Hansen
7	*Gemeinderundschreiben*, c/o Knuth Hansen, Donizettistr. 47, DDR-1147 Berlin
8	
9	a, b, c, d
10	
11	
12	
13	
14	
15	

16	1	21	b	26	7
17	5	22	1–3	27	1
18	240	23		28	0
19	168	24	a	29	b
20	a	25	1	30	

Europe
Europe
Europa
Europa

Great Britain, Ireland
Grande Bretagne, Irlande
Gross Britanien, Irland
Gran Bretania, Irlanda

British Conference of Mennonites

Irish Mennonite Movement

1	c/o London Mennonite Centre, 14 Shepherds Hill, London N6 5AQ, Great Britain ☎ [44] (1) 340-8775 (1987)		
2	English		
3	Robert Buchan *Chair*		
4	Frederick Yocum *Treasurer*		
5	Sean Gardiner *Secretary*		
6	Robert Buchan		
7			
8			
9	c, e		
10	London Mennonite Centre, 14 Shepherds Hill, London N6 5AQ ☎ [44] (1) 340-8775		
11	4		
12	£50,400 ± (US $81,000)		
13			
14			
15			

16	1	21	b	26	3
17	2	22	1	27	1/2
18	60	23	80	28	0
19	27	24	a	29	b, c
20	c	25	5	30	MC

1	4 Clonmore Villas, 92 Ballybough Rd., Dublin 3, Eire (1978)		
2	English		
3	Brian Judge		
4	Paul Nelson		
5	Mike Garde		
6	Mike Garde		
7			
8			
9	c, e		
10			
11			
12			
13			
14			
15			

16	1	21	a	26	1
17	1	22	2	27	0
18	30	23	200	28	0
19	10	24	a	29	b
20	b, c	25	4	30	MC

Europe
Europe
Europa
Europa

Italy, Luxembourg
Italie, Luxembourg
Italien, Luxemburg
Italia, Luxemburgo

Chiesa Evangelica Mennonita Italiana

Association Mennonite Luxembourgeoise

1	Via Rinaldo d'Aquino 9, 90135 Palermo, Italia (1981)
2	Italiano
3	Francesco Picone *Presidente*
4	Giovanni Quartararo *Tesoriere*
5	Francesco Sapienza *Segretario*
6	Francesco Picone
7	*Il Messaggero*, c/o Via Rinaldo d'Aquino 9, 90135 Palermo
8	
9	a, b, c, d
10	
11	
12	
13	
14	
15	

1	82 Rosswinkel, L-6251 Scheidgen, Luxembourg (1953)
2	Deutsch, Français
3	René Nafziger *Président*
4	
5	Armand Schertz *Secrétaire*
6	René Nafziger
7	
8	
9	
10	
11	
12	
13	
14	
15	

16	5	21	a	26	0
17	6	22	2	27	1
18	270	23	75	28	0
19	129	24	a	29	a, b, c
20	b, c (98%)	25	4	30	MC

16	2	21		26	
17		22		27	
18		23		28	
19	100 ±	24		29	
20		25		30	

Europe
Europe
Europa
Europa

The Netherlands
Pays-Bas
Niederlande
Los Países Bajos

Algemene Doopsgezinde Sociëteit (ADS)

1	Singel 450, NL-1017 AV Amsterdam, Nederland ☎ [31] (20) 230914 (1811)
2	Nederlands
3	S.A. Vis *Voorzitter*
4	F.A. Slikker *Penningmeester*
5	Ed van Straten *Algemeen Secretaris*
6	Ed van Straten
7	*Algemeen Doopsgezind Weekblad*; *Woord over Daad*
8	
9	a, b, c, d, e
10	Doopsgezinde Zendings Raad ☎ [31] (50) 259001; EMEK
11	
12	
13	Stichting voor Bijzondere Noden ☎ [31] (23) 248000
14	
15	514.630 hfl. (US $270,000)

16	139	21	b	26	
17	150	22	1	27	
18		23		28	2
19	18,000	24	a	29	a, b
20	a	25		30	ADS

Europe
Europe
Europa
Europa

Spain
Espagne
Spanien
España

Comunidad Cristiana de los Hermanos Menonitas de España

1	Avenida Dr. Federico Rubio y Gali 73, E-28040 Madrid, España
	(1982)
2	Español
3	
4	Antonio Frías Lozoya *Tesorero*
5	Marisa Gimenez *Secretaria*
6	Marisa Gimenez
7	*Tiempo de encuentro*, Avenida Dr. Federico Rubio y Gali 73, E-28040 Madrid
8	
9	a, b, c, d
10	
11	
12	
13	
14	
15	

16	2	21	a	26	0
17	2	22	2	27	0
18	70	23	80	28	0
19	24	24	a	29	b
20	c	25	0	30	MB

Comunidades Cristianas Unidas de Burgos

1	Apartado 533, E-09080 Burgos, España
	(1989)
2	Español
3	Dionisio Byler *Presidente*
4	Carlos Bartolome *Pastor*
5	José Gallardo *Vice-Presidente*
6	José Gallardo
7	
8	
9	a, b, c, d, e
10	
11	
12	
13	Accorema, Calle Mayor 23, E-09197 Quintanadueñas (Burgos) ☎ [34] (947) 202704
14	2
15	3.500.000 Ptas (US $32,000)

16	3	21	b	26	2
17	3	22	3	27	3
18	300 ±	23	90	28	0
19	190	24	c	29	a, b, c
20	c	25	4	30	

Europe
Europe
Europa
Europa

Switzerland, USSR
Suisse, URSS
Schweiz, Sowjetunion
Suiza, URSS

Konferenz der Mennoniten der Schweiz (Alttäufer)

Mennonites in the Union of Soviet Socialist Republics

Konferenz der Mennoniten der Schweiz (Alttäufer)	Mennonites in the Union of Soviet Socialist Republics
1 Kehr 398, CH-3550 Langnau, Schweiz ☎ [41] (35) 23218 (c. 1890) 2 Deutsch, Français	1 Includes members who adhere to one of the following groups: Inclut les membres qui adhèrent à un des groupes suivants: Einschließlich der Glieder, die zu den nachstehenden Gruppen gehören: Incluye miembros afiliados a uno de los siguientes grupos:
3 Charly Ummel *Präsident* 4 Daniel Engel *Kassier* 5 Esther Braun *Sekretärin* 6 Charly Ummel, Foyer 6, CH-2400 Le Locle	Council of Churches of Evangelical Christians and Baptists Evangelical Christian Baptist Union Mennonite (Kirchliche Mennoniten) registered and unregistered congregations
7 *Der Zionspilger*, Postfach, CH-2533 Evilard 8	Mennonite Brethren registered and unregistered congregations
9 a, c, e	2 Deutsch, Russian
10 SMEK, Baselstrasse 95, CH-4142 Münchenstein ☎ [41] (61) 460237 11 12 CHF 227.619 (US $162,300)	9 a
13 SMO, Fenatte 2, CH-2854 Bassecourt 14 15 CHF 257.179 (US $183,400)	

16	15	21	a	26	52
17	20 ±	22	1–2	27	7
18		23	50	28	1
19	3,000 ±	24	a	29	b
20	a (70%), c	25	39	30	

16		21	a	26	
17		22	2–4	27	
18	60,000 ±	23		28	
19	26,200 ±	24	a	29	a, b, c
20	b, c	25		30	GC, MB

North America
Amérique du Nord
Nordamerika
América del Norte

Canada
Canada
Kanada
Canadá

Bergthaler Churches in Alberta and Saskatchewan

Chortitzer Mennonite Conference

1	
2	Deutsch, English
3	
4	
5	
6	
7	
8	
9	c
10	
11	
12	
13	
14	
15	

16	11 ±	21		26		
17		22		27	0	
18		23		28		
19	900 ±	24		29		
20		25		30		

1	Box 968, Steinbach, MB R0A 2A0 Canada ☎ [1] (204) 326-4342 (c. 1890)
2	English, Deutsch
3	Wilhelm Hildebrandt *Bishop*
4	Elmer Martens *Treasurer*
5	Richard Martens *Secretary*
6	Wilhelm Hildebrandt
7	*CMC Chronicle*, Box 968, Steinbach, MB R0A 2A0
8	
9	c
10	CMC Board of Missions, Box 403, Steinbach, MB R0A 2A0 ☎ [1] (204) 326-4342
11	
12	
13	MCCC
14	
15	

16	11	21	a	26	0
17	11	22	1	27	3
18	4,000	23	70	28	0
19	2,400	24	c	29	b
20	b	25	18	30	

Canada
Canada
Kanada
Canadá

Conference of Mennonites in Canada

1	600 Shaftesbury Blvd., Winnipeg, MB R3P 0M4 Canada ☎ [1] (204) 888-6781 (1902)
2	English, Cantonese, Deutsch, Español, Français, Lao, Mandarin, Saulteaux, Vietnamese
3	Walter Franz *Chairperson*
4	Edgar Rempel *Treasurer*
5	Larry Kehler *General Secretary*
6	Larry Kehler
7	*Mennonite Reporter*, 3–312 Marsland Dr., Waterloo, ON N2J 3Z1
8	
9	c, e
10	Native Ministries; European Min.; COM
11	
12	
13	MCCC
14	
15	

16	156	21	a	26	43
17	176	22	1	27	177
18		23	65–70	28	1
19	28,994	24	a	29	b
20	a, b, c	25	378	30	GC

Evangelical Mennonite Conference (Canada)

1	440 Main Street, Box 1268, Steinbach, MB R0A 2A0 Canada ☎ [1] (204) 326-6401 (1956)
2	English, Deutsch
3	Harvey Plett *Moderator*
4	
5	Edwin Friesen *Conference Pastor*
6	Harvey Plett
7	*The Messenger*, Box 1268, Steinbach, MB R0A 2A0
8	
9	c
10	EMCC
11	
12	
13	MCCC
14	
15	

16	48	21	a	26	8
17	48	22	1–2	27	65
18		23	152	28	1
19	5,813	24	a	29	a, b, c
20	b, c	25	220	30	EMCC

North America
Amérique du Nord
Nordamerika
América del Norte

Canada
Canada
Kanada
Canadá

Markham-Waterloo Conference

New Reinland Mennonite Church of Ontario

1	(1939)
2	English, Deutsch
3	
4	
5	
6	Clare Frey, Route 2, Elmira, ON N3B 2Z2 Canada
7	
8	
9	c
10	
11	
12	
13	
14	
15	

16	10	21	a	26	0
17		22	1	27	0
18	1,930	23	90	28	0
19	1,035	24	c	29	
20	b	25	20	30	

1	(1984)
2	Deutsch, English
3	Cornelius Quiring *Bishop*
4	
5	Peter Wiebe *Minister*
6	Peter Wiebe, 190 Elk Street, Aylmer West, ON N5H 1S9
7	
8	
9	c
10	
11	
12	
13	
14	
15	

16	3	21	a	26	0
17	3	22	1	27	0
18	1,200 ±	23	70	28	0
19	464	24	a	29	
20	b	25	6	30	

Canada
Canada
Kanada
Canadá

Old Colony Mennonite Church—Alberta

Old Colony Mennonite Church—British Columbia

#	Alberta		#	British Columbia
1	La Crete, AB T0H 2H0 Canada (c. 1939)		1	(c. 1961)
2	Deutsch, English		2	Deutsch, English
3	John Klassen *Bishop*		3	Peter Klassen *Deacon*
4			4	
5	Herman Friesen *Minister*		5	
6	John Klassen		6	
7			7	
8			8	
9	c		9	c
10			10	
11			11	
12			12	
13	MCCC		13	MCCC
14			14	
15			15	

Alberta:

16	4	21	a	26	0		
17	4	22	1	27	0		
18	2,200	23	80	28	0		
19	1,050	24	a	29			
20	b	25	10	30			

British Columbia:

16	3	21	a	26	0		
17	3	22	1	27	0		
18	700 ±	23	25	28	0		
19	349	24	a	29			
20	b	25	5	30			

North America
Amérique du Nord
Nordamerika
América del Norte

Canada
Canada
Kanada
Canadá

Old Colony Mennonite Church—Manitoba

Old Colony Mennonite Church—Ontario (and Unaffiliated)

	Old Colony Mennonite Church—Manitoba		Old Colony Mennonite Church—Ontario (and Unaffiliated)
1	Box 601, Winkler, MB R6W 4A8 Canada (1936)	1	1020 Oak Street East, Leamington, ON N8H 3V7 Canada (1960)
2	Deutsch, English	2	Deutsch, English
3	John P. Wiebe *Bishop*	3	Cornelius Enns *Bishop*
4	Abram Driedger *Deacon*	4	
5	Jacob J. Elias *Minister*	5	Henry Friesen *Deacon*
6	Abram Driedger	6	Henry Friesen
7		7	
8		8	
9	c	9	c
10		10	
11		11	
12		12	
13	MCCC	13	MCCC
14		14	
15		15	

Old Colony Mennonite Church—Manitoba

16	4	21	a	26	0
17	4	22	1	27	0
18	2,018	23	80	28	0
19	1,036	24	a	29	
20	b	25	7	30	

Old Colony Mennonite Church—Ontario (and Unaffiliated)

16	6	21	a	26	0
17	6	22	1	27	0
18		23	75–80	28	0
19	3,300 ±	24	a	29	
20	b	25	11	30	

North America
Amérique du Nord
Nordamerika
América del Norte

Canada
Canada
Kanada
Canadá

Old Colony Mennonite Church—Saskatchewan

Old Order Mennonites

1	Box 424, Hague, SK S0K 1X0 Canada (c. 1897)				
2	Deutsch, English				

3	Peter Wolfe *Bishop*
5	
6	Peter Wolfe

7	
8	

9	c

10	
11	
12	

13	MCCC
14	
15	

16	4	21	a	26	0
17	4	22	1	27	0
18	750 ±	23	50	28	0
19	415	24	a	29	
20	b	25	11	30	

Old Order Mennonites

1	Ontario, Canada
2	Deutsch, English

3	
4	
5	
6	

7	
8	

9	c

10	
11	
12	

13	
14	
15	

16	17	21		26	
17		22		27	
18		23		28	
19	2,470	24		29	
20		25		30	

North America
Amérique du Nord
Nordamerika
América del Norte

Canada
Canada
Kanada
Canadá

Reinland Mennonite Church

Sommerfeld Mennonite Church

1	P.O. Box 96, Rosenfeld, MB R0G 1X0 Canada (1958)
2	Deutsch
3	W.H. Friesen *Ältester*
4	
5	
6	W.H. Friesen
7	
8	
9	c
10	
11	
12	
13	
14	
15	

1	Box 14, Halbstadt, MB R0A 0S0 Canada (1894)
2	Deutsch, English
3	John A. Friesen *Bishop*
4	Diedrich Schroeder *Deacon*
5	
6	Diedrich Schroeder
7	
8	
9	c
10	Sommerfeld Church Mission Committee, Box 412, Altona, MB R0G 0B0 ☎ [1] (204) 324-6174
11	5
12	Canadian $82,282
13	MCCC
14	
15	

Reinland Mennonite Church

16	8	21	a	26	0
17	8	22	1	27	0
18		23	75	28	0
19	1,590	24	c	29	
20	b	25	12	30	

Sommerfeld Mennonite Church

16	26 ±	21		26	
17		22	1	27	
18		23		28	0
19	5,500 ±	24	c	29	
20	b	25	22	30	

North America
Amérique du Nord
Nordamerika
América del Norte

Canada/United States
Canada/Etats-Unis
Kanada/Vereinigte Staaten
Canadá/Estados Unidos

Beachy Amish Mennonite Fellowship

Brethren in Christ General Conference (North America)

Beachy Amish Mennonite Fellowship	Brethren in Christ General Conference (North America)
1 c/o Bishop Steve Yoder, Contact Person, 28064 CR 52, Nappanee, IN 46550 USA (1927)	1 P.O. Box 245, Upland, CA 91785 USA ☎ [1] (714) 946-0088 (1871)
2 English, Deutsch	2 English
3	3 John A. Byers *Moderator*
4	4 Harold D. Chubb *Director of Finance*
5	5 R. Donald Shafer *General Secretary*
6 Steve Yoder	6 R. Donald Shafer
7 *Calvary Messenger*	7 *Evangelical Visitor*, 301 N. Elm St., P.O. Box 166, Nappanee, IN 46550
8	8 Evangel Publishing House
9 c	9 c, e
10 Amish Mennonite Aid, 9650 Iams Rd., Plain City, OH 43064 ☎ [1] (614) 873-8140; Mission Interests Committee ☎ [1] (215) 593-5764	10 BICWM
11	11
12	12
13 MCC	13 MCC
14	14
15	15

Beachy Amish Mennonite Fellowship						Brethren in Christ General Conference					
16	105	21	a	26		16	225	21	a	26	25
17		22	2	27	6	17	225	22	1–2	27	200
18		23	90	28	0	18	20,789	23		28	0
19	7,238	24	a	29	b	19	19,853	24	a, c	29	a, b
20	b	25	300	30	BA	20	c (90%)	25	342	30	BIC

North America
Amérique du Nord
Nordamerika
América del Norte

Canada/United States
Canada/Etats-Unis
Kanada/Vereinigte Staaten
Canadá/Estados Unidos

Church of God in Christ, Mennonite

1	420 North Wedel, P.O. Box 230, Moundridge, KS 67107 USA ☎ [1] (316) 345-2532 (1859)
2	English
3	
4	
5	
6	
7	*Messenger of Truth*, P.O. Box 230, Moundridge, KS 67107
8	Gospel Publishers
9	c
10	General Mission Board/Missions in USA/Missions in Canada
11	
12	US $3,135,180
13	Christian Service International
14	
15	US $851,414

16	111	21	a	26	0
17		22	2	27	0
18		23	90–100	28	
19	12,694	24	b	29	
20	b	25	490	30	CGC

Eastern Pennsylvania Mennonite Church and Related Areas

1	
2	English
3	
4	
5	
6	Jesse Neuenschwander, 325A West Newport Road, Lititz, PA 17543
7	*Eastern Mennonite Testimony*
8	Eastern Mennonite Publications, 431 Royer Road, Lititz, PA 17543
9	c
10	Mennonite Messianic Mission, Inc., 325A West Newport Road, Lititz, PA 17543 ☎ [1] (215) 693-5708
11	
12	
13	
14	
15	

16	55	21		26	
17		22		27	
18		23		28	1
19	3,255	24		29	
20		25		30	

North America
Amérique du Nord
Nordamerika
América del Norte

Canada/United States
Canada/Etats-Unis
Kanada/Vereinigte Staaten
Canadá/Estados Unidos

Evangelical Mennonite Mission Conference

1	Box 126, Winnipeg, MB R3C 2G1 Canada ☎ [1] (204) 477-1213 (1959)
2	English, Deutsch
3	Leonard Sawatzky *Moderator*
4	Henry Thiessen *Business Administrator*
5	Henry Dueck *Executive Secretary*
6	Henry Dueck, Leonard Sawatzky
7	*EMMC Recorder*, Box 126, Winnipeg, MB R3C 2G1
8	
9	c
10	EMMC
11	
12	
13	MCC
14	
15	

16	24	21	a	26	7
17	32	22	2	27	28
18	4,600	23	130	28	1
19	3,470	24	a	29	b
20	b (50%), c	25	55	30	EMMC

General Conference of the Mennonite Brethren Churches

1	4–169 Riverton Avenue, Winnipeg, MB R2L 2E5 Canada; 315 South Lincoln, Hillsboro, KS 67063 USA ☎ [1] (316) 947-3151 (USA) (1879)
2	Engl., Canton., Comanche, Deutsch, Español, Franç., Hindi, Khmu, Lao, Mandar., Portu., Punjabi, Russian, Sioux, Vietnam.
3	Herbert Brandt *Moderator*
4	J. Neufeld (Canada); M. Reimer (USA)
5	Ronald Reimer *Secretary*
6	315 South Lincoln, Hillsboro, KS 67063
7	*MB Herald; Christian Leader*
8	Kindred Press
9	c, e
10	MBM/S
11	
12	
13	MCC
14	
15	

16	317	21	a	26	40 ±
17	317	22	2	27	406
18		23	90	28	6
19	43,452	24	a, b	29	a, b, c
20	c	25		30	MB

North America
Amérique du Nord
Nordamerika
América del Norte

Canada/United States
Canada/Etats-Unis
Kanada/Vereinigte Staaten
Canadá/Estados Unidos

Hutterian Brethren

Mennonite Church General Assembly

	Hutterian Brethren
1	(1874)
2	English, Deutsch
3	Jacob Kleinsasser *Head Elder*
4	
5	
6	Jacob Kleinsasser, Crystal Spring Colony, Ste. Agathe, MB R0G 1Y0 Canada
7	
8	
9	c
10	
11	
12	
13	
14	
15	

	Mennonite Church General Assembly
1	421 South Second Street, Suite 600, Elkhart, IN 46516-3243 USA ☎ [1] (219) 294-7131 (1898/1971)
2	English, Choctow, Cree, Creek, Español, Français, Hmong, Indonesian, Navajo, Ojibway, Vietnamese
3	George R. Brunk III *Moderator*
4	Timothy J. Burkholder *Treasurer*
5	James M. Lapp *Executive Secretary*
6	James M. Lapp
7	*Gospel Herald*, 616 Walnut Ave., Scottdale, PA 15683
8	Mennonite Publishing House
9	c, e
10	MBM
11	
12	
13	MCC
14	
15	

Hutterian Brethren

16	353	21		26	
17	353	22		27	
18	35,000 ±	23		28	
19	14,000 ±	24		29	
20		25		30	

Mennonite Church General Assembly

16	1,055	21	a	26	177
17	1,000 ±	22	1–2	27	800 ±
18	159,165	23	70	28	3
19	102,276	24	a	29	a, b, c
20	b (90%), c	25	2,624	30	MC

Canada/United States
Canada/Etats-Unis
Kanada/Vereinigte Staaten
Canadá/Estados Unidos

Mennonite Church (Independent and Unaffiliated Groups)

Old Order Amish

1					1	(c. 1870)			
2	English				2	Deutsch, English			

3		3	
4		4	
5		5	
6		6	

7		7	
8		8	Ben J. Raber (Baltic, Ohio)

9		9	c

10		10	
11		11	
12		12	

13		13	
14		14	
15		15	

16	288	21		26		16	784	21	a	26	0
17		22		27		17	784	22	Ev. 2	27	0
18	17,577	23		28		18	127,800	23	100	28	0
19	13,878	24		29		19	56,200 ±	24	a, c	29	
20		25		30		20	b	25	2,200	30	A

North America
Amérique du Nord
Nordamerika
América del Norte

United States
Etats-Unis
Vereinigte Staaten
Estados Unidos

Evangelical Mennonite Church

General Conference Mennonite Church (USA)

	Evangelical Mennonite Church		General Conference Mennonite Church (USA)
1	1420 Kerrway Ct., Ft. Wayne, IN 46805 USA ☎ [1] (219) 423-3649 (1865)	1	Box 347, Newton, KS 67114 USA ☎ [1] (316) 283-5100 (1860)
2	English	2	English, Arapaho, Blackfeet, Cantonese, Cheyenne, Choctaw, Creole, Deutsch, Español, Hmong, Hopi, Lao, Mandarin, Navajo, Taiwanese, Vietnamese
3	Douglas Habegger *Chairman*	3	Florence Driedger *Moderator*
4	Dennis Zimmerman *Treasurer*	4	Ted W. Stuckey *Treasurer*
5	Donald Roth *President*	5	Vern Preheim *General Secretary*
6	Donald Roth	6	Vern Preheim
7	*EMC Today*, 1420 Kerrway Ct., Ft. Wayne, IN 46805	7	*The Mennonite*, Box 347, Newton, KS 67114
8		8	Faith and Life Press
9		9	c, e
10	Department of International Ministries, 1420 Kerrway Ct., Ft. Wayne, IN 46805 ☎ [1] (219) 423-3649	10	COM
11	40	11	
12	US $443,768	12	
13	MCC	13	MCC
14		14	
15		15	

Evangelical Mennonite Church

16	26	21		26	
17	26	22		27	
18	4,700	23	117	28	0
19	3,888	24		29	
20		25		30	EMC

General Conference Mennonite Church (USA)

16	258	21	a	26	
17	258	22	1	27	338
18	43,162	23		28	1
19	33,812	24	a	29	c
20	a, b, c	25	756	30	GC

North America
Amérique du Nord
Nordamerika
América del Norte

United States
Etats-Unis
Vereinigte Staaten
Estados Unidos

Hutterian Brethren (Society of Brothers)

Old Order Mennonites

1	Woodcrest, Rifton, NY 12471 USA
	☎ [1] (914) 658-3141
	(1954)
2	English, Deutsch

3	Johann C. Arnold *Elder*
4	Marcus Mommson *Steward*
5	Christopher Winter *Servant of the Word*
6	Johann C. Arnold

7	*The Plough*, Hutterian Brethren, Ulster Park, NY 12487
8	Plough Publishing House

9	c

10	Woodcrest Service Committee, Hutterian Brethren, Rifton, NY 12471
	☎ [1] (914) 658-3141
11	20
12	

13	Woodcrest Service Committee
14	
15	

16	6	21	a	26	18
17	6	22	4–5	27	0
18	1,800	23	98	28	0
19	800	24	b	29	
20	b, c	25	14	30	

1	(1845–)
2	English, Deutsch

3	
4	
5	
6	c/o Lloyd Weiler, R.D. 3, Box 429 K, Manheim, PA 17545

7	
8	

9	c

10	
11	
12	

13	MCC
14	
15	

16	49	21	a	26	0
17	74	22	1, Ev. 2	27	0
18		23		28	0
19	10,000 ±	24	b	29	
20	b	25		30	

North America
Amérique du Nord
Nordamerika
América del Norte

United States
Etats-Unis
Vereinigte Staaten
Estados Unidos

Old Order River Brethren

1	c/o Stephen Scott, Contact Person, Route 1, Box 362, Columbia, PA 17512 USA (c. 1780)
2	English
3	
4	
5	
6	Stephen Scott
7	
8	
9	c
10	
11	
12	
13	
14	
15	

16	7	21	b	26	0
17		22	1	27	0
18	522	23	188	28	0
19	326	24	a	29	
20	c	25	32	30	

Agencies

Mennonite Christian Service Fellowship of India

Yayasan Pengutusan Injil & Pelayanan Kasih

To encourage and promote Christian service in the spirit of Christ in the educational, social, medical, philanthropic, and religious fields. And to seek ways and means to strengthen the Fellowship among its cooperating and associated members and churches and to promote evangelism and peace witness for the purpose of the foregoing objectives.

The Vision: Proclaim the Whole Gospel to the Whole Nation.
The Guiding Idea: Holistic ministry.
The Purpose: Church planting and community development.
The Goal for the Year 2000: Plant 50 new churches; establish 10 new independent churches.

1	MCSFI	1	Yayasan PIPKA
2	c/o Mennonite Central Committee, 22 Girish Chandra Bose Road, Calcutta 14, India	2	Kosambi I/7, Kalibaru, P.O. Box 8/TPK, Jakarta 14001, Indonesia
3		3	☎ [62] (21) 492831
4		4	
5		5	
6		6	
7	1963	7	1965
8	P.B. Arnold *Chairperson*	8	Eddy Sutjipto
9	R.S. Lemuel *Director*	9	Yahya Chrismanto
10	Z.B. Gardia *Treasurer*	10	Stefanus Haryono
11	Six Mennonite conferences in India, Council of International Ministries (CIM), Mennonite Central Committee (MCC)	11	Gereja Kristen Muria Indonesia (GKMI), Eastern Mennonite Board of Missions and Charities (EMBMC), Mennonite Brethren Missions/Services (MBM/S), Mennonite Central Committee (MCC)

12	US Dollars	17	5,000	12	US Dollars	17	75,500
13	4,300	18	2,000	13	75,000	18	42,200
14	4,300	19	1,300	14	61,150	19	33,300
15		20	2	15	11,150	20	62
16		21	0	16	2,700	21	15
		22				22	0

South America
Amérique Sud
Südamerika
América del Sur

Asociación de Servicios de Cooperación Indígena-Mennonita

Associação Menonita de Assistência Social

Acompañar a las Comunidades Indígenas del Chaco Central en su desenvolvimiento socio-económico. Orientar este proceso de acompañamiento en base de una cooperación recíproca, respetando iniciativa y responsabilidad propia de cada comunidad indígena.

AMAS ist ein mennonitisches, missionarisch ausgerichtetes, soziales Hilfswerk der deutschsprachigen Mennonitengemeinden Brasiliens. Das Werk will armen, notleidenden Kindern und Familien, ohne Unterschied von Rasse, Nation und Religion, Gottes Liebe in Wort und Tat nahebringen, nach dem Motto: Dienen in der Liebe Christi.

1	ASCIM	1	AMAS
2	Filadelfia, c.d.c. 984, Asunción, Paraguay	2	Rua Francisco Derosso 2660, 81.500 Curitiba, Brasil
3	☎ [595] (91) 231	3	☎ [55] (41) 277-3482
4		4	
5		5	
6		6	
7	1962	7	1972

8	Cornelius B. Sawatzky *Presidente*	8	Henrique Ens *Presidente*
9	Helmut Giesbrecht *Director*	9	Heinrich Koop *Gerente Administrativo*
10	Willi W. Reimer *Tesorero*	10	Gerhard Klassen *Tesoureiro*

11	Las iglesias menonitas del Chaco Paraguayo	11	Associação das Igrejas Menonitas do Brasil (AIMB), Ev. Kirchengemeinde Eibelshausen BRD, Internationale Mennonitische Organisation (IMO), Mennonite Central Committee (MCC)

12	Guaranies	17	739.267.039	12	US Dollars	17	123,000
13	739.267.039	18	496.626.039	13	123,000	18	53,000
14	496.571.948	19	242.641.000	14	63,000	19	70,000
15	203.889.021	20	226	15	32,000	20	70
16	38.806.070	21	0	16	28,000	21	18
	[1 Gs=US $.0008]	22	4			22	7

Europe
Europe
Europa
Europa

Europäisches Mennonitisches Evangelisations Komitee

Europäisches Mennonitisches Friedenskomitee

Les anabaptistes ont toujours souligné que la vie d'obéissance doit aller de pair avec l'annonce de la doctrine évangélique. Michaël Sattler disait à Bucer: "Oui, nous sommes sauvés par la foi, sans les œuvres, mais pas sans les œuvres de la foi". Ainsi, nos Eglises soutiennent, en plus de la mission, des œuvres de secours. Nous recherchons, partout où c'est possible, une coordination et une collaboration franche entre Mission et Oeuvre de Secours.

EMFK facilitates the exchange of news among European Mennonite peace groups. When needed, it helps to coordinate common projects of peace groups and provides a forum where European Mennonites organized in peace groups can be addressed as a whole. If necessary, bigger common interests are organized in the form of interest groups (e.g., NATO WATCH). EMFK believes that international exchange and coordination add a new and necessary dimension to the peace witness in this time of ever larger-scale communications and economic dependencies.

1	EMEK		
2	2a, rue de Bischwihr, F-68280 Andolsheim, France		
3	☎ [33] (89) 714301		
4			
5			
6			
7	1951		

8	Alle Hoekema		
9	Raymond Eyer *Secrétaire Exécutif*		
10	Heinrich Zeisset		

11	Les Eglises mennonites des Pays-Bas, d'Allemagne Fédérale, de Suisse et de France et leurs Comités de Missions: DZR, DMMK, SMEK, CMMF

12	DM	17	622.185
13	622.185	18	403.998
14	622.185	19	218.187
15		20	0
16		21	1
	[1 DM=US $.5918]	22	0

1	EMFK, European Mennonite Peace Committee, EMPC
2	Mesdaghout 38, NL-8072 JJ Nunspeet, Nederland
3	☎ [31] (3412) 52438
4	
5	[31] (3412) 60346
6	
7	1985

8	
9	Maarten van der Werf *Secretary*
10	D. Nielsen *Treasurer*

11	Schweizersches Mennonitisches Friedenskomitee (SMFK), Deutsches Mennonitisches Friedenskomitee (DMFK), Doopsgezinde Vredesgroep (DVG), Irish Mennonite Movement, Centre Mennonite de Bruxelles, MCC

12	Dutch Guilders	17	21.500
13	21.500	18	12.000
14	21.500	19	9.500
15		20	0
16		21	1
	[1 hfl.=US $.5241]	22	5–10

Europe
Europe
Europa
Europa

Internationale Mennonitische Organisation e.V.

Mennonitische Umsiedlerbetreuung

Aufgabe ist Hilfswerk orientiert am Evangelium Jesu Christi. Wo immer möglich bietet es Hilfe zur Selbsthilfe. In der praktischen Ausführung heißt das fast immer Zusammenarbeit mit vor Ort tätigen Organisationen in vereinbarten Projekten. Dazu werden auch Freiwillige vermittelt und ausgesandt.

Ministry and assistance to emigrants from the Soviet Union to Bundesrepublik Deutschland.

1	IMO	1	MUB
2	Langendorfer Str. 29, D-5450 Neuwied 1, Bundesrepublik Deutschland	2	Langendorfer Str. 29, D-5450 Neuwied 1, Bundesrepublik Deutschland
3	☎ [49] (2631) 31440	3	☎ [49] (2631) 31871
4	867785 MCC D	4	867785 MCC D
5	[49] (2631) 25808	5	[49] (2631) 25808
6		6	
7	1967	7	

8	Rolf-Rüdiger Schuster *Vorsitzender*	8	
9	Volker Horsch *Geschäftsführer*	9	Hans von Niessen *Geschäftsführer*
10		10	

11	"Aus Großer Freude" e.V., Bund europäischer Mennoniten Brüdergemeinden, Mennonitisches Hilfswerk "Christenpflicht" e.V., Stichting voor Bijzondere Noden in de Doopsgezinde Broederschap en Daarbuiten, Vereinigung der Deutschen Mennonitengem.	11	IMO, MCC

12	DM	17	1.661.000	12		17	
13	1.661.000	18	567.400	13		18	
14	633.000	19	1.093.600	14		19	
15	700.000	20	1	15		20	
16	338.000	21	2	16		21	
	[1 DM=US $.5918]	22	25			22	

North America
Amérique du Nord
Nordamerika
América del Norte

Africa Inter-Mennonite Mission

Brethren in Christ World Missions

AIMM believes in the primacy of communicating the Gospel of Christ by sharing the truth of Scripture and demonstrating the love of God through Christian compassion, nurture, and service.

The Brethren in Christ are committed to worship and obey the triune God. The chief purpose of the Brethren in Christ Church is to establish groups of fellowshiping believers in obedience to the Great Commission. Our goal is to establish groups of fellowshiping believers (congregations) in at least 20 countries of the world. It is our goal to see them develop into self-governing and self-propagating churches.

	Africa Inter-Mennonite Mission		Brethren in Christ World Missions
1	AIMM	1	BWM, BICWM
2	Box 518, Elkhart, IN 46515 USA	2	500 South Angle Street, P.O. Box 390, Mount Joy, PA 17552 USA
3	☎ [1] (219) 875-5552	3	☎ [1] (717) 653-8067
4		4	
5	[1] (219) 875-6576	5	
6		6	BICMISSION
7	1912	7	1898
8	Henry Klassen *President of Board*	8	Lowell D. Mann *Chairman*
9	Earl Roth *Executive Secretary*	9	A. Graybill Brubaker *Executive Director*
10	Art Janz *Associate Executive Secretary/ Finances*	10	W. Edward Rickman *US Treasurer*
11	Evangelical Mennonite Church, Evangelical Mennonite Conference, Evangelical Mennonite Mission Conference, Fellowship of Evangelical Bible Churches, General Conference Mennonite Church, Mennonite Brethren Missions/Services	11	Brethren in Christ Church

12	US Dollars	17	1,403,646	12	US Dollars	17	1,500,000
13	1,403,646	18	1,318,839	13	1,500,000	18	
14	1,179,524	19	84,807	14		19	
15	117,945	20	65	15		20	126
16	106,177	21	1	16		21	5
		22	3			22	15+

North America
Amérique du Nord
Nordamerika
América del Norte

Christian Peacemaker Teams

Commission on Overseas Mission

Christian Peacemaker Teams is a unique initiative at peacemaking among cooperating Mennonite and Brethren churches. The concept emphasizes the art of nonviolent direct action in addition to research, prayer, negotiations, and careful organization. This action when done from a biblical point of view is a timely gift of ministry for the late-twentieth-century church.

COM is a channel for General Conference Mennonite churches to fulfill corporately in other nations the biblical missionary mandate of reconciliation and love, proclaiming to all peoples by word and deed, in a servanthood stance, that Jesus Christ is the only Savior and Lord, and seeking the formation of caring communities of believers (churches) which in turn have a mission outreach. COM is ready to serve with the churches of the world as a channel for joint mission and for cultivating fellowship across national boundaries.

1	CPT	1	COM
2	1821 West Cullerton, Chicago, IL 60608 USA	2	722 Main Street, Box 347, Newton, KS 67114 USA
3	☎ [1] (312) 421-5513	3	☎ [1] (316) 283-5100
4		4	281854
5		5	[1] (316) 283-0454
6		6	
7	1987	7	1860

8	Edgar Metzler	8	William Block *Chairperson*
9	Gene Stoltzfus *Coordinator*	9	Erwin Rempel *Executive Secretary*
10		10	Ted Stuckey *Business Manager and Treasurer*

11	Brethren in Christ, Church of the Brethren, General Conference Mennonite Church, Mennonite Church	11	General Conference Mennonite Church

12	US Dollars	17	15,000	12	US Dollars	17	3,200,000
13	15,000	18	12,000	13	3,250,000 ±	18	
14	8,000	19	3,000	14	2,925,000 ±	19	
15	7,000	20	0	15	325,000 ±	20	120
16	0	21	1	16	0	21	
		22	400 ±			22	

North America
Amérique du Nord
Nordamerika
América del Norte

Conservative Mennonite Board of Missions and Charities

Eastern Mennonite Board of Missions and Charities

The primary missionary goal of the church is a spiritual ministry of evangelism in which individuals are won to a saving faith in Jesus Christ and are brought into a circle of fellowship, edification, and witness. Responsive persons are gathered into indigenous churches with eventual indigenous leadership. The goal of relief, social, and developmental projects is to relieve human suffering. These projects may utilize education, facilitation, and advocacy in behalf of the sufferers. These programs contribute to the primary goal of evangelism and provide settings for spiritual ministry.

EMBMC is commissioned by Lancaster Mennonite Conference to cultivate a vision for world mission and to be a channel for congregations to fulfill corporately the biblical mandate for reconciliation and wholeness of all people in Christ Jesus. We proclaim by word and deed that Jesus Christ is the only Savior and Lord. We invite people to yield to God's rule and become caring communities. We partner with others near and far to carry out ministries of compassion and evangelism, plant churches, make and equip disciples, train leaders, work for justice, and cultivate fellowship.

1	Rosedale Mennonite Missions, RMM
2	9920 Rosedale-Milford Center Road,
	Irwin, OH 43029 USA
3	☎ [1] (614) 857-1068
4	
5	
6	
7	1919

8	Jesse L. Yoder *Chairman of the Board of Directors*
9	David I. Miller *President*
10	Levi Miller *Treasurer*

11	Conservative Mennonite Conference

1	EMBMC, Eastern Mennonite Board
2	Oak Lane and Brandt Boulevard,
	Salunga, PA 17538 USA
3	☎ [1] (717) 898-2251
4	90-2210 MENCENCOM AKRP
5	[1] (717) 898-8092
6	MENMISSION
7	1914

8	Jay C. Garber *Chairman*
9	Paul G. Landis *President*
10	Dale E. Witmer *Treasurer*

11	Lancaster Mennonite Conference

12	US Dollars	17	1,044,304
13	1,029,503	18	
14	630,486	19	
15	131,062	20	40
16	0	21	15
		22	45

12	US Dollars	17	5,674,648
13	5,723,057	18	3,674,648
14	4,904,768	19	2,000,000
15	765,745	20	309
16	52,544	21	15
		22	168

North America
Amérique du Nord
Nordamerika
América del Norte

Evangelical Mennonite Conference Board of Missions

Evangelical Mennonite Mission Conference Bd. of Missions and Service

The primary goal is to glorify God and to establish local autonomous churches in areas of ministry and that these churches form a national conference in their particular country. To fulfill the primary goal involves various types of ministries such as evangelism, church planting, leadership training, radio, medical, literature, and educational development programs.

EMMC regards the Great Commission as a mandate to disciple peoples by preaching the Gospel of Christ, baptizing those who respond in repentance and faith, and teaching them to observe the Lord's commands. This outreach has several emphases, but the primary goal is to establish churches which will themselves develop into sending churches in their own way. EMMC believes it should minister to people according to their needs. EMMC is committed to the Anabaptist-Mennonite tradition and recognizes its loyalty to Jesus Christ as the determining principle in all of its activities.

1	EMCC Board of Missions	1	EMMC Board of Missions
2	Box 1268, Steinbach, MB R0A 2A0 Canada	2	526 McMillan Avenue, Box 126, Winnipeg, MB R3C 2G1 Canada
3	☎ [1] (204) 326-6401	3	☎ [1] (204) 477-1213
4		4	
5		5	
6		6	
7	1953	7	1959

8	Jonathan Bonk *Chairman*	8	George A. Hildebrand *Chairman*
9	Henry Klassen *Executive Secretary*	9	Lawrence Giesbrecht *Director of Missions*
10		10	Henry Thiessen *Business Administrator*

11	Evangelical Mennonite Conference (Canada)	11	Evangelical Mennonite Mission Conference

12	Cdn Dollars	17	1,388,263	12	Cdn Dollars	17	435,463
13	1,388,263	18		13	435,463	18	225,690
14		19		14		19	
15		20	100	15		20	12
16		21	6	16	1,000	21	1
	[1 Cdn=US $.8635]	22			[1 Cdn=US $.8635]	22	6 ±

North America
Amérique du Nord
Nordamerika
América del Norte

Mennonite Board of Missions

Mennonite Brethren Missions/Services

In joyful response to God's forgiving grace, Christ's redeeming ministry, and the Spirit's empowering presence, the Mennonite Board of Missions seeks to lead and enable the Mennonite Church, through its conferences and congregations, to fulfill its evangelizing mission by proclaiming hope and wholeness for all people in the kingdom of our Lord; sharing God's love in Christ with alienated persons through our lives, witness, and service; calling people to repentance, faith, and discipleship in caring communities around the world.

Mennonite Brethren Missions/Services is an agency of the Mennonite Brethren church whose mission, empowered by the Holy Spirit, is to glorify God by bringing the gospel of Christ to the unevangelized of the world, and by ministering to the needs of mankind, to the end that people of all nations are discipled into vibrant, active, reproducing churches (Acts 1:8, Matt. 28:19).

1	MBM
2	500 South Main Street, Box 370, Elkhart, IN 46515 USA
3	☎ [1] (219) 294-7523
4	6503231818 MCIUW
5	
6	MENBOARD
7	1906

8	Ronald B. Schertz *Chairperson, Board of Directors*
9	Paul M. Gingrich *President*
10	Edward L. Burkholder *Treasurer*

11	Mennonite Church in North America

12	US Dollars	17	8,202,109
13	8,329,270	18	4,021,735
14	3,632,920	19	4,180,374
15	4,696,350	20	191
16		21	23
		22	174

1	MBM/S
2	2–169 Riverton Avenue, Winnipeg, MB R2L 2E5 Canada
3	☎ [1] (204) 669-6575
4	
5	[1] (204) 667-0680
6	
7	1900

8	Henry H. Dick *Chairman*
9	Victor Adrian *General Secretary*
10	S.V. Epp *Secretary for Finances*

11	Conference of Mennonite Brethren Churches of North America

12	US/Cdn $	17	
13	5,545,500	18	3,954,000
14	4,572,500	19	
15		20	162
16	551,600	21	2
		22	

North America
Amérique du Nord
Nordamerika
América del Norte

Mennonite Central Committee

Mennonite Central Committee Canada

MCC is the service ministry of Mennonite and Brethren in Christ churches of North America. As an inter-Mennonite organization, its specific concerns are emergency relief, community development, peace, and reconciliation. The primary vehicle of fulfilling its mission is through the placement of volunteers.

MCC is the cooperative relief and service agency of North American Mennonite and Brethren in Christ churches and conferences. MCC Canada directs programs in Canada and participates in international activities through MCC in Akron, Pennsylvania.

1	MCC
2	21 South 12th Street, Akron, PA 17501 USA
3	☎ [1] (717) 859-1151
4	90-2210 MENCENCOM AKRP
5	[1] (717) 859-2622
6	MENCENCOM 17501
7	1920

1	MCCC, MCC Canada
2	134 Plaza Drive, Winnipeg, MB R3T 5K9 Canada
3	☎ [1] (204) 261-6381
4	0757525 MENCENCOM WPG
5	[1] (204) 269-9875
6	MENCENCOM
7	1963

8	Ron Mathies *Chairperson*
9	John A. Lapp *Executive Secretary*
10	Paul Quiring *Treasurer*

8	Jake Harder *Chairperson*
9	Daniel Zehr *Executive Director*
10	Arthur Driedger *Treasurer*

11	Mennonite and Brethren in Christ churches of the US and Canada, including Beachy Amish, BIC, Emmanuel Mennonite Church, Evangelical Mennonite Church, Evangelical Mennonite Conf., EMMC, GC, MB, MC, Old Colony, Sommerfeld

11	Brethren in Christ, Chortitzer, Conference of Mennonites in Canada, Evangelical Mennonite Conference, EMMC, Mennonite Brethren Church, Mennonite Conference of Eastern Canada, Northwest Mennonite Conference, Old Colony, Sommerfeld

12	US Dollars	17	31,714,000
13	33,785,000	18	7,723,000
14	13,754,000	19	11,110,208
15		20	90
16	5,491,000	21	
		22	500 (+ 15,000)

12	Cdn Dollars	17	18,000,000
13	18,000,000	18	
14		19	
15		20	60
16		21	25
[1 Cdn=US $.8635]		22	190

North America
Amérique du Nord
Nordamerika
América del Norte

Mennonite Central Committee U.S.

Mennonite Economic Development Associates

1. To carry overall responsibility for MCC domestic programming in the United States.
2. To generate constituency support for the worldwide ministries and programs of MCC.
3. To work at the area of constituency relations in cooperation with MCC.
4. To encourage inter-Mennonite cooperation in local and regional groupings in the United States.

Mennonite Economic Development Associates is an association of people who are committed to the nurture and expression of their Christian faith in a business or work setting. MEDA exists to enable members to integrate biblical values and business principles in their daily lives and to address the needs of the disadvantaged through programs of economic development. MEDA programs are designed with the assumption that people in business are called to honor God in the world of work and economics by extending God's reign to all their activities.

1	MCC U.S.		1	MEDA	
2	21 South 12th Street, Akron, PA 17501 USA		2	402–280 Smith Street, Winnipeg, MB R3C 1K2 Canada	
3	☎ [1] (717) 859-1151		3	☎ [1] (204) 944-1995	
4	90-2210 MENCENCOM AKRP		4		
5	[1] (717) 859-2622		5	[1] (204) 943-2597	
6	MENCENCOM 17501		6		
7	1979		7	1953	

8	Phil Rich *Chairperson*	8	LeRoy Troyer *Chairperson of the Board of Directors*	
9	Lynette Meck *Executive Secretary*	9	Neil Janzen *President*	
10	Paul Quiring *Treasurer*	10	Charles Loewen *Treasurer*	

11	Beachy Amish, Brethren in Christ, Emmanuel Mennonite Church, Evangelical Mennonite Church, General Conference Mennonite Church, Mennonite Brethren Church, Mennonite Church	11	Membership of about 2,000 mostly business and professional people drawn from Mennonite and Brethren in Christ churches

12	US Dollars	17	3,330,000		12	US Dollars	17	1,912,917
13	3,738,000	18			13	1,971,210	18	
14		19			14	0	19	
15		20	50		15	574,735	20	23
16		21			16	1,396,475	21	2
		22	110				22	2

North America
Amérique du Nord
Nordamerika
América del Norte

Mennonite Health Services

Virginia Mennonite Board of Missions

Mennonite Health Services is a subsidiary corporation of MCC, commissioned to carry out the biblical injunction to help people toward health and hope. Serving in the name of Christ and recognizing the value of all human life, MHS sponsors healthcare and human service institutions/programs, promotes the potential of Christian community for healing, and fosters new opportunities of service.

As an agency of Virginia Mennonite Conference, the Virginia Mennonite Board of Missions exists to challenge and enable the Church to be faithful in keeping Christ's commandment to proclaim the Gospel and to make disciples in all the world by following His example in ministering to the whole person. We seek to plant indigenous congregations both overseas and within the United States, primarily in our geographical area.

1	MHS		
2	21 South 12th Street, Akron, PA 17501 USA		
3	☎ [1] (717) 859-1151		
4			
5	[1] (717) 859-2622		
6			
7	1952		

8	Larry Nikkel *Chairperson*
9	Carl L. Good *Executive Director*
10	Harold Loewen *Treasurer*

11	Mennonite Central Committee

12	US Dollars	17	360,332
13	360,332	18	201,387
14	109,000	19	
15	18,950	20	6
16		21	
		22	

1			
2	901 Parkwood Drive, Harrisonburg, VA 22801 USA		
3	☎ [1] (703) 434-9727		
5			
6			
7	1919		

8	Richard Bowman *Chairman of the Board*
9	Paul T. Yoder *President*
10	Richard K. Lantz *Treasurer*

11	Virginia Mennonite Conference

12	US Dollars	17	736,214
13	629,517	18	521,851
14	315,753	19	13,626
15	248,795	20	17
16	17,537	21	7
		22	9

cilitation

International Mennonite Peace Committee

Mennonite World Conference

IMPC is a subcommittee of MWC with the following purposes: (1) to listen to, share, and discern the experience of the Mennonite church worldwide in regard to the issues of justice, peace, and preservation of creation, with special attention to the role of the church in the state and society, (2) to support peace and justice education in churches, (3) to provide assistance in planning MWC events, (4) to provide an entity within MWC that is dedicated to periodic analysis and reflection around the Bible on selected themes, (5) to promote interchurch peace efforts and a witness to the larger world.

Acknowledging and appreciating our diversity, MWC promotes the vision of a more unified, global body where the biblical principles of justice, love, and mutual concern can be lived out daily. MWC identifies three areas of continuing activity: fellowship, facilitation, and communication.

1	IMPC, Comité International Mennonite pour la Paix (CIMP), Internationales Mennonitisches Friedenskomitee (IMFK), Comité Internacional Menonita de Paz (CIMP)
2	c/o Mennonite World Conference
3	
4	
5	
6	
7	1978
8	
9	Hansulrich Gerber, Executive Secretary
10	
11	Mennonite World Conference

1	MWC, Conférence Mennonite Mondiale (CMM), Mennonitische Weltkonferenz (MWK), Congreso Mundial Menonita (CMM)
2	465 Gundersen Drive, Suite 200, Carol Stream, IL 60188 USA
	1990: + Strasbourg, France
3	☎ [1] (708) 690-9666
4	4931833 MWC UI
5	[1] (708) 260-0114
6	MENNOWORLD
7	1925
8	Ross T. Bender *President*
9	Paul N. Kraybill *Executive Secretary*
	Larry Miller *Executive Secretary 1990–*
10	Ray Schlichting *Treasurer*
11	Mennonite, Brethren in Christ, and related churches worldwide

12	US Dollars	17	18,800
13	18,800	18	11,800
14	18,800	19	0
15	0	20	0
16	0	21	1
		22	0

12	US Dollars	17	200,000
13	200,000	18	60,000
14	107,000	19	0
15	84,000	20	3
16	0	21	1
		22	0

Facilitation
Coordination
Handreichung
Facilitación

Africa Mennonite and Brethren in Christ Fellowship

Asia Mennonite Conference

AMBCF is an organization of Mennonite and Brethren in Christ conferences in Africa. Its purpose is to promote fellowship, communication, and mission.

AMC is a fellowship of Mennonite and Brethren in Christ conferences in Asia and Australia. Its purpose is (1) to provide fellowship among these church members, (2) to facilitate sharing of information through a semiannual newsletter, (3) to encourage international exchange visits, (4) to sponsor work camps and other activities for youth, (5) to organize and sponsor a General Assembly, (6) to encourage and facilitate missionary outreach, (7) to promote the study of the Anabaptist peace witness and discipleship and apply this in each national and regional context.

1	AMBCF		
2	P.O. Box 14299, Nairobi, Kenya		
3			
4			
5			
6			
7	1962		
8	Stephen Ndlovu *Chair*		
9	Million Belete *Secretary/Treasurer*		
10			
11	Mennonite and Brethren in Christ conferences in Africa		
12	Kenya Shillings	17	815 (US $38)
13	6675 (US $315)	18	
14	6675 (US $315)	19	
15		20	
16		21	
		22	

1	AMC		
2	c/o Eastern Mennonite Board of Missions and Charities, 76 Waterloo Road 1/F, Kowloon, Hong Kong		
3	☎ [852] 7134271		
4			
5			
6			
7	1971		
8	Joshua Chang *Chairman, AMC Steering Committee*		
9	Yorifumi Yaguchi *Secretary, AMC Steering Committee*		
10	Paul Wing-Sang Wong *AMC Treasurer*		
11	Mennonite churches in Asia, Council of International Ministries (CIM)		
12	US Dollars	17	3,000–4,000 ±
13		18	
14	2,000 ±	19	
15	2,500 ±	20	
16		21	
		22	

Facilitation
Coordination
Handreichung
Facilitación

Canadian Council of Mennonite & Brethren in Christ Moderators

Centro Latinoamericano de Recursos Anabautistas

A forum for consultation and discussion among Canadian Mennonite and Brethren in Christ conferences and with Mennonite Central Committee Canada.

CLARA es un Centro de Coordinación, Divulgación, y Producción de Recursos Anabautistas para América Latina. CLARA es un esfuerzo conjunto de organizaciones y personas que tienen el interés de promover la visión de la reforma radical en América Latina. CLARA funcionará en forma "decentralizada" y tratará de responder a iniciativas de convenciones, instituciones, y congregaciones. CLARA ayudará con la coordinación o producción de recursos necesarios.

1	CCMBCM	1	CLARA
2	Box 1554, Steinbach, MB R0A 2A0 Canada	2	Cra. 15 No. 32-78, Apartado Aéreo 57-527, Bogotá 2, Colombia
3	☎ [1] (204) 326-2759	3	☎ [57] (91) 2452256
4		4	
5		5	
6		6	
7	1986	7	1989

8	Herb Neufeld *Chair*	8	
9	Leonard Sawatsky *Secretary*	9	Roberto Suderman *Director*
10		10	

11	BIC, Conf. of Mennonites in Canada, Evangelical Mennonite Conf., EMMC, Markham-Waterloo Conf., Mennonite Brethren, Mennonite Church, Mennonite Conf. of Eastern Canada, Old Colony Mennonites, Reinland Mennonite Church, Sommerfeld Mennonite	11	Igl. Evangélica Menonita de Colombia, Convención Hispana Menonita (USA), Junta Admin. Menonita Boliviana, CEMTA, CAMCA, SEMILLA, Agrupación Menon. Lat. de Comunicaciones, MCC, MBM, COM, Concilio de las Igl. Evan. Menonitas en Venezuela

12	17	12	17
13	18	13	18
14	19	14	19
15	20	15	20
16	21	16	21
	22		22

Facilitation
Coordination
Handreichung
Facilitación

Comité National Inter-Mennonite

Congreso Menonita Latinoamericano del Cono Sur

Notre organisation a pour but de servir de cadre de rencontres tendant au renforcement et à l'enrichissement des relations fraternelles, aux réflexions théologiques sur la vision anabaptiste-Mennonite et à la promotion de l'identité Mennonite Africaine.

El Congreso Menonita Latinoamericano del Cono Sur es un encuentro que se realiza cada dos años. El propósito es estrechar vínculos entre las iglesias de la Conferencia General, Menonita y Hermanos Menonitas, estudiar temas de interés común, y buscar maneras de unir esfuerzos para dar testimonio de Cristo y servir en su nombre.

1	CONIM, National Inter-Mennonite Committee		
2	Kwango No. 7, Zone de Kintambo, B.P. 12.639, Kinshasa 1, Zaire		
3	☎ [243] (12) 25-503		
4	21435		
5			
6			
7	1987		

8	
9	Mukanza Ilunga *Secrétaire Exécutif*
10	Kumbi-Kumbi Kamwenyi

11	Communauté Mennonite au Zaire (CMZ), Communauté des Eglises de Frères Mennonites au Zaire (CEFMZ), Communauté Evangélique Mennonite (CEM), Mennonite Central Committee (MCC—Zaire)

12	US Dollars	17	13,180
13	30,621	18	5,980
14	480	19	7,200
15	15,000	20	1
16	0	21	4
		22	4

1	Cono Sur, Southern Cone	
2	c/o 3 de Febrero 4381, 12900 Montevideo, Uruguay	
3		
4		
5		
6		
7	1981	

8	
9	
10	

11	Las iglesias Menonitas del Cono Sur: Argentina, Bolivia, Brasil, Paraguay y Uruguay

12		17	
13		18	
14		19	
15		20	
16		21	
		22	

Facilitation
Coordination
Handreichung
Facilitación

Consulta Anabautista Menonita de Centro América

Council of International Ministries

El propósito: (1) reunirnos una vez al año en un ambiente de fraternidad y solidaridad, para compartir toda experiencia, con el fin de crecer, apoyarnos, acompañarnos y emplazar acciones directas en respuesta a las necesidades surgidas y que demanden especial atención; (2) fomentar las relaciones fraternales entre el liderazgo de las iglesias; (3) promover el crecimiento de las iglesias por medio de la evangelización; (4) cultivar los principios bíblicos interpretados a través de nuestra historia anabautista; (5) realizar proyectos en beneficio de las iglesias; (6) promover la superación ministerial.

The Council seeks to encourage the worldwide witness to the love of God in Jesus Christ by word and deed, to provide a channel for communication and broader understanding among North American Mennonite and Brethren in Christ mission and service agencies involved in work overseas, with opportunity for reporting and sharing activities, program, strategy and problems, plan projects of common interest, and coordinate mutual concerns and overlapping programs.

1	CAMCA
2	19 Avenida 5-94, Zona 11, Ciudad de Guatemala, Guatemala
3	☎ [502] (2) 772631
4	
5	[502] (2) 519680
6	
7	1975

8	Hector Caballero *Coordinador General*
9	
10	

11	12 convenciones de iglesias Menonitas de Centro América, y Puerto Rico como un nuevo miembro

12		17	
13		18	
14		19	
15		20	0
16		21	0
		22	1

1	CIM
2	500 South Main Street, Box 370, Elkhart, IN 46515 USA
3	☎ [1] (219) 294-7523
4	6503231818 MCIUW
5	
6	MENBOARD
7	1958/1976

8	John A. Lapp *Chairperson*
9	Ronald E. Yoder *Executive Secretary*
10	

11	Brethren in Christ, Evangelical Mennonite Church, General Conference Mennonite Church, Mennonite Brethren, Mennonite Church

12	US Dollars	17	56,750
13	56,750	18	6,300
14	56,750	19	
15		20	0
16		21	2
		22	

Facilitation
Coordination
Handreichung
Facilitación

Council of Moderators and Secretaries

Japan Mennonite Fellowship

This is a forum for Mennonite and Brethren in Christ moderators and secretaries to share ideas and common concerns and to facilitate communication and activities that no other group is doing.

1. Promoting mutual cooperation and solidarity among Mennonite/Brethren in Christ churches in Japan.
2. Providing fellowship and study meetings.
3. Settling the identity of the Mennonite church in Japan.

1	CMS	1	JMF, Nihon Mennonite Senkyokai
2	P.O. Box 245, Upland, CA 91785 USA	2	c/o Michio Ohno, 1789-14 Tokecho,
3	☎ [1] (714) 946-0088		Chiba-Shi, Chiba-Ken 299-31, Nippon
4		3	
5		4	
6		5	
7		6	
		7	1971
8	George Brunk III *Chairman*	8	Takanobu Tojo *Chairman*
9	R. Donald Shafer *Secretary*	9	Michio Ohno *Secretary*
10	James Lapp *Treasurer*	10	Mitsuko Yaguchi *Treasurer*
11	Brethren in Christ, General Conference Mennonite Church, Mennonite Brethren, Mennonite Church	11	Japan Mennonite Christian Church Conference, Nihon Menonaito Kirisuto Kyokai Kaigi, Tokyo Chiku Menonaito Kyokai Rengo, Nihon Kirisuto Keiteidan

12		17		12	Yen (US $)	17	400.000 (2,800)
13		18		13	400.000 (2,800)	18	250.000 (1,700)
14		19		14	350.000 (2,400)	19	150.000 (1,000)
15		20		15	50.000 (350)	20	0
16		21		16	0	21	0
		22				22	4

Facilitation
Coordination
Handreichung
Facilitación

Komite Kerjasama GKMI-GITJ

Mennonitische Europäische Regional Konferenz

1. To build a better relationship between GKMI and GITJ.
2. To become a facilitator for GKMI and GITJ churches, enhancing broader relations with Mennonite churches abroad.

MERK ist 1975 als Versuch entstanden, einmal möglichst alle europäischen Mennoniten zusammen zu bringen. Das Echo war so gut, daß seither etwa alle sechs Jahre eine solche Versammlung stattfand. Damit ist MERK zu einem Instrument der Gemeinschaft, des Zusammenwachsens und des gegenseitigen Verstehens unter den Mennoniten Europas geworden. MERK ist aber keine Organisation mit festen Strukturen.

1	Joint Committee for GKMI and GITJ
2	Jl. Sompok Lama 60, Semarang, Indonesia 50242
3	☎ [62] (24) 312-795
4	
5	
6	
7	1987

8	Drie Susantyo
9	Yesaya Abdi K.J.
10	Evan Paul Gunawan

| 11 | Gereja Kristen Muria Indonesia, Gereja Injili di Tanah Jawa |

12		17	
13		18	
14		19	
15		20	
16		21	
		22	

1	MERK
2	Liestalerstraße 18, CH-4412 Nuglar, Schweiz
3	☎ [41] (61) 969500
4	
5	
6	
7	1975

8	Samuel Gerber *Kontaktperson*
9	
10	

| 11 | Algemene Doopsgezinde Sociëteit, Association des Eglises Evangéliques Mennonites de France, Konferenz der Mennoniten der Schweiz, Verband deutscher Mennonitengemeinden, Vereinigung der Deutschen Mennonitengemeinden |

12		17	
13		18	
14		19	
15		20	
16		21	
		22	

Training

Training
Formation
Ausbildung
Capacitación

Name Nom Name Nombre	Address Adresse Adresse Dirección	Affiliation* Affiliation* in Verbindung mit* Afiliación*	Type of Training** Type de formation** Typ** Tipo de capacitación**	Students Etudiants Studenten Estudiantes
Africa				
Tanzania				
TEE-North Mara Diocese	c/o KMT, Dayosisi ya Mara Kaskazini, Private Bag, Shirati Hospital, Musoma	Kanisa la Mennonite Tanzania	TEE	90
Zaire				
Kikwit Bible Institute	B.P. 81, Kikwit	CEFMZ, MBM/S	Bible School	135
TEE-Kikwit	c/o CEFMZ, Kikwit	CEFMZ, MBM/S	TEE	900
Institut Supérieur Théologique de Kinshasa	B.P. 4742, Kinshasa II	AIMM, COM, MBM/S	Seminary	36
TEE-Kituba	B.P. 4081, Kinshasa II	AIMM	TEE	200
Kalonda Bible Institute	B.P. 18, Tshikapa	AIMM	Bible School	18
TEE-Tshiluba	B.P. 18, Tshikapa	AIMM	TEE	223
Zambia				
Sikalongo Bible Institute	P.O. Box 630131, Choma	BIC	Bible School/TEE	12+
Zimbabwe				
Ekuphileni Bible Institute	Private Bag M5218, Bulawayo	BIC	Bible School	10
Asia				
India				
Mennonite Brethren Bible Institute	Shamshabad via Hyderabad, Ranga Reddy Dist. A.P. 509 218	MBM/S	Bible School	75
Indonesia				
Pendidikan Guru Agama-Agama Kristen	Jl. Diponegoro 33, Pati, Central Java	GITJ	Bible School	137
Sekolah Tingji Agama Kristen Wiyata Wacana	Jl. Diponegoro 33, Pati, Central Java	GITJ	Seminary	80

Name Nom Name Nombre	Address Adresse Adresse Dirección	Affiliation* Affiliation* in Verbindung mit* Afiliación*	Type of Training** Type de formation** Typ** Tipo de capacitación**	Students Etudiants Studenten Estudiantes

Caribbean, Central and South America

Argentina

| Centro Evangélico de Estudios Bíblicos | José Bonifacio 4252, 1407 Buenos Aires | Mennonite churches in Argentina | TEE | |

Brasil

| Centro Evangélico Menonita de Teología (CEMTE) | R. Venezuela 330, Jardim Nova Europa, 13035 Campinas, S.P. | COM, MBM, Mennonite churches in Brasil | TEE | 100 |
| MB Bible Institute/ Seminary | C.P. 2445, 80.000 Curitiba, Paraná | MB | Bible School/ Seminary | 120 |

Colombia

| Seminario Bíblico Menonita | A.A. 53024, Bogotá | COM | Seminary/TEE | 43 |

Guatemala

| SEMILLA | Apartado 1779, Cd. de Guatemala | Latin American Mennonite churches | Seminary | 135 |

Paraguay

Instituto Bíblico Asunción	c.d.c. 1154, Asunción	MBM/S and MB churches in Paraguay	Bible School	40
TEE-Asunción	c.d.c. 166, Asunción	EMCC	TEE	8
TEE-Asunción	c.d.c. 1154, Asuncjón	MBM/S	TEE	300
Yalve Sanga Bible School	c.d.c. 984, Asunción	COM, Konferenz der MBG von Paraguay, Vereinigung der MG von Paraguay	Bible School	35
Centro Evangélico Menonita de Teología Asunción (CEMTA)	Correo San Lorenzo, Casilla 35, Tte. Maschio Casi San Felipe, San Lorenzo	COM, Mennonite churches in Brasil, Paraguay, and Uruguay	Bible School/ Seminary	63

Uruguay

| Centro de Entrenamiento de los Hermanos Menonitas | Casilla 122, Montevideo | MBM/S | Bible School | 30 |
| Centro de Estudios de las Iglesias Menonitas | 3 de Febrero 4381, Montevideo | COM, MBM, Mennonite churches in Uruguay | Seminary | 35 |

Venezuela

| EMC International Ministries | Apartado 75304, Caracas D.F. 1041-A | EMC | TEE | 5 |

Name Nom Name Nombre	Address Adresse Adresse Dirección	Affiliation* Affiliation* in Verbindung mit* Afiliación*	Type of Training** Type de formation** Typ** Tipo de capacitación**	Students Etudiants Studenten Estudiantes

Europe

Nederland

Het Seminarium	Singel 450, NL-1017 AV Amsterdam ☎ [31] (20) 230914	ADS	Seminary	20 ±

Schweiz

Europäische Mennonitische Bibelschule	CH-4410 Liestal ☎ [41] (61) 9014501	KMS, AEEMF, AMBD, MCC, VdM, VDM	Bible School	60 ±

North America

Canada

Columbia Bible College	2940 Clearbrook Rd., Clearbrook, BC V2T 2Z8 ☎ [1] (604) 853-3358	GC, MB	Bible School	188
Canadian Mennonite Bible College	600 Shaftesbury Blvd., Winnipeg, MB R3P 0M4 ☎ [1] (204) 888-6781	GC	Bible School	171
Mennonite Brethren Bible College	1–169 Riverton Ave., Winnipeg, MB R2L 2E5 ☎ [1] (204) 669-6575	MB	Bible School	112
Steinbach Bible College	Box 1420, Steinbach, MB R0A 2A0 ☎ [1] (204) 326-6451	EMCC, EMMC, Chortitzer, Steinbach Evan. MB Church, Christian Fellow- ship Church (Mennonite)	Bible School	81
Winkler Bible Institute	121 Seventh St. South, Winkler, MB R6W 2N4 ☎ [1] (204) 325-4242	MB	Bible School	72
Conrad Grebel College	Westmount Rd. N., Waterloo, ON N2L 3G6 ☎ [1] (519) 885-0220	GC, MC	Liberal Arts	300
Institut Biblique Laval	1775 Edouard-Laurin, Ville St. Laurent, PQ H4L 2B9 ☎ [1] (514) 331-0878	MB	Bible School	19
Bethany Bible Institute	Box 160, Hepburn, SK S0K 1Z0 ☎ [1] (306) 947-2175	MB	Bible School	117
Swift Current Bible Institute	Box 1268, Swift Current, SK S9H 3X4 ☎ [1] (306) 773-0604	GC	Bible School	31

Name Nom Name Nombre	Address Adresse Adresse Dirección	Affiliation* Affiliation* in Verbindung mit* Afiliación*	Type of Training** Type de formation** Typ** Tipo de capacitación**	Students Etudiants Studenten Estudiantes
United States of America				
Fresno Pacific College	1717 S. Chestnut Ave., Fresno, CA 93702 ☎ [1] (209) 453-2000	MB	Liberal Arts	876
Mennonite Brethren Biblical Seminary	4824 E. Butler Ave., Fresno, CA 93727 ☎ [1] (209) 251-8628	MB	Seminary	93
Assoc. Mennonite Biblical Seminaries	3003 Benham Ave., Elkhart, IN 46517 ☎ [1] (219) 295-3726	GC, MC	Seminary	204
Goshen College	1700 S. Main St., Goshen, IN 46526 ☎ [1] (219) 535-7000	MC	Liberal Arts	1,094
Bethel College	300 E. 27 St., North Newton, KS 67117 ☎ [1] (316) 283-2500	GC	Liberal Arts	589
Hesston College	P.O. Box 3000, Hesston, KS 67062 ☎ [1] (316) 327-4221	MC	Liberal Arts	503
Tabor College	400 S. Jefferson, Hillsboro, KS 67063 ☎ [1] (316) 947-3121	MB	Liberal Arts	414
Bluffton College	Bluffton, OH 45817 ☎ [1] (419) 358-8015	GC	Liberal Arts	580
Rosedale Bible Institute	2270 Rosedale Rd., Irwin, OH 43029 ☎ [1] (614) 857-1311	MC	Bible School	94
Messiah College	Grantham, PA 17027 ☎ [1] (717) 766-2511	BIC	Liberal Arts	2,246
Eastern Mennonite College	Harrisonburg, VA 22801 ☎ [1] (703) 433-2771	MC	Liberal Arts	906
Eastern Mennonite Seminary	Harrisonburg, VA 22801 ☎ [1] (703) 433-2771	MC	Seminary	74

*Affiliation pertains to the relationship with Mennonite/Brethren in Christ groups and does not exclude other affiliations.
En relation avec des groupes Mennonite/Brethren in Christ; des relations avec d'autres organisations ne sont pas exclues.
Bezieht sich nur auf Verbindung zu Mennonitischen/Brethren in Christ Gruppen und schließt Verbindungen zu anderen Gruppen nicht aus.
Afiliación se refiere a la relación con grupos Menonitas y Hermanos en Cristo, sin excluir la posibilidad de otras afiliaciones.

Seminary=Faculté de théologie, theologisches Seminar, Seminario
Bible School=Ecole Biblique, Bibelschule, Instituto bíblico
Theological Education by Extension (TEE)=Formation théologique décentralisée, theologisches Fernstudium, Educación teológica por extensión
Liberal Arts=Liberal Arts college, North America